THE SPY OF THE REBELLION

Frontispiece.

Allan Pinkerton and General McClellan in Private Consultation.

P. 153.

THE
SPY _{OF THE} REBELLION;

BEING

A TRUE HISTORY
OF THE
SPY SYSTEM OF THE UNITED STATES ARMY

DURING THE LATE REBELLION.

REVEALING MANY SECRETS OF THE WAR HITHERTO NOT MADE PUBLIC.

COMPILED FROM OFFICIAL REPORTS

PREPARED FOR

PRESIDENT LINCOLN, GENERAL McCLELLAN AND THE PROVOST-MARSHAL-GENERAL.

BY

ALLAN PINKERTON,

WHO

(UNDER THE NOM-DE-PLUME OF MAJOR E. J. ALLEN)

WAS

CHIEF OF THE UNITED STATES SECRET SERVICE.

WITH NUMEROUS ILLUSTRATIONS.

Introduction by Patrick Bass

University of Nebraska Press
Lincoln and London

Introduction copyright © 1989 by the University of Nebraska Press
Manufactured in the United States of America

First Bison Book printing: 1989
Most recent printing indicated by the last digit below:
10   9   8   7   6   5   4   3   2   1

Library of Congress Cataloging-in-Publication Data
Pinkerton, Allan, 1819–1884.
    The spy of the rebellion: being a true history of the spy system of
the United States Army during the late rebellion, revealing many
secrets of the war hitherto not made public / by Allan Pinkerton:
introduction by Patrick Bass.
    p. cm.
    ''Compiled from official reports prepared for President Lincoln,
General McClellan, and the provost-marshal-general.''
    Reprint. Originally published: Hartford, Conn.: M. A. Winter &
Hatch, 1883.
    ISBN 0-8032-3686-7 (alk. paper) ISBN 0-8032-8722-4 (pbk.)
    1. United States—History—Civil War, 1861–1865—Secret service.
2. United States—History—Civil War, 1861–1865—Personal narra-
tives. 3. Pinkerton, Allan, 1819–1884. I. Title.
E608.P65 1989
973.7'86—dc20   89-33081 CIP

Reprinted from the 1883 edition published by M. A. Winter & Hatch,
Hartford, Connecticut. An appendix, ''Rebel Forces before Richmond,''
has been omitted from this Bison Book edition.

∞

CONTENTS.

CHAPTER IV.

CHAPTER V.

CHAPTER VI.

CHAPTER VII.

CHAPTER VIII.

CHAPTER IX.

CHAPTER X.

CHAPTER XI.

CHAPTER XII.

CHAPTER XIII.

CHAPTER XVIII.

CHAPTER XIX.

CHAPTER XX.

CHAPTER XXI.

CHAPTER XXII.

CHAPTER XXIII.

CHAPTER XXIV.

CHAPTER XXV.

CHAPTER XXVI.

CHAPTER XXVII.

CHAPTER XXVIII.

CHAPTER XXIX.

ii

CHAPTER XXX.

CHAPTER XXXI.

CHAPTER XXXII.

CHAPTER XXXIII.

CHAPTER XXXIV.

CHAPTER XXXV.

CHAPTER XXXVI.

CHAPTER XXXVII.

CHAPTER XXXVIII.

LIST OF ILLUSTRATIONS.

INTRODUCTION.

By Patrick Bass

———◆———

For those of us who have reached maturity in the age of radio and television, the private investigator, the gumshoe detective, has been a common fictional companion. From Sir Arthur Conan Doyle's "consulting detective," the upright, acerbic Sherlock Holmes, to the more modern—and less ethical—American private eyes, Samuel Spade and Philip Marlowe, the adventures and mysteries associated with them have an enduring appeal. Although seldom the subject of such fanciful accounts, the most famous genuine organization of private detectives has long been the Pinkerton agency, founded by Mr. Allan Pinkerton in Chicago, Illinois, in the raw and violent years before the American Civil War. For this act, if for no other, Mr. Pinkerton would remain a historical curiosity, memorable to many. But his intimate involvement in the great events surrounding the climactic years of 1861 and 1862 merits him and his works scholarly, and even popular, attention. Fortunately, Mr. Pinkerton produced a record of his exploits as a Union operative during these first, key years of the Civil War, entitled *The Spy of the Rebellion: Being a True History of the Spy System of the United States Army During the Late Rebellion*. Published in 1883, the few currently surviving editions

of this vitally important work have been moldering and dis-
integrating, defying the preserver's art, in the few libraries
lucky enough to still have copies in possession. Thus, this
timely reissue of *The Spy of the Rebellion* by the University
of Nebraska Press will gladden the hearts of all those who
pursue American history as a profession. But this reprint should
also excite those who love to read Civil War history as recreation, and even those who thrill to factually based espionage
and adventure stories. Indeed, Mr. Pinkerton's narrative is
lively, fast-paced, and descriptive, replete with narrow escapes, violent episodes, nefarious schemes, and candid conversations with the most famous and powerful people of the
time. It is, in fact, just good reading.

Historically speaking, these last "virtues" are not particularly virtuous at all. By Mr. Pinkerton's own admission, his
records were lost in the Chicago fire of 1871; thus the majority
of his account relies upon a few scraps of notes, official reports,
and that most unreliable of sources, human memory—made
especially unreliable by twenty years of elapsed time. Moreover, Pinkerton supplies narrative-enhancing dialogue, even in
those instances when he was not present. Veracity must suffer
from such cavalier treatment. Indeed, his object in writing *The
Spy of the Rebellion* was not necessarily the production of
accurate history at all. He had, instead, more mundane motives: among other things, money and the defense of his wartime reputation.

Financial gain was the least important of these two factors
influencing the production of the work, although it was un-
mistakably present. The period from the late 1860s to the early
1880s had been lucrative for publishing Civil War memoirs,
and by all evidence, nearly every survivor of the war was eager
to rush into print to share in the profits. Some of these published
"war accounts" were spurious, some of limited scope, others

sentimentally irrelevant. Some enterprising authors published and republished the same account time and again, often bothering only to change the title. Nevertheless, the public demand for these works seemed inexhaustible. In such a market, Mr. Pinkerton's memoirs were a valuable commodity, partly because of the nature of his wartime activities and partly because of his subsequent fame as a private investigator. By gently inflating his own importance and influence, by carefully deleting the less colorful portions of his organization's experiences, by enhancing the most romantic aspects of his operations, and by completely ignoring his inauspicious career in the West from 1863 onward, he produced a story specifically designed for the consumption of the American reading public. In doing so, Pinkerton took great liberties with the truth, although these liberties were not, in general, historically substantive.

The more serious problem for the scholar—although not for the general reader—is the second influence, the necessity the author feels to defend the Pinkerton Spy System's record in Virginia during the first years of the war. After President Abraham Lincoln called Major General George B. McClellan to command the Army of the Potomac in the East in the fall of 1861, the general came to rely upon "Major E. J. Allen's" reports of enemy activities, "Maj. Allen" being none other than Allan Pinkerton. Indeed, General McClellan had but little choice, for the undertrained Union cavalry (the usual source of army intelligence) was no match for the cavalry of the Army of Northern Virginia, and the Virginia populace was understandably uncooperative. Into this void stepped "Maj. Allen's" espionage organization, ingeniously planted throughout Virginia, a seemingly detailed and accurate source of information on Confederate troop numbers, dispositions, and command structures. (By the way, Mr. Pinkerton's anecdotes concerning the methods by which he established, contacted, and managed these agents are most entertaining, and provide much of the heart of the narrative.) Despite the ingenuity involved, however, these intelligence reports, upon which General McClellan based Union strategic and tactical planning, were greatly exaggerated; in some cases, they were on the verge of the fantastic. The effects were hardly salubrious to the fortunes of the Army of the Potomac in 1862, leading to the presidential dismissal of General McClellan and the resignation of "Maj. Allen" at the end of the year. After the war's conclusion, as Confederate sources became available in the North, the scope of the Pinkerton Spy System's errors became manifest. Mr. Pinkerton and his wartime organization came to suffer some popular criticism. *The Spy of the Rebellion* was his rejoinder to these criticisms.

Because it is by nature, then, an apologia, *The Spy of the Rebellion* is not entirely reliable. Too much was at stake. Pinkerton's investigative reputation, and the reputation of his growing detective agency, in large part rested upon his war exploits. Every incentive existed for Pinkerton to strengthen his wartime case (whether truly or falsely); every incentive existed for him to detail the painstaking, often heroic, methods of intelligence collection to "prove" (whether truly or falsely) the accuracy of the reports that he delivered to Union commanders. No reader can now ascertain whether Mr. Pinkerton, in fact, even records the truth as he knew it; no independent source on the minutiae of his Spy System exists. These factors must give the historian pause—not in considering the accuracy of the intelligence, for Mr. Pinkerton lost that battle years ago, but rather in granting full credence to the narrative details that the author uses to support these now discredited reports. Yet no reliable contrary evidence exists concerning these details, either. The case remains unproven, and scholarly caution is in order.

These professional scruples aside, *The Spy of the Rebellion* is nonetheless invaluable as a first-class primary source in Civil War history. Mr. Pinkerton was a close confidant of important Unionists in Washington, D.C., in 1861 and 1862, and he was an informed member of the highest political circles. For the portraits of these people that he draws, for the insights into these political circles that he provides, for the information concerning military espionage and counterespionage that he produces, Mr. Pinkerton's work is one that no Civil War historian can afford to ignore. *The Spy of the Rebellion* is as vital to any serious student of the early Virginia campaigns as it is to any examination of Civil War intelligence operations; it is as important to any understanding of the national political situation in 1862 (with its puzzling partisan subtexts) as it is to any appreciation of the colorful adventures of individual Union spies, such as Timothy Webster. Now, fortunately, this seminal work will be more readily available for scholarly research and contemplation.

But Mr. Pinkerton's memoirs go far beyond merely conveying historical information, narrowly understood. *The Spy of the Rebellion* also serves historical comprehension in the same manner that good fiction often does, through almost subconscious means, through an indefinable "feel" for the milieu that it imparts to the reader. Here a weary Mr. Lincoln, on his meandering path to his first inauguration, hears, ponders, and reluctantly heeds Mr. Pinkerton's advice concerning possible assassination plots. Here also the beleaguered General McClellan, in order to counter the phantom Confederate hordes constructed by the Spy System, indecisively alters vital military strategy, strategy upon which the lives of thousands, and the life of the nation, rests. Here, as well, the gallant Mr. Webster pays the ultimate cost of a spy captured in time of war. In part, or as a whole, *The Spy of the Rebellion* is a stirring account of war and politics; it is well worth the most careful attention of both scholars and general readers.

These same aspects, of course, also contribute to *The Spy of the Rebellion*'s additional appeal, the appeal of the first-class adventure story, written by an author who understands the American public's reading tastes, of whatever era. The famous and the picturesque inhabit these pages: the benign President Lincoln, the villainous Secretary Edwin Stanton, the notorious Rebel spy Mrs. Rose Greenhow, the heroic Webster, and countless others, of lesser renown but of great interest. The descriptions are lively; the characters well drawn; the movement fast-paced. Although Mr. Pinkerton's prose sometimes betrays racial "insensitivity" to a degree jarring to modern sensibilities, such forms of expression were then common, and his ardent abolitionism goes far toward mitigating the unintentional offense. If the reader can forgive these few indiscretions, the reward is palpable. The vivid narrative reads quickly and enjoyably, as any action-filled combination of mystery, war story, and detective drama is wont to do. Indeed, this work contains all of the most accessible elements of polite popular fiction—reading it is a treat for anyone, irrespective of historical knowledge or background.

PREFACE.

NEARLY a score of years have passed since the occurrence of the events related in the following pages. The "Rebellion," with its bloody scenes, has ended, and the country is at peace. The grass is waving green and beautiful over many Southern fields that once ran with human blood, as the contending forces met in the deadly encounter. The birds are carolling sweetly in the air, which then was laden with the clarion notes of the trumpet; the fierce, wild yell of assaulting soldiery; the booming of cannon, and the groans of the wounded and dying. The merchant, the mechanic, and the husbandman have returned to the pursuits which they followed before the dark clouds of war had overshadowed this fair land, and they shouldered their muskets in defense of the Union. From the desolation and the ravages of war, the country has emerged into the sunshine of abiding peace, and now, in the evening twilight, the gray-haired veterans gather around their family hearthstones to repeat the stories of bravery and devotion associated with those trying hours of their country's history.

In the twilight of my days I have been tempted to the recitals which follow, and in relating my experiences as the Chief of the Secret Service of the Government during the Rebellion, I have been governed by a desire to acquaint the public with the movements of those brave men who rendered invaluable service to their country, although they never wore a uniform or carried a musket. Working quietly, and frequently under diguises, their assistance to the Union commanders was of incalculable advantage, and many acts of courage and daring were performed by these men which, until now, have never been revealed. Indeed, as to my own *nom-de-plume,* "E. J. Allen," many of the officers of the army and officials of the Government, with whom I was in constant communication, never knew me by any other name, and the majority of them are to this day in ignorance of the fact that E. J. Allen, late Chief of the Secret Service, and Allan Pinkerton are one and the same person.

During the progress of the struggle, and the years

which have since elapsed, many of my old acquaintances, who held important positions in the army and
in governmental departments, have passed away from
earth. Some of them falling in the heat of battle,
in the courageous discharge of duty, while others,
passing through the fiery ordeal, have died amid
the comforts and the charms of home.

President Lincoln, Edwin M. Stanton, William
H. Seward and Salmon P. Chase, all giants in their
day, have departed from the sphere of their usefulness, and have gone to their long home. Soldiers
and civilians, generals and privates, with whom I was
connected, and their name is legion, have taken up
their journey to "that bourne from whence no traveler
e'er returns."

In detailing the various events which follow, I
have been careful to offer nothing but that which
actually transpired. I have avoided giving expression to any thoughts or feelings of antagonism to the
South, because the time for such utterances has
passed. Indeed, except for the existence of slavery,
I always cherished a warm affection for the Southern
people. But this institution of human bondage
always received my most earnest opposition. Believing it to be a curse to the American nation, and an
evidence of barbarism, no efforts of mine were ever

spared in behalf of the slave, and to-day I have not a single regret for the course I then pursued.

Many times before the war, when I was associated with those philanthrophic spirits who controlled the so-called "Underground Railroad," I have assisted in securing safety and freedom for the fugitive slave, no matter at what hour, under what circumstances, or at what cost, the act was to be performed. John Brown, the white-haired abolitionist of Kansas fame, was my bosom friend; and more than one dark night has found us working earnestly together in behalf of the fleeing bondman, who was striving for his liberty. After his gallant effort at Harper's Ferry, and while he was confined in a Virginia prison, my efforts in his behalf were unceasing; and had it not been for the excessive watchfulness of those having him in charge, the pages of American history would never have been stained with a record of his execution. As it is, though his fate may have been in accordance with the decrees of the laws then existing, I can recall with all the old enthusiasm that I then experienced, the thundering effect of thousands of our brave "boys in blue," joining in that electric war cry, the refrain of which was:

"John Brown's body lies mouldering in the grave,
But his soul goes marching along,"

while they harried in solid phalanx to meet the enemy upon the field of battle.

In the preliminary chapters, I have detailed with accuracy the facts connected with the conspiracy to assassinate Abraham Lincoln, when he was first elected to the Presidency. The part I took in discovering the existence of that plot and the efforts of my men in ferreting out the prime movers of that murderous compact, are told for the first time in these pages, and the correctness of their relation is undoubted; though in the dark days that followed, the bullet of the assassin removed the martyred President, while engaged in the fulfillment of his mission. I cannot repress a sense of pride in the fact, that at the commencement of his glorious career I had averted the blow that was aimed at his honest, manly heart.

In the events which transpired during the years 1861 and 1862, I took an active part. From the early days of April until after the battle of Antietam had been fought and won, I was connected with the military operations of the government. In Washington I acted under the directions of the Secretaries of War, and Colonel Andrew Porter, the provost-marshal; and in the field, I was under the immediate direction of General George B. McClellan.

My relations with the various departments were

always of the most cordial and confidential character
To particularize in this matter is almost impossible;
but I cannot refrain from mentioning, in the highest
terms of respect and friendship, Colonel Thomas
A. Scott of Pennsylvania. In the early days of the
nation's peril, he occupied the position of Assistant
Secretary of War. In him I always found a warm
friend and advocate, and in many emergencies his
prompt and intelligent action was most potent in accomplishing good results in that era of confusion, of
doubt and hesitation.

Of my service with the military department while
in active duty, little needs to be said here. From the
time of his commission by Governor Dennison of
Ohio, to the day when he was relieved, after his
splendid victory at Antietam, I followed the fortunes
of General McClellan. Never doubting his ability or
his loyalty—always possessing his confidence and
esteem, I am at this time proud and honored in rank-
ing him foremost among my invaluable friends.
When secret enemies were endeavoring to prejudice
the mind of the President against his chosen commander ; when wily politicians were seeking to be-
little him in the estimation of the people, and when
jealous minded officers were ignorantly criticising
his plans of campaign, General McClellan pursued

his course with unflinching courage and with a devotion to his country unsurpassed by any who have succeeded him, and upon whose brows are entwined the laurels of the conqueror.

His marvelous reorganization of the army, the enthusiasm with which his presence invariably inspired the soldiers under his command, and the grand battles which he fought against enemies in front and in rear, have all passed into history—and to-day the intelligent and unprejudiced reader finds in a calm and dispassionate review of his career, an ample and overwhelming justification of his course as a loyal and capable commander-in-chief.

Self-constituted critics, whose avenues of information were limited and unreliable, have attempted to prove that the force opposed to General McClellan was much less than was really the case ; and upon this hypothesis have been led into unjust and undeserved censure of the commanding general. From my own experience, I *know* to the contrary. My system of obtaining knowledge upon this point was so thorough and complete, my sources of information were so varied, that there could be no serious mistake in the estimates which I then made and reported to General McClellan. From every available field the facts were gleaned. From prisoners of war, contrabands, loyal

Southerners, deserters, blockade-runners and from
actual observations by trustworthy scouts, my estimates were made, and to-day I affirm as strongly as
I then did, that the force opposed to General Mc-
Clellan before Richmond approximated nearer to
200,000 men, than they did to the numerous estimates of irresponsible historians who have placed the
strength of the rebel forces at that time below
100,000 men. In this connection I must refer also
to the valuable assistance rendered both General Mc-
Clellan and myself by that indefatigable Aid-de-camp
Colonel Key. Though he no longer mingles with
the things of earth, the memory of his devotion and
his intelligent services to the cause of the Union is
imperishable. No truer, braver man ever drew a
sword than did this noble and efficient staff officer,
now deceased.

Of Timothy Webster, who so ably assisted me in
my various and delicate duties, and whose life was
sacrificed for the cause he held so dear, I have only
words of warmest commendation. Brave, honest and
intelligent, he entered into the contest to perform his
whole duty, and right nobly did he fulfill his pledge,
No danger was too great, no trust too responsible,
no mission too delicate for him to attempt, and
though executed as a spy in a Richmond prison, his

name shall ever be cherished with honor and friend-ship by those who knew his worth, and who appreciated the unswerving devotion of a loyal heart. No dishonor can ever attach to the memory of a patriot who died in the service of his country.

The events narrated have all occurred. The record is a truthful one. Although not so complete as I could wish, they must serve the purpose for which they are intended. In the disastrous fire which swept over Chicago in 1871, my records were mainly destroyed, and to this fact must be attributed the failure to more elaborately detail the multitudinous operations of my men. With the able assistance of Mr. George H. Bangs, my efficient General Superintendent, "we did what we could," and the approbation of our commanding officers attest the efficiency of our efforts.

After leaving the service, the conduct of the war passed into other hands. Other men were chosen to the command of the armies, and other sources of information were resorted to. Succeeding battles have been fought, defeats have been sustained, victories have been achieved, and the war is happily ended. The slave is free, and in the enjoyment of the rights of citizenship. The country is at peace, her prosperity is assured, and now that passion and prejudice have died away, and honest judgments are given of the events that have transpired, I leave to the impartial reader, and historian, the question whether the course I pursued, and the General whom I loved and faithfully served, are deserving of censure, or are entitled to the praises of a free and enlightened people.

ALLAN PINKERTON.

THE SPY

OF

THE REBELLION.

CHAPTER I.

"An Unwritten Page of History."—A Political Résumé.— Mr. Lincoln is Elected President.

MANY years have elapsed since the occurrence of the events which I am about to relate. Years that have been full of mighty import to the nation. A bitter, prolonged and bloody war has laid its desolating hands upon a once united country. For years the roar of cannon and the clash of steel reverberated through the bright valleys and the towering hills of the fruitful South. In those years when brother arose against his brother, when ties of kindred and association were broken asunder like frail reeds, glorious deeds were wrought and grand results have been accomplished. America has taught the world a lesson of bravery and endurance ; the shackles

have been stricken from the slave; an error of a
century has been crushed, and freedom is now no
longer an empty name, but a beautiful and enduring
realism.

To-day peace spreads her broad, sheltering arms
over a reunited and enlightened nation.   The roll of
the drum and the tramp of armed men are now no
longer heard.   North and South have again clasped
hands in a renewal of friendship and in a perpetuity
of union.

But a short time ago a Republican President
elected by but a slight majority of the voters of this
great community, left his peaceful home in the West
and journeyed to the capital of the nation, to take
the oath of office and to assume the high duties of
a chief magistrate. As he passed through the
towns and cities upon his route a general plaudit
of welcome was his greeting, even noted political
foes joining in the demonstrations. His road was
arched with banners and his path was strewn with
flowers. Everywhere he found an enthusiasm of
welcome, a universal prayer for success, and the
triumphal train entered the capital amid the ovations
of the populace, which reached almost a climax of
patriotic and effervescing joy.

Twenty years ago witnessed a different condition
of affairs. The political horizon was dark and obscured. The low mutterings of the storm that was
soon to sweep over our country, and to deluge our

fair land with fratricidal blood, were distinctly heard. Sectional differences were developing into wide-spread dissensions. Cherished institutions were threatened with dissolution, and political antagonism had aroused a contented people into a frenzy of hate.

On the twenty-second of May, 1856, an American Senator was assaulted in the Senate-house by a political opponent for daring to give utterance to opinions that were hostile to the slave-holding interests of the South. Later in the same year a Republican candidate, with professed anti-slavery views, was nominated for the presidency, and although defeated, gave evidence of such political strength that Southern leaders became alarmed.

At this time the Hon. Stephen A. Douglas was a prominent leader of the Democratic party, but through his opposition to what was known as the Lecompton Bill, he incurred the displeasure of his political friends of the South, who vainly endeavored to enact such legislation as would practically lead to his retirement from the party.

In 1858 the famous contest between Abraham Lincoln and Stephen A. Douglas for the United States Senatorship from Illinois took place, and during its progress absorbed public attention throughout the country. The two candidates indulged in open discussions of questions of public policy, which were remarkable for their brilliancy and for the force and vigor with which their different views were uttered.

It was during this canvass that Mr. Lincoln made the forcible and revolutionizing declaration that: " *The Union cannot permanently endure half slave and half free.*" Mr. Lincoln was defeated, however, and Mr. Douglas was returned to the Senate, much against the wishes of those Democrats who desired the unlimited extension of the institution of Slavery.

In the following year occurred the slave insurrection in Virginia, under the leadership of that bold abolitionist, John Brown. The movement was frustrated, however, and John Brown, after a judicial trial for his offense, was sentenced to be hung. Up to the day of his execution he remained firm in the belief that he had but performed his duty toward enslaved humanity, and he died avowing the justice of his cause and the hope of its ultimate success.

All of these occurrences tended to engender a spirit of fierce opposition in the minds of the Southern leaders. The growing sentiment of abolitionism throughout the North, and the manifest disposition to prevent its increase or extension, aroused the advocates of Slavery to a degree of alarm, which led to the commission of many actions, both absurd and unjustifiable.

The year of 1860 opened upon a scene of political agitation which threatened to disrupt long united associations, and to erect sectional barriers which appeared almost impossible to overcome.

In April, 1860, the Democratic National Convention assembled in Charleston, South Carolina, for the purpose of nominating a candidate for the presidency. During its session loud and angry debates occurred, in which the Southern element indeavored to obtain a strong indorsement of the institution of Slavery, and of the right to carry slaves into the Territories of the United States. They were met by the more conservative portion of the party, who desired to leave the question to be decided by the States themselves. After a prolonged discussion the majority of the Southern States withdrew their delegates from the convention, and the remainder proceeded to ballot for a candidate of their choice.

After a protracted sitting, during which several ballots were taken and no decided result obtained, the convention adjourned, to meet in the city of Baltimore on the eighteenth day of June succeeding. Stephen A. Douglas, of Illinois, received a large percentage of the votes that were cast, but failed to obtain a sufficient number to secure his nomination.

The withdrawing delegates organized a rival convention, but, without transacting any business of a decisive character, also adjourned, to meet in Baltimore at a date nearly coincident with that of the regular body.

On the nineteenth day of May, the Constitutional Union (being the old American) party held their convention in the city of Baltimore, and nominated John

Bell, of Tennessee, for President, and Edward Everett, of Massachusetts, for the Vice-Presidency,

The Republican Convention was held on the sixteenth day of May, in the city of Chicago, and upon the third ballot nominated Abraham Lincoln, of Illinois, for the office of President, and Hannibal Hamlin, of Maine, for the second office.

This convention also adopted a platform very pronounced upon the subject of Slavery, and which was calculated to give but little encouragement to the extension or perpetuity of the slave-holding power.

On the eighteenth day of June the regular Democratic Convention assembled, pursuant to adjournment, in the city of Baltimore, and named Stephen A. Douglas, of Illinois, and Herschel V. Johnson, of Georgia, as their standard-bearers in the political conflict that was to ensue.

On the twenty-eighth day of the same month the seceding delegates met in the same city, and after pronouncing their ultra views upon the question of Slavery, nominated John C. Breckinridge, of Kentucky (then the Vice-President of the country), and General Joseph Lane, of Oregon, as the candidates of their choice.

The lines of battle were now drawn, and from that time until the election, in November, a fierce contest was waged between the opposing parties. Never before in the history of parties was a canvass conducted with more bitterness or with a greater amount of vituperation. The whole country was engrossed with the gigantic struggle. Business interests, questions of finance and of international import were all made subservient to the absorbing consideration of the election of a national President.

The Southern " Fire-eaters," as they were called, fully realized their inability to elect the candidates they had named, but strove with all their power to prevent the success of the regular Democratic nominees, and when at last the day of election came, and the votes were counted, it was found that the Republican party had been victorious and that Abrahm Lincoln had been elected.

In many portions of the South this result was hailed with joyful enthusiasm. The anti-slavery proclivities of the successful party was instantly made a plausible pretext for secession and the withdrawal of the slave-holding States from the Union was boldly advocated.

The same power that threatened in 1856, in the words of Governor Wise of Virginia : " That if Fremont had been elected, he would have marched at the head of twenty thousand men to Washington, and taken possession of the capital, preventing by force Fremont's inauguration at that place "—was again aroused, and an open opposition to the Republican inauguration was for a time considered.

The absorbing and exciting question in the South was : " Would the South submit to a Black Repub-

lican President and a Black Republican Congress ?"
and the answer to the question was a loud and decisive negative.

Among the bolder advocates of secession the election of Mr. Lincoln was regarded with pleasure, and
meetings were held in Charleston, rejoicing in the
triumph of the Republican party. Secession and disunion were loudly advocated, and the slave oligarchy
of South Carolina regarded this event as the opportunity to achieve her long-cherished purpose of breaking up the Union, and forming a new confederacy,
founded upon the peculiar ideas of the South.

Says Horace Greeley : " Men thronged the streets,
talking, laughing, cheering, like mariners long be-
calmed upon a hateful, treacherous sea, when a sudden breeze had swiftly wafted them within sight of
their looked for haven, or like a seedy prodigal, just
raised to affluence by the death of some far-off, unknown relative, and whose sense of decency is not
strong enough to repress his exultation."

Open threats were made to withdraw at once from
the Union, and these demonstrations seemed to find
sympathy among other nations than our own, and
soon foreign intrigue was hand and glove with domestic treason, in the attempt to sap the foundations of
our government, and seeking peculiar advantages from
its overthrow.

It is unnecessary to detail the various phases of
this great agitation, which, firing the Southern heart

with the frenzy of disunion, finally led to the secession of the Southern States. Various compromises
were attempted, but all failed of beneficial result.
The "masterly inactivity" of the administration contributed in no small degree to the accomplishment of
this object, and in the end the Southern Confederacy
was organized and Jefferson Davis was elected as its
President.

The Palmetto waved over the custom-house and
post-office at Charleston ; government forts and
arsenals were seized by the volunteers to the Southern cause, and on February 1, 1861, the Federal mint
and custom-house at New Orleans were taken possession of by the secessionists.

The removal of Major Anderson from Fort Moul-
trie to the more secure stronghold of Fort Sumter,
in Charleston harbor, had been accomplished, and as
yet no measures had been taken by the government
to prevent further demonstrations of a warlike character on the part of the Southern Confederacy. The
administration remained passive and inert, while every
effort was being made to calm the public fears of hostilities, and the organization of an open revolt.

The city of Baltimore was, at this time, a slave-
holding city, and the spirit of Slavery was nowhere
else more rampant and ferocious. The mercantile and
social aristocracy of that city had been sedulously and
persistently plied, by the conspirators for disunion,
with artful and tempting suggestions of her future

greatness and advancement as the chief city of the new government.

If a Confederacy composed of the fifteen slave-holding States was organized, Baltimore, it was urged, would naturally be the chief city of the new Republic. In time it would become the rival of New York, and occupy to the Confederacy the same relations which New York does to the Union, and would be the great ship-building, shipping, importing and commercial emporium.

These glittering prophecies had not been uttered without effect. The ambition of the aristocracy was aroused. Already they saw the ocean whitened with her sails, and the broad domain of Maryland adorned with the palaces reared from her ample and ever-expanding profits. Under these hallucinations, their minds were corrupted, and they seemed eager to rush into treason.

Being a border State, Maryland occupied a position of particular importance. Emissaries were sent to her from South Carolina and elsewhere, and no effort was spared to secure her co-operation in these revolutionary movements. It is to be regretted that they were too successful, and the result was that the majority of the wealthier classes and those in office were soon in sympathy with the rebellion, and the spirit of domestic treason, for a time, swept like a tornado over the State.

Added to the wealthier classes was the mob

element of the city of Baltimore—reckless and unscrupulous, as mobs generally are—and this portion of her community were avowedly in full accord with the prospective movement, and ready to do the bidding of the slave power. Between these, however, there existed a great middle class, who were loyally and peacefully inclined. But this class, large as it was, had hitherto been divided in their political opinions, and had as yet arrived at no common and definite understanding with regard to the novel circumstances of the country and the events which seemed to be visibly impending.

The government of the city of Baltimore was under the control of that branch of the Democracy who supported Breckinridge, and who had attained power under a popular cry for reform, and it was soon learned that these leaders were deep in the counsels of the secessionists.

The newspaper press was no small factor of this excitement—their utterances had much to do in leading public opinion, and though their efforts " to fire the Southern heart," many were led to sanction the deeds of violence and outrage which were contemplated.

Especial efforts had been made to render Mr. Lincoln personally odious and contemptible, and his election formed the pretexts of these reckless conspirators, who had long been plotting the overthrow of the Union. No falsehood was too gross, no statement too exaggerated, to be used for that purpose, and so zealously did these misguided men labor in the cause of disunion, and so systematically concerted was their action, that the mass of the people of the slave States were made to believe that this pure, patient, humane, Christian statesman was a monster whose vices and passions made him odious, and whose political beliefs made him an object of just abhorrence.

This was the condition of affairs at the dawning of the year 1861.

A COUNCIL OF WAR.

CHAPTER II.

*Opposition to Mr. Lincoln's Inauguration.—A Plot to Assassi-
nate him.—The Journey from Springfield.*

WITH the opening of the new year, the political
condition evinced alarming symptoms. As
the day of the inauguration of the new President drew
near, the excitement became intense. Loud threats
were made that Mr. Lincoln should never be permitted to take the oath of office, and the hostility of
the South manifested itself in such a manner as to
excite the fears of those who desired the peaceful
solution of the important question of continued
union.

The events about to be related have been for a
long time shrouded in a veil of mystery. While
many are aware that a plot existed at this time to
assassinate the President-elect upon his contemplated
journey to the capital, but few have any knowledge
of the mode by which the conspiracy was detected, or
the means employed to prevent the accomplishment
of that murderous design.

Considerations which affected the personal safety
of those who actively participated in this detection,
precluded a disclosure at the time, but that such a

conspiracy existed no doubt can be entertained. Now, however, that the dark clouds have passed away, and the bright sunshine of an enduring peace is throwing its beneficient rays over a united country, the truth may be disclosed, and a desire to peruse a hidden page of history may now be gratified.

Early in the year 1861 I was at my headquarters in the city of Chicago, attending to the manifold duties of my profession. I had, of course, perused the daily journals which contained the reports of doings of the malcontents of the South, but in common with others, I entertained no serious fears of an open rebellion, and was disposed to regard the whole matter as of trivial importance. The same tones had been listened to before, and although the disunionists had hitherto never taken such aggressive steps, I was inclined to believe that with the incoming of the new administration, determined or conciliatory measures would be adopted, and that secession and rebellion would be either averted or summarily crushed.

At this time I received a letter from Mr. Samuel H. Felton, the president of "The Philadelphia, Wilmington and Baltimore Railroad," requesting my presence in Philadelphia upon a matter of great importance. From his communication it appeared that rumors were afloat as to the intention of the roughs and secessionists of Maryland to injure the road of which he was the President. From what had already been learned, it was feared that their designs were to prevent travel upon the road either by destroying the ferry-boats which then carried the trains across the Susquehanna river at Havre de Grace or by demolishing the railroad bridges over the Gunpowder river and other streams. This road was the great connecting link between the metropolis of the country and the capital of the nation, and it was of the utmost importance that no interruption should be permitted to the free communication between Washington and the great cities of the North and West.

This letter at once aroused me to a realization of the danger that threatened the country, and I determined to render whatever assistance was in my power towards preventing the successful operation of these ill-advised and dangerous men.

I lost no time, therefore, in making my arrangements, and soon after receiving Mr. Felton's communication, in company with four members of my force was upon the train speeding towards Philadelphia. Upon arriving in that city, I went directly to the office of Mr. Felton and obtained from him all the information he possessed of the movements and designs of the Maryland secessionists. I also had a consultation with Mr. H. F. Kenney, the superintendent of the road, with reference to a plan of operation which I proposed, and which was considered would result in obtaining the information so much to be desired.

I resolved to locate my men at the various towns along the road, selecting such places where, it was believed, disaffection existed. With a view, therefore of acquiring the facts necessary for an intelligent prose cution of the inquiry, I took passage on one of the trains of the road, intending to see for myself how affairs stood, and to distribute my men in such a manner as to me seemed best.

At the city of Wilmington, in Delaware, I found evidences of a great political excitement, but nothing that indicated a hostile disposition or which led me to believe that any danger was to be apprehended at this place. Nothing that savored of organization was apparent, and I was therefore compelled to look fur· ther for the existence of any antagonism to the rail· road or any desire to prevent the running of their trains.

At Perryville I found the same excitable condition of affairs, but nothing of a more aggressive character than at Wilmington. Men indulged in fierce arguments, in which both sides were forcibly represented, but aside from this I discovered no cause for apprehension, and no occasion for active detective work as yet.

At Havre de Grace, however, the lines were more clearly drawn and the popular feeling much more bitter. It was at this point that the boats which carried the trains crossed the Susquehanna river, and where serious damage might be done to the company, should the ferries be destroyed. I therefore left one man at this place, with instructions to become ac·

quainted with such men as he might, on observation, consider suspicious, and to endeavor to obtain from them, by association, a knowledge of their intentions.

At Perrymansville, in Maryland, the feeling was considerably more intense. Under the influence of bad men the secession movement had gained many supporters and sympathizers. Loud threats were uttered against the railroad company, and it was boastfully asserted that "no d—d abolitionist should be allowed to pass through the town alive."

I have always found it a truism that "a barking dog never bites," and although I had but little fear that these blatant talkers would perform any dangerous deeds, I considered it best to be fully posted as to their movements, in order to prevent a catastrophe, if possible.

I accordingly directed Timothy Webster, a daring and discreet man upon my force, to locate himself at this point, and to carefully note everything that transpired which had any relation to attempted violence or a disposition to resort to aggressive measures.

As I neared the city of Baltimore the opposition to the government and the sympathy with secession was manifestly more intense. At Magnolia, particularly, I observed a very dangerous feeling, and among men of all classes the general sentiment was in favor of resistance and force. Another operative, John Seaford, was accordingly left at this place, with instructions similar to those which had been given to the others.

I then proceeded on to Baltimore, and there I found the greatest amount of excitement that I had yet experienced. I took quarters at the Howard House, and proceeded to inquire closely and carefully into the political situation. I soon found that the fears of the railroad officials were not wholly without foundation. The opposition to Mr. Lincoln's inauguration was most violent and bitter, and a few days' sojourn in this city convinced me that great danger was to be apprehended, and that the sentiment of disunion was far more widespread and deeply rooted than I had before imagined.

The police force of the city was under the control of Marshal George P. Kane, and was almost entirely composed of men with disunion proclivities. Their leader was pronouncedly in favor of secession, and by his orders the broadest license was given to disorderly persons and to the dissemination of insurrectionary information. This individual was subsequently arrested, and, after a brief sojourn in Fort McHenry, fled in 1863 to the more congenial associations of Richmond.

From the knowledge I gained of the situation in Baltimore, I resolved to establish my headquarters in that city. I accordingly engaged a building situated on South street, and in a position where I could receive prompt reports from all quarters of the metropolis. I also sent for an additional force of men, whom I distributed among the people of all grades and conditions of life. The building I had selected was admirably adapted for my purpose, and was so constructed that entrance could be gained to it from all four sides, through alleyways that led in from neighboring streets.

Day by day, the reports of my men contained many important revelations of the designs of the opposition, and as a matter of additional precaution, I advised Mr. Felton to employ a small number of men to guard the various bridges and ferries, who could be warned in time to resist attack should such be made.

The chief opposition seemed to be to the inauguration of President Lincoln, and the plan of the conspirators was to excite and exasperate the popular feeling against the President-elect to the utmost, and so successfully had this been done that a majority of the wealthier classes, with few exceptions—those in office—and the mob element in general were in full accord in their desire to prevent the inauguration from taking place.

On the eleventh day of February, Mr. Lincoln, with a few of his personal friends, left his quiet home in Springfield to enter upon that tempestuous political career which eventually carried him to a martyr's grave. Among the party who accompanied the President were Norman B. Judd, Esq., Col. Ward

H. Lamon, Judge Davis, Col. Sumner, a brave and impetuous officer, Major Hunter, Capt. John Pope, Col. Ellsworth, whose heroic death took place shortly afterwards, and John G. Nicolay, the President's private secretary.

As the President was about leaving his home, the people turned out en masse to bid him farewell, and to them Mr. Lincoln addressed the following pathetic words of parting :

" My Friends : No one who has never been placed in a like position can understand my feelings at this hour, nor the oppressive sadness I feel at this parting. For more than a quarter of a century I have lived among you, and during all that time I have received nothing but kindness at your hands. Here I have lived from youth until now I am an old man ; here the most sacred ties of earth were assumed ; here all my children were born, and here one of them lies buried. To you, dear friends, I owe all that I have, and all that I am. All the strange checkered past seems now to crowd upon my mind. To-day I leave you. I go to assume a task more difficult than that which devolved upon Washington. Unless the great God who assisted him shall be with me and aid me, I must fail ; but if the same Omniscient Mind and Almighty Arm that directed and protected him shall guide and support me, I shall not fail—I shall succeed. Let us all pray that the God of our fathers may not forsake us now. To Him I commend you all. Permit me to ask that with equal sincerity and faith you will invoke His wisdom and guidance for me. With these few words I must leave you, for how long I know not. Friends, one and all, I must bid you an affectionate farewell."

How touchingly simple and earnest seem these words. A strange and almost weird presentiment of grief and suffering give his utterances a pathos that becomes profoundly impressive when linked with subsequent events. How prophetic too—full of tears and fraught with the prescience of a future terrible and bloody war—they bear yet an echo like that of the voice that sounded in the ear of Halleck's dying hero—for surely in their tones are heard the thanks of millions yet to be. How more than prophetic they seemed when, four years later, "a funeral train, covered with the emblems of splendid mourning, rolled into the same city, bearing a corpse whose obsequies were being celebrated in every part of the civilized world."

From Springfield the passage was a perfect continuous ovation. Cities and towns, villages and hamlets, vied with each other in testifying their devotion to Union and their determination to uphold the chief magistrate in the great trial before him. Immense crowds surrounded the stations at which the special train halted, and in the cities of Indianapolis, Cincinnati, Columbus, Pittsburg, Cleveland, Erie, Buffalo, Albany, New York, Trenton, Newark, Philadelphia and Harrisburg, public demonstrations of an imposing character were given in his

honor, and vast concourses of people assembled to
greet him.   Everywhere he was received and honored
as the chief of a free people, and in reply to complimentary addresses which he day by day received, the
President endeavored to utter cheering words, and
indicated a disbelief in any bloody issue of our
domestic complications.

On the day prior to the departure of Mr. Lincoln
from his home, I received a letter from the master
mechanic of the railroad, of which the following is an
extract :

"I am informed that a son of a distinguished
citizen of Maryland said that he had taken an oath
with others to assassinate Mr. Lincoln before he gets
to Washington, and they may attempt to do it while he
is passing over our road.   I think you had better look
after this man, if possible.   This information is
perfectly reliable.   I have nothing more to say at
this time, but will try to see you in a few days."

This communication was confirmatory of reports
of an indefinite character which had reached me prior
to this, and the information was far too important to
be disregarded.   I determined, therefore, to probe
the matter to the bottom, and obtaining the authority
of Mr. Felton for such action, I immediately set about
the discovery of the existence of the conspiracy and
the intention of its organization, and then, if coolness,
courage and skill could save the life of Mr. Lincoln,
and prevent the revolution which would inevitably

follow his violent death, I felt sure of accomplishing it.

My plans were soon perfected, and they were to have several of my men, together with myself, announced as residents of Charleston and New Orleans, and by assuming to be secessionists of the most ultra type, to secure entrance into their secret societies and military organizations, and thus become possessed of their secret designs. In looking over the qualifications of the members of my corps I found two men admirably adapted to the object I had in view. They were both young and both fully able to assume and successfully carry out the character of a hot-blooded, fiery secessionist.

One of these men, whom I shall call Joseph Howard, was a young man of fine personal appearance, and of insinuating manners. He was of French descent, and in his youth had been carefully educated for a Jesuit priest, but finding the vocation distasteful to him, he had abandoned it. Added to his collegiate studies, he possessed the advantage of extensive foreign travel, and the ability to speak, with great facility, several foreign languages. He had a thorough knowledge of the South, its localities, prejudices, customs and leading men, which had been derived from several years residence in New Orleans and other Southern cities, and was gifted with the power of adaptation to persons whom they wish to influence, so popularly attributed to the Jesuits.

Howard was instructed to assume the character of an extreme secessionist, to obtain quarters at one of the first-class hotels, and register his name, with residence at New Orleans. This was done because he was well acquainted with the city, having resided there for a long time, and was consequently enabled to talk familiarly of prominent individuals of that city whom he had met.

The other man whom I selected for this important work was Timothy Webster. He was a man of great physical strength and endurance, skilled in all athletic sports, and a good shot. Possessed of a strong will and a courage that knew no fear, he was the very man to operate upon the middle and lower classes who composed the disunion element.

His subsequent career as a Union spy—one of the most perilous and thankless positions—and his ignominious death at Richmond, at the hands of the rebels, have passed into history, but no historian will ever relate the thousand perils through which he passed in the service of his country ; of his boldness and ingenuity in acquiring information that was of incalculable value to the Union officers, nor of his wonderful fertility of invention, which frequently enabled him to escape from dangers which would have appalled a less brave or less devoted man. Arrested at last, he was condemned as a spy, and on the thirtieth day of April, 1862, he was executed in the City of Richmond, by order of Jefferson Davis. Even then he would have succeeded in effecting a well-devised plan of escape, had he not been rendered incapable of movement by reason of a prostrating sickness. His name is unknown to fame, but fewer hearts beat truer to the Union, and fewer arms performed more devoted service in its cause, and a record of his daring and romantic adventures as a Union spy, would certainly equal, if not surpass, those of the Harvey Birch of Cooper.

It was not long before I received undoubted evidence of the existence of a systematized organization whose avowed object was to assist the rebellious States, but which was in reality formed to compass the death of the President, and thus accomplish the separation of the States. I learned also that a branch of this conspiracy existed at Perrymansville, under the guise of a company of cavalry, who met frequently and drilled regularly. Leaving Harwood to operate in Baltimore with the others, I dispatched Timothy Webster back to Perrymansville, and in twenty-four hours thereafter he had enrolled himself as a member of the company, and was recognized as a hail fellow among his rebel associates.

CHAPTER III.

The Conspirators at Work.—Detectives on Their Trail.— Webster as a Soldier.

EVERY day reports would be brought to me from the numerous men I had detailed along the line of the railroad, and regularly on alternate days I would make the journey from Baltimore to Philadelphia for consultation with the officers of the company.

At every visit which I made to the suspected localities, I could not fail to notice an increase in the excitement and the indications of a disposition to open revolt became more evident. Everywhere the ruling principle seemed to be opposition to the new administration and a decided inclination to aid the Confederacy. As the daily papers, which chronicled the events which occurred upon the journey of Mr. Lincoln towards Washington, or the desperate movements of the Southern ringleaders, were perused by the people, or were read aloud in tavern or store, they would be greeted by alternate expressions of hate and malignity for the abolitionist and wild cheers for the rebellion.

This feeling, too, was largely increased by the

visits which prominent villagers would make to Baltimore, and who, upon their return, would relate marvelous stories of what they had seen and heard of the courage, the unity and the determination of the Southern people. Everything calculated to inflame the popular mind was seized upon, and the wonderful spirit of invention which these men evinced was simply astonishing. As a consequence, the ignorant residents of these villages and towns, having no authoritative information of their own, relied implicitly upon the exaggerated statements and untruthful reports of their leaders, and were kept in a condition of excitement that made them ready tools of their unscrupulous and better-informed managers. As far as could be learned, however, no definite plan of action had been arranged, and no public outbreak had as yet occurred.

Barnum's Hotel, in Baltimore, appeared to be the favorite resort of the Southern element. The visitors from all portions of the South located at this house, and in the evenings the corridors and parlors would be thronged by the tall, lank forms of the long-haired gentlemen who represented the aristocracy of the slaveholding interests. Their conversations were loud and unrestrained, and any one bold enough or sufficiently indiscreet to venture an opinion contrary to the righteousness of their cause, would soon find himself in an unenviable position and frequently the subject of violence.

As this hotel was so largely patronized by the so-called "Fire-eaters," I instructed Howard to go there in order to secure quarters and to ingratiate himself with these extremists. It was not long after this, that, joining a company of gentlemen who were loudly declaiming against the ruling powers of the country, he entered into their discussion, and by blatant expressions of the most rebellious nature, he was warmly welcomed by the coterie and instantly made one of their number.

Hailing as he did from New Orleans, his residence was a ready passport to their favor and confidence, and his fine personal appearance, gentlemanly address and the fervor of his utterances soon won the favor of those with whom he associated. To a general inquiry he stated that private affairs of a financial nature required his presence in Baltimore, but as his acquaintance with the trustworthy emissaries of rebeldom increased, he quietly insinuated that affairs of a national character were far more dear to him than individual interests or private concerns.

By continued intercourse with these men, he greatly increased the circle of his acquaintances, and soon became a welcome guest at the residences of many of the first families of that refined and aristocratic city. Here his accomplishments appeared to the best advantage. His romantic disposition and the ease of his manner captivated many of the susceptible hearts of the beautiful Baltimore belles, whose eyes grew brighter in his presence, and who listened enraptured to the poetic utterances which were whispered into their ears under the witching spell of music and moonlit nature.

He gradually neared the circle of which Marshal George P. Kane appeared to be the leader, and in a short time he had succeeded in entirely winning his confidence, and from this gentleman Howard acquired many important items of information. The entire police force of the city—officers and men—were in full sympathy with the rebellion, and it became apparent to him that a strict watch was kept over every man who expressed Northern opinions, or who was not identified with the cause which they had espoused.

To all of these arrangements Howard signified his hearty indorsement, and by every means in his power he sought to convince the leaders of his full sympathy with their efforts and his resolve to take a leading part in the struggle that seemed to be impending.

Accepting the invitation of Mr. Kane, he one evening accompanied that gentleman to a meeting of one of the secret societies that then existed, the first one he had succeeded in gaining entrance to. Arriving at the place of assembly, he was surprised at the many familiar faces which greeted him. Men whose aristocratic doors had opened to his entrance and whose social positions were unquestioned ; **young**

men who traced their lineage through several genera-
tions, and whose wealth and intelligence gave them
a social status of no ordinary character, were found in
full accord and upon perfect equality with tradesmen,
artificers, and even with those whose vocation was
decidedly doubtful, and some of whom had heard
the key of a prison lock turned upon them for offenses
committed in days gone by.

The leader and President of this society was a
Captain Fernandina, who was known as one of the
most active of the conspirators. This individual at
one time occupied the exalted position of a barber at
Barnum's Hotel, but treason and conspiracy had
elevated him to the station of a military captain whose
orders were to be obeyed, and a leader whose man-
dates compelled respect. He was an Italian or of
Italian descent, and having lived in the South for a
number of years he was thoroughly impressed with
the idea of Southern wrongs, and that the election
of Mr. Lincoln was an outrage which must not be
tamely submitted to by the high-toned and chivalrous people of the South.

He was an enthusiast and fanatic, a dangerous
man in any crisis, and particularly so in the one now
impending, which threatened a civil war and all its
direful consequences. Educated with Italian ideas and
possessed of the temperament of his people, he openly
justified the use of the stiletto, and fiercely advocated
assassination as the means of preventing the Presi-

dent-elect from taking his seat in the executive chair.
He was also the captain of a military company which
drilled regularly and whose members were believed
to fully indorse the views of their chief.

At this meeting Fernandina delivered an address
which, for its treasonable nature and its violent opposition to all laws, human or divine, has scarcely a
parallel. He boldly advocated the doctrine of State
rights ; he fiercely denounced the party who had succeeded in obtaining power ; he inveighed in violent
language against the policy of the so-called abolitionists, and his arraignment of Mr. Lincoln was most
vile and repulsive. As these words fell from his lips
the excitement became intense. Faces were eagerly
turned towards him, eyes glistened with the fires of
hate, and hands were clenched as though each one
present was imbued with the same feelings which
animated their sanguinary leader.

As he proceeded, overcome by the violence of his
emotions, he drew from his breast a long, glittering
knife, and waving it aloft, exclaimed :

" This hireling Lincoln shall never, never be President. My life is of no consequence in a cause like
this, and I am willing to give it for his. As Orsini
gave his life for Italy, I am ready to die for the
rights of the South and to crush out the abolitionist."

As he stood before them, his black eyes flashing
with excitement, his sallow face pale and colorless
and his long hair brushed fiercely back from his low

forehead, he seemed a fitting representative of so desperate a cause, and his influence over the assemblage was wonderful to behold. Loud cheers and wild clapping of hands greeted his utterances, and all seemed in perfect accord with his declared intentions.

There could be no mistaking the fact, that the object of these men was dangerous, and that they had fully determined to oppose and prevent the inauguration of Mr. Lincoln, but the exact plan of operation had not as yet been agreed upon.

Upon these facts being conveyed to me by Howard on the following morning, I resolved to interview this desperate leader of the conspiracy myself, and endeavor to learn from him further particulars of their movements and designs.

In the immediate vicinity of Barnum's Hotel at that time there was a famous restaurant, popularly known as "Guy's," and this place was much frequented by the secessionists who were in the city. Fernandina spent much of his time there, either in drinking or in consultation with his numerous political friends, who all seemed to regard him as an important personage, and one who was eventually to perform giant service in the cause.

Howard having effecting an introduction to Fernandina, and convinced him of his devotion to the interests of the South, I experienced no difficulty in obtaining the desired interview. About three o'clock on the following afternoon Howard and myself care-

P. 65.

"*He must die, and if necessary we will die together!*"

lessly entered the saloon, and were gratified to perceive that Fernandina was also there, accompanied by several members of the military company which he commanded. Walking directly up to these gentlemen, Howard introduced me as a resident of Georgia, who was an earnest worker in the cause of secession, and whose sympathy and discretion could be implicitly relied upon.

Fernandina cordially grasped my hand, and we all retired to a private saloon, where, after ordering the necessary drinks and cigars, the conversation became general, and to me, absorbingly interesting.

The question of assassinating the President was freely discussed, and Captain Fernandina expressed himself vehemently in its favor.

Some one in the party remarked :

" Are there no other means of saving the South except by assassination ?"

" No," replied Fernandina; " as well might you attempt to move the Washington Monument yonder with your breath, as to change our purpose. He must die—and die he shall. And," he continued, turning to Captain Trichot, a fellow-conspirator who stood near, " if necessary, we will die together."

" There seems to be no other way," interposed Howard, " and while bloodshed is to be regretted, it will be done in a noble cause."

Fernandina gazed approvingly at Howard, and then added :

5

"Yes, the cause is a noble one, and on that day every captain will prove himself a hero. With the first shot the chief traitor, Lincoln, will die, then all Maryland will be with us, and the South will be forever free."

"But," said I, "have all the plans been matured, and are there no fears of failure? A misstep in so important a direction would be fatal to the South and ought to be well considered."

"Our plans are fully arranged," answered the Captain, "and they cannot fail; and," he added, with a wicked gleam in his eyes—"if I alone must strike the blow, I shall not hesitate or shrink from the task. Lincoln shall certainly not depart from this city alive."

"Yes," added Captain Trichot, "it is determined that this G—d d—d Lincoln shall never pass through here alive, and no d—d abolitionist shall ever set foot upon Southern soil except to find a grave."

"But about the authorities"—I asked—"is there no danger to be apprehended from them?"

"Oh, no," said the Captain, assuringly, "they are all with us. I have seen Col. Kane, the Chief Marshal of Police, and he is all right. In a week from to-day the North shall want another President, for Lincoln will be a corpse."

All the company gave approving responses to these threats, with but one exception, and he remained silent, with a doubtful, troubled expression upon his face. This young man was one of the fast "bloods" of the city, who proudly wore upon his breast a gold Palmetto badge, and who was a Lieutenant in the Palmetto Guards, a secret military organization of Baltimore, and I determined to select this man for the purpose of obtaining the information I so much desired; and as the company shortly afterwards broke up, Howard and myself accompanied Lieutenant Hill from the saloon.

Hill soon proved a pliant tool in our hands. Being of a weak nature and having been reared in the lap of luxury, he had entered into this movement more from a temporary burst of enthusiasm and because it was fashionable, than from any other cause. Now that matters began to assume such a warlike attitude, he was inclined to hesitate before the affair had gone too far, but still he seemed to be enamored with the glory of the undertaking.

By my directions Howard, the ardent secessionist from Louisiana, and Hill, of the Palmetto Guards, became bosom friends and inseparable companions. They drank together, and visited theaters and places of amusement in each other's company.

By reason of his high social position Hill was enabled to introduce his friend to the leading families and into the most aristocratic clubs and societies of which the city boasted, and Howard made many valuable acquaintances through the influence of this rebellious scion of Baltimore aristocracy.

Finally the young man was induced to open to his companion the secrets of the plot to assassinate the President. It was evident, however, that Hill was playing his part in the conspiracy with great reluctance, and one day he said to Howard :

" What a pity it is that this glorious Union must be destroyed all on account of that monster Lincoln." From Hill it was learned that the plans of the conspirators were first to excite and exasperate the popular feeling against Mr. Lincoln to the utmost, and thus far this had been successfully accompanied. From the published programme Mr. Lincoln was to reach Baltimore from Harrisburg by the Northern Central Railroad on the twenty-third day of February, now but a few days distant. He would, therefore, reach the city about the middle of the day. A vast crowd would meet him at the Calvert street depot, at which point it was expected that he would enter an open carriage and ride nearly half a mile to the Washington depot. Here it was arranged that but a small force of policemen should be stationed, and as the President arrived a disturbance would be created which would attract the attention of these guardians of the peace, and this accomplished, it would be an easy task for a determined man to shoot the President, and, aided by his companions, succeed in making his escape.

Agents of the conspirators had been dispatched to all the principal Northern cities, to watch the movements of the presidential party, and ready to telegraph to Baltimore any change of route or delay in arrival. A cipher had been agreed upon between them, so that the conspirators could communicate with each other without the possibility of detection, and everything seemed to be satisfactorily arranged except to depute one of their number to commit the fatal deed. This was to be determined by ballot, and as yet no one knew upon whom might devolve the bloody task.

Meanwhile, the idea of assassination was preying heavily upon the mind of the Lieutenant of the Palmetto Guards; he grew sad and melancholy, and plunged still deeper into dissipation. Howard had now become a necessity to him and they were scarcely ever separated. Under the influence of the master spirit, the disposition of Hill underwent wonderful changes. At times, he would be thoughtful and morose, and then would suddenly break out into enthusiastic rhapsodies. His sleep became tormented with dreams in which he saw himself the martyr to a glorious cause and the savior of his country.

At such times he would address himself to Howard, in the most extravagant language.

"I am destined to die," said he one day, "shrouded with glory. I shall immortalize myself by plunging a knife into Lincoln's heart."

Howard endeavored to calm his transports, but without avail. Raising himself to his full height, he exclaimed: "Rome had her Brutus, why should not we? I swear to you, Howard, if it falls to me I will kill Lincoln before he reaches the Washington depot, not that I love Lincoln less, but my country more."

As the day drew nearer for the arrival of the President, he became more nervous and excited, and would more frequently indulge in extravagant expressions, which would have been regarded as absurd, but for the fact that he was but one of a large number of fanatics, who seriously entertained the same ideas of murder, and his expressions but the reflex of others, more determined.

Timothy Webster was still at Perrymansville, and by this time had fully identified himself with the rebel cause, and the company of cavalry of which he was a member. On several occasions he had given undoubted indications of his loyalty and devotion to the South, and was generally looked upon as a man who could be trusted. He became quite intimate with the officers of the company, and succeeded in gaining their entire confidence. As yet, however, he had learned but little of the important movement which we believed was in contemplation, as all conversations upon that subject appeared to be between the officers of the company, at their secret meetings, to which he had not been able as yet to gain an entrance.

At length one morning, after the usual daily drill,

and when the company had been dismissed, the Captain addressed Webster and requested him to be present at his house that evening, as he desired to consult with him upon important affairs, at the same time cautioning him to say nothing to any one concerning the matter.

Promptly at the time appointed Webster presented himself at the residence of the Captain, and was ushered into a room upon the upper floor, where there were several men already assembled. The cur tains had been drawn close, and heavy quilts had been hung over the windows, which effectually prevented any one from the outside from discovering a light in the room. On his entrance he was introduced to the gentlemen present, three of whom were unknown to him, who were members of the secret league from Baltimore, and who were evidently impressed with the solemnity and importance of their undertaking. They greeted Webster cordially, however, and made room for him at the table around which they were sitting.

A few minutes satisfied Webster as to the nature of the meeting, and that it was a conclave of the conspirators, who had met to discuss a plan of action. Intensely eager as he was to acquire all possible information, he was obliged to restrain his impetuosity and to listen calmly to the developments that were made. From what transpired that evening there could be no doubt of the desperation of the men engaged in the conspiracy, or of the widespread interest which was taken in their movements.

The plans for the assassination of the President had been fully matured, and only needed the selection of the person to perform the deed, in order to carry them into effect. In the meantime, however, other important measures required attention and consideration. If the affair stopped simply with the assassination of the President, but little, if any, good would be accomplished. The North would rise as one man to avenge the death of their leader, and they would only hasten a disaster they were anxious to avoid. It was necessary, therefore, that the work should be thoroughly done, and the plan suggested was as follows :

As soon as the deed had been accomplished in Baltimore, the news was to be telegraphed along the line of the road, and immediately upon the reception of this intelligence the telegraph wires were to be cut, the railroad bridges destroyed and the tracks torn up, in order to prevent for some time any information being conveyed to the cities of the North, or the passage of any Northern men towards the eapital.

Wild as the scheme was, it found instant favor with the reckless men assembled together, and all signified their hearty assent to the propositions and offered their aid in successfully carrying them out. Among the most earnest in their protestations was Timothy Webster, and as he announced his intention

to perform his duty in the affair he was warmly congratulated.

Matters were evidently getting warm, and but
little time was left for action.

"WARMING UP."

CHAPTER IV.

The Conspirators in Council.—My Operative Joins the Conspiracy.

I HAD already written to Mr. Norman B. Judd as the party reached Cincinnati, informing him that I had reason to believe that there was a plot on foot to murder the President on his passage through Baltimore, and promising to advise him further as the party progressed eastward.

This information Mr. Judd did not divulge to any one, fearing to occasion undue anxiety or unnecessary alarm, and knowing that I was upon the ground and could be depended upon to act at the proper time.

When the party reached Buffalo another note from me awaited Mr. Judd, informing him of the accumulation of evidence, but conveying no particulars. The party were now journeying towards New York city, and I determined to learn all that there was to learn before many hours.

Previous to this, in addition to the men engaged in Baltimore, I had sent for Mrs. Kate Warne, the lady superintendent of my agency. This lady had arrived several days before, and had already made

remarkable progress in cultivating the acquaintance of the wives and daughters of the conspirators.

Mrs. Warne was eminently fitted for this task.
Of rather a commanding person, with clear-cut,
expressive features, and with an ease of manner that
was quite captivating at times, she was calculated to
make a favorable impression at once. She was of
Northern birth, but in order to vouch for her
Southern opinions, she represented herself as from
Montgomery, Alabama, a locality with which she was
perfectly familiar, from her connection with the detection of the robbery of the Adams Express Company,
at that place. Her experience in that case, which is
fully detailed in " The Expressman and the Detective," fully qualified her for the task of representing
herself as a resident of the South.

She was a brilliant conversationalist when so
disposed, and could be quite vivacious, but she also
understood that rarer quality in womankind, the art
of being silent.

The information she received was invaluable, but
as yet the meetings of the chief conspirators had not
been entered. Mrs. Warne displayed upon her
breast, as did many of the ladies of Baltimore, the
black and white cockade, which had been temporarily
adopted as the emblem of secession, and many hints
were dropped in her presence which found their way
to my ears, and were of great benefit to me.

As I have said, the Presidential party were in Buffalo, and I had resolved upon prompt and decisive measures to discover the inward workings of the conspirators. Accordingly I obtained an interview with Howard, and gave him such instructions as I deemed necessary under the circumstances. He was to insist upon Hill taking him to the meeting at which the ballots were to be drawn, and where he, too, would have an opportunity to immortalize himself, and then, that being accomplished, the rest would be easy and all further danger would be over.

Accordingly, that day Howard broached the matter to Hill in a manner which convinced him of his earnestness, and the young Lieutenant promised his utmost efforts to secure his admission. At five o'clock in the afternoon they again met, and Hill joyfully informed his companion that his request had been granted, and that, upon his vouching for the fidelity of his friend, he had succeeded in obtaining permission for him to enter their society.

That evening Howard accompanied his friend Hill to the rendezvous of the league, and as they entered the darkened chamber, they found many of the conspirators already assembled. The members were strangely silent, and an ominous awe seemed to pervade the entire assembly. About twenty men comprised the number, but many entered afterward. After a few preliminary movements, Howard was conducted to the station of the President of the

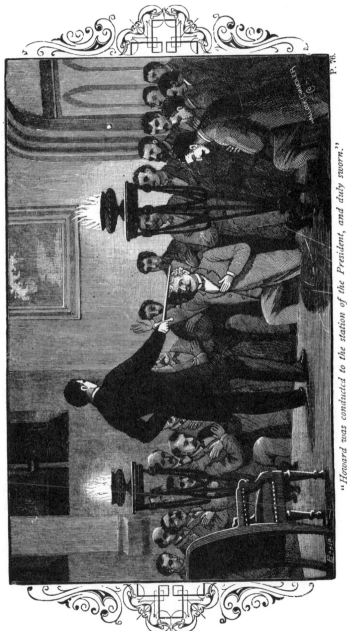

"Howard was conducted to the station of the President, and duly sworn."

P. 76.

assembly and duly sworn, the members gathering around him in a circle as this was being done.

Having passed through the required formula, Howard was warmly taken by the hand by his associates, many of whom he had met in the polite circles of society. After quiet had been restored, the President, who was none other than Captain Fernandina, arose, and in a dramatic manner detailed the particulars of the plot.

It had been fully determined that the assassination should take place at the Calvert street depot. A vast crowd of secessionists were to assemble at that place to await the arrival of the train with Mr. Lincoln. They would appear early and fill the narrow streets and passages immediately surrounding it. No attempt at secrecy was made of the fact that the Marshal of Police was conversant with their plans, and that he would detail but a small force of policemen to attend the arrival, and nominally clear and protect a passage for Mr. Lincoln and his suite. Nor was the fact disguised that these policemen were in active sympathy with the movement. George P. Kane's animus was fully shown when he was subsequently arrested by General Banks, and afterwards became an officer in the rebel army.

When the train entered the depot, and Mr. Lincoln attempted to pass through the narrow passage leading to the streets, a party already delegated were to engage in a conflict on the outside, and then the policemen were to rush away to quell the disturbance. At this moment—the police being entirely withdrawn —Mr. Lincoln would find himself surrounded by a dense, excited and hostile crowd, all hustling and jamming against him, and then the fatal blow was to be struck.

A swift steamer was to be stationed in Chesapeake Bay, with a boat awaiting upon the shore, ready to take the assassin on board as soon as the deed was done, and convey him to a Southern port, where he would be received with acclamations of joy and honored as a hero.

The question to be decided this evening was: "Who should do the deed?" "Who should assume the task of liberating the nation of the foul presence of the abolitionist leader?" For this purpose the meeting had been called to-night, and to-night the important decision was to be reached.

It was finally determined that ballots should be prepared and placed in a box arranged for that purpose, and that the person who drew a *red* ballot should perform the duty of assassination.

In order that none should know who drew the fatal ballot, except he who did so, the room was ren dered still darker, and every one was pledged to secrecy as to the color of the ballot he drew. The leaders, however, had determined that their plans should not fail, and doubting the courage of some of their number, instead of placing but *one red ballot* in the box, they placed *eight* of the designated color, and these eight ballots were drawn—each man who drew them believing that upon him, his courage, strength and devotion, depended the cause of the South—each supposing that he alone was charged with the execution of the deed.

After the ballots had been drawn the President again addressed the assembly. He violently assailed the enemies of the South, and in glowing words pointed out the glory that awaited the man who would prove himself the hero upon this great occasion, and finally, amid much restrained enthusiasm, the meeting adjourned, and their duties had thus far been accomplished.

My time for action had now arrived ; my plans had been perfected and I resolved to act at once. Taking Mrs. Warne with me I reached New York city on the same day that the presidential party arrived there, and leaving Mrs. Warne to perfect arrangements, I proceeded at once to Philadelphia. That evening Mrs. Warne repaired to the Astor House and requested an interview with Mr. Judd. Her request being granted, Mrs. Warne informed that gentleman, that, fearing to trust the mail in so important a matter, she had been delegated by me to arrange for a personal interview, at which all the proofs relating to the conspiracy could be submitted to him. It was suggested that immediately after the arrival of the party in Philadelphia, I should inform Mr. Judd of my plans for an interview, and that he would be governed accordingly.

While they were conversing, Col. E. S. Sandford, President of the American Telegraph Company, called, and was introduced by Mrs. Warne to Mr. Judd. This gentleman had been made fully acquainted with what I had learned, and had promised all the assistance within his power, and he accordingly tendered to Mr. Judd his own personal service and the unlimited use of the telegraph lines under his control, for any communications he might desire to make.

On arriving at Philadelphia, I proceeded directly to the office of Mr. Felton, and acquainted him with all the information I had received, of the designs of the conspirators with regard to Mr. Lincoln, and of their intention to destroy the railroad should their plot be successful. The situation was truly alarming, and cautious measures were absolutely necessary. It was therefore resolved to obtain an interview with Mr. Lincoln, submit the facts to him, and be governed by his suggestions, whatever they might be.

This interview took place on the 20th day of February, and Mr. Lincoln was expected to arrive on the following day. Great preparations had been made for his reception, and the military, of which Philadelphia was justly proud, were to escort the President-elect from the depot to the Continental Hotel, where quarters had been engaged for him, and where he would receive the congratulations of the people.

CHAPTER V.

THE twenty-first dawned bright and sunny, and the streets were alive with the eager populace, all anxious to do honor to the new President, and to witness the scenes attendant upon his reception. In due time the train containing the party arrived, and after an informal welcome they took carriages, and, escorted by the troops, the procession took up the line of march for the hotel. Vast crowds lined the sidewalks and the enthusiasm of the people was unbounded. The President graciously acknowledged their courtesies as he passed along. On each side of the carriage in which Mr. Lincoln was seated, accompanied by Mr. Judd, was a file of policemen, whose duty it was to prevent the mass of people from pressing too closely to the vehicle. As the procession reached the corner of Broad and Chestnut streets, a young man approached the file of policemen and endeavored to attract the attention of the occupants of the carriage. Finding this impossible, he boldly plunged through

6 [81]

the ranks of the officers, and coming to the side of the carriage, he handed to Mr. Judd a slip of paper, on which was written :

" *St. Louis Hotel, ask for J. H. Hutchinson.*"

This young man was Mr. George H. Burns, an attache of the American Telegraph Company and confidential agent of E. S. Sandford, Esq., who acted as my messenger, and who afterwards distinguished himself for his courage and daring in the rebellion. It is needless to add that J. H. Hutchinson was the name I had assumed in registering at the hotel, in order to avoid any suspicion or curiosity in case any emissary of the conspirators should ascertain my real name and thus be warned of the discovery of their scheme.

Shortly after the arrival of Mr. Lincoln at the Continental, Mr. Judd was announced at the St. Louis Hotel as desiring to see me. Mr. Felton was with me at the time, and in a few miuutes Mr. Judd made his appearance. More than an hour was occupied in going over the proofs which I produced of the existence of the conspiracy, at the end of which time Mr. Judd expressed himself fully convinced that the plot was a reality, and that prompt measures were required to secure the safety of the President.

" My advice is," said I, after I had succeeded in convincing Mr. Judd that my information was reliable, "that Mr. Lincoln shall proceed to Washington this evening by the eleven o'clock train, and then once safe at the capital, General Scott and his soldiery will afford him ample protection."

"I fear very much that Mr. Lincoln will not accede to this," replied Mr. Judd; "but as the President is an old acquaintance and friend of yours and has had occasion before this to test your reliability and prudence, suppose you accompany me to the Continental Hotel, and we can then lay this information before him in person and abide by his decision."

This idea was at once adopted and we proceeded to the hotel. Here we found the entrances blocked up by a surging multitude which effectually prevented our admission, and we were obliged to enter by the rear of the building through a door used by the servants.

On reaching the room occupied by Mr. Judd that gentleman summoned Mr. Nicolay, the President's private secretary, and dispatched him with a note requesting the presence of Mr. Lincoln upon a matter of urgent importance.

The President at that time was in one of the large parlors surrounded by a number of ladies and gentlemen, all eager to extend to him the hospitalities of the city and to express their good wishes for the success of his administration. Upon receiving the message, however, he at once excused himself, and forcing his way through the crowd came directly to us.

Up to this time Mr. Lincoln had been kept in entire ignorance of any threatened danger, and as he listened to the facts that were now presented to him, a shade of sadness fell upon his face. He seemed loth to credit the statement, and could scarce believe it possible that such a conspiracy could exist. Slowly he went over the points presented, questioning me minutely the while, but at length finding it impossible to discredit the truthfulness of what I stated to him. he yielded a reluctant credence to the facts.

After he had been fully made acquainted with the startling disclosures, Mr. Judd submitted to him the plan proposed by me, that he should leave Philadelphia for Washington that evening.

"But," added Mr. Judd, "the proofs that have just been laid before you cannot be published, as it will involve the lives of several devoted men now on Mr. Pinkerton's force, especially that of Timothy Webster, who is now serving in a rebel cavalry company under drill at Perrymansville in Maryland."

Mr. Lincoln at once acknowledged the correctness of this view, but appeared at a loss as to what course to pursue.

"You will therefore perceive"—continued Mr. Judd—"that if you follow the course suggested—that of proceeding to Washington to-night—you w'll necessarily be subjected to the scoffs and sneers of your enemies, and the disapproval of your friends who cannot be made to believe in the existence of so desperate a plot."

"I fully appreciate these suggestions," replied Mr. Lincoln, "and I can stand anything that is necessary, but," he added rising to his feet, "I cannot go to-night. I have promised to raise the flag over Independence Hall to-morrow morning, and to visit the legislature at Harrisburg in the afternoon—beyond that I have no engagements. Any plan that may be adopted that will enable me to fulfill these promises I will accede to, and you can inform me what is concluded upon to-morrow."

Saying which Mr. Lincoln left the room and joined the people in the parlor. During the entire interview, he had not evinced the slightest evidence of agitation or fear. Calm and self-possessed, his only sentiments appeared to be those of profound regret, that the Southern sympathizers could be so far led away by the excitement of the hour, as to consider his death a necessity for the furtherance of their cause.

From his manner, it was deemed useless to attempt to induce him to alter his mind, and after a few minutes' further conversation, which was participated in by Mr. Sandford, who had entered the room, I left for the purpose of finding Thomas A. Scott, Esq., the Vice-President of the Pennsylvania Central Railroad, in order to make arrangements for the carrying out of a plan which had occurred to me, and which would enable Mr. Lincoln to fulfill his engagements.

I was unable, however, to find Mr. Scott, but succeeded in reaching Mr. G. C. Franciscus, the general manager of the road, and at twelve o'clock that night, in company with that gentleman and Mr. Sandford, we called again upon Mr. Judd.

At this meeting a full discussion of the entire matter was had between us, and after all possible contingencies had been considered, the following programme was agreed upon.

After the formal reception at Harrisburg had taken place, a special train, consisting of a baggage-car and one passenger-coach, should leave there at six o'clock P. M. to carry Mr. Lincoln and one companion back to Philadelphia; this train was to be under the immediate control of Mr. Franciscus and Mr. Enoch Lewis, the general superintendent. In order to avoid the possibility of accident, the track was to be cleared of everything between Harrisburg and Philadelphia from half-past five o'clock until after the passage of the special train. Mr. Felton was to detain the eleven o'clock P. M. Baltimore train until the arrival of the special train from Harrisburg, Mrs. Warne in the meantime engaging berths in the sleeping-car bound for Baltimore.

I was to remain in Philadelphia in order that no accident might occur in conveying the President

"*Mr. Lincoln raising the flag on Independence Hall.*"

from one depot to another, and Mr. Judd was to manage the affair at Harrisburg. Everything that could be suggested in relation to this matter was fully considered, and having at length perfected our plans, the party separated at half-past four o'clock in the morning, fully prepared to carry out the programme agreed upon.

At six o'clock on the morning of the 22d, a vast concourse of people assembled in front of Independence Hall on Chestnut street, and at precisely the hour appointed, Mr. Lincoln made his appearance. With his own hands he drew to the top of the staff surmounting the edifice a beautiful new American flag, and as its Stripes and Stars floated out gracefully to the breeze, the air was rent with the shouts of the multitude and the music of the band.

Mr. Lincoln's speech upon this occasion was the most impressive and characteristic of any which he had delivered upon his journey to the capital, while a tinge of sadness pervaded his remarks, never noticed before, and which were occasioned no doubt by the revelations of the preceding night. He gave a most eloquent expression to the emotions and associations which were suggested by the day and by the historic old hall where he then stood. He declared that all his political sentiments were drawn from the inspired utterances of those who had sat within the walls of that ancient edifice.

He alluded most feelingly to the dangers and toils and sufferings of those who had adopted and made good the Declaration of Independence—a declaration which gave promise that "in due time the weight would be lifted from the shoulders of all men." Conscious of the dangers that threatened his country, and feeling also that those dangers originated in opposition to the principles enunciated in the Declaration of Independence, knowing that his own life was even then threatened because of his devotion to liberty, and that his way to the national capital was beset by assassins, he did not hesitate to declare boldly and fearlessly "that he would rather be assassinated on the spot than surrender those principles" so dear to him.

After these proceedings, Mr. Lincoln was driven back to the Continental Hotel, and sending for Mr. Judd, he introduced him to Mr. Frederick H. Seward, a son of the late William H. Seward, who was in the room with the President. Mr. Lincoln then informed Mr. Judd that Mr. Seward had been sent from Washington by his father and General Scott to warn him of the danger of passing through Baltimore, and to urge him to come direct to Washington.

From whom this information was originally obtained did not appear, but the facts were deemed of sufficient moment to be brought to the ears of the President, and hence Mr. Seward's visit to Philadelphia. Mr. Lincoln evinced no further hesitancy in the matter, and signified his readiness to do whatever was required of him. Mr. Judd then directed Mr. Seward to inform his father that all had been arranged, and that, so far as human foresight could predict, Mr. Lincoln would be in Washington before the evening of the following day, and cautioned him to preserve the utmost secrecy in regard to the matter. No particulars were given and none were asked.

At the time appointed Mr. Lincoln started for Harrisburg, and I busied myself with the preparations that were necessary to successfully carry our plans into operation. From reports which I received from Baltimore, the excitement in that city had grown more intense, and the arrival of the President was awaited with the most feverish impatience. The common and accepted belief was that Mr. Lincoln would journey from Harrisburg to Baltimore over the Northern Central Railroad, and the plans of the conspirators were arranged accordingly.

It became a matter of the utmost importance, therefore, that no intimation of our movements should reach that city. I had no doubt but that trusty agents of the conspirators were following the presidential party, and after the absence of Mr. Lincoln had been discovered, the telegraph would be put into active operation to apprise the movers of this scheme of the change that had been made. To effectually prevent this I determined that the telegraph wires which connected Harrisburg with her neighboring

cities should be so "fixed" as to render communication impossible.

To arrange this matter Capt. Burns was sent to
the office of the American Telegraph Company, and
obtaining from Mr. H. E. Thayer, the manager of
the company, a competent and trustworthy man for
the purpose, departed for Harrisburg, in order to
carry out the proposed measures. Mr. Thayer, in the
meantime, was to remain in the office during the
night, in order to intercept any dispatches that might
be sent over the wires from any point between
Harrisburg and Baltimore, and to immediately deliver
any messages that might be sent to me.

Mr. W. P. Westervelt, the superintendent, and
Mr. Andrew Wynne, the line-man of the telegraph
company, were delegated to Harrisburg to "fix" the
wires leading from that place in such a manner as to
prevent any communication from passing over them,
and to report to Capt. Burns upon their arrival.

After the train containing Mr. Lincoln and his
party had left Philadelphia, Mr. Judd sought the first
favorable opportunity of conversing with Mr. Lincoln
alone, and fully detailed to him the plan that had
been agreed upon, all of which met with the hearty
approval of the President, who signified a cheerful willingness to adapt himself to the novel circumstances.

It was evident, from the manner of several of the
gentlemen of the party, that they suspected something was transpiring of which they had not been ad-

vised, but they all very judiciously refrained from asking any questions. Mr. Judd, however, who felt the
responsibility of his position, finally suggested to Mr.
Lincoln the propriety and advisability of informing
them of what had taken place, and of consulting with
them upon the proper carrying out of the contemplated journey. To this Mr. Lincoln yielded a ready
assent, adding, with an amused smile :

"I suppose they will laugh at us, Judd, but I
think you had better get them together."

It was therefore arranged that after the reception
at the State House had taken place, and before they
sat down to dinner, the matter should be fully laid
before the following gentlemen of the party : Judge
David Davis, Col. Sumner, Major David Hunter,
Capt. John Pope and Ward H. Lamon, Esq.

Mr. Lincoln arrived at Harrisburg at noon, and
was introduced to the people from the balcony of the
Jones House, where an address was delivered by Gov.
Andrew G. Curtin, whose fame became widespread
during the dark days of the rebellion that followed,
as the "War Governor of Pennsylvania." From the
hotel the party proceeded to the House of Representatives, where he was welcomed by the Speaker, to
which he replied in a few well-chosen words.

After a short time spent in congratulations and
hand-shaking they returned to the hotel, and the gentlemen who have been previously named were invited
(in company with the Governor) to confer with the

President in the parlor. At this meeting the information of the discovery of the plot to assassinate the President was laid before them, and also the details of the
proposed journey to Washington. After the matter
had been fully explained, a great diversity of opinion
manifested itself among the gentlemen present, and
some warm discussion was indulged in. Finally, Judge
Davis, who had expressed no opinion upon the subject
as yet, addressed the President, saying :

"Well, Mr. Lincoln, what is your own judgment
upon this matter ?"

"I have thought over this matter considerably
since I went over the ground with Mr. Pinkerton last
night," answered Mr. Lincoln, "and the appearance of
Mr. Frederick Seward, with warning from another
source, confirms my belief in Mr. Pinkerton's statement ; therefore, unless there are some other reasons
than a fear of ridicule, I am disposed to carry out
Mr. Judd's plan."

Judge Davis turned to the others, and said :

"That settles the matter, gentlemen."

"So be it," exclaimed Col. Sumner. "It is
against my judgment, but I have undertaken to go to
Washington with Mr. Lincoln, and I shall do it."

Mr. Judd endeavored in vain to convince the gallant old soldier that every additional person only
added to the risk, but the fiery spirit of the veteran
was aroused and debate was useless.

Having arranged the matter thus satisfactorily

the party, at about four o'clock in the afternoon, repaired to the dining-room for dinner.

All the preliminaries had now been successfully
arranged. The special train, ostensibly to take the
officers of the railroad company back to Philadelphia,
was waiting upon a side track just outside of the
town. The telegraph operators had performed their
work admirably. Walking out of the city nearly two
miles, Mr. Wynne climbed the poles and placing fine
copper ground wires upon the regular lines, the city
was soon entirely isolated from her neighbors. No
message could possibly be sent from Harrisburg, and
the capital of Pennsylvania was cut off temporarily
from the rest of the world.

The preparations in Philadelphia had also been
fully made. Mrs. Warne had succeeded in engaging
the rear half of a sleeping-car for the accommodation
of her invalid brother, and that portion of the car was
to be entirely separated from the rest by a curtain, so
arranged that no one in the forward part of the car
would be aware of the occupants of the same coach.

In order to detain the Baltimore train until the
arrival of Mr. Lincoln, the conductor was directed
not to start his train until he received personal instructions to that effect from Mr. H. F. Kinney, the
superintendent, who would hand him an important
parcel, which President Felton desired should be delivered early on the following morning to Mr. E. J.
Allen at Willard's Hotel, in Washington. (E. J.

Allen was the nom-de-plume I generally used when on detective operations.)

At a quarter to six o'clock everything was in readiness. A carriage was in waiting at the side entrance of the hotel, and the entire party were still at the table. A message was delivered to the President by Mr. Nicolay, and upon receiving it, he immediately arose, and, accompanied by Mr. Curtin, Mr. Lamon and Mr. Judd, he left the dining-room. Mr. Lincoln exchanged his dinner dress for a traveling suit, and soon returned with a shawl upon his arm and a soft felt hat protruding from his coat pocket.

The halls, stairways and pavement were filled with a mass of people, who, seeing the President in company with the Governor, at once imagined that they were going to the executive mansion, where a reception was to be held in the evening.

Mr. Judd whispered to Mr. Lamon to proceed in advance, adding :

"As soon as Mr. Lincoln is in the carriage, drive off."

As the party, consisting of Mr. Lincoln, Governor Curtin, and Mr. Lamon, entered the carriage, Col. Sumner attempted to follow them, but Mr. Judd gently put his hand upon the old gentleman's shoulder, and as he turned quickly around to inquire what was wanted, the carriage was driven rapidly away.

Thus far everything had passed off admirably, and in a short time Mr. Lincoln was upon the special

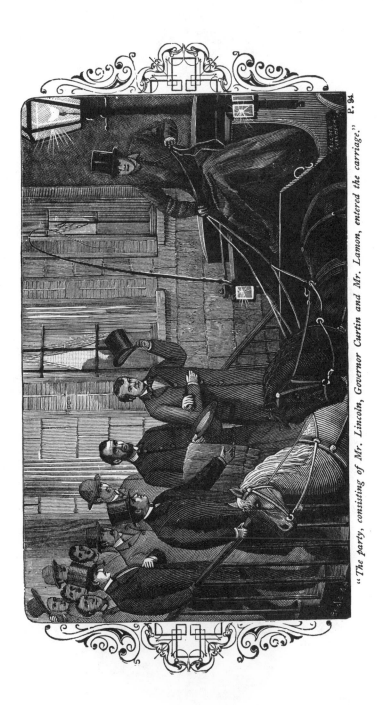

"The party, consisting of Mr. Lincoln, Governor Curtin and Mr. Lamon, entered the carriage."

P. 94.

train, accompanied only by Mr. Lamon and the railroad officials, and speeding along toward Philadelphia.

Without accident the party arrived at the Quaker City shortly after ten o'clock, where I was waiting with a carriage, in company with Mr. Kinney. Without a word Mr. Lincoln, Mr. Lamon and myself entered the vehicle, while Mr. Kinney seated himself alongside of the driver, and we proceeded directly to the depot of the Philadelphia, Wilmington and Baltimore Railroad.

Driving up to the sidewalk on Carpenter street, and in the shadow of a tall fence, the carriage was stopped and the party alighted. As we approached the train, Mrs. Warne came forward, and, familiarly greeting the President as her brother, we entered the sleeping-car by the rear door without unnecessary delay, and without any one being aware of the distin guished passenger who had arrived.

A carefully inclosed package, which resembled a formidable official document, but which contained only some neatly folded daily papers, was placed in the hands of the unsuspecting conductor—the whistle sounded, and soon the train was in motion, whirling on towards the capital of the nation.

So carefully had all our movements been conducted, that no one in Philadelphia saw Mr. Lincoln enter the car, and no one on the train, except his own immediate party—not even the conductor, knew of his presence, and the President, feeling fatigued from the labors and the journeys of the day, at once retired to his berth.

In order to prevent the possibility of accident, I had arranged with my men a series of signals along the road. It was barely possible that the work of destroying the railroad might be attempted by some reckless individuals, or that a suspicion of our movements might be entertained by the conspirators, and therefore, the utmost caution must be observed.

As the train approached Havre de Grace, I went to the rear platform of the car, and as the train passed on a bright light flashed suddenly upon my gaze and was as quickly extinguished, and then I knew that thus far all was well.

From this point all the way to Baltimore, at every bridge-crossing these lights flashed, and their rays carried the comforting assurance " All's Well !"

We reached Baltimore at about half-past three o'clock in the morning, and as the train rumbled into the depot an officer of the road entered the car and whispered in my ear the welcome words " All's Well !"

The city was in profound repose as we passed through. Darkness and silence reigned over all. Perhaps, at this moment, however, the reckless conspirators were astir perfecting their plans for a tragedy as infamous as any which has ever disgraced a free country—perhaps even now the holders of the *red* ballots were nerving themselves for their part in the

dreadful work, or were tossing restlessly upon sleepless couches.

Be that as it may, our presence in Baltimore was
entirely unsuspected, and as the sleeping-car in which
we were, was drawn by horses through the streets
from the Philadelphia, Wilmington and Baltimore
depot, until we reached the Washington station, no
sign of life was apparent in the great slumbering city.
At the depot, however, a number of people were
gathered, awaiting the arrival and departure of the
various trains, and here the usual bustle and activity
were manifested.

We were compelled to remain here fully two
hours, owing to the detention of the train from the
West, and during that time, Mr. Lincoln remained
quietly in his berth, joking with rare good humor with
those around him.

Ever and anon some snatches of rebel harmony
would reach our ears, as they were rather discordantly
sung by the waiting passengers in and around the
depot. "My Maryland" and "Dixie" appeared to
be the favorites, and once, after an intoxicated individual had roared through one stanza of the latter
song, Mr. Lincoln turned quietly and rather sadly to
me and said :

"No doubt there will be a great time in Dixie by
and by."

How prophetic his words were, the succeeding
years too fully proved.

7

At length the train arrived and we proceeded on our way, arriving in Washington about six o'clock in the morning.   Mr. Lincoln wrapped his traveling shawl about his shoulders, and in company with Mr. Lamon, started to leave the car.   I followed close behind, and on the platform found two of my men awaiting our arrival.   A great many people were gathered about the depot, but Mr. Lincoln entirely escaped recognition, until as we were about leaving the depot, Mr. Washburne, of Illinois, came up and cordially shook him by the hand.

The surprise of this gentleman was unbounded, and many of those standing around, observing his movements, and the tall form of Mr. Lincoln exciting curiosity, I feared that danger might result in case he was recognized at this time.   I accordingly went up to them hurriedly, and pressing between them whispered rather loudly:

"No talking here !"

Mr. Washburne gazed inquiringly at me, and was about to resent my interference, when Mr. Lincoln interposed :

"That is Mr. Pinkerton, and everything is all right."

Thus satisfied, Mr. Washburne quickly led the way to a carriage in waiting outside, where we met Mr. Seward, who warmly greeted the President, and then the party were rapidly driven down Pennsylvania Avenue to Willard's Hotel — I following

P. 98.

"*The safe arrival at Washington.*"

closely behind them with my men, in another vehicle.

On his arrival at the hotel Mr. Lincoln was warmly greeted by his friends, who were rejoiced at his safe arrival, and leaving him in the hands of those whose fealty was undoubted, I withdrew, and engaged temporary quarters at another hotel.

Dnring the forenoon I received a note from Mr. Lincoln requesting an interview, and received his warm expressions of thankfulness for the part I had performed in securing his safety, after which, finding that my object had been fully accomplished, I took the train and returned to Baltimore.

Here I found the utmost excitement prevailing. The news of the safe arrival of Mr. Lincoln had already reached there, and a general sentiment of rage and disappointment pervaded the entire circle of conspirators and secessionists. I lost no time in securing an interview with Howard, and learned from him the particulars attendant upon the discovery that Mr. Lincoln had outwitted his enemies and was now safely quartered in Washington. Finding that their plans had been discovered, and fearing that the vengeance of the government would overtake them, the leading conspirators had suddenly disappeared. All their courage and bravado was gone, and now, like the miserable cowards that they were, they had sought safety in flight.

A curious episode occurred at Harrisburg immediately after the departure of Mr. Lincoln from that city. Two newspaper correspondents connected with prominent New York journals had accompanied the party from Springfield, and had faithfully noted the incidents which had occurred upon the journey. As soon as the train which carried Mr. Lincoln away from Harrisburg was on its way, a gentlemanly individual, *well-known to me*, went to the room occupied by these journalists, and found them engaged in preparations to witness the further proceedings of the presidential party

The visitor quickly informed the gentlemen that Mr. Lincoln had left the city and was now flying over the road in the direction of Washington, which he would no doubt reach in the morning. This was the signal for renewed activity, and both gentlemen hastily arose, and, grasping their hats, started for the door. Their visitor however, was too quick for them, and standing before the door with a revolver in each hand, he addressed them : "You cannot leave this room, gentlemen, without my permission !"

"What does this mean ?" inquired one of the surprised gentlemen, blinking through his spectacles.

"It means that you cannot leave this room until the safety of Mr. Lincoln justifies it," calmly replied the other.

"I want to telegraph to the *Herald*," said the second correspondent—"what is the use of obtaining news if we cannot utilize it ?"

"You cannot utilize anything at present, gentle-men. The telegraph will not be of any service to you, for the wires are all down, and Harrisburg will be separated from the rest of the world for some hours yet."

"When do you propose to let us out?" humbly asked one.

"Well, I'll tell you, gentlemen. If you will sit down calmly, and bide your time and mine, I will make matters interesting for you, by informing you all about this flank movement on the Baltimoreans."

Their indignation and fright subsided at once, and they quietly sat down. Refreshments were sent for, and soon the nimble pencils of the reporters were rapidly jotting down as much of the information as was deemed advisable to be made public at that time. After they had heard all, they prepared their dis-patches for New York, both correspondents writing long and interesting accounts of the affair.

When daylight dawned, and the gladsome tidings had been received that Mr. Lincoln was safe, these knights of the quill were liberated, and, rushing to the telegraph offices, which were now in running order again, the news was transmitted to New York, and in less than an hour the types were being set which would convey to the public the startling news of the discovered conspiracy, and the manner in which the conspirators had been outwitted.

As the later train arrived at Baltimore, I went to

the depot and found the remaining members of the President's party, who also brought Mrs. Lincoln with them.

Mr. Judd was jubilant at the success of the adventure, but Col. Sumner had not yet recovered his good humor. I have no doubt, however, that Mr. Lincoln succeeded in placating his irascible friend, and I know that in the bloody scenes which followed Col. Sumner bore an honorable and courageous part.

Thus ends the narration of this important episode in one of the most interesting epochs of the country's history, and a truthful record has been given. Exaggerated stories and unauthorized statements have been freely made with regard to this journey of Mr. Lincoln. The caricaturist has attempted to throw ridicule upon the great man who now sleeps in a martyr's grave. A silly story of his being disguised in a Scotch cap and plaid obtained a temporary currency, but the fact remains that Mr. Lincoln, as a gentleman, and in the company of gentlemen, successfully passed through the camp of the conspirators and reached in safety the capital of the country.

Now the war is ended. Peace reigns throughout the borders of the great Republic. And when, during the last dying throes of the rebellion, this great man was stricken down by the hand of an assassin, North and South alike united in lamenting his death, and in execrating the damnable deed and its reckless perpetrators.

I had informed Mr. Lincoln in Philadelphia that I would answer with my life for his safe arrival in Washington, and I had redeemed my pledge.

A CAMP SONG.

CHAPTER VI.

My Connection with the Rebellion.—Timothy Webster Accepts a Mission.

M Y connection with the " Great Rebellion " of 1861 began almost from the inception of that gigantic struggle. During the days that intervened between the inauguration of Abraham Lincoln and the memorable 12th day of April, 1861, treason was busy in the South, and secession resolved itself into an accomplished fact. Scarcely had the reverberating tones of the guns upon the batteries in Charleston Harbor died away upon the air, than I was called into the service of the military branch of the government. At that time I was engaged in the energetic practice of my profession as a detective, which, large as it was, and constantly increasing, required a personal supervision, which absorbed my undivided attention. When, however, it became evident that a conflict was unavoidable, I soon found my services were needed, and putting aside all considerations of a private or business nature, I yielded a ready and cheerful response to the call, and during my connection with what was afterwards known as the secret service of the government, I rendered every assistance that lay in my power to further the cause of union, and to serve the country of my adoption.

The month of April, 1861, was an important one in the history of the country. Whatever fears and apprehensions had filled the minds of the Northern people as to the solution of the great political questions then pending, a resort to arms had, until that time, been regarded as not likely to occur. A people who had been reared amid the blessings of a long and undisturbed peace, and whose lives, under this benign influence, had been prosperous and happy, they were almost entirely unprepared for a serious contest or a warlike struggle. Many times before the political horizon had grown dark and threatening, but the storm had subsided almost instantly, under that wise yielding of obedience to law and to the will of majorities, which it was hoped would now exercise its power for the preservation and continuance of amity.

When, therefore, on the 12th of April, the attack upon Fort Sumter in Charleston Harbor was made, the Northern people were almost startled by surprise. Though entirely unprepared for such an event, it was clearly demonstrated to all that war could now no longer be honorably avoided. It was now too late to inquire into original causes of the contest; it remained only for the loyal heart to resent the insult to a nation's flag, and to sustain the government in upholding its constitution

and in enforcing its laws. This act fired the patriotic heart and solidified the patriotic ranks, and,
with the crumbling of the walls upon Fort Sumter, were shattered all the hopes previously entertained of a peaceful solution of the problems which
were then before the country. I have very little
doubt that the assault upon Fort Sumter was ordered
by the rebel government, under the fallacious hope
and groundless belief that it would not provoke
immediate or wide-spread civil war. The Southern
leaders were well aware of the fact that the frontier
could not be entirely stripped of regulars, and assuming, or pretending to, that the existing laws
contained no provision authorizing a call of the
militia, they inferred that it would be difficult for
the new administration to obtain at once legislation
of a coercive character. Then, too, they relied, in
a great measure, upon a friendly feeling toward the
South from their late political associates in the
North ; but in this their reckoning was at fault,
and the roar of Beauregard's guns in Charleston
Harbor cleared up the political horizon as if by
magic.

There could no longer be any doubt as to the
position and intentions of the Confederates. Seven
disloyal States, with all their machinery of a separate
government, stood behind those batteries, and the
cool deliberation of the assault gave evidence of
plan, of purpose and of confidence. What had been

believed to be a mere conspiracy for the gaining of certain political ends, now gave way to a revolution, which menaced the perpetuity of the government and which required the armed force of the govern-ment to combat and subdue.

The news of the assault upon Sumter reached Washington on Saturday, the 13th day of April, and on the following day, Sunday though it was, President Lincoln assembled his Cabinet to discuss the duty of the hour, and on Monday morning a proc-lamation was issued, calling forth an army of seventy-five thousand men, for objects entirely lawful and constitutional.

The effect of this proclamation upon the people of the North was almost electrical, and the heart of the whole nation throbbed with its patriotic emotions as that of a single individual. The general sentiment appeared to be in entire accord with the utterance of Stephen A. Douglas, a live-long Democrat, that " every man must be for the United States, or against it ; there can be no neutrals in this war—only patriots and traitors." More than double the number of men that were required tendered their services, and before the lapse of forty-eight hours armed companies and regiments of volunteers were in motion toward the expected border of conflict. Nor was there exhibited that division of Northern sentiment that had been so boastfully predicted by the Southern leaders, and all men, of every belief, Democrats and Republicans,

Conservatives and Radicals, natives and foreigners, from Maine to Oregon, responded to the call, and came to the defense of the constitution, the government and the Union.

At this time the position of Maryland was rather a precarious one. There could be no doubt that the Unionists were greatly in the majority, but it was also true that there was a large and influential minority of her people in favor of secession. Here, as elsewhere, conspiracy had been at work for months, and many of the prominent political leaders were in full accord with the rebel government. The legislature was believed to be unreliable, and treason had obtained so firm a foothold in the populous city of Baltimore, that a secret recruiting office was sending enlisted men to Charleston. The venomous germ of treason, once planted, grew in magnitude and virulence, until it finally culminated in the infamous riot of April 19th, when the blood of the citizen soldiery of Massachusetts was first shed in defense of the Union. A spirit of opposition to the passage of Northern troops through the city, on their way to the seat of government, had been engendered among the " rough " element of Baltimore, and the excitement reached its climax upon the arrival of the Sixth Massachusetts Regiment, which was the first to answer the call for troops. When their presence became known the traitorous element could no longer be restrained, and while the men were passing quietly through the city, on their way from one railroad station to another, they were murderously attacked by a reckless, howling mob, which resulted in bloodshed and carnage, and some of the most fiendish outrages were perpetrated that ever blackened a page of American history.

The crowning act of disloyalty, and one which threatened the most serious consequences to the government, was committed about midnight of the same day. A secret order was issued by the mayor and police officers to burn the nearest bridges on the railroads leading into Baltimore from the free States, and parties, under the command of the police authorities were dispatched to execute the order.

Before daylight the following morning, the bridges at Melvale, Relay House and Cockeysville, on the Harrisburg road and over the Bush and Gunpowder rivers and Harris Creek, were completely destroyed by fire, thus effectually severing railroad communication with the North. The telegraph wires leading to and from the capital were also cut, completely shutting off Washington, and the government from the loyal Northern States. These acts, commited by the orders of the very men who that morning had risked their lives in defending the soldiers of the Union, are sufficient to show the rapid and overmastering influence of revolutionary madness.

Of course, the news of these outrages spread far and wide over the country, and while they aroused universal indignation, they nevertheless were the occasion of grave fears for the safety of the capital.

It was on the 21st of April, two days after the occurrence of these events that my services were required. Several gentlemen of prominence in Chicago, intimate friends of President Lincoln, and men of influence and intelligence in the State, desired to communicate with the President upon questions connected with the existing condition of affairs, and applied to me for the purpose of having letters and dispatches conveyed directly to Washington by the hands of a trusty messenger.

I at once accepted the duty, and selected a man for its performance. Experience proved that I was not mistaken in my selection, and as the messenger chosen for this duty is to bear an important part in the event, which I am about to relate, a description of him will at once acquaint the reader with his personal appearance.

He was a tall, broad-shouldered, good-looking man of about forty years of age. In height he was about five feet ten inches; his brown hair, which was brushed carelessly back from a broad, high forehead, surmounted a face of a character to at once attract attention.

There was such a decided mixture of sternness and amiability, of innate force and gentle feelings, of frankness and resolution stamped upon his features, that he instinctively impressed the beholder at a glance.

The deep gray eyes could twinkle and sparkle with good humor, or they would grow dark and menacing, and seem to flash under the influence of anger. The mouth, almost concealed by the heavy brown mustaches which he wore, and the square, firm chin evinced a firmness that was unmistakable. His nose, large and well-formed, and the prominent cheek bones all seemed in perfect harmony with the bold spirit which leaped from the eyes, and the strong will that lurked about the set lips. In figure, he was rather stout, but his shoulders were so broad, his feet and hands so shapely, and the lithe limbs so well formed, that he did not appear of as full habit as he really was. A casual observer on meeting this man would almost immediately and insensibly be impressed with the conviction that he was a man who could be trusted; that any duty devolving upon him would be sacredly kept; and as he stood before me on this sunny afternoon in April, I felt that I could implicitly rely upon him in any emergency in which he might be placed, and to perform any service for which he might be selected.

This man was Timothy Webster, a faithful officer, a true friend, and an ardent patriot.

I had known this man for years. He had been in my employ for a long time, and had been engaged upon operations of a varied and diverse nature, consequently I knew precisely what his capabilities were, and how entirely he could be trusted. Though not a man of great enlightenment, he was gifted with a large amount of natural shrewdness, which enabled him to successfully meet any emergency which might arise. From his association with people in the various walks of life, he had acquired that habit of easy adaptation which made him appear, and feel, perfectly at home in almost any society, whether in the drawing-room or the tavern, in the marts of trade, or laboring at the plow.

From my knowledge of Timothy Webster, and my confidence in his wisdom and reliability, I had chosen him to be the bearer of the dispatches to Mr. Lincoln. I therefore called him into my office and explained to him the nature of the duties he was to perform, the possible dangers he would encounter, and the importance of the trust that was to be reposed in him, and when I had concluded, I asked:

"Timothy, knowing what you do of the task before you, will you undertake its performance?"

"I understand all perfectly," he replied, drawing himself up to his full height, while his eyes flashed with a patriotic fire, "I know that my country demands my services, and that, if it shall cost me my life, I am ready to perform my full duty."

The preparations for his departure did not occupy a very long time; the services of Miss Kate Warne, my female superintendent, were requested, and in a few minutes the important dispatches, some twelve in number, were securely sewed between the linings of his coat collar, and in the body of his waist-coat, and Timothy Webster was on his way to the capital of the country.

8

A COLORED CONTRABAND

CHAPTER VII.

*Webster on his Way to the Capital.—Wrecked Trains and
Broken Bridges.—An Adventure with a Cavalryman.—
Rebel Emissary.—President Lincoln and Timothy Webster.*

EVERYWHERE along the route the greatest
excitement prevailed, and the people were
in a state of wildest commotion. A rumor had
spread throughout the country that the government, indignant at the riotous conduct of the
Baltimoreans, had ordered the guns of Fort Mc-
Henry to fire upon the city, that the bombardment
was now going on, and that half the town was
reduced to ashes. This rumor was false, as Webster learned on arriving in Philadelphia, although
even in the staid old Quaker City there was
manifest a degree of excitement scarcely to be
expected in a community so sedate and easy-
going as Philadelphians usually are.

Leaving the train at Philadelphia, Webster made
his way through the crowded streets to the center
of the city. He deemed it best to take counsel
with some of the railroad and express officials, with
whom he was very well acquainted, by reason of his
connection with the discovery of the conspiracy to

assassinate President Lincoln in Baltimore in the month of February immediately preceding.

At that time Webster had been enrolled as a member of a volunteer company of cavalry at Perrymansville, in Maryland, and, gaining the confidence of his officers, had assisted in discovering the plans of the conspirators, and partly through his efforts, I had been successful in frustrating their murderous designs. This operation had brought him in close association with several gentlemen who were connected with the railroad and express companies, whose travel lay between Philadelphia and the now riotous and isolated city of Baltimore. As he was walking leisurely down Chestnut street he was accosted by Mr. Dunn, a gentleman who was connected with a leading express company in the city, and who was now upon his return from a visit to the Philadelphia, Wilmington and Baltimore depot. After an interchange of salutations, Webster inquired of Mr. Dunn the condition of affairs in and around Baltimore.

"Very bad, indeed," replied that gentleman ; "the bridges are all down, and the tracks have been torn up all along the road from Perrysville to Baltimore. The telegraph-wires have been cut, and no communications have been received from Baltimore or Washington except through couriers. The roads are guarded with soldiery, whose sympathies are with the rebellion, and it is almost impossible for any one who cannot identify himself as a Southern man to pass the guards who are stationed along the highways."

"It does not look very favorable for my reaching Washington to-morrow, then?" said Webster, inquiringly.

"No, sir. I am afraid that you will find it difficult, if not dangerous, to attempt such a journey, particularly by the way of Baltimore; and perhaps you had better delay your departure until it can be more safely accomplished," said Mr. Dunn.

"It may be as you say," replied Webster, "but I left Chicago for Washington, and my line of travel was laid out through Baltimore. I will obey my orders to the letter, and I will arrive in Washington to-morrow night, or lose my life in attempting it!"

"I see that you are determined to go," said Mr. Dunn, "and further argument would be of no avail; but I assure you, that you cannot travel further by rail than Perrysville; you may succeed in getting across the river to Havre de Grace, but after that you will have to rely entirely upon yourself."

"Never fear for me," replied Webster, with a smile, "I will get through all right, I feel confident. I will have but little time now to catch the train, Mr. Dunn, and if you will be kind enough to telegraph to Mr. Pinkerton according to my directions, I will esteem it a great favor."

"Certainly, Webster; anything I can do for you, or Mr. Pinkerton, will be done cheerfully."

Writing out a message, informing me of his arrival in Philadelphia and of his intentions, he requested Mr. Dunn to forward the same, and then, bidding that gentleman good-bye, he made his way to the Baltimore depot, and was soon on the road to that city.

As the train went speeding along upon its journey, Webster had ample time for the consideration of his plans. He was pretty well acquainted with the country between Havre de Grace and Baltimore, and had no fear of losing his way, even if the journey must be made by foot. He was impressed, however, with the necessity of using the utmost caution. While he did not fear for his own personal safety—for fear was an element entirely unknown to him—he realized the importance of his mission too well to rashly imperil its success by any useless exposure, or unnecessary risk. To reach Washington, however, he was determined, and to accomplish that object no danger would be too great, no hardship too severe. He nevertheless felt that he must rely solely upon himself, that he would have no one to advise him, and his own discretion and wisdom would have to be depended upon under all circumstances. Arriving at the Perrysville station, he found that the train could go no further, and that, to reach Havre de Grace, upon the opposite side of the Susquehanna River, the passengers would be requied to take small boats and be rowed over, after which each man must make his way as best he could.

As the boat touched the land Webster sprang ashore, and, going directly to the hotel, inquired for the landlord. He found that gentleman engaged in earnest conversation with an individual who at once instinctively awakened the suspicions of my operative. This gentleman was a tall, fine-looking man, with the erect carriage and and self-reliant air of the soldier, but there was something in the nervousness of his manner, and in the furtive glances of his eyes, which convinced Webster that he was concealing something and would bear watching.

Approaching the spot where the two men were conversing, Webster at once addressed the landlord in a hearty manner. " Landlord, I must get to Baltimore to-day.   How am I going to do it ?"

" I do not know," replied the hotel-keeper, " this gentleman is anxious to do the same thing, but I am afraid I cannot help either of you."

The gentleman thus referred to turned to Webster, saying :

" Yes, I am very anxious to get through.   I am a bearer of dispatches to the British Consul at Washington, and it is of the utmost importance that they should be delivered at once."

While he was speaking a man drove up to the front of the hotel with a fine, strong team of horses attached to a covered road wagon, and throwing the reins across the back of his horses, leaped lightly to the ground.

" Here is a man who can help you," said the land-lord, as the new-comer entered the room; and then he called out:

" Harris, come here !"

The driver of the team came over to where the three men were standing, and the landlord at once made known to him the wishes of Webster and the messenger of the British Consul.

" Harris, these gentlemen want to get to Balti-more to-day. Do you think you can manage it for them ?"

The man addressed as Harris gazed at Webster and his companion in a scrutinizing manner, and finally, apparently satisfied with his investigation, signified his willingness to make the attempt, provided the price he demanded, which was fifty dollars, was agreed to.

Both men assented to the payment of the sum named, and after dinner had been partaken of, the two men took their seats in the vehicle, the driver cracked his whip, and they were upon their way.

" I cannot promise to take you through to Balti-more," remarked the driver, after they had started ; " I was stopped twice on the road yesterday, and I may not be able to pass the guards to-day."

" Do the best you can," said Webster, good-na-turedly, " and we will take the risk of a safe arrival."

Webster then turned to his companion, who had remained silent and watchful ever since they had set

out, and endeavored to engage him in conversation.
The bearer of dispatches, however, was very little inclined to be sociable, and Webster had great difficulty in breaking through the reserve which he resolved to maintain.

The further they journeyed, the more Webster
became convinced that this man was not what he assumed to be, but he vailed his suspicions carefully,
and appeared as frank and cordial in his manner as
though they were brothers.

Nothing worthy of note transpired upon the route
until the party arrived at the outskirts of Perrymansville, which had been the scene of Webster's first experience in military service, and where, a few months
before, he had been a member of a company of cavalry.   They were trotting along quietly, and as the
day was balmy and bright the ride was quite an en-
joyable one, and for a moment the detective forgot
the grave duties which he had undertaken and the
dangers that might surround him, and gave himself
up to the full enjoyment of the scenes around him.
His pleasant reflections were short-lived, however, for
just as they were entering the town they saw a
mounted cavalryman approaching, who, as he reached
the carriage, commanded them to halt.

The driver suddenly pulled up his horses, and then
the soldier, in a tone of authority : " Who are you,
and where are you going ?"

" We are residents of Baltimore," answered Webster, not at all dismayed by the stern appearance and manner of his soldierly interlocutor, "and we are endeavoring to get home."

"You will have to go with me," replied the soldier, decisively, "you can't go any further without permission."

Here was a detention as unwelcome as it was unexpected, but Webster had recognized the uniform worn by the soldier as that of the very company of cavalry he had previously been a member of, and a duplicate of one in which he had previously arrayed himself. The man who had accosted him, however, was unknown to him, and he could, therefore, do nothing but submit quietly to his orders and await a favorable operation of circumstances.

As Webster glanced casually at his companion, the British messenger, he was surprised at the change which was apparent in the expression of his features. Instead of the calm, dignified air of watchful repose which he had observed before, his face had grown pale, and there was such an unmistakable evidence of fear about the man, that Webster's suspicions were confirmed, and come what might he resolved to ascertain the nature of his business before they parted company.

They had traveled but a short distance under the escort of their guard when they met another man dressed in a similar uniform, and evidently a member of the same company, and as Webster gazed at the new-comer he experienced a sensation of relief and joy, for in him he recognized an old companion in arms.

As this man approached nearer, Webster called out from the carriage, in a cheery voice:

"Hello, Taylor! how are you?"

Thus suddenly accosted, the soldier rode up to the vehicle, and after a momentary glance at the features of the detective, he reached forth his hand and cordially saluted him.

"Why, Webster, how do you do? The boys said you would not come back, now that the war had commenced, but I knew better, and I am glad to see you."

The face of the reputed Englishman cleared in an instant, as he found that his companion was among friends, and this effect was not lost upon Webster, who had been furtively observing him. He turned his attention, however, to the soldier who had addressed him.

"Oh, yes," he replied, "I have come back; and my friend here and I are anxious to get to Baltimore as soon as possible."

"That will be all right," said the soldier; and then, turning to his comrade, he said: "These men are all right, you will permit them to pass."

After a few minutes spent in a pleasant conversation, the soldier handed to Webster a pass which would prevent further interruption to their journey, and with a mutual pull at a flask with which Webster had provided himself before starting, the parties separated, and they proceeded on their way.

This little incident produced a marked change in the demeanor of Webster's companion, and on being informed that the soldiers were Southerners, and not Federals, he seemed quite relieved.

By the time they were approaching the suburbs of Baltimore the stranger had grown exceedingly communicative, and upon Webster hinting to him that he also was engaged in the cause of the South, he without hesitation informed my operative that he was similarly employed, and that he was at present carrying dispatches to prominent Southern sympathizers then residing in Washington.

As he communicated this important item of information Webster grasped him warmly by the hand, and greeted him as a fellow-patriot, after which, with rare good humor, they cemented their acquaintance and confidence with a friendly draught from the spirit bottle.

Several times on their journey they were halted by the guards along the roads, but the talismanic pass obtained at Perrymansville avoided all questioning, and gained for the travelers a safe passage to their destination. Arriving safely at the outskirts of Baltimore, the two men left the carriage, and walking a short distance, they entered a street car, and were driven to a retired hotel, where Webster had frequently stopped when in the city on former occasions. Here they engaged quarters for the night, and Webster's companion had by this time formed such an attachment for his fellow-traveler that communicating rooms were engaged, and after partaking of a hearty repast, the two men lighted their cigars and strolled out through the city.

There were still many evidences of the riotous affrays which had but lately taken place. The people were in a feverish state of excitement, the drinking saloons and the corridors of the hotels were filled with crowds of excited men, each of whom seemed to vie with the other in giving loud expressions of their opinions, and of denouncing the attempt of the government to transport armed troops through the streets of a peaceful city. Ever mindful of the important duty devolving upon him, Webster wisely forebore to engage in any conversation with those whom he met, and among the number of the most outspoken of the Southern sympathizers were many whom he had previously met, and to whom he was known as an adherent of the South. At an early hour he and his newly found companion returned to their hotel, and shortly afterward retired for the night.

Arising early on the following morning, they found the same difficulty was to be encountered that had been successfully overcome at the commencement of their journey. The railroads between Baltimore and Washington had also been torn up, so as to render the running of the trains an impossibility. This fact necessitated the procuring of a team that would convey them to the capital; but this time Webster's acquaintance with the proprietors of the hotel, and several of the permanent guests of the house, enabled them without difficulty or delay to secure a pair of horses and a road wagon, with a trusty driver, who guaranteed to carry them to Washington for the same amount which had been paid upon the other portion of their journey, and at an early hour they were upon the road to the seat of government.

Meantime Webster had been seriously considering his course of action with regard to his fellow-passenger. That he was an agent of the Confederacy he had already admitted, and that he was the bearer of dispatches to prominent sympathizers with the South who were now living in Washington, was also well known to the detective. How, therefore, to arrange his plans, so that these papers would be intercepted and the ambassador detained without arousing his suspicion? It must be accomplished so that no delay should result to his own journey, as he had resolved that his dispatches must be delivered that day. Just before starting out an idea occurred to him, and requesting the driver to wait a few minutes, as he had forgotten something in his room, he re-entered the hotel, and going to the room they had occupied the

evening before, he hurriedly wrote a note which he
folded up and placed in his pocket.   The note was as
follows :

" To Whom it may Concern :
   "My companion is an emissary of the Confederacy,
carrying dispatches to Southern sympathizers in
Washington.   Apprehend him, but do so discreetly
and without compromising me.   T. W."

He then descended the stairs, and entering the
wagon, they were driven away towards Washington.
The day was exceedingly warm, and the horses, unused to long journeys, early began to show signs of
weakness, but they kept on without incident, save an
occasional question from a passer-by as to their
destination, and about noon arrived at a hotel known
as the " Twelve-Mile House," so called from its being
located at that distance from Washington.

Here the party halted for dinner, and while engaged at their repast Webster noticed at an opposite
table a friend of years ago, who wore the uniform of
a Lieutenant of infantry.   Fortunately, however, the
officer did not appear to recognize him, and during
the progress of the dinner Webster kept his face
hidden as much as possible from his new-found friend.
As the Lieutenant ceased eating and arose from the
table, Webster, who also had about completed the
bill of fare, arose, and excusing himself to the driver
and his companion, passed out into the hallway and

met the officer face to face. Cordial greetings were interchanged, and in a few minutes Webster had detailed to his friend the circumstances attending his meeting with the so-called British messenger, and his suspicions concerning them. It was not long before a plan had been arranged for the carrying out of the project of arresting the pseudo Englishman without occasioning the slightest suspicion to fall upon Timothy Webster, and shortly afterwards the Lieutenant mounted his horse and rode off in the direction of Washington.

After smoking their after-dinner cigars, Webster and his companion again resumed their journey. By this time they had become thoroughly acquainted, and they enlivened their drive with many a pleasing anecdote of experience or of invention, until they came in sight of Washington city. Here a difficulty awaited them, apparently unexpected by both travelers. A Lieutenant at the head of eight men emerged from a house by the wayside, and in a voice of authority directed the driver to stop his horses, after which he advanced to the vehicle and saluted the occupants with the utmost courtesy, saying:

"Gentlemen, I am sorry to discommode you, but I have orders to intercept all persons entering the city, and hold them until they can satisfactorily account for themselves. You will be kind enough to consider yourselves under arrest and follow me."

Blank astonishment was depicted on the countenances of both Webster and his companion, but realizing that to parley would be useless, the two men dismounted and followed the lieutenant and his men into the building, which proved to be a military guard-house.

Here they were separated and conducted to different apartments, where they were securely locked in, Webster's companion standing outside of the door of the room in which Webster was placed, and after witnessing the operation which confined Webster a prisoner, he was conducted to the room assigned to him, and the key was turned upon him.

In a few minutes afterwards Webster was quietly released by the Lieutenant who had effected his arrest, and who was none other than the friend to whom he had given the information. In less than half an hour thereafter my detective was ascending the steps of the White House, inquiring for his Excellency, the President of the United States.

Having also been provided with a letter to the President's private secretary, Mr. Nicolay, Webster was soon ushered into the presence of Mr. Lincoln, to whom he made known the nature of his business, and taking off his coat and vest, he removed the dispatches and letters, and handed them to the President, who had been silently watching his movements with a great deal of amused interest.

"You have brought quite a mail with you, Mr. Webster," said the President, "more, perhaps, than it would be quite safe to attempt to carry another time."

"Yes, sir," replied Webster. "I don't think I would like to carry so much through Baltimore another time."

The President carefully looked over the papers he had just received, and finding that they required more consideration than could be given to them at that time, he turned to Webster and said :

"Mr. Webster, I have a Cabinet conference this evening, and I will not be able to give these matters my attention until to-morrow. Come to me at ten o'clock and I will see you at that time."

Again thanking the detective for the service he had so successfully rendered, he bade him good evening, and Webster sought his hotel, thoroughly exhausted with his journey, and soon after he was sound asleep.

The next morning, on repairing to the White House, he was at once admitted, and the President greeted him with marked evidences of cordiality.

"Mr. Webster, you have rendered the country an invaluable service. The bearer of dispatches who was arrested last evening by your efforts, proved, as you suspected, to be an emissary of the South, and the letters found upon him disclose a state of affairs here in Washington quite alarming. Several prominent families here are discovered to be in regular communication with the Southern leaders, and are

9

furnishing them with every item of information. Until this time we had only a suspicion of this, but suspicion has now resolved itself into a certainty. You have performed your duty well, and before many days there will be an account demanded of some of these people which they are far from expecting."

"I am glad to be of any service," replied Webster; "and I have done nothing more than my duty. If you have any further commands for me, Mr. President, I am ready to obey them."

"Very well," said the President; "take these telegrams, and when you have reached a point where communication is possible, send them to General McClellan, at Columbus, Ohio; they are important and must be sent without delay. Also telegraph to Mr. Pinkerton to come to Washington at once; his services are, I think, greatly needed by the government at this time."

Rolling up the papers which he received, Webster placed them in the center of a hollow cane, which he carried; then, replacing the handle, and promising to attend faithfully to the duties assigned him, he left the executive mansion.

CHAPTER VIII.

*Timothy Webster in Washington.—The Return to Philadel-
phia.—I go to the Capital.—An Important Letter.*

AFTER leaving the White House, Timothy
Webster went immediately in quest of a conveyance that would enable him to reach Baltimore
without unnecessary delay. He expected to encounter greater difficulties in obtaining what he desired
here in Washington than he had met with in Baltimore, for the reason that in the capital he was a
comparative stranger, while in the latter city he had
numerous friends, who believed him to be in sympathy with the Confederacy, and whose assistance
he could rely upon on that account. His only hope,
therefore, lay in his being able to find some friendly
Baltimorean, upon whose influence he could depend
to procure him a mode of conveyance for his return. Having arrived late on the preceding evening and being terribly fatigued by the journey he
had made, Webster had retired almost immediately
after he reached his hotel, and consequently he
was surprised at the busy scenes which greeted
him now. The capital was swarming with soldiers
and civilians. Regiments continually arriving and

were being assigned to quarters and positions around the city, and the streets were filled with eager and excited multitudes. The position which Maryland had assumed was vehemently discussed everywhere, and the riotous conduct of the Baltimoreans was loudly denounced by Northern men, and secretly applauded by those whose sympathies were with the cause of the South. The prompt action of General Butler, with his regiment of Massachusetts soldiers, who followed quickly after the sixth, in going by boat directly to Annapolis, in order to reach Washington without hindrance or delay, and his patriotic and determined response to those in authority, who sought to induce him to change his plans for reaching the capital, were everywhere warmly commended. There could be no doubt that the North was thoroughly aroused, and were dreadfully in earnest in their determination to suppress a rebellion which they believed to be causeless, unlawful and threatening the future of a great country.

As Webster walked along Pennsylvania Avenue, carefully scanning the faces of every one he met in the hope of discovering some one whom he knew and who might be of service to him, he recognized the driver who had brought him from Baltimore on the day before, and who started in astonishment at finding the man whom he had last seen a prisoner in the hands of United States troops now walking the streets free and unattended. This man was accompanied by three others, with two of whom Webster was slightly acquainted, and he at once advanced toward them and greted them cordially.

" Why, Webster, is that you?" inquired the foremost of the party, a well-known " sympathizer " of the name of John Maull. " We heard you had been taken prisoner—how did you get out so soon?"

" That is easily accounted for," said Webster, with a laugh ; " I was simply arrested on suspicion, and when they could find nothing about me that was at all suspicious, they were compelled to let me go."

" This country is coming upon strange times," remarked a sallow-faced Baltimorean who boasted of having been one of the most prominent of the rioters a few days before, " when a man can be arrested in this way and have no means of redress."

" That is very true," replied Webster, " but we will have a decided change before long, or I am very much mistaken. ' Uncle Jeff ' means business, and there will be long faces in Washington before many days."

" Give me your hand, old boy," exclaimed Maull heartily, " you are of the right stripe ; but don't talk so loud ; let us go around the corner to a quiet little place where we can talk without danger."

The party repaired to a drinking saloon, in a retired neighborhood, and on entering it they were greeted warmly by several parties who were standing before the bar. Webster was immediately intro-

duced to these gentlemen, and it was not long before
he had firmly established himself in their good opinions as a devoted friend of the South.

The conversation soon became general, and the
most extravagant ideas were expressed with regard to
the wonderful achievements that were expected of
the Southern soldiers, and no doubt was entertained
that the Yankees, as they called the Northern men,
would be quickly vanquished by the chivalrous armies
of the "Sunny South."

To all of these suggestions Webster yielded a
ready assent, and not one among the number was
more pronounced in his belief in the needs of the
Southern cause than was my trusty operative, who, in
the cane he flourished so conspicuously, carried important dispatches from the President of the United
States to a General in command of Northern soldiers.

All the time, however, he was growing very
restive under the enforced delay in his journey, and
seeking a favorable opportunity during a lull in the
conversation, he turned to the driver of the wagon
and inquired of him when he was going to return to
Baltimore.

"Not for a day or two, at least," replied the man.

"That is very bad," said Webster. " I must get
there this evening; it is of the utmost importance that
I should do so."

At this one of the party approached Webster and

informed him that he was going back that day and had engaged a conveyance for that purpose, and as there was room enough for two, he would be most happy to have his company. Webster at once accepted the invitation, and having thus relieved his anxiety upon the point of reaching Baltimore, he joined heartily in the conversation that was going on around him. No one, to have heard him, would doubt for a moment his loyalty to the South, or his firm belief in the eventual triumph of her armies.

After remaining in the saloon for some time, Webster noticed that the men were becoming intoxicated, and fearing that they would become noisy and probably get into trouble, he suggested to the gentleman with whom he was to drive to Baltimore the propriety of leaving the rest to their enjoyment while they arranged matters for their departure. His advice was at once accepted, and the two men bade their associates farewell and repaired to the hotel, where they had their dinner, and about two o'clock they were upon their journey. Webster's fears were proven to be well-founded, for as they were passing the locality where they had spent the morning, they saw their former companions between a file of soldiers, and there was little doubt that they had allowed their libations to overcome their judgments, and that they would be allowed to recover their reason in a guard-house.

The journey was made without event, the carriage

and driver being apparently very well known along the
route, and Webster arrived in Baltimore late that
evening.   He was desirous of pushing on without
delay, as it was important that the dispatches which
he carried should be forwarded at once, and he therefore went immediately to the hotel he had occupied
when he first arrived in the city.   Requesting the
landlord to use his best efforts to procure him a conveyance to Havre de Grace, he sat down to his
supper, and did ample justice to a plenteous repast.
When he had finished the landlord entered the room
and informed him that he had succeeded in providing
a team for his service, but that grave doubts were
entertained whether he would succeed in reaching his
destination.   Expressing his willingness to assume
any responsibility of that kind, Webster bade his
entertainer good-bye, and entering the wagon, he
started upon his midnight journey to Havre de
Grace.

Again fortune favored him, and although repeat-
edly halted, he was able to give such a straightforward account of himself that they were allowed to
proceed, and he arrived in Havre de Grace in time
for breakfast.   Crossing the river, he went directly to
the headquarters of Colonel Dare, who was in charge
of the Union troops at Perrysville, and requested
that officer to forward the telegram to General
McClellan at once.   This the Colonel promised to do,
and in a few minutes the important message was fly-

ing over the wires to its destination at Columbus, Ohio, and the President's request for my appearance at Washington followed soon after, and was received by me in due time.

Recognizing the importance of the call, I lost no time in answering the dispatch of Mr. Lincoln, and started at once on my journey to Washington, accompanied only by a trusty member of my force. Before leaving I left orders that should I fail to meet with Webster upon the way he should be directed to await my return in the city of Pittsburg.

On my arrival at Perrysville I found that a mode of communication had been hurriedly established with Washington, by means of a boat which sailed down the Chesapeake Bay and landed their passengers at Annapolis, from which point the railroad travel to Washington was uninterrupted.

Arriving at the capital I found a condition of affairs at once peculiar and embarrassing, and the city contained a strange admixture of humanity, both patriotic and dangerous. Here were gathered the rulers of the nation and those who were seeking its destruction. The streets were filled with soldiers, armed and eager for the fray; officers and orderlies were seen galloping from place to place; the tramp of armed men was heard on every side, and strains of martial music filled the air. Here, too, lurked the secret enemy, who was conveying beyond the lines the coveted information of every movement made or contemplated.   Men who formerly occupied places of dignity, power and trust were now regarded as objects of suspicion, whose loyalty was impeached and whose actions it was necessary to watch.   Aristocratic ladies, who had previously opened the doors of their luxurious residences to those high in office and who had hospitably entertained the dignitaries of the land, were now believed to be in sympathy with the attempt to overthrow the country, and engaged in clandestine correspondence with Southern leaders.   The criminal classes poured in from all quarters, and almost every avenue of society was penetrated by these lawless and unscrupulous hordes.   An adequate idea can be formed of the transformation which had been effected within a few short weeks in this city of national government.

On the day following my arrival I wended my way to the White House and sought an interview with the President.   Around the executive mansion everything was in a state of activity and bustle. Messengers were running frantically hither and thither; officers in uniform were gathered in clusters, engaged in animated discussions of contemplated military operations; department clerks were bustling about, and added to these was a crowd of visitors, all anxious, like myself, to obtain an interview with the Chief Executive.

I was not required to wait an unusual length of time, and I was soon ushered into the presence of

Mr. Lincoln, who greeted me cordially and introduced me to the several members of the Cabinet who were engaged with him. I was at once informed that the object in sending for me was that the authorities had for some time entertained the idea of organizing a secret-service department of the government, with the view of ascertaining the social, political and patriotic status of the numerous suspected persons in and around the city. As yet, no definite plans had been adopted, and I was requested to detail my views upon the subject, in order that the matter might be intelligently considered, and such action taken as would lead to definite and satisfactory results. I accordingly stated to them the ideas which I entertained upon the subject, as fully and concisely as I was able to do at the time, and, after I had concluded, I took my departure, with the understanding that I would receive further communications from them in a few days.

It was very evident to me, however, that in the confusion and excitement which were necessarily incident to the novel and perplexing condition of affairs then existing, that anything approaching to a systematized organization or operation would be for a time impossible. The necessity for war had come so suddenly upon a peaceful community that there had been as yet but little time for thorough preparation or system. The raising of a large army, with all the various contingencies of uniforming, arming and drilling; the furnishing of supplies, and the assigning of quarters, were occupying the attention of the rulers of the government, and I felt confident that I would be required to wait a longer time than I could then conveniently spare from my business, ere I would be favored with any definite instructions from those in authority. This opinion was fully confirmed, after several unsuccessful attempts to obtain satisfying particulars from the heads of several of the departments, and leaving my address with the secretary of the President, I returned to Philadelphia.

I had directed, prior to leaving Chicago, that all important communications addressed to me should be forwarded to that city, and on my arrival there I found a number of letters which required immediate attention.

Among the number was the following, which had been somewhat delayed in its transmission.

"COLUMBUS, OHIO,
April 24, 1861.

"ALLAN PINKERTON, Esq.,
"Dear Sir :—

"I wish to see you with the least possible delay, to make arrangements with you of an important nature. I will be either here or in Cincinnati for the next few days—here to-morrow—Cincinnati next day. In this city you will find me at the Capitol, at Cincinnati at my residence.

"If you telegraph me, better use your first name

alone. Let no one know that you come to see me, and keep as quiet as possible.

"Very truly yours,

"GEO. B. McCLELLAN,

"Maj. Gen'l Comd'g Ohio Vols.

This letter at once decided me. Anxious as I was to serve the country in this, the hour of her need, I sought the first opportunity for active duty that presented itself, and I left Philadelphia at once, in order to comply with the instructions contained in this message of Gen. McClellan.

STORMING A FORT.

CHAPTER IX.

An Adventure in Pittsburg.—A Mob at Bay.—An Explanation.—Good-feeling Restored.

SEVERAL influences operated in my mind to induce me to respond at once to this letter, and some of them of a directly personal nature. I had been acquainted with General McClellan for a long time before this, and had been intimately associated with him while engaged upon various important operations connected with the Illinois Central and the Ohio and Mississippi Railroads, of the latter of which he was then president. From the friendship and esteem I entertained for him growing out of my relations with him in those matters, both as an individual and as an executive officer, I felt the more anxious to enter into his service, now that he had assumed the command of a military department, and was about to take an active part in the impending struggle.

At Philadelphia I ascertained that Timothy Webster had already departed for Pittsburg, according to previous instructions, and hastily telegraphing to the General that I would instantly respond to his letter in person, I took the first train leading westward and was soon upon my way.

Timothy Webster, meanwhile, had proceeded on his journey from Perrysville, and arrived without accident or adventure in Philadelphia. He immediately repaired to the office of Mr. Dunn, who informed him that he had just received a dispatch for him from Chicago. Webster hastily opened the message and found my directions for him to await my return at the city of Pittsburg. Remaining in the Quaker City until the following day, he took the western train and in due time arrived at his destination. On inquiring at the telegraph office in Pittsburg he received another message to the same effect as the first one, and he therefore engaged quarters at a hotel, patiently awaiting my coming. On the second day after his arrival in the Smoky City, which was Sunday, he again went to the telegraph office, where he received information that I would probably arrive there in the course of that day.

Returning to the hotel, Webster entered the barroom, and while he was being attended to two men came in, apparently engaged in excited conversation. They advanced to the bar and requested drinks. The excitement in the city, attendant upon the news from Baltimore, had not abated in the least since Webster had passed through several days before, and these two men were discussing the action of the government in regard to this matter. One of them, an excitable, empty-headed fellow, was cursing the President and General Scott, in very loud tones and in unmeasured terms, for not burning the city of Baltimore to ashes, and thus teaching the rebels a lesson they would be apt to remember. The remonstrances of his friend seemed only to excite him still more, and Webster, feeling desirous of avoiding any controversy at that time, started to leave the saloon, when the angry disputant turned to him, and arrogantly demanded his opinion of the matter.

"I think," said Webster, "that the President and General Scott understand their duties much better than I can inform them, and I suppose they do not wish to destroy the property of many who are true to the government."

"That is all nonsense," replied the other, sharply, "there is not a single Union man in the whole city."

"I think you are mistaken," said Webster, coolly. "I am sure there are thousands of them there."

This answer seemed to infuriate the man, and striding up to Webster, he asked, with an air of impertinence :

"Are you a Southern man?"

"No, sir, I was born in New York," was the reply.

"What is your name?" impudently demanded the fellow.

"You will find my name upon the register of the hotel, if you desire it, and as I do not wish to have any further controversy with you, I bid you good morning," replied Webster, still remaining cool and unruffled.

By this time a crowd of about twenty men had

gathered about them, and as Webster turned to leave the room, one of them demanded to know the contents of the telegram he had just received.

This demand, added to the previous suggestion that Webster was a Southern man, was sufficient to excite the entire crowd, who had been living upon excitement for more than a week, and they began to press around him in a threatening manner, one of them calling out:

"I believe he is a d—d spy; let us see what he has got!"

Webster broke loose from those nearest to him, and retreating backwards toward the door, exclaimed, in a determined voice:

"Gentlemen, I am no spy, and if any of you attempt to trouble me further, some of you will assuredly get hurt!"

At this the crowd grew boisterous and violent, and several called out, "Hang him!" "Hang the spy!" while some of them made a rush toward where he stood.

Drawing his revolver, Webster faced his angry assailants, who drew back involuntarily when they saw that he was both well armed and undismayed.

"Gentlemen, we have had enough of this nonsense. You can talk about hanging me, and perhaps there are enough of you to do it, but, by God, the first one that attempts to put his hands upon me is a dead man!"

10

Matters began to look serious. It seemed evident that these excited people were determined to resort to violence, and that there would be bloodshed in consequence. Webster, whose relations with the government were of so intensely loyal a character, was filled with regret at having allowed himself to become a party to a conversation which would lead to such serious consequences. He was resolved, however, to maintain his position. To show signs of weakness, therefore, would be dangerous, if not fatal, to him, and he stood bravely in front of the angry mob, who had drawn back at the sight of the revolver which was leveled so menacingly at them.

Only for a moment, however, did the crowd stand awed and irresolute—one moment of silence, in which every man appeared to be deciding for himself his course of action. Then one tall, stalwart man stepped from their midst, and waving his hand toward his companions, he cried out :

" Come on, he is only one against twenty, and we will take him dead, or alive !"

The crowd took a few steps in advance, and Webster had braced himself to receive their attack, when suddenly, close beside him stood a form, and a loud voice called out :

" Stop, gentlemen, where you are ! This man is no traitor, and I will defend him with my life !" and the muzzles of two revolvers ranged themselves beside

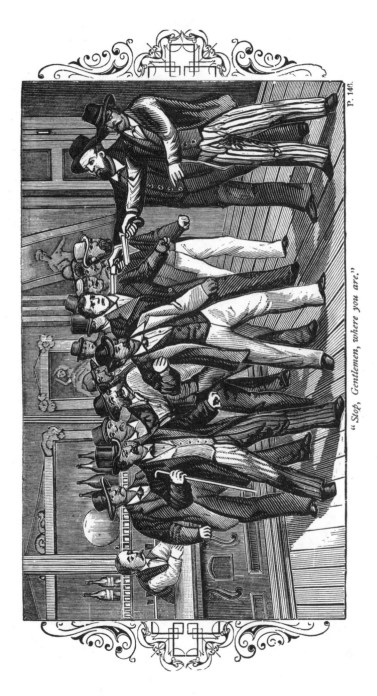

"Stop, Gentlemen, where you are."

P. 146.

that presented by the suspected, but undismayed detective.

Involuntarily the crowd stood still at this unexpected arrival of reinforcements, and Webster, who had recognized the voice, looked up in surprise and relief at this unlooked-for, though timely, assistance.

I had arrived just in the nick of time, and I was resolved to defend my undaunted operative to the last.

At this moment the proprietor of the hotel entered the saloon, and in a calm voice and quiet manner attempted to subdue the angry feelings of the bystanders.

" Gentlemen, " said he, " there need be no trouble about this matter; Mr. Webster can fully explain his position, and I think the best plan would be for you all to repair to the office of the mayor, where any explanation can be given."

" I am perfectly willing to do that," said I; "I know this man, and will answer for him under any circumstances; we will accompany you to the office of the mayor at once, and I think I can convince him that he is no spy."

This proposition was eagerly accepted by some, ar.d reluctantly by others, and finally the entire party marched out of the hotel on their way to the office of the chief magistrate of the city; Webster and myself walking together.

The crowd increased as we went on, and frequent calls were still made to " hang the traitor," but no further attempts were made to molest us, and we reached the office without any event of a troublesome nature occurring.

The noise of the crowd attracted the attention of the chief of police, who, during the temporary absence of the mayor, was in charge of affairs of this nature, and he came to the door to ascertain the occasion of the tumult.

As the crowd, with Webster and myself in the van, reached the steps which led up to the municipal office, I at once recognized the chief of police, having been connected with him some time before in the detection of some burglars from the city of Pittsburg, and that officer was not slow to identify me as the detective, who had frequently enabled him to secure the desperate criminals whom the law had at various times pursued.

As we reached the platform where the officer was standing, I stretched forth my hand, which the chief cordially grasped.

" Why, Mr. Pinkerton, what are you doing here ?" inquired the chief, with some surprise.

" I have come to defend one of my men, whom these people insist upon hanging as a rebel spy, but who is loyal to the core," I answered, laughingly.

" I will take care of that," replied the chief, " and your word is sufficient for me," at the same time extending his disengaged hand and warmly greeting Webster, who stood beside me.

As the crowd noticed the evident acquaintance and good-feeling that existed between the reputed spy and their chief of police, they drew back instinctively, while some of them looked as if they were not insensible to a feeling of shame. The chief realized the state of affairs at once, and turning to the now crestfallen and subdued gathering, he addressed them :

"Gentlemen, I will be responsible for the loyalty and integrity of these gentlemen, and you will instantly disperse."

The leaders of this assault on Webster looked terribly ashamed of themselves when they found how ridiculously they had been acting, and as the door of the chief's office closed on our retreating figures, they slowly and silently retired.

In an hour afterwards, when Webster and I returned to the hotel, we found the gentlemen who a short time before were anxious to hang him, awaiting our arrival, and we received from them their heartfelt apologies for their hasty and inconsiderate conduct, all of which were received with a spirit of good nature that won the regards of all present, and when the time of our departure arrived, they accompanied us to the depot in a body, and cheered us lustily as the train slowly moved away.

Thus an adventure, which promised to be very

serious in its results, terminated in a manner satisfactory to all, and Webster and myself, instead of being lynched by a Pittsburg mob, departed in safety on our journey, and arrived in Cincinnati upon the following day, prepared to receive from General McClellan such instructions as were deemed necessary by him for the furtherance of the cause in which he was engaged.

BETRAYED BY HIS BOOTS.

CHAPTER X.

General McClellan in Command of Ohio.—I am Engaged
for the War.—The Secret Service.—A Consultation.—
Webster starts for Rebeldom.

AT the outbreak of the rebellion many difficulties
were encountered which the people and their
leaders were ill-prepared to surmount, and many
expedients were resorted to in order to equip and
officer the troops as they arrived. The State of
Ohio, the militia of which General McClellan had
been called upon to command by Governor Dennison,
was no exception to this rule; but that gentleman
realized the importance of calling some one to the
command of the volunteers, upon whose knowledge,
judgment and experience he could place implicit
reliance. He therefore turned to Captain McClellan,
who was a graduate of West Point, and had been a
captain in the regular army, but who had for some
years past been devoting himself to the management
of a prominent railroad enterprise in the State.

The Governor at once sent a communication to
the general government, requesting that McClellan
should be restored to his old rank in the army, and

that the duty of organizing the Ohio volunteers should be assigned to him. To this request no answer was received, and it was afterwards learned that the Governor's letter, owing to the interruption of communications with Washington from all points, had not reached its destination. Failing, therefore, to receive any reply from the general government, and being thus forced to rely upon his own resources, Governor Dennison at once summoned McClellan to Columbus, where the latter applied himself earnestly to the work of organizing the numerous volunteer regiments which offered their services to the country. The State laws were changed in such a manner as to allow the Governor to select commanding officers for these volunteers outside of the members of the State militia, and very soon afterward the Ohio troops were commanded by thoroughly competent men, who had made military movements the subject of scientific study.

On the third day of May a "Department of the Ohio" was formed, consisting of the combined forces of Ohio, Indiana and Illinois, and this department, by order of General Scott, was placed under the command of General McClellan.

The Ohio troops, as they arrived, were mainly located at Camp Dennison, which was situated in a valley about sixteen miles northwesterly from the city of Cincinnati. This was the largest and the chief camp in the State, and here the volunteers received that

thorough instruction and training so essential in preparing for the rigors of war.

As I have stated, my personal acquaintance with
George B. McClellan had, from its earliest incipiency,
been of the most agreeable and amicable nature, and
when I called at his house in Ludlow street, as I did
immediately upon my arrival in Cincinnati, I was received with genuine cordiality. After we were
closeted together I explained fully to him the character of the business that had called me to Washington,
and how the complication of affairs at the seat of
government necessitated so much delay that I had
found it imperative upon me to leave without arriving at any definite understanding with the President.

The General had already been advised of his elevation in rank, and among other things desired to
consult with me in relation to his affairs at the War
Department.

I need not stop to give the details of that interview. His object in sending for me was to secure
my aid and co-operation in the organization of a
secret service for his department, and finding me
more than willing to do all in my power to help along
the cause of the Union, he immediately laid before
me all his plans.

Our business was settled. It arranged that I
should assume full management and control of this
new branch of the service, and that I should at once
enter upon the discharge of the multifarious duties

attending so responsible a position. The General then informed me that he would write to General Scott for permission to organize this department under his own personal supervision; and he also agreed to submit the project to Governor Dennison, of Ohio, with a request to that gentleman to solicit the co-operation of the Governors of Illinois, Indiana, Michigan and Wisconsin, in sustaining the organization.

To this arrangement I gave a ready assent, and we then entered upon the discussion of affairs requiring immediate attention. Several measures, more or less important, had suggested themselves to my mind while the General was talking, and in the course of the conversation which followed, I presented them for his consideration. It was a relief to me to find that at the outset there was no clash of opinion between us, and I felt confident that there was not likely to be any in the future.

For several days my time was principally taken up in private consultations with General McClellan, in laying out a line of operations, by which I was to assist in making arrangements for bringing my own force into active duty at the earliest possible hour. I rented a suite of rooms and fitted up an office in Cincinnati, where I called about me some of the most capable and trustworthy detectives in my employ, and impressed upon them the great importance of the tasks that were about to be imposed upon them.

The general informed me that he would like observations made within the rebel lines, and I resolved to at once send some scouts into the disaffected region lying south of us, for the purpose of obtaining information concerning the numbers, equipments, movements and intentions of the enemy, as well as to ascertain the general feeling of the Southern people in regard to the war. I fully realized the delicacy of this business, and the necessity of conducting it with the greatest care, caution and secrecy. None but good, true, reliable men could be detailed for such service, and knowing this, I made my selections accordingly; my thoughts reverting first of all to Timothy Webster.

Within six hours after the commander had expressed his wishes to me, Timothy Webster was on his way to Louisville, with instructions to proceed southward from that city to Memphis, stopping at Bowling Green and Clarkesville on the way.

In Webster's case it was not necessary to devote much time to instructions, except as to his line of travel, for he was a man who understood the whole meaning of a mission like this, and one who would perform his duty with that faithfulness and ability by which he had fairly earned the confidence I now reposed in him.

Within a few days I also sent out other scouts, singly and in pairs, on the different routes that had been carefully prepared for them, and in a short time quite a number of my best operatives were engaged upon more or less difficult and dangerous tasks, all tending to the same end.

In organizing and controlling this secret service, I endeavored to conceal my own individual identity so far as my friends and the public were concerned. The new field of usefulness into which I had ventured was designed to be a secret one in every respect, and for obvious reasons I was induced to lay aside the name of Allan Pinkerton—a name so well known that it had grown to be a sort of synonym for detective. I accordingly adopted the less suggestive one of E. J. Allen ; a *nom de guerre* which I retained during the entire period of my connection with the war. This precautionary measure was first proposed by the General himself, and in assenting to it I carried out his views as well as my own. This ruse to conceal my identity was a successful one. My true name was known only to General McClellan, and those of my force who were in my employ before the breaking out of the rebellion, and by them it was sacredly kept. Indeed, I doubt if McClellan has ever divulged it to this day, if I may judge by the frequent occurrence of such incidents as the following :

A short time since, while on a visit to my New York agency, I chanced to meet one of my old army friends, General Fitz-John Porter. He recognized me, gave me a hearty greeting, and proceeded to address me as Major Allen, after the custom of by-gone days. I permitted the conversation to go on for some time, and then said :

"Are you not aware, General, that the name of E. J. Allen, which I used during the war, was a fictitious one?"

He looked at me, as if to satisfy himself that I was not jesting, and then exclaimed:

"Fictitious ! You are not in earnest, Major ?"

I assured him that I was never more so.

"Why, I never suspected such a thing. What, then, is your true name ?"

"Allan Pinkerton," I replied.

"Allan Pinkerton !" he ejaculated.

His astonishment knew no bounds, and he declared it was the first intimation he had ever had that Allan Pinkerton and Major Allen were one and the same person.

It was on the thirteenth of May that Timothy Webster left Cincinnati on his trip southward. He arrived at Louisville, Ky., late in the night, and remained there until the following day, when he pursued his course into the heart of that self-satisfied State which only desired to be " let alone."

It is not my purpose to give in detail all the events of Webster's journey, as there was much that would only prove tedious at this late day, though at that time regarded as of the utmost importance to the country. Shrewd, wide-awake, and keen as a bloodhound on the scent, he allowed nothing to escape him, but quietly jotted down every item of intelligence that could possibly be of advantage to the Union army, and picked up many important points, which would have escaped the notice of a man of less detective experience and ability.

He stopped a day or two at Bowling Green, Ky., and then proceeded on to Clarkesville, Tenn. He made friends of all he met, and cleverly ingratiated himself into the good graces of those whom he believed might be of service to him. He was a " Hail, fellow ! well met," "A prince of good fellows," a genial, jovial, convivial spirit, with an inexhaustible fund of anecdote and amusing reminiscences, and a wonderful faculty for making everybody like him. He partook of soldiers' fare in the rebel camp, shook hands warmly with raw recruits, joked and laughed with petty officers, became familiar with colonels and captains, and talked profoundly with brigadier-generals. He was apparently an enthusiastic and determined rebel, and in a few cunningly-worded sentences he would rouse the stagnant blood of his hearers till it fairly boiled with virtuous indignation against Yankees in general, and " Abe Linkin " in particular.

Webster's talent in sustaining a *role* of this kind amounted to positive genius, and it was this that forced me to admire the man as sincerely as I prized his services. Naturally, he was of a quiet, reserved disposition, seldom speaking unless spoken to, and never betraying emotion or excitement under any pressure of circumstances. His face always wore that calm, imperturbable expression denoting a well-balanced mind and a thorough self-control, while the immobile countenance and close-set lips showed that he was naturally as inscrutable as the Sphinx. Many of his associates were of the opinion that he was cold and unfeeling, but *I* knew there could be no greater mistake than this; *I* knew that a manlier, nobler heart never existed than that which beat within the broad breast of Timothy Webster; and I knew that, reserved and modest as he was, he was never wanting in courtesy, never derelict in his duty, never behind his fellows in acts of kindness and mercy.

It was when he was detailed for such operations as the one in question that his disposition underwent a complete metamorphosis. Then his reserve vanished, and he became the chatty, entertaining boon companion, the hero of the card-table, the story-teller of the bar-room, or the lion of the social gathering, as the exigencies of the case might require. He could go into a strange place and in one day surround himself with warm friends, who would end by telling him all he desired to know. In a life-time of varied detective experience, I have never met one who could more readily and agreeably adapt himself to circumstances.

Webster represented himself as a resident of Baltimore, and gave graphic accounts of the recent troubles in that city; of the unpleasant position in which the "friends of the cause" were placed by the proximity and oppression of Northern troops, and of the outraged feelings of the populace when the "Lincoln hirelings" marched through the streets of the Monumental City. His eyes seemed to flash with indignation during the recital, and it would have been difficult indeed to induce his audience to believe that he was acting a part, or that his heart was not with the South.

On the morning of his departure from Clarkesville quite a number of soldiers and citizens, who had become attached to him during his brief sojourn with them, accompanied him to the depot, shook him warmly by the hand at parting, and earnestly wished him God-speed. He told them all that he hoped to see them again soon, and waved them a smiling adieu from the platform of the car, as the train whirled him away toward Memphis.

As the train stopped on the east bank of the Tennessee river, and the passengers swarmed out of the cars, Webster noticed a man take the conductor aside and engage in earnest conversation with him for a few moments. This man was a dark-complexioned, sharp-visaged, long-haired individual, clad in civilian's garb, and wearing a broad-brimmed hat. There was an air of mystery about him which attracted more than a passing glance from the scout, and caused the latter to keep an eye on him there-after.

The passengers were obliged to cross the river in a ferry-boat. The train going south was in waiting on the other side, and its conductor stood on the bank alone, making entries in his memorandum-book. As soon as the boat touched the land the man with the long hair and broad-brimmed hat sprang ashore and approached the conductor, to whom he began to talk in the same hurried, nervous manner that he had done to the one on the other side. As the time for starting approached, the mysterious stranger and the conductor walked toward the train together, conversing excitedly as they went.

"There's something up," thought Webster, as he boarded the train. "Perhaps that fellow is on the look-out for new-comers like myself; but we'll see whether he is sharp enough to catch a weasel asleep."

For the first twenty miles after leaving the Tennessee river, the road lay through an uncultivated region of swamps and heavy timber. At every station along the route uniformed men, heavy guns, car-loads of muskets and ammunition were seen, indicating general and active preparations for war, while the secession flag was flying in the breeze, and the music of fife and drum was frequently borne to the ear. At Humboldt, where the train arrived at four o'clock in the afternoon, they were delayed for some time, and Webster improved the opportunity to look around him and to procure his dinner. The man with the broad-brimmed hat seated himself almost opposite

11

Webster at table, who noticed that his restless, inquisitive eyes were kept busy scrutinizing every face that
came within range of his vision.   He did not address
himself to any one during the progress of the repast,
and after hurriedly satisfying his own appetite, he
walked out upon the platform of the depot, where he
stood intently watching the other passengers as they
returned to the train.

Webster, as he crossed the platform, instinctively
felt that those searching eyes were riveted upon him
as if they would pierce him through, but he did not
evince the slightest degree of trepidation or uneasiness under the ordeal.   Assuming an air of quiet unconsciousness, he sauntered past the man without
seeming to notice him, and entered the smoking-car,
coolly lighted a cigar, drew a Nashville newspaper from his pocket, and settled himself to his reading.   He saw no more of the mysterious stranger
during the remainder of the journey, but on alighting
from the train at the Memphis depot, the first object
that met his gaze was the wearer of the broad-brimmed hat.

Arriving in Memphis at nine o'clock in the evening, Webster went directly to the Worsham House,
where he intended to stay while in the city.   While
registering his name he observed a military officer in
full uniform standing at his elbow, watching him
closely as he wrote. Several other new arrivals
placed their signatures after Webster, and he then no-

ticed that the officer was engaged in making a copy of names and addresses on a piece of paper.

While watching this proceeding, his attention was distracted by some one hastily entering the hotel office. It was his mysterious fellow-traveler, who, stepping into the center of the room, glanced quickly around, apparently looking for some particular face. The search was evidently successful, for, walking up to one of the men who had just arrived on the train from the North, he tapped him on the shoulder and beckoned him.

After a few moments' conversation, during which the new-comer appeared to be both surprised and frightened, the two left the hotel together and walked up the street arm in arm.

Two citizens who were lounging near the door had been interested spectators of this incident, and Webster heard one of them inquire :

" What does that mean ?"

" It means that the stranger is under arrest," replied his companion.

" Under arrest ? And who is the man who arrested him ?"

" Oh, he is a member of the safety committee."

" But what crime has the stranger committed, that he should thus be taken into custody ?"

" Nothing, perhaps ; but the fact that he is a stranger from the North, is sufficient to mark him as an object of suspicion."

"Isn't that a little severe?"

"Severe? It's a necessity in these times. For my part, I am in for hanging every Northern man who comes here, unless he can give the most satisfactory proof that he is not a spy."

The rest of the conversation did not reach Webster's ear, and, being much fatigued by his day's journey, he soon retired, to seek that much needed rest which slumber only could afford.

He rose at an early hour in the morning, feeling much refreshed. On entering the dining-room he found it crowded with guests, the majority of whom wore the uniform and shoulder-straps of Confederate officers. The conversation around the table was upon the all-absorbing theme which at that time was uppermost in every mind, and the scout was both amused and edified by what he heard. He did not long remain a silent listener, but taking his cue at the proper moment he entered easily and naturally into the conversation himself, and his pleasing address and intelligent observations commanded at once the respectful attention of those around him.

After breakfast Webster determined to ascertain whether or not he was under the surveillance of the vigilance committee, and he accordingly left the hotel, and wended his way toward the post-office.

He had not proceeded far when he noticed a man who appeared to be following him on the opposite side of the street. Desiring to satisfy himself upon this point he walked on for several blocks, and then dropped into a saloon. Remaining there a sufficient length of time for the man to pass from view, in case he did not stop in his onward course, he emerged from the saloon and retraced his steps toward the hotel. As he did so he noticed the stranger on the other side of the street, dogging him as before. This left no doubt in his mind that he was being shadowed, and he resolved to be guarded in his movements, to refrain from writing any reports or making any notes that could possibly betray him. He returned to the office and bar-room of the Worsham Hotel, and spent an hour or two reading and smoking. While thus occupied, three military officers entered and stood near the bar engaged in animated conversation. Webster sauntered toward them, and heard one of the trio—a man whom the others addressed as "Doctor"—remark emphatically:

"Yes, gentlemen, that is a true principle. It will not do to let a man set foot on Kentucky soil until the Northern troops disregard the neutrality of that State."

Catching the drift of the conversation, Webster stepped forward and said:

"I beg pardon, sir; will you permit me to ask one question?"

The three officers turned toward him, with expressions of mild surprise in their faces, and the Doctor replied:

"Certainly, sir; certainly."

"Do you suppose," added Webster, "that Kentucky will allow the Northern army to march through the State without showing fight?"

"Not by a jug-full," was the prompt response. "The moment the Northern army crosses the Ohio river, Kentucky will rise in arms and take sides with the South."

"If she doesn't," said Webster, with much apparent warmth, "she will prove herself unworthy of the respect of any true Southern men!"

The Doctor's face brightened up, and he laid his hand approvingly on the scout's shoulder.

"May I ask where you are from?"

"I was born in Kentucky and reared in Maryland," was the quiet reply, "and I am now direct from Baltimore."

"Baltimore!" ejaculated the whole trio in chorus; and the next moment were all shaking hands in the most vigorous fashion.

"Baltimore!" repeated the Doctor, his face red with his recent exertion. "My friend, we are always glad to meet a Baltimorean, for we know there is many a true man in that city who would help us if he could. May I ask your name, sir?"

"Webster—Timothy Webster."

"A devilish good name. Mine is Burton. My friends all call me Doctor Burton. Allow me to introduce you to Colonel Dalgetty and to Captain Stanley of the Arkansas Rifles."

The introduction was cordially acknowledged on both sides, and Webster then said :

"Gentlemen, I was about to call for a drink when I heard you speak of Kentucky. I am happy to know that there is still hopes for that State. Will you drink her health with me?"

And in the clinking of the glasses, and the quaffing of their favorite beverages, the new link of friendship was forged.

RUN DOWN BY CAVALRY.

CHAPTER XI.

Webster Fraternizes with the Rebel Officers.—A Secession Hat.—A Visit to a Rebel Camp.—" The Committee of Safety."—A Friendly Stranger.—A Warning.—The Escape.

WEBSTER'S new friends were men whom he believed he could use to good advantage, and he determined to improve the chance that had thrown him in contact with them. He found them not only very well informed, but disposed to be communicative, and he therefore applied the " pumping " process with all the skill at his command. He experienced no difficulty in making this mode of operation effectual, for these officers were exceedingly willing to air their knowledge for the benefit of their Baltimore friend, and enjoyed his frequent expressions of agreeable surprise at the extent of the preparations made by the people of the South to defend their rights.

Dr. Burton was the most conspicuous one of the group, from his very pompousness. He wore a superfluity of gorgeous gold lace on his uniform, and assumed the dignity of a major-general. He was a flabby-faced, bulbous-eyed individual, with a wonderful stomach for harboring liquor, and that unceasing flow of spirits arising from a magnified sense of his own importance. It was evident, even upon a short acquaintance, that the doctor found his chief entertainment in listening to himself talk, a species of recreation in which he indulged with great regularity, sharing the pleasure with as many others as would grant him a hearing.

In Webster he found an attentive auditor, which so flattered his vanity that he at once formed a strong attachment for my operative, and placed himself on familiar and confidential terms with him.

" Webster, we've got to do some hard fighting in these parts, and that before we are many days older," said the Doctor, with a wise shake of the head.

" I think you are right," conceded the scout. " We must fight it out. From what you have told me, however, I am sure the Lincoln troops will find you fully prepared to give them a warm reception here."

" That they will, sir ; that they will !" was the emphatic rejoiner. " We have one full regiment and four or five companies besides, at Camp Rector, and General Pillow has thirty-seven hundred men at the camp in the rear of Fort Harris, which is a little above us on this side of the river. We expect to move with him, and if there is an attack made upon us every man in the town will instantly become a soldier."

" Have you arms enough for all of them ?"

"Arms? Let the Yankees count on our not having arms, and they will meet with a surprise party. In two hours' notice we can have from eight to ten thousand men ready to march."

"No doubt of it, Doctor; but how do you expect to get two hours' notice?"

"Lord bless you, Webster, we have men watching the movements of the Yankees at Cairo, and the minute they make a move we are notified. Then our signal gun is fired, and every man is mustered."

"A good arrangement, truly," said the detective, quietly.

"You look as if you could do some hard fighting yourself, Mr. Webster," remarked Colonel Dalgetty.

The detective smiled.

"I have been fighting against great odds for the past two months in Baltimore. The last battle I fought was to get away from there with my life."

"Yes, and we are confounded glad to receive you here," exclaimed the enthusiastic Doctor, shaking Webster by the hand for the twentieth time. "Come, gentlemen, we must have another drink. Step up and nominate your 'pizen.'"

The glasses were filled, and some one proposed the toast: "Death to the Yankees!" Under his breath, however, the detective muttered, "Confusion to the rebels!" and drained his glass. The toast was no sooner drank than Lieutenant Stanley, who was

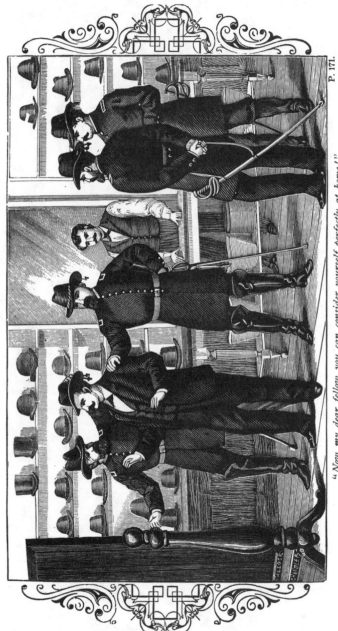

"Now, my dear fellow, you can consider yourself perfectly at home!"

P. 171.

evidently beginning to feel the influence of the liquor he had drank, took off his uniform hat and put it on Webster's head.

"Excuse me, Mr. Webster," he said, "I merely wish to see how you look in one of our hats." Then stepping back, he added: "By the gods, nothing could be more becoming! My dear fellow, you must have one by all means, if you stay among us."

Webster endeavored laughingly to object, but they all refused to accept "no" for an answer. So, finding it impossible to resist, he went with them to a neighboring hat store.

"Fit a hat to Mr. Webster's head—a hat just like mine," said Dr. Burton, to the proprietor; then turning to the scout, he added: "We will have you a cord and tassel of blue, as that will show that you are true to the cause, although you do not belong to the military."

The hatter produced a secession chapeau of the kind and size required, and Webster at once put it on, much to the delight of the Doctor, who slapped Webster familiarly on the shoulder, with the exclamation:

"Now, my dear fellow, you can consider yourself at home!"

"Perfectly at home," echoed Colonel Dalgetty.

"Henceforward you are one of us," put in the Lieutenant.

Webster thanked them cordially for their kindness, and promised to wear it in preference to any other. As they stepped outside of the store, however, all thoughts of the new hat were temporarily driven from his mind, for, standing on the sidewalk, within a few yards of the store door, and looking directly at him, was the identical individual whom he had noticed on the train, who had arrested the Northern stranger the night before.

The gaze which this vigilant agent of the safety committee now bent upon Webster was full of dark suspicion, but after one swift glance at him the detective turned away with an air of perfect composure and unconcern, and walked off between his companions. To say that he felt some uneasiness at this evidence that he was still being closely followed, would be only to tell the truth. His first impulse was to speak to his companions about it, but a second thought decided him not to mention the matter to any one, nor to betray by word or act that he had the slightest hint of a suspicion that he was being watched.

The three officers introduced Webster to a large number of soldiers and citizens, and before the day was over he had quite an extended circle of acquaintance in Memphis. Dr. Burton, who had conceived a fancy for him, as sudden as it was pronounced, assumed a sort of paternal control over Webster, hovering about him with an air of protection and solicitude, and drawing the scout's arm through his when they walked together.

That afternoon, Webster, desiring to be alone for awhile, hired one of the hackmen at the door of the hotel to drive him three or four miles into the country. He went down the river road, and as it was a beautiful day, he enjoyed himself admiring the picturesque scenery along the way.

Just below the town, on the bank of the river, he found a small encampment of soldiers with a battery, who were on the lookout for boats coming up the river, and during his ride he saw several encampments of the same nature. After spending several hours inspecting the fortifications along the river, Webster returned to the hotel, which he reached about dark.

The next day Doctor Burton and several of his military friends sought out the detective, and urged him to go with them to Camp Rector.

"Gentlemen, I am at your service," said Webster, earnestly. " I think I would enjoy a visit to your camp to-day above all things."

They went to the levee, and at ten o'clock were on the boat, steaming up the river toward Mound City, where Camp Rector was located.

A distance of some six or seven miles, passing on their way up, various objects of interest, among them Fort Harris, which was merely an embankment thrown up, to answer the purpose. Arriving at Mound City, the party disembarked and walked to the hotel. After dinner the party visited the camp-ground, a distance of about one-fourth of a mile from the hotel, and here Dr. Burton and the other officers took much pride in showing Webster around. They talked volubly about the unexampled bravery of the Confederate soldier; had much to say on the subject of Southern chivalry as opposed to Northern braggadocio; told how well they were prepared to meet the onslaught of the enemy; and found a special delight in exhibiting to the visitor a portion of General Bragg's artillery, which they had in the camp.

After that they seated themselves around a table in one of the larger tents, to rest and enjoy the grateful shade, as it was a warm and sunny afternoon. While engaged in the most bombastic utterances of their prowess, and of the wonderful exploits that might be expected of the Southern army, their conversation was interrupted by a shadow falling across the strip of sunlight that streamed in through the opening of the tent. Every one around the table glanced up, and there at the entrance stood the man with the broad-brimmed hat! The intruder did not tarry a moment, but turned and walked away. Evidently he had stopped only to look in; but in that single instant he had shot a keen, and apparently satisfactory, glance at Timothy Webster, which was fortunately not observed by any one save the detective himself.

"That fellow is one of the safety committee," said Dr. Burton, filling his glass.

"He appears to be looking **for some one**," remarked Lieutenant Stanley.

"Reckon he is," answered the Doctor. "He's always looking for some one. And, by-the-bye, those chaps are doing a heap of good for the cause just now. A Northern man stands no show for his life in these parts if the safety committee spots him. They hang 'em on suspicion."

"That's right," said Webster, coolly. "I believe in hanging every Northern man that comes prowling around. They don't deserve a trial, for they have no right here anyway."

But cool and collected as Webster outwardly appeared, it must be admitted that he was inwardly ill at ease. There was now no longer the shadow of a doubt in his mind that this long-haired agent of the safety committee was following him and watching his every movement, and that any attempt on his part to return to the North would betray him and cause his arrest.

"The only reason I have not already been arrested," mused the scout, "is because they are not sure whether I came from the North or not. They merely *suspect*, and are watching me to see if I undertake to return northward. Such an act would confirm their suspicions, and I would be arrested and probably put to death as a spy. It stands me in hand to give them the slip before I take the back track."

After spending a very pleasant day at the camp, he returned to Memphis on the latest boat that night, informing Dr. Burton that he was going to Chattanooga to look up a brother whom he had not seen in twelve years.

"You'll come back?" said the Doctor, as he wrung his hand.

"Oh, certainly," was the cheerful response.   "I'll be with you again before long."

Colonel Gaines, of the artillery, who heard this conversation, now grasped the scout's hand.

"Webster, you'd make a good soldier," he said, bluntly.   "Hang me if I wouldn't like to have you on my force."

Webster smiled good-naturedly.

"I have some family business to attend to before I could think of entering the army.   After that I may remind you of your remark."

"All right," said the Colonel, "any time that you are ready, come ; I will make room for you."

On his way down the river Webster found, to his relief, that the man with the broad-brimmed hat was not aboard the boats.   He now had a hope of being able to give his shadow the slip by leaving Memphis on early train in the morning.

Arriving in sight of their destination, the passengers on the ferry-boat were surprised to see that the levee was crowded with people.   Shortly after, they learned that this unusual gathering was caused by the capture of the steamboat "Prince of Wales" by the rebels.

Webster went to the Worsham Hotel, where he

spent the night, and at five o'clock in the morning, after making a few preparations, and dispatching an early breakfast, he repaired to the depot. Arriving there he looked carefully about on all sides, but saw no one who seemed to take any interest in his movements. "So far, so good," he muttered, as he boarded the train; and the next minute he was leaving the scene of his most recent exploits with the speed of the wind.

He was himself too shrewd and cunning to feel absolutely sure that he was not followed. His own experience in the art of "shadowing" told him he had not yet escaped the vigilant eyes of the safety committee, but he resolved to elude them if it was possible to do so.

Innumerable troops were being transported at this time, and the train was crowded with soldiers. Webster amused himself by making the acquaintance of the officers, and skillfully drawing on their fund of information, until the train arrived at Grand Junction, where he decided to change cars for Jackson, Tennessee.

Accordingly, he abandoned the Chattanooga cars and boarded the north-bound train, which was in waiting at the junction, and again he was whirled away across the verdure-clad country, this time toward the "land of the free." But no sooner was the train well under way than something which came under Webster's observation removed from his mind all doubt as to whether he would be permitted to pursue his journey unmolested. He occupied a seat in the forward part of the car, and on turning carelessly away from the window after gazing out upon the landscape for awhile, he was somewhat surprised at seeing an individual standing on the front platform of the car, looking in through the glass door.

It was a person whose face and figure had already become quite familiar to him, being no other than the man who had so persistently followed him for the past few days.

"He seems determined not to let me get away," thought the scout; but neither in his face nor manner did he betray any of the disappointment he felt.

He noticed that his pursuer was not alone this time, but was accompanied by another person—an ill-looking man of herculean proportions—with whom he conversed in an earnest, confidential way.

When the train arrived at Jackson, Webster stepped out upon the platform of the depot, and the two agents of the safety committee did the same. The conductor stood near by, and Webster spoke to him in a tone which he meant his shadows to hear, asking:

"How soon will there be a train for Humboldt?"

"In twenty minutes," replied the conductor.

"Do you know anything about the hotels there?" inquired the scout. "I've got to stop two or three days in the town, and it's a strange place to me."

The conductor recommended him to a good house convenient to the depot, and thanking him for the information, Webster turned away. He had spoken in a tone that he knew must have been distinctly heard by his enemies, and he hoped this bit of stratagem would have the desired effect.

He boarded the train for Humboldt, and the brace of shadows promptly followed him, taking seats in the same car.

While the train was speeding on its way, Webster was aroused from a reverie by the voice of a woman saying:

"Pardon me, sir; may I occupy a portion of this seat?"

He looked up; a tall, very respectable looking lady was standing in the aisle, and he saw in an instant that she was the person who had addressed him.

"Certainly, madam, certainly;" he replied; and quickly made room for her.

She sat down beside him, and then, to his great surprise, she began to talk to him in a low, earnest tone, without once turning her face toward him.

"You are going to Humboldt?" she inquired.

"I am," he answered, surprised at the question.

"You are a Northern man?"

"Madam!" A suspicion flashed, lightning-like, across his mind.

"Believe me, I am not an enemy," the lady went

on, "I have been sitting in the rear part of this car I heard two men talking, and have reason to believe they were speaking about you. They said they would stop at the same hotel with you in Humboldt, and keep a close watch over you, and if you attempt to go northward they will arrest you, take you back to Memphis, and deal with you as they would with any Northern spy. I advise you to be very careful, sir, for your life depends upon it."

The train by this time was approaching Humboldt, and the lady arose and disappeared before the astonished detective could tender his thanks for the warning. She was destined to remain an utter stranger to him for all time to come, for he never heard of her afterwards. As they entered the depot, Webster passed out at the rear end of the car, and he noticed, with a smile of satisfaction, that his attendant shadows were making their way out at the front. As he stepped from the car he noticed a pile of baggage near him, and quickly stepping behind this, he watched the movements of the two men. Apparently fully satisfied that their game would be safely bagged at the hotel, they left the depot and walked rapidly away in the direction of the public-house. His ruse worked to a charm. A violent shower happened to be passing over at this time, and it was only natural for the two "safety" men to suppose that Webster had stopped to seek shelter in the depot for a few minutes.

The express train from Memphis was soon due, and as it came dashing in " on time," Webster jumped aboard, and was on his way toward Louisville, smiling in his sleeve as he thought of those two crafty foxes, whose cunning had overreached themselves, patiently awaiting his arrival at the hotel in Humboldt.

Before crossing the Kentucky line, Webster put his rebel hat out of sight, and once more donned the one he had worn from the North.

The remainder of his journey was made without incident, and in due time he arrived in Cincinnati, and reported to me.

A HOT LUNCH.

CHAPTER XII.

I take a Trip to the South.—Danger in Memphis.—A Timely Warning.—A Persistent Barber.—An Unfortunate Memory.—Return to Cincinnati.

TIMOTHY WEBSTER had scarcely departed upon his trip to Memphis, when I was summoned for consultation with General McClellan. Upon repairing to his office, which I did immediately on receiving his message, I found him awaiting my arrival, and in a few minutes I was informed of his wishes. He was desirous of ascertaining, as definitely as possible, the general feeling of the people residing South of the Ohio river, in Kentucky, Tennessee, Mississippi and Louisiana, and requested that measures be at once taken to carry out his purposes.

It was essentially necessary at the outset to become acquainted with all the facts that might be of importance hereafter, and no time offered such opportunities for investigations of this nature as the present, while the war movement was in its incipiency, and before the lines between the opposing forces had been so closely drawn as to render traveling in the disaffected district unsafe, if not utterly impossible.

As this mission was of a character that required

coolness and tact, as well as courage, and as most of my men had been detailed for duties in other sections of the rebellious country, I concluded to make the journey myself, and at once stated my intention to the General, who received it with every evidence of satisfaction and approval.

"The very thing I should have proposed, Major," said he; "and if you will undertake this matter, I have no fears of a failure, and every confidence in obtaining important developments."

My action had been prompted by two impelling reasons. The first was the absence of the men whom I had thus far engaged, and who, as I have before stated, had been detailed upon missions of investigations in various parts of the South and West, and the other was a desire to see for myself the actual condition of affairs as they existed at that time. I have invariably found that a personal knowledge is far more satisfactory than that gleamed from others, and whenever it was possible, I have endeavored to acquire my information by such means. Another advantage to be derived from a personal observation was that I would be necessarily forced to rely in many matters to which it would be impossible for me to devote my personal attention.

Having arranged everything to my satisfaction, in order that my absence would occasion no disarrangement in the proper conduct of the investigations already commenced, I left my office in the charge of

Mr. George H. Bangs, my general superintendent, and started upon my journey, intending to be as rapid in my movements as circumstances would per· mit, and to return at as early a date as I could, consistently with the proper performance of the duties intrusted to me.

My first objective point was the city of Louisville, in Kentucky. The position of this State at the present time was a peculiar one. Her Governor, if not a Southern conspirator, was, if his own language was to be relied upon, both in opinion and expecta· tion, a disunionist. He had at first remonstrated against the action of the Cotton States, but after that action had been taken, he was unqualifiedly opposed to coercing them back to obedience, and in addition to this, he had endeavored to excite his own people to a resistance to the principles and policy of the party in power.

The people, however, did not sustain his views, and while the popular sentiment was deeply pro-slavery, and while her commerce bound her strongly to the South, the patriotic example and teachings of Henry Clay had impressed upon them a reverence and love for Union higher and purer than any mere pressing interests or selfish advantage.

At Louisville, therefore, I found a degree of excitement prevailing that was naturally to be ex-pected from the unsettled condition of public affairs. The Governor had refused to comply with the President's call for troops, and the State had been in a state of hopeless bewilderment and conflict of opinion in consequence. A strong minority, arrogating to themselves an undue importance, were endeavoring, by self-assertion and misapplied zeal, to carry the State into the secession fold, but thus far they had made no substantial progress against an overwhelming undercurrent of Union sentiment. Failing in this, their energies were now devoted to an effort to place the State in a neutral attitude, which would prevent her from taking a decided stand upon the question of supporting the Union. Thus far they had been temporarily successful, and on the 16th day of May the house of representatives passed resolutions declaring that Kentucky "should during the contest occupy the position of strict neutrality."

This was the existing condition of affairs when I arrived in Louisville, and which I found prevalent throughout all the sections of the State I passed.

Representing myself as a Southern man, a resident of Georgia, I had no difficulty in engaging in conversation with the prominent men of both elements, and I decided then, from my own observations, that Kentucky would not cast her fortunes with the South, but that, after the bubble of unnatural excitement had burst and expended itself, the loyal heart would be touched, and " Old Kaintuck " would eventually keep step to the music of the Union. Results proved that I was not mistaken, and not many weeks

elapsed before Union camps were established within
her domain, and the broad-shouldered Kentuckians
were swearing allegiance to the old flag, and, shoul-
dering their muskets, entered into the contest with a
determination to support the government.

Passing on undisturbed, but everywhere on the
alert, and making copious notes of everything that
transpired, that I considered at all material to the
furtherance of the loyal cause, I reached Bowling
Green.

At this place I found a very decided Union sentiment, the Stars and Stripes were floating from the
various buildings, and the Union men were largely in
the majority. There was one great cause for dis-
quietude, however, which was very manifest even to
a casual observer. Many residents of Bowling Green
and the vicinity were slave owners, and the impression had become general throughout the negro communities that the opening of the war naturally and
inevitably involved their freedom, an opinion, however, without sure foundation, at that time, but
which was eventually to be justified by subsequent
events. The slaves had heard their masters discussing the various questions which naturally grew out
of a conflict of this chance character, and in which it
was generally admitted, that emancipation must follow the commencement and continuance of hostilities
between the two sections. It was not surprising
therefore, that this opinion should spread among the

entire colored element, or that it should be greedily accepted by these down-trodden blacks as the harbinger of a freedom for which they had been praying. In conversation with one of the leading men of Bowling Green, I was thoroughly impressed with the importance of this phase of circumstances.

"Mr. Allen," said he, "you have no idea of the danger we are apprehending from the blacks. We know that the moment that Lincoln sends his abolition soldiers among our niggers, they will break out and murder all before them. Why, sir," continued he, "we cannot sleep sound at nights for fear of the niggers. They think Lincoln is going to set them free."

"Why," I interrupted, "what can they know about Lincoln?"

"They know too much about him," he replied; "there has been so much talk about this matter all through the State, that the niggers know as much about it as we do."

"You should not talk before your niggers; it is not safe, and I never do it." As I never owned a negro this was perfectly true.

"I know we should not, but it is too late now; they know as much as we do, and too much for our safety or peace of mind. Why, sir, we are compelled to mount guard at nights ourselves for mutual protection, and though there has been no outbreak as yet, and I believe that this is the only thing that keeps them in check."

"It would be a good plan," said I, anxious to preserve my reputation as a Southern pro-slavery man, "to take all the men and boys over fifteen years of age and sell them South."

"That's the devil of it," he replied, "we cannot do that; it was tried only last week, and a nigger that I was offered $1,500 for last year, I could not sell at any price."

Already, it seemed, the fruits of the slavery agitation were being made apparent. The very institution for which these misguided men were periling their lives, and sacrificing their fortunes, was threatened with demolition; and the slaves who had so long and so often felt the lash of their masters, were now becoming a source of fear to the very men who had heretofore held them in such utter subjection.

This state of affairs I found to be prevalent all over the country which I visited. Bright visions of freedom danced before the eyes of the slaves, and they awaited anxiously the dawning of the day, when the coming of the soldiers of the North would strike from their limbs the shackles they had worn so long. In the after years of this bloody struggle, many deeds of self-sacrifice were performed by these slaves, when, resisting the dazzling opportunities to obtain their coveted liberty, they cast their lot with the families of their old masters, whose male members were fighting to continue their bondage. Many cases could be cited where, but for the faithful labors and devotion

of the despised slave, the families of many of the
proud aristocrats would have starved. But the faithful heart of the negro ever beat warmly for those
whom he had served so long, and disregarding the
tempting allurements of freedom, he devoted himself
to the service and to the maintenance of those who
had regarded him as so much merchandise, or simply
as a beast of burden.

At Bowling Green I purchased a splendid bay
horse, whose swiftness and powers of endurance I felt
assured could be relied upon, intending to make the
rest of my journey on horseback. By this means I
would be the better able to control my movements
than if I were compelled to depend upon the railroads for transportation. I would also be enabled to
stop at any place where I might find the necessity, or
a favorable opportunity for observation. I had no
cause to regret the purchase I had made, for right
nobly did the spirited animal which I had selected
perform the arduous duties that were imposed upon
him. Day after day he would be urged forward, and
under his flying feet the distance sped away almost
imperceptibly, and each morning found my charger
rested and refreshed, and ready for the day's journey,
be the weather fair or foul, or the roads easy or
rugged.

I reached Nashville, Tennessee, in due season, and
resolved to devote several days to my investigations.
Here the disunion element was more united and out-

spoken, but even here, I detected evidences of a
Union sentiment which was none the less profound,
because of the danger which its utterances would
have incurred. There could be no doubt that this
State had resolved to cast her fortunes with the confederacy, and the rebel General Pillow had been for
some time engaged in fortifying the city of Memphis.
At Nashville I met a number of officers of the rebel
army, all of whom were full of enthusiasm, and whose
bombastic utterances in view of the eventual results,
seem at this time almost too absurd to be repeated.
Here also I came in contact with an army surgeon,
whose head was full of wild *Quixotic* schemes for destroying the Northern armies by other processes than
that of legitimate warfare. One of his plans I
remember was to fill a commissary wagon with
whisky, in which had been previously mixed a gen-
erous quantity of strychnine. The wagon was then
to be broken and abandoned and left upon the road
so as to fall into the hands of the Union soldiers.
Of course, the liquor would be consumed by the
finders, and the valiant Doctor, with evident satisfaction to himself, but to the equally evident disgust of
his companions, loudly vaunted his death-dealing and
barbarous scheme. This brave warrior, however, I
learned afterward, had fled in terror at the first fire,
and was afterwards dishonorably dismissed from the
service he was so well calculated to disgrace. So far
as I was afterward able to learn, this grand project

for wholesale slaughter, of the valorous Doctor, received no sympathy or support from his more honorable associates, and the soldiers were enabled to drink their whiskey untainted with any other poisonous influences than is naturally a part of its composition.

Leaving Nashville, I spurred on in the direction of Memphis, and in due time reached the city, which now presented a far different aspect than when I visited it only a few years before. Then the country was at peace. The war cloud had not burst with all its fury over a happy land, and the people were quietly pursuing their avocations. I was engaged in a detective operation which required my presence in the city, and had been in consultation with some of the express company's officials, for whom I was attempting to discover the perpetrators of a robbery of one of their safes. Turning a corner I came upon a scene that stirred my feelings to the utmost.

It was the market square, and the merchandise disposed of were human beings. There was the auction-block and the slave-pen. Men, women and children were being knocked down to the highest bidder. Wives were sold away from their husbands, and children from their parents. Old and young were submitted to the vulgar speculators in flesh and blood, and their value was approximated by their apparent age, strength and healthfulness. My blood boiled in my veins as I witnessed, for the first time, the heart-rendering scenes which I had only heard or read of before. The cold cruelty of the buyers and abject misery of the sold, filled me with a spirit of opposition to this vile traffic that gave me renewed strength to fulfill my duty as an active abolitionist, and to labor earnestly in the cause of emancipation. I shall never forget the events of that day, and I can recall the feeling of intense satisfaction which I experienced on my second visit, when even then, I could see the dawning of that liberty for which I had labored, and I knew that the day of emancipation could not be far distant. Then the fair fame of independent America would no longer be blackened by the pressure of the slave or the master, but all men under the protection of the starry banner would be free and equal under the law.

Now the streets were filled with soldiers, some of them fully armed and equipped, and others provided with but ordinary clothing, and furnished with such inefficient arms as they had brought with them from their homes. A most motley gathering they were, and their awkward and irregular evolutions at this time gave but little promise of the splendid army of which they were destined in the near future to form so important a part. The work of fortifying the city had been progressing in earnest ; earthworks had been thrown up all along the banks of the Mississippi, and batteries were already in position, whose guns frowned threateningly upon the river.

Here to be known or suspected as a Union man was to merit certain death, and to advocate any theory of compromise between the two sections was to be exiled from the city. Here rebeldom was rampant and defiant, and I had some difficulty in evading the suspicions of the watchful and alert Southron, who regarded all strange civilians with doubtful scrutiny, and whose "committee of safety" were ever on the *qui vive* to detect those whose actions savored in the least of a leaning towards the North. Fearlessly, however, I mingled with these men, and as I lost no opportunity in pronouncing my views upon the righteousness of the cause of secession, and of my belief in its certain triumph, I obtained a ready passport to the favor and confidence of the most prominent of their leaders. I talked unreservedly with the private soldier and the general officer, with the merchant and the citizen, and by all was regarded as a stanch Southern man, whose interests and sympathies were wedded to rebellion.

General Pillow was in command at this point, and almost every citizen was enrolled as a soldier, whose services would be cheerfully and promptly rendered whenever the call should be made upon them.

Even this redoubtable chieftain was not proof against my blandishments, and he little dreamed when on one occasion he quietly sipped his brandy and water with me, that he was giving valuable information to his sworn foe, and one to whom every

13

idea gained was an advantage to the government he was attempting to destroy.

It is needless to relate the valuable items of information which I was enabled to glean upon this journey—information which in later days was of vast importance to the Union commanders, but which at this time would only burden a narrative of the events which they so ably assisted to successful results.

Here, as in many other places, I found that my best source of information was the colored men, who were employed in various capacities of a military nature which entailed hard labor. The slaves, without reserve, were sent by their masters to perform the manual labor of building earthworks and fortifications, in driving the teams and in transporting cannon and ammunition, and, led by my natural and deep-seated regard for these sable bonsmen, I mingled freely with them, and found them ever ready to answer questions and to furnish me with every fact which I desired to possess.

Here and there I found an unassuming white man whose heart was still with the cause of the Union, but whose active sympathy could not at this time be of service to the country, as he dared not utter a voice in defense of his opinions. From all these sources, however, I was successful in posting myself fully in regard to the movements and intentions of the rebel authorities and officers, and, as I believed, had also succeeded in concealing my identity.

"Fo' God, Massa Allen, ye'll be a dead man in de mo'nin'!"

On the third evening of my sojourn in Memphis, however, my dreams of fancied security were suddenly dispelled, and I was brought face to face with the reality of danger.

I had retired early to my room, according to my general custom, and had scarcely been seated when I was disturbed by a faint but quick and distinct knocking at my door. I arose hastily, as it was something unusual for me to receive visitors after I had retired, and throwing open the door, I was somewhat surprised to see, standing before me, in a state of unmistakable excitement, the colored porter of the hotel.

Before I had time to question him, he sprang into the room and closed the door behind him. His countenance evinced a degree of terror that immediately filled me with alarm. His eyes were fixed wildly upon me, his lips were quivering, and his knees trembled under him, as though unable to sustain the weight of his body. Indeed, so frightened was he, that he appeared to be struggling forcibly to do so.

"What is the matter, Jem?" I inquired, in as calm a tone as I could assume, and with a view of reassuring him. "What has happened to frighten you so?"

"'Fore God, Massa Allen," ejaculated the black, succeeding by a great effort in finding his voice, "you done can't sleep in this housn to-night, ef ye do, ye'll be a dead man before morning."

As may be imagined, this information was not of a very agreeable nature, indefinite as it was; I felt assured that my informant could be relied on that something had occurred to endanger my safety, and I became impatient to learn what he knew.

"Out with it, Jem," said I, "and let me know what it is all about." I spoke cheerfully and confidently, and the coolness of my manner had the effect of restoring the equilibrium of my sable friend, and, recovering himself with an effort, he began to explain :

"I tell you what it is, Massa Allen, and I'se gwan to tell it mighty quick. Ye see, de General hab got a lot of spies up de river at Cairo, a watching of the Linkum sogers, and one o' dem fellows jes came in as you were going up stairs. De berry minit dat he seed you he said to de man what was wid him, 'Dat man is 'spicious ; I seed him in Cincinnati two weeks ago, and he ain't down here for no good,' and he started right off for de General, to tell him all about it. I kem right up heah, massa, and you must git away as fast as ye can."

This was too important to be ignored. I had no desire to be captured at that time, and I had no doubt of the correctness of the porter's story. I resolved to act at once upon the suggestion, and to make good my escape before it was too late. My admonitory friend was fearfully in earnest about getting me away, and he quickly volunteered to procure my horse, which I had quartered in close proximity to the hotel, and to furnish me with a guide who would see me safely through the lines and outside of the city. Bidding Jem make all possible haste in his movements, I gathered together my few belongings, and in a few minutes I descended the stairs and made my exit through the rear of the house. Through the faithfulness of Jem, and the careful guidance of the watchful negro he had provided me with, I was soon riding away from threatened danger and ere morning broke I had proceeded far upon my way. How much service these faithful blacks had been to me, I did not fully learn until some time afterwards, when I was informed by Timothy Webster, who arrived in Memphis following my departure, and who thus learned the full particulars of the exhausting pursuit of one of Lincoln's spies, who had mysteriously disappeared from the chief hotel, while a guard was being detailed to effect his arrest.

I met the faithful Jem several years later, when he had worked his way as a refugee from his native State and entered the Union lines in Virginia, and he was soon afterwards attached to my force, where he proved his devotion in a manner that was quite convincing. My faithful steed, who had become thoroughly rested after his long journey, bore me safely through this danger, and in due time I entered the State of Mississippi. Here rebellion and disunion were the order of the day, and a wide-spread deter-

mination existed to fight the cause of the South to
the bitter end.   Stopping one night at Grenada, I
pushed on my way to Jackson, and here I resolved to
remain a day or two, in order to make a thorough investigation of the place and its surroundings.

Putting up my horse, I engaged quarters for myself at the principal hotel in the city, and feeling very
much fatigued with my long journey, I retired early to
my room and passed a long night in refreshing sleep.

In the morning I arose about five o'clock, as is
my general custom.   I was feeling in excellent health
and spirits ; my journey had thus far been fully as
successful as I could have desired ; and safely concealed about my person I had items of value that
would amply repay me for the fatigues I had undergone and the dangers I had passed.   I had plans of
the roads, a description of the country, a pretty correct estimate of the troops and their various locations
and conditions, and altogether I felt very well satisfied with myself and with the results of my mission.

As I descended the stairs, I noticed a fine soldierly officer standing in the doorway, and after bidding him a hearty good-morning, I invited him to
accompany me to the saloon of the hotel, where we
mutually indulged in a decoction as is the universal
custom in Southern cities.   After I had obtained my
breakfast, it occurred to me that, before attempting
any active measures for the day, I owed it to myself
to procure the services of a barber for a much-needed

shave. I had been traveling for a number of days, and my face had been a stranger to a razor for a long time. and I concluded I would be more presentable if I consulted a tonsorial artist.

This was an unfortunate idea, and I soon had occasion to regret having entertained it for a moment. I would have been far more contented if I had bestowed no thoughts upon my grizzled beard, and allowed nature to take its course with my hirsute appendage.

Entirely unconscious, however, of what was in store for me, I entered the well-fitted saloon of the hotel, and patiently waited my turn to submit myself to the deft fingers of the knight of the razor.

In response to the universal and well-understood call of "next!" I took my seat in the luxuriously upholstered chair, and in a few minutes my face was covered with the foamy lather applied by the dapper little German into whose hands I had fallen.

I noticed when I sat down that the man wore a puzzled and speculative look, as though he was struggling with some vexing lapse of memory, and as he drew the keen edge of the razor across my face, his eyes were fixed intensely upon my features. His manner annoyed me considerably, and I was at a loss to account for his strange demeanor. Whatever ideas I may have entertained with regard to this singular action were, however, soon set at rest, only to give place to a feeling of unrestful anger.

He had just cleared one side of my face of its stubby growth of hair, when a smile irradiated his face, and with a look of self-satisfied recognition and pride, he addressed me :

"Vy, how do you do, Mr. Bingerdon ?"

Had a thunderbolt fallen at my feet I could not have been more perfectly amazed, and for a moment I could scarcely tell whether I was afoot or on horseback. I devoutly wished that I was anywhere than with this Dutch barber, whose memory was so uncomfortably retentive.

I had been too accustomed to sudden surprises, however, to lose my self-control, and I replied to him, with an unmoved face and as stern a voice as I could command :

"I am not Mr. Bingerdon, and I don't know the man."

"Oh yes, your name is Bingerdon, and you leev in Geecago."

The face of the German was so good-natured, and he appeared quite delighted at recognizing me, but for myself I was feeling very uncomfortable indeed. I did not know the man, nor what he knew of me. I knew, however, that he was perfectly right about my identity, and I knew also that it would be very dangerous for his knowledge to become general.

"I tell you I don't know the man you are speaking of," said I, sternly.

"Oy, Mr. Bingerdon," he replied, in a grieved

"If you say another word to me, I'll whip you on the spot."

tone, " I know you well. Don't you mind me shaving you in the Sherman House in Geecago, you was a customer of mine."

The pertinacity of the man was simply exasperating, and fearing that his memory would be likely to get me into trouble, as several people were listening to our conversation, I resolved to end the difficulty at once. Jerking the towel from around my neck and wiping the lather from the unshaved portion of my face, I leapt from the chair, exclaiming angrily :

" I tell you I know nothing of you Mr. Bingerdon, or any other d—d Yankee abolitionist, and if you say another word to me upon this subject, I'll whip you on the spot !"

The barber presented a most ridiculous appearance; he was utterly frightened at my manner, and yet so convinced was he that I was the man he took me for, that he appeared more amazed at my denial, than at my threats of violence.

Meanwhile, the occupants of the saloon began to crowd around us, and several came in from the adjoining rooms. Turning to them with well-simulated anger, I told them the story I had invented; I lived near Augusta, Georgia ; never was in Chicago, did not know Mr. Pinkerton or any of his gang. Then I denounced the discomfited barber in round terms, and finished by inviting the entire crowd to take a drink with me.

This they all did with alacrity, and by the time

they had drained their glasses, every one of the party were strong adherents of mine. We then returned to the barber-shop, and so thoroughly was the crowd convinced of my truthfulness, that they were eager to punish the innocent occasion of my anger. One impetuous individual wanted to hang him on sight, and his proposition was received with general favor; but finding I had succeeded in evading detection for myself, I interfered in the poor fellow's behalf and he was finally let off.

After another drink all round I managed to get away from the party, and it was not long before I was upon my horse, and traveling away from the possibility of a recurrence of such an accidental discovery. I procured a razor and shaving materials, and performed that operation for myself, as I did not care to excite curiosity by exhibiting my half-shaved face to any more inquisitive barbers.

A few miles outside of the town I sold my horse, and concluding that I had obtained as much information as was desirable at that time, and as I had already been absent from head-quarters longer than I had intended, I made my way back to Cincinnati by a circuitous route, and reached there in safety, well pleased with my work, and quite rejoiced to find that General McClellan was fully satisfied with what I had learned.

CHAPTER XIII.

East and West Virginia.—Seceding from Secession.—My Scouts in Virginia.—A Rebel Captain Entertains " My Lord."—An old Justice Dines with Royalty.—A Lucky Adventure.—A Runaway Horse.—A Rescue.

AT this time the condition of affairs in the State of Virginia—the " Old Dominion," as it was generally denominated—presented a most perplexing and vexatious problem. The antagonistic position of the two sections of that state demanded early consideration and prompt action on the part of the Federal Government, both in protecting the loyal people in the Western section, and of preserving their territory to the Union cause. Within the borders of this commonwealth there existed two elements, directly opposed to each other, and both equally pronounced in the declaration of their political opinions. The lines of demarkation between these diverse communities were the Allegheny Mountains, which extended through the very middle of the state, from north-east to south-west, and divided her territory into two divisions, slightly unequal in size, but evidently different in topographical features and personal characteristics.

From the nature of its earlier settlement, and by reason of climate, soil and situation, Eastern Virginia remained the region of large plantations, with a heavy slave population, and of profitable agriculture, especially in the production of tobacco. West Virginia, on the contrary, having been first settled by hunters, pioneers, lumbermen and miners, possessed little in common with her more wealthy and aristocratic neighbors beyond the mountains. They made their homes in the wilds of the woods, and among the rocky formations, under which was hidden the wealth they were seeking to develop, and in time this western country became the seat of a busy manufacturing industry, with a diversified agriculture for local consumption, while the east was largely given up to the production of great staples for export. As a natural result, the population and wealth of the eastern portion, which was thus made to stand in the relation of a mere tributary province to her grasping neighbor, who selfishly absorbed the general taxes for local advantage.

The slave interest also entered largely into the creation and continuance of this antagonistic feeling. According to a census, which had been recently taken, it was ascertained that Eastern Virginia held but a few thousands. It was not a matter of surprise, therefore that secessionism should be rampant in the east, and that a Union sentiment should almost universally prevail in the west. As the institution of slavery was more or less the cause of the war, here, as in other parts of the South, secession reared its most formidable front where the slave interest predominated, and treason was more alert in the centers of accumulated wealth and family pride, whose foundations were laid by the suffering and the toil of the African bondsmen. The war had been waged to defend the " Divine institution," and it was scarcely to be expected that such a cause would be valiantly championed by men whose self-reliance and personal independence had endeared to them the rights of free and honorable manhood.

When the Convention of Virginia met to consider the question of secession, the slave-holding dignitaries were somewhat startled by the logical, but novel, declaration of one of the western members, that "the right of revolution can be exercised as well by a portion of the citizens of a State against their State government, as it can be exercised by the whole people of a State against their Federal Government." This was followed by another, more pointed and revolutionary, " that any change in the relation Virginia now sustains to the Federal Government, against the wishes of even a respectable minority of her people, would be sufficient to justify them in changing their relation to the State government by separating themselves from that section of the State that had thus wantonly disregarded their interests and defied their will."

The convention, however, denying the pertinency of this logic, passed its secret ordinance of secession on the 17th day of April, and within a week popular movements were on foot in the various towns and counties of Western Virginia, to effect a division of the State. The people united in a unanimous protest against the efforts of the slave-holding aristocrats to carry them into a cotton confederacy, and a determination to "secede from secession," was manifested everywhere. The loyal determination was rapidly followed by popular organization, an appeal for assistance was made to the government at Washington, who promised them countenance and support, and on the 13th day of May, delegates from twenty-five counties of West Virginia met at Wheeling, to devise such action as would enable them to fully and finally repudiate the treasonable revolt of East Virginia.

Many circumstances favored their position. The state of Ohio, immediately adjoining, was organizing her military force of volunteers, and Western Virginia was, not long after, attached to the department of the Ohio under command of General McClellan. The blockade of Washington, and other events, had operated to keep the Western troops on the Ohio line, and the Unionists of West Virginia found a protecting military force at once in their immediate vicinity, with a commanding officer who was instructed to give them every encouragement and support.

Meanwhile, Governor Letcher, of Virginia, ignoring the attitude assumed by the people of the West, had issued his proclamation calling for the organization of the state militia, and including Western Virginia in the call. Prompted by a spirit of arrogance or over-confidence, he at an early day dispatched officers to that locality to collect and organize the militia of Western Virginia. Owing to the sparsity of the population, and the hilly and mountainous situation of the country, there were but two principal localities or lines of travel, where a concentration of forces could be best effected—one of these being the line of the Baltimore and Ohio Railroad, and the other the valley of the Great Kanawha river. In these districts Governor Letcher sent his recruiting agents, but they soon returned reports of a very discouraging character. The rebel emissaries found the feeling very bitter: that Union organizations existed in most of the counties, and that while fragments of rebel companies were here and there springing up, it was very evident that no local force sufficient to hold the country, would respond to the Confederate appeal, while the close proximity of Union forces at several points along the Ohio, pointed to a short tenure of Confederate authority.

This information was not at all cheering to the rebel Governor of the State, and he determined to maintain his authority in the disaffected districts with armed forces from the eastern portion of the State. To accomplish this, he detailed a few available companies from Staunton to march toward Beverly, from which point they could menace and overawe the town of Grafton, the junction of the main stem of the Baltimore and Ohio Railroad, with its branches extending to Parkersburg and Wheeling. The inhabitants showed more alacrity, however, to take up arms for the government than for Governor Letcher or General Lee. A Union Western Virginia regiment, under the command of Colonel Kelley, began to gather recruits rapidly at Wheeling, while the rebel camps between Beverly and Grafton were comparatively deserted, and Colonel Porterfield, who had been sent under orders of Governor Letcher, found his efforts at recruiting decidedly unsuccessful.

On the 23d day of May the State voted upon the ordinance of secession, and East Virginia, under complete military domination, accepted the ordinance, while West Virginia, comparatively free, voted to reject the idea of secession.

Immediately after the result was ascertained, the rebel troops became aggressive, and Colonel Porterfield dispatched several of his companies to burn the bridge on the Baltimore & Ohio Railroad.

The appearance of these troops was quickly brought to the notice of the Federal authorities at Washington. On the 24th day of May the Secretary of War and General Scott telegraphed this information to General McClellan, and inquired "whether its influence could not be counteracted." General McClellan at once replied in the affirmative, and this was the sole order he received from Washington regarding a campaign in Virginia.

On the 26th, the General ordered two regiments to cross the river at Wheeling, and two others at Parkersburg. They were to move forward simultaneously by the branch railroads from each of these points to their junction at Grafton. The burnt bridges were restored in their passage, and after a most brilliant strategic movement, Porterfield was completely surprised, and the rebels were forced to disperse, in utter rout and confusion.

This complete success of the first dash at the enemy had the most inspiriting effect upon the Union troops, and also encouraged and fortified the Western Virginia unionists, in their determination to break away from the East and to form a new State. This movement was successfully accomplished, and early in July they elected two United States senators, who were admitted to, and took part in the national legislature.

Governor Pierpont, who was head of this provisional State government, organized at Wheeling, made a formal application to the United States for aid to suppress the rebellion and protect the people against domestic violence. General McClellan, in furtherance of this object, ordered additional forces into the State from his department.

In order to act intelligently in the matter, it was

14

necessary that some definite information should be derived respecting the country which was now to be protected, and from which it was necessary the invading rebels should be driven. For this purpose the General desired that I should dispatch several of my men, who, by assuming various and unsuspicious characters, would be able to travel over the country, obtain a correct idea of its topography, ascertain the exact position and designs of the secessionists.

For this duty I selected a man named Price Lewis, who had just returned from a trip to the South, and whom I had reason to be satisfied was equal to the task. I resolved, therefore, that he should be one of the party to make this journey, together with several others who were delegated for the same purpose. In order to afford variety to the professions of my operatives, and because of his fitness for the character, I decided that Price Lewis should represent himself as an Englishman traveling for pleasure, believing that he would thus escape a close scrutiny or a rigid examination, should he, by any accident, fall into the hands of the rebels.

Procuring a comfortable-looking road-wagon and a pair of strong gray horses, which were both substantial-looking and good roadsters, I stocked the vehicle with such articles of necessity and luxury as would enable them to subsist themselves if necessary, and at the same time give the appearance of truth to such professions as the sight-seeing Englishman

might feel authorized to make. I provided him also
with a number of English certificates of various kinds,
and I also supplied him with English money which
could be readily exchanged for such currency that
would best suit his purposes in the several localities
which he would be required to visit.

Lewis wore a full beard, and this was trimmed in
the most approved English fashion, and when fully
equipped for his journey he presented the appearance
of a thorough well-to-do Englishman, who might
even be suspected of having "blue blood" in his
veins. In order that he might the more fully sustain
the new character he was about to assume, and to
give an added dignity to his position, I concluded to
send with him a member of my force who would act
in the capacity of coachman, groom and body servant, as occasion should demand. The man whom I
selected for this role was a jolly, good-natured, and
fearless Yankee named Samuel Bridgeman, a quick,
sharp-witted young man, who had been in my employment some time, and who had on several occasions
proved himself worthy of trust and confidence in matters that required tact as well as boldness, and good
sense as well as keen wit.

Calling Sam into my office, I explained to him
fully the nature of the duties he would be required to
perform, and when I had concluded I saw by the
merry twinkle in his eyes, and from the readiness
with which he caught at my suggestions, that he

thoroughly understood and had decided to carry out his part of the programme to the very letter.

In addition to these, I arranged a route for two other men of my force. They were to travel through the valley of the Great Kanawha river, and to observe carefully everything that came under their notice, which might be of importance in perfecting a military campaign, in case the rebels should attempt hostile measures, or that General McClellan might find it necessary to promptly clear that portion of Virginia from the presence of secession troops. These two men were to travel ostensibly as farm laborers, and their verdant appearance was made to fully conform to such avocations.

Everything being in readiness, the two parties were started, and we will follow their movements separately, as they were to travel by different routes.

Price Lewis, the pseudo Englishman, and Sam Bridgeman, who made quite a smart-looking valet in his new costume, transferred their horses, wagon and stores on board the trim little steamer "Cricket," at Cincinnati, intending to travel along the Ohio River, and effect a landing at Guyandotte, in Western Virginia, at which point they were to disembark and pursue their journey overland through the country.

I accompanied Lewis to the wharf, and after everything had been satisfactorily arranged, I bade him good-bye, and the little steamer sailed away up the river.

There were the usual number of miscellaneous passengers upon the boat, and added to these were a number of Union officers, who had been dispatched upon various missions throughout that portion of the State of Ohio. These men left the steamer as their points of destination were reached, and after they had departed, several of the passengers who had hitherto remained silent, became very talkative. They began in a cautious manner to express their opinions, with a view of eliciting some knowledge of the sympathies of their fellow-travelers in the important struggle that was now impending. Lewis had maintained a quiet, dignified reserve, which, while it did not forbid any friendly approaches from his fellow-passengers, at the same time rendered them more respectful, and prevented undue familiarity. Sam Bridgeman contributed materially to this result; his deference to "my lord" was very natural, and the respect with which he received his commands convinced the passengers at once that the English-looking gentleman was a man of some importance.

The passengers all appeared to be Union men, and while they expressed their regrets that the war had commenced, they regarded their separation from Eastern Virginia, with undisguised satisfaction.

At midnight, on the second evening, the boat landed at Guyandotte, and Samuel, with a great deal of importance, attended to the transfer of his master and the equipage from the boat to the wharf. Here they found a number of men in uniform, who were ascertained to be representatives of the "Home Guard," and in a few minutes Bridgeman had secured the services of two of them, to assist him in safely landing their effects. This being satisfactorily accomplished, he, apparently in a sly manner, treated them to a drop of good whisky, which formed part of the stores they had been provided with. Stopping at the hotel over night, they continued their journey on the following morning. They drove leisurely along, and at about ten o'clock they stopped at a farm-house to rest their horses. They remained here until nearly three o'clock in the afternoon, conversing with the old farmer, who seemed to be much pained at the condition of affairs, but who had two sons who had joined the rebel army. They renewed their journey in the afternoon, and in about two hours reached the little village of Colemouth, where there was a rebel encampment. On passing this they were halted by the guard, who inquired their business and destination. Lewis told him he was an Englishman, accompanied only by his servant, and that he was traveling through the country for pleasure. The guard informed them that he could not let them pass, and asked Lewis to go with him to the Captain's headquarters, which was located in a large stone house, a few hundred yards distant. My operative willingly consented, and leaving Sam in charge of his carriage, he accompanied the soldier to the officer's quarters. He was ushered

An English Lord and a Rebel Captain.

into a large and well-furnished apartment on the second floor, and in a few minutes the Captain came in.

He greeted my operative pleasantly, and informed him that he regretted the necessity of detaining him, but orders had to be obeyed. Lewis related in subssance what he had already stated to the guard, which statement the Captain unhesitatingly received, and after a pleasant conversation, he invited the detective to accept the hospitality of the camp.

An English gentleman traveling for pleasure was not to be treated with discourtesy, and upon Lewis' accepting of his invitation, a soldier was dispatched to bring the horses and carriage and their impatient driver into camp.

Supper was ordered, and in a short time the Captain and his guest were discussing a repast which was far more appetizing than soldiers' fare usually is. During the meal Sam stood behind the chair of Lewis, and awaited upon him in the most approved fashion, replying invariably with a deferential,

"Yes, my lord."

After full justice had been done to the repast, Price directed Bridgeman to bring in from the carriage a couple of bottles of champagne, and by the time the hour of retiring had arrived the detective had succeeded in impressing his entertainer with a very exalted opinion of his rank and standing when at home.

Lewis, being an Englishman by birth, was very well posted about English affairs, and he entertained his host with several very well invented anecdotes of the Crimea, in which he was supposed to have taken an active part, and his intimacy with Lord Raglan, the commander of the British army, gained for him the unbounded admiration and respect of the doughty Captain.

From this officer Lewis learned that there were a number of troops in Charleston, but a few miles distant, and that General Wise, who was then in command, had arrived there that day.

After a refreshing sleep and a bounteous breakfast, Lewis informed the Captain that he would continue his journey toward Charleston, and endeavor to obtain an interview with General Wise. The Captain cordially recommended him to do so, and furnished him with passports which would carry him without question or delay upon the road. As they were about taking their leave the Captain put into Lewis' hands an unsealed letter, at the same time remarking with great earnestness :

"My lord, I beg of you to accept the inclosed letter of introduction to General Wise; as I am personally acquainted with him, this letter may be of some service to you, and I should be only too happy if it will be so."

"Thank you," replied Lewis, "but you have been far too kind already, and believe me I shall always recall my entertainment at your hands with pleasure."

The valiant Captain was not aware that he had been furnishing very valuable information to his gentlemanly visitor, and that while he was unsuspectingly answering his well-directed questions, his servant, the quiet Sam Bridgeman, was unobservedly making notes of all that he heard in relation to the situation of affairs and with regard to the probable movements of the rebel troops.

A rather ridiculous incident occurred to our two travelers after leaving the camp. They had proceeded but a short distance upon their way, when one of the horses they were driving cast a shoe, which made it necessary for them to stop at a little village and secure the services of a blacksmith.

Driving up to the hotel, Lewis alighted from the wagon, while Bridgeman drove to the blacksmith-shop in order to have his horse attended to. As Lewis ascended the steps of the hotel he noticed a tall, rather commanding-looking gentleman seated upon the porch, who was evidently scrutinizing his appearance, very carefully. The stranger was a man about sixty years of age, but remarkably well preserved, and the lines on his face scarcely gave but little indication of his years. There was an air of seeming importance about him which impressed Lewis with the fact that he must be one of the dignitaries of the place, and as he approached him he very politely raised his hat and saluted him.

The old gentleman returned the salutation with an inquiring gaze, and Lewis, in order to pave the way to his acquaintance, invited him to partake of a drink, which was cordially accepted. In a few minutes, under its influence, the two men were conversing with all the freedom of old friends.

Lewis ascertained that his companion was a justice of the peace, an office of some importance in that locality, and that the old gentleman was disposed to give to his judicial position all the dignity which a personal appreciation of his standing demanded. In a quiet manner, Lewis at once gave the justice to understand his appreciating the honor he had received in meeting him, and by a few well-administered flatteries, succeeded in completely winning the kind regards of the old gentleman. Their pleasant conver· sation was progressing with very favorable success, when Sam Bridgeman drove up with the team, having succeeded in finding a smithy and in having the lost shoe replaced.

With a deferential, semi-military salute, he addressed Lewis :

"We are all ready, my lord." At the mention of the title the old fellow jumped to his feet in blank amazement, and in the most obsequious manner, and with an air of humility, that, compared with his bombastic tone of a few moments before, was perfectly ridiculous. Jerking off his hat and placing it under his left arm, he advanced, and said :

"If my lord would do me the honor to accept my poor hospitality, I would only be too happy to have the pleasure of his company for dinner ; my house is only a short distance off, on the road to Charleston, and will detain you no longer than to rest and feed your horses, and partake of a true Southern meal."

Lewis hesitated a moment, and then remembering that he had represented himself as traveling purely for pleasure, he did not see how he could avoid accepting his kind invitation.

"I have heard, sir, of the hospitable character of the Southern gentlemen, and I assure you I shall be most happy to avail myself of your kindness."

The old Justice could not conceal his pleasure at the prospect of entertaining a "live lord" in his own house, and with evident delight he accepted a seat in Lewis' carriage. He directed the way to his dwelling, which stood back from the road, surrounded by a grove of lofty pines, and then invited his guest within ; intrusting the care of the team to the care of Sam and one of the servants, they entered the house, and were soon engaged in discussing the situation of affairs, both North and South. Lewis informed the old Justice that his name was Henry Tracy, of Oxford, England, and that his object was to reach Charleston, but that he was not aware that the country was so unsettled, or he would not have ventured on this trip. He then related his adventure of the day before, and commented favorably on the gentlemanly bearing of the Captain, and the manner in which he had been treated. They indulged in pleasant conversation, on various topics, until dinner was announced.

When they had done justice to an excellent repast, they repaired to a shaded porch in the rear of the house, and Lewis instructed Sam to bring out a bottle of champagne and a bottle of brandy. These, as already intimated, had been labeled with foreign wrappers, so that the deception was complete. The brandy was a very ordinary article, and the wine of an inferior quality, but the old gentlemen went into ecstasies over it, and under its mellowing influence, he became familiar and confidential, and gave to my shrewd operative much valuable information. Finally the justice grew profusely demonstrative, and leaning across the table, he said :

" My lord, I have never tasted such brandy as you carry in all my life, I have a couple of warm friends outside whom I have taken the liberty to send for, and whom I know will be delighted to see you, and still more pleased to taste this excellent liquor."

" Certainly," replied Lewis, "bring them in; I shall be happy to meet them."

Lewis supposed, of course, that the two men whom he had referred were planters and neighbors, but imagine his surprise when the justice returned, accompanied by the blacksmith and cobbler of the village.

After being introduced to "my Lord Tracy," Lewis invited them to take a glass with them, and with evident pleasure, yet with visible embarrassment, they accepted the invitation and seated themselves at the table.

It was now that the old gentleman grew loquacious; he was loud and profuse in his praises of the brandy; he asserted again and again, that it had never been his good fortune to taste such liquor, in which encomiums the blacksmith and cobbler heartily joined. As the afternoon wore away, and the present supply was exhausted, Sam was dispatched after another bottle, and the social meeting continued until evening. Lewis was careful as to the amount he drank, and intensely enjoyed the whole affair. The idea of the blacksmith and cobbler hobnobbing with an English lord, struck him as being so ridiculously funny, that he laughed again and again at the absurdity of the situation. Often during the evening he laughed immoderately, at what they supposed their own jokes and wit, when he was really thinking of the ridiculous comedy in which he was playing the leading part. When the hour for retiring arrived, the old man begged as a special favor that he would be allowed to keep one of the empty bottles, as a memento of the occasion of his lordship's dining with him, and to remind him of the pleasure he had enjoyed of drinking some rare old imported brandy (made in Cincinnati). The blacksmith and cobbler also looked so longingly at the empty bottles before them, that Lewis could scarcely refrain from laughing heartily, as he graciously complied with their request for a souvenir of the occasion. The evident satisfaction with which they appropriated a bottle apiece, as they started for home, and their hearty thanks as they bid him good-night, was heartily echoed by the old justice, who carefully laid his bottle away as a sacred relic of a never-to-be-forgotten event.

While the party were enjoying themselves on the porch, Sam Bridgeman had been using his time well among the servants, and had gleaned much valuable information from them. They remained over night with the old gentleman, and on the following morning, after bidding him a kind farewell, they started on their journey. Lewis did not forget, however, before leaving, to take a parting glass with his host, who seemed very reluctant to have them depart. They continued on their way towards Charleston, traveling but slowly, as the roads were heavy from the recent rains. About noon they arrived at a farm-house, to which they had been recommended by their host of the night before. Here they stopped for dinner, and after refreshing themselves, they again went on The afternoon was warm and pleasant, and their journey lay through a beautiful stretch of country. Driving quietly along, they beguiled the time admiring the beautiful scenery spread before them, and in pleasant converse. Their enjoyment was, however, suddenly interrupted by the sound of loud voices and the clattering of horses' hoofs immediately behind him. Quickly turning around, the cause of this unusual excitement was at once apparent. A fine black horse, covered with foam, was tearing down the turnpike at break-neck speed, and evidently running away. Upon his back was seated a young lady, who bravely held her seat, and who was vainly attempting to restrain the unmanageable animal. Some distance behind were a party of ladies and gentlemen on horseback, all spurring their horses to the utmost, as if with the intention of overtaking the flying steed in front of them. Intense fear was depicted upon the countenances of those in the rear, and not without reason, for the situation of the young lady was dangerous indeed.

Quick as a flash, my operatives realized the situation of affairs, and the necessity for prompt action. Without uttering a word, Sam Bridgeman turned his horses directly across the road, intending by that means to stop the mad course of the fiery charger approaching them. As he did so, Lewis sprang from the wagon, and with the utmost coolness advanced to meet the approaching horse. On came the frightened animal at a speed that threatened every moment to hurl the brave girl from her seat, until he approached nearly to the point at which my operatives had stationed themselves, and then, evidently perceiving the obstructions in his path, he momentarily slackened pace. In that instant Lewis sprang forward, and grasping the bridle firmly with a strong hand, he forced the frightened animal back upon his haunches. The danger was passed. The horse, feeling the iron grip upon the bridle, and recognizing the voice of authority, stood still and trembling in every joint, his reeking sides heaving, and his eyes flashing fire. The young lady, with a sudden revulsion of feeling, fell back in the saddle, and would have fallen but that Sam Bridgemen, hastening to the relief of his companion, was fortunately in time to catch the fainting figure in his arms. Extricating her quickly from the saddle, he set her gently on the ground, and as he did so the fair head fell forward on his shoulder, and she lost consciousness.

By this time Lewis had succeeded in quieting the excited animal, and had fastened him to a tree by the wayside, and as he turned to the assistance of Bridgeman, the companions of the unconscious girl rode up. Hastily dismounting, they rushed to her aid, and in a few minutes, under their ministrations, the dark eyes were opened, and the girl gazed wonderingly around.

After being assisted to her feet, she gratefully expressed her thankfulness to the men who had probably saved her life, in which she was warmly joined by the remainder of the party.

Sam Bridgeman received these grateful expressions with an air of modest confusion, which was indeed laughable, and then said :

"It ain't no use thanking me, Miss, it was my lord here, that stopped the the animal."

At the words "my lord," a look of curiosity came over the faces of the new-comers, and Lewis stepped gracefully forward and introduced himself.

"I am glad, ladies and gentlemen, to have been of service to this young lady, and permit me to introduce myself as Henry Tracy, of Oxford, England, now traveling in America."

The three gentlemen who were of the riding party grasped the hand of their new-made English acquaintance, and in a few words introduced him to the ladies who accompanied them, all of whom were seemingly delighted to make the acquaintance of a gentleman who had been addressed by his servant as "my lord."

This adventure proved to be a most fortunate one for my two operatives. The gentlemen, upon introducing themselves, were discovered to be connected with the rebel army, and to be recruiting officers sent by Governor Letcher to organize such rebel volunteers as were to be gathered in Western Virginia. By them Lewis was cordially invited to join their company to Charleston, which he as cordially accepted. Suggesting that as the young lady, who had scarcely recovered from the accident, might not feel able to ride her horse into town, he politely offered her a seat in his carriage, which offer was gratefully accepted, and attaching the runaway horse to the rear of the vehicle, the party proceeded on their way to Charleston, at which point they arrived without further event or accident.

The young lady whom Lewis had so providentially rescued was the only daughter of Judge Beveridge, one of the wealthiest and most influential men in the State, and upon conducting her to her home, the detective was received with the warmest emotions by the overjoyed father. Lewis was pressed to make the house of the Judge his home during his stay, but gratefully declining the invitation, he took up his quarters at the hotel, where he could more readily extend his acquaintance, and where his movements would be more free.

The young officers whom he had met upon the road had their quarters at the hotel at which Lewis had stopped, and under their friendly guidance no one thought of questioning his truthfulness, or impeaching his professions.

By this means he was enabled to acquire a wonderful amount of information, both of value and importance to the cause of the North, all of which was duly reported to me at headquarters, and by me communicated directly to General McClellan.

CHAPTER XIV.

The Rebels Attempt to Occupy West Virginia.—General McClellan Ordered to Drive them Out.—Early Battle.— The Federals Victorious.—West Virginia Freed from Rebel Soldiers.

RECOGNIZING the importance of holding West Virginia, and of preventing the Union forces from penetrating through the mountains in the direction of Staunton, the rebel authorities had sent two new commanders into that region. Ex-Governor Wise was dispatched to the Kanawha Valley, and General Garnett, formerly a Major in the Federal army, was sent to Beverly to attempt to gather up and reorganize the remnants of Colonel Porterfield's scattered command, and to adopt immediate measures to reinforce them.

General Wise having been assigned to the Kanawha Valley, was expected to arrive at Charleston on the day following the appearance of my operatives, and the city was in a state of subdued excitement in anticipation of his coming.

In the evening, Lewis, in company with the officers whom he had met in the morning, proceeded to the residence of Judge Beveridge, where he was cordially received by that gentleman and his charming daughter, who had now thoroughly recovered from the effects of her dangerous ride. With rare grace she greeted my operative, and her expressions of thankfulness were couched in such delicate language, that the pretended Englishman felt a strange fluttering in his breast, which was as novel to him as it was delicious. He passed a very delightful evening, and by his knowledge of English affairs, and his unqualified approval of the cause of the South, added to the fact that he was believed to be a gentleman of rank and fortune, he succeeded in materially increasing the high opinion which had previously been entertained regarding him.

The next morning General Wise arrived, and his appearance was hailed with delight by the disunion element of the city, while those whose sympathies were with the North looked with apprehension and disfavor upon the demonstrations that were being made in his honor.

At the first opportune moment, Price Lewis, with the assistance of his new-found friends, the rebel officers, succeeded in obtaining an introduction to the ancient-looking individual whose career had been marked by such exciting events, and who was so prominent a figure in the tragedy that was now being enacted. He was a small, intelligent-looking man, whose age appeared to be nearly seventy years, and whose emaciated appearance gave every token that he had not long to live. His eyes shone with the brilliancy of youth, and the fires of ambition seemed to be burning brightly in his breast. Perhaps no other man in the South had contributed in so great a degree to hasten the folly of secession, and certainly none rejoiced more heartily at its final realization.

By his eloquence, and the magnetic power of his presence, he had led the ignorant classes of the State to firm belief in the justice of his cause, and by his teachings he had imbued them with a firm conviction that they were acting for their own best interests, and for the furtherance of the Southern supremacy and success.

Stern and determined, he allowed nothing to stand between him and the accomplishment of his purposes. But a few months before, he had ordered the execution of John Brown, who, with a mere handful of men, had attempted to strike a blow in behalf of the slave. This ardent abolitionist attacked and captured Harper's Ferry, a government arsenal, by overpowering the men who were stationed at that place, but the authorities had been called upon, and then, yielding to superior numbers, he was compelled to surrender. In this encounter the majority of his men were slain, and John Brown, with six of his associates, was taken prisoner. This occurred on the 16th day of October, 1859, and on the 22d day of December, after a hurried trial, the prisoners were ordered by Governor Wise to be publicly hanged. The sentence was duly carried into effect, and the action of John Brown was used by the secession advocates to inflame the minds of the Southern people against the North. Now that secession had become an established fact, it was a matter of question whether the leaders of the Southern cause would not, in the end, strike a far more forcible blow in favor of the emancipation of the slave, than did the impetuous old man who gave up his life at the behest of the Southern leaders.

The General had been previously informed of the presence of Lewis in the hotel, and of his adventure on the day previous, consequently, when he was presented to the new commander, he was received with warm cordiality. The General inquired particularly into his history, and his present movements, all of which were replied to by Lewis in a dignified and satisfactory manner. Under the influence of Lewis' good-nature the General became social and familiar, and invited him to dine with him in his apartments.

Leaving no opportunity that offered, the detective took advantage of every available suggestion, and the result was he became fully posted upon everything that was of importance, and was enabled to render such an account of his labors as was satisfactory in the extreme. Sam Bridgeman, too, had not been idle, but mingling freely with the soldiers, he had succeeded in learning much of the conditions of the country that was of immense advantage in the after events of the campaign in Western Virginia.

They remained in Charleston about eight days, and then, taking leave of the many friends they had made, they made their way safely back to Cincinnati and reported. The other two men whom I had dispatched upon the same mission traveled by rail across the State of Ohio and reached the West Virginia line at Point Pleasant. Here they began their investigations, and passing unquestioned they roamed through the country, passing eastward as far as Lynchburg. Thence, they made a detour to the South, and journeyed as far as Chattanooga and Nashville, in Tennessee, and thence to Louisville, Ky. Throughout their entire pilgrimage they were ever on the alert to acquire knowledge, and the immense amount of information which they gathered would only prove tedious to both myself and the reader. It is enough to say that they performed their duty in a manner creditable to themselves and valuable to the cause they represented, and I will simply summarize the situation.

General Garnett had posted himself in the pass at Laurel Hill, with an additional force at Beverly, while another, detachment, under Col. Pegram, had established himself in the pass at Rich Mountain. Here he had intended to fortify himself and to await a favorable opportunity for breaking the railroad. He found affairs upon his arrival in a miserable condition; the troops were disorganized and without discipline, arms or ammunition, and General Lee immediately sent him re-enforcements.

This was the condition of affairs, when, early in July, General McClellan resolved to take the offensive and drive the rebels from West Virginia. In this campaign he received material aid and assistance from that brave officer General Rosecrans, who by superhuman exertions penetrated the pathless forest cutting and climbing his way to the very crest of Rich Mountain.

This movement, difficult as it was, to the South of the rebels, was a complete surprise to the enemy, who was expecting their arrival from the North.

They made a gallant resistance, however, but the Union forces had such an advantage that the contest was quickly decided. The rebel forces were driven from their breast-works and were compelled to take refuge in thickets or the mountains. Their confusion was deplorable, and their defeat unmistakable.

This victory placed the enemy in a very precarious position. McClellan was in his front and Rosecrans in secure possession of the road behind him, and Pegram, realizing the danger that threatened him, returned to his camp and, hastily spiking his guns, he abandoned all his stores and equipments, and endeavored to escape by marching northward along the mountain, intending, if possible, to join Garnett at Laurel Hill.

For the time being, he was successful in eluding the Federal commanders, and after a most laborious march of eighteen hours, found himself within three miles of Leedsville. Here he was doomed to disappointment, for he learned that Garnett had also retreated, and that a strong Union column was in close pursuit. Thus he was again caught between two Union armies, and despairing of effecting his escape, he sent a proposal to General McClellan, offering a total surrender of his command. The Union General accepted the proposition, and on the following day the half-famished rebel fugitives laid down their arms and became prisoners of war, only too glad to receive once more comfortable quarters and hunger-appeasing rations.

The fugitives who had escaped from the battle of Rich Mountain carried the news of that disaster to Beverly, and to General Garnett, at Laurel Hill, and an immediate retreat was ordered. But he was closely pressed by the advancing Union armies, and when General Garnett reached Leedsville, he heard that General McClellan was at Beverly, thus cutting off effectually his further passage southward. He now resolved upon the desperate attempt of turning to the North and reaching St. George and West Union by a rough and difficult mountain road, during which his troops naturally became very much scattered and disorganized. Although he was nearly fifteen hours in advance of his pursuers, they gained rapidly upon him, and notwithstanding every effort was made by the rebels to impede his progress by felling trees in the narrow mountain defiles, the Union advance overtook the rebel wagon-train at Carrick's Ford, one of the crossings of Cheat River, about twenty-six miles north-west of Laurel Hill. Here Garnett resolved to risk an encounter, and facing about his troops, he took a position on a favorable and precipitous elevation on the river bank, and planting his guns so as to command the ford and the approaching road, he prepared to defend his retreat. A brisk engagement at once ensued, and after a sharp contest the rebel lines broke and fled, abandoning one of their guns.

Retreat and pursuit were once more commenced, and at the next ford, a quarter of a mile further on, during a desultory skirmish fire between small parties of sharpshooters, General Garnett was killed. Here the Federal pursuit was discontinued, and the rebels left in the hands of the victors their entire baggage train, one gun, two stands of colors and fifty prisoners.

Estimated according to mere numbers, these battles of Rich Mountain and Carrick's Ford appear somewhat insignificant in contrast with the great battles of the rebellion, which occurred during the succeeding three years. Hundreds of engagements of greater magnitude, and attended with much more serious loss of life, followed these encounters, and decided the mighty problem of Northern success, but this early skirmish with the rebels on Rich Mountain, and this rout of Garnett's rear-guard at Carrick's Ford, were speedily followed by great political and military results, which exercised a powerful influence upon the after-conduct of the war. They closed a campaign, dispersed a rebel army, which had for a long time been harassing a State whose sympathies were with the Union, and they permanently pushed back the military frontier to the borders of rebellious territory. Now, is it too much to say that the brilliant success which attended this first aggressive movement of General McClellan had a marked effect upon the public mind? That they gave a general impression of his military skill is not to be doubted, and he was from that time the hero of the hour. Certain it is that a train of circumstances started from these achievements which eventually led to his being called to Washington after the reverses at Manassas and Bull Run, and made him, on the first day of November following, the General-in-Chief of all the armies of the United States.

It is not necessary for me to follow the subsequent operations in West Virginia, as my duties were connected with General McClellan and his campaigns in that district ended with the death of General Garnett and the dispersion of his army. About a week afterwards he was called to a new field of duty at Washington city, and it is not my purpose to touch upon events in which I took no part. It is enough to say that, with somewhat fluctuating changes, the rebels were gradually forced back from the Great

Kanawha Valley, and the eventual result left West Virginia in possession of the Federal troops, her own inherent loyalty having contributed largely in producing this condition. The Union sentiment of the people was everywhere made manifest, and the new State government was consolidated and heartily sustained, ending in her ultimate admission as a separate member of the Federal Union in June, 1863.

CHAPTER XV.

General McClellan is called to Washington and placed in
Command of the Armies, after the Battle of Bull Run.—
The Secret Service Department.—Its Duties and Respon-
sibilities.

AS I am not attempting to write a history of the
Civil War, but merely relating, as best I can,
the leading incidents connected with my labors in the
secret service, I shall not dwell upon the details of
the military movements of the war, except as they are
necessarily connected with my own movements. It
is necessary, however, to make cursory mention of
that remarkable chain of circumstances which followed General McClellan's campaign in West Virginia, resulting in entire and unexpected change of
circumstances to him, and a consequent enlargement
of my own field of operations. Therefore, without
pausing to describe the various movements and enter-
prises in West Virginia during the remainder of the
year 1861, or detailing the campaign of the three
months' volunteers under General Patterson, and
their bloodless victory at Harper's Ferry, I will pass
on to other scenes and events which lead directly to
the turning-point in my story.

Patriotism in the North was excited to such a pitch that the people were impatient of delay, and eager to strike a decisive blow—a blow that would at once annihilate treason and wipe out the insult to a nation's flag, and maintain a nation's honor. The resounding echoes of the rebel guns that had done their work of destruction on Sumter's walls, were still vibrating in the air.

The Confederate seat of government had been transferred from Montgomery to Richmond, immediately after Virginia's indorsement of the secession ordinance, and this enthronement of rebellion so close to the very stronghold of freedom, caused patriotic resentment to blaze up with fresh intensity.

In the month of June a determined movement against Manassas was resolved upon at Washington.

As a preliminary step to the advancement upon the rebel capital, General Scott gave Patterson orders to offer Johnston battle, or detain him in the Shenandoah Valley by other demonstrations, in order that his army might not unite with Beauregard's and defeat the movement. But Patterson failed to perform the task assigned to him, and his failure lost to the Union cause the first great battle of the war.

General Beauregard was in possession of Manassas with six thousand men, and this force was being very materially increased by the arrival of reinforcements from time to time; but notwithstanding this fact, it was believed that every chance of success would be provided for by the strength of the Union army at the capital, if only Johnston could be held in check for a few days.

Delay in starting this expedition against the enemy's works was unavoidable, and it was not until the afternoon of the 16th of July that the march of McDowell's army commenced. Even then the progress was painfully slow, owing to inexperience and lack of discipline on the part of the troops.

Manassas Junction was defended by about two thousand rebels, with fourteen or fifteen heavy guns, while at Bull Run, some three miles east of Manassas, was stationed Beauregard's main army, over twenty thousand strong, posted at the various fords of the stream, in a line fully eight miles long. McDowell, as a strategic movement to conceal his real purpose, directed his march upon Centerville, at which place Tyler's Division arrived on the morning of July 18th, to find that it had been evacuated by the rebels, who were all behind Bull Run. From Centreville, which is situated on a hill, Tyler and his men had a view of the whole valley spread out before them, with Manassas on the high plateau beyond. It has been hinted that Tyler was inspired with over confidence by the utter absence of opposition to his advance, and was thus betrayed into the indiscretion of a further advance and an experimental assault. This provoked a skirmish, which speedily culminated in the battle of

Blackburn's Ford, the result of which was much loss
and demoralization.

Two more days elapsed before the great fight
occurred. Those two days were occupied by the en-
gineers in efforts to find an unfortified ford over Bull
Run, which was accomplished in time to permit
McDowell to call his officers together on Saturday
night, and announce to them his plan of battle for
the following day. This brought the main contest on
Sunday, July 21st, and before daylight on the morning
of that eventful day, both armies were up and astir,
each intending to take the initiative. There was much
unnecessary confusion and delay, mingled with undue
excitement and impetuosity, showing that everything
was raw and awkward on both sides. Perhaps no
troops ever engaged in warfare with as little knowledge of the privations, hardships and dangers of
soldier-life, as did the Union and Confederate armies
on this bloody field.

The day passed ; the shades of evening fell, and
the battle of Bull Run had been fought and lost !
Victory had perched itself on the rebel banners, and
the Union army was in full retreat towards Washington. The engagement had been well contested, and
fought with equal courage and persistence by both
sides, and the result was quite as unexpected to the
Confederates as to the Federals.

But Johnston had not been kept out of the fray,
as it was calculated he would be. His army had

been permitted to arrive on the battle-field in the nick of time to take a decisive part in the famous conflict, and to turn the fortunes of the day at a moment when the signs of victory were all in favor of the Federal troops. Totally unconscious of the fact that they had been fighting Johnston all day, the Union soldiers had not once lost confidence in themselves, and fully believed that they must win ; but when a fresh assault from a new quarter convinced them that Johnston's forces had arrived, the realization and acknowledgment of coming defeat pervaded the whole army, and the quick instinct of retreat was aroused. They believed that success had now become hopeless, and nothing could change this belief, or check or control the impulse of flight, once started. The day was lost; the evidence of a great disaster became suddenly overwhelming to the non-combat- ants in the rear ; the retreating brigades, and the nearer approach of cannonade and musketry soon confirmed the worst fears of a terrible defeat and a hot pursuit ; and then began that insane scramble and stampede for safety.

The sights and scenes encountered on the way to Fairfax Court-House will never be effaced from the memory of those who witnessed it. The story of that memorable retreat has been told over and over again ; of the mad flight of civilians, in carriages and on horseback, lashing their steeds to the top of their speed ; of soldiers of all regiments mingled confusedly

16

together, some in complete uniform, others stripped
of everything but trousers, shirts and shoes, and all
footsore, haggard and half-starved ; of arms, clothing
and other valuables abandoned, that the progress of
the runaways might not be impeded by such incum-
brances ; of vehicles, and even ambulances, bearing
wounded men, left standing in the road, while the
frightened teamsters rode away like the wind, on
horses unhitched or cut out of their harness ; of army
wagons emptied of their loads and filled with
stragglers, thundering along the crowded highway ; of
the dash and clatter of artillery carriages ; of confusion, panic, demoralization and headlong hurry
everywhere along the route.

By midnight, mounted officers and civilians began
to arrive in Washington ; but not until the next day,
when the rain was pouring down in torrents—that
dreadful, drenching rain that continued for thirty-six
hours, with but slight intermission—did the poor,
hungry, fagged-out soldiers commence straggling in.
That they were promptly and properly fed by the
people, rich and poor, who threw open their doors
and gave what they could to alleviate the suffering of
these brave but unfortunate men, speaks volumes for
the unselfish generosity of the loyal families of the
capital during that period.

It was while this discouraging state of affairs existed that General McClellan was called to Washington, to assume control of the lately defeated troops

General Rosecrans having succeeded him in the command of the Army of the West. Considering his recent success in West Virginia, and the military skill and judgment there displayed by him, it is but natural that McClellan should have been selected to re-create the army, which was destined to defend the Capital for the next three years.

His arrival in Washington, on the 27th of July, was hailed with genuine delight by officers and citizens, for at that date he held the esteem and confidence and admiration of all loyal people. It was an immense responsibility which devolved upon him, but he accepted it cheerfully, and took up his task with that energy, tact and perseverance which precluded all possibility of failure. When first called to the command, he found a mere collection of regiments, undisciplined, undrilled and dispirited, cowering on the banks of the Potomac, and with only such material to work upon, he soon organized, equipped, and trained with rare skill, that grand body of troops, which he afterwards led in the campaign of the Peninsula.

The war was but just commenced, at a time when most people thought it would be over. The "ninety days" theory was completely exploded. Those who had flattered themselves that the conflict would be "sharp and short"—that a single victorious and glorious campaign would crush the rebellion—were now undeceived. My own hopes had controlled my judgment on this subject, and made me visionary. I had

hoped for myself to be able speedily to return to congenial pursuits and my domestic circle, and that a
speedy collapse of their frenzy would save the Southern people from the inevitable ruin which must
result from a protracted war. I had hoped for my
country, that the spectacle she now presented to
the world—exciting the derision of her enemies, and
the melancholy pity of her friends—would soon be
changed by the "returning good sense of the people,"
as it was so easily and egotistically phrased by many
individuals at that time. Above all, I had hoped
for the oppressed and shackled race of the South,
that the downfall of slavery would be early accomplished, and their freedom permanently established.
Being myself an old line abolitionist, and by no
means the least active or energetic of those who had
controlled and operated the famous " under-ground
railroad," I had the Anti-Slavery cause very much at
heart, and would never have been satisfied until that
gigantic curse was effectually removed.

Indeed, during the whole time that I labored for
the cause of the Union, the dearest object I had in
view was the abolition of the most cruel system of
oppression that ever cursed any people—an oppression long ago so justly characterized by John Wesley
as " the sum of all villainy"—in comparison with
which Egyptian bondage appeared simply burden-
some. All these hopes were dissipated by the results
of the late campaign. The war had developed into a

reality to estimate. "The Federal Union—it must and shall be preserved!" was the sentiment that now prevailed, and all realized that the time for doubt and hesitation had gone by.

There was no mistaking the duty of every loyal heart—the Republic must be saved at whatever cost.

As I have previously stated, my connection with General McClellan was not interrupted by this change in his position. By my own preference, as well as at his request, I accompanied him to Washington, and cast my lot with those who were rallying there to protect and defend the government of the United States.

Among the first things the General did, after being assigned to the command of the troops around that city, was to organize a secret service force, under my management and control. I was to have such strength of force as I might require ; my headquarters were for the time located in Washington. It was arranged that whenever the army moved I was to go forward with the General, so that I might always be in close communication with him. My corps was to be continually occupied in procuring, from all possible sources, information regarding the strength, positions and movements of the enemy. All spies, "contrabands," deserters, refugees and prisoners of war, coming into our lines from the front, were to be carefully examined by me, and their statements taken in writing.

This was the first real organization of the secret service. How much benefit was rendered to the country by this branch of the army will probably never be known—the destruction of nearly all my papers in the great fire of Chicago preventing their full publication—but that our operations were of immense practical value to the Union commander is a fact attested to by every one connected with the leading movements of our forces.

It was about this time that the city of Washington was placed under martial law—a measure deemed necessary to correct the serious evils which existed, and to restore order in the city. Colonel Andrew Porter, of the Sixteenth United States Infantry, was appointed Provost-Marshal, and under his command was placed all the available infantry, a battery, and a squadron of cavalry. In addition to these, the assistance of a detective police force was deemed indispensable, and in answering this requirement I found work enough to keep myself and entire corps busy during our stay in Washington. A better understanding of my position and the nature of my duties at this time may be gained from the following extracts from a letter which I addressed to General McClellan when the organization of this department was yet in its incipiency.

" General :

" In accordance with your expressed desire, I beg leave to submit to you my views with regard to the duties of my detective police force, should the services of the same be required by the government.

"In order to promote the efficiency of such a force, it is highly necessary that its existence should be known to as few persons as possible. It is an admitted and self-evident fact that the movements of the various departments of the government, civil and military, are closely watched, and it is beyond a doubt that from some source the rebels have received early, and to them, valuable notice of the intended actions of the government. I am also led to believe that the rebels have spies who are in the employment of this government, or who possess facilities for acquiring information from the civil and military authorities, or bureaus, and that this information is imparted to others, and transmitted, within a very short time, to the rebel government. Many of the parties thus leagued with the enemy are said to be persons of wealth and position.

"In operating with my detective force, I shall endeavor to test all suspected persons in various ways. I shall seek access to their houses, clubs, and places of resort, managing that among the members of my force shall be ostensible representatives of every grade of society, from the highest to the most menial. Some shall have the *entree* to the gilded salon of the suspected aristocratic traitors, and be their honored guests, while others will act in the capacity of valets, or domestics of various kinds, and try the efficacy of such relations with the household to gain evidence. Other suspected ones will be tracked by the 'shadow' detective, who will follow their every foot-step, and note their every action.

"I also propose to employ a division of my force for the discovery of any secret traitorous organization which may be in existence ; and if any such society is discovered, I will have my operatives become members of the same, with a view to ascertaining the means employed in transmitting messages through the lines, and also for the purpose of learning, if possible, the plans of the rebels. All strangers arriving in the city, whose associations or acts may lay them open to suspicion, will be subjected to a strict survillance.

*   *   *   *   *   *

"Another and more dangerous feature of the service contemplated to be rendered to the government by my detectives, is that of entering the rebel lines, and endeavoring to obtain accurate information of the nature of their defences, the number of troops under their command at various points, etc.

"In order to give efficiency to this movement, operations should be commenced in Baltimore as well as at Washington.

*   *   *   *   *   *

"Considering the amount of labor to be done and the necessity of immediate action on my part, in case these plans are to be carried out, I purpose concentrating my entire detective force of *both sexes* into this work.   *   *   *   *   *

"The amount of force necessary to carry out such an undertaking as I have indicated, will necessarily be very large, and the assumption of disguises and characters by my operatives, will be a very important item in itself," etc., etc., etc.

My views were carried out just as they were set

forth in this letter, and I was soon hard at work in my efforts to "regulate" the District of Columbia. It was too true that a great majority of the local police were disloyal, and could not be depended upon to faithfully discharge their duties to the government that employed them; therefore, in addition to my other work, I exerted myself to the utmost in aiding the municipal authorities to reorganize and discipline the police of the district.

Many personal incidents worthy of note occurred during this period, but there was one which I recall at this moment with a laugh at my own expense—an incident in which I was reluctantly compelled to occupy the wrong side of a guard-house over night, and instead of capturing a prisoner became a prisoner myself.

GUARD-HOUSE PRISONERS.

CHAPTER XVI.

DURING the earlier stages of the rebellion, a number of Southern sympathizers were domi· ciled in the city of Washington, and among the number were many ladies of refinement and wealth, from the South, who had been leaders of fashion and of society in the brilliant days of previous administrations. Many of these ladies were extremely fascinating in their manners, and being gifted with great personal beauty and with rare conversational qualities, they had gathered around them a brilliant circle of acquaintances, to whom they dispensed regal hospitalities and most delicate courtesies.

When the war broke out, these ladies thoroughly identified themselves with the cause of the South, and upon all occasions were unreserved in the expression of opinions favorable to the rebels, and of fervent hopefulness for the eventual success of the disunionists. But little attention was paid to these *grand dames* of the old regime, as it was not deemed possible that any danger could result from the utterances of non-combatant females, nor was it considered chivalrous that resolute measures should be adopted toward those of the weaker sex.

That this policy was a mistaken one was soon fully proved, and when it was discovered that these fine ladies were secretly giving information to the enemy, it was deemed of great importance that such means should be adopted as would prevent their treasonable actions from being made valuable to the opponents of the government, and who were seeking its overthrow.

From information received from reliable sources, it was shown that the rebel authorities were as fully conversant with the plans of the Union commanders as they were themselves. That they knew of the position of every regiment and brigade, and the contemplated movements of the commanders, and the time of proposed action, far in advance of any publicity being given to them, and when the utmost secrecy was the only true passport to victory. Indeed, it was openly boasted that the secret information given to the rebel generals had been mainly the cause of the defeat of our armies at Bull Run and Manassas.

Upon these facts being fully proven, the government resolved to effectually prevent a continuance of these practices, and that if they were persisted in, the guilty parties should either be confined or exiled to the more congenial climate of Dixie.

My department was in its infancy when the event occurred which I am about to relate. I had secured a house in Washington, and had gathered around me a number of resolute, trustworthy men and discreet women, who were devoted to the cause of their country, but were scarcely in such a condition as to move properly or with any systematized regularity. I had not been many days in the city when one afternoon I was called upon by the Hon. Thomas A. Scott, of Pennsylvania, who was then acting as the Assistant-Secretary of War, who desired my services in watching a lady whose movements had excited suspicion, and who, it was believed, was engaged in corresponding with the rebel authorities, and furnishing them with much valuable information.

This lady was Mrs. Rose Greenhow, a Southern woman of pronounced rebel proclivities, and who had been unsparing in her denunciation of the "Abolition North," and who had openly declared that "instead of loving and worshiping the old flag of the Stars and Stripes," she saw "in it only the symbol of murder, plunder, oppression and shame." Mrs. Greenhow had occupied a prominent position in the social circles of the capital, and was personally acquainted with all of the leading men of the country, many of whom had partaken of her hospitality and had enjoyed a social intercourse that was both pleasurable and fascinating.

She had now become an avowed hater of the

Union, and it was feared, from her previous association with officers in the army, that she was using her
talents in procuring information from them which
would be immediately communicated to the rebel
government at Richmond.

The residence of Mrs. Greenhow was situated at
the corner of Thirteenth and I streets—quite a
fashionable quarter of the city, and within a short
distance of the White House. The building, while
not at all imposing in appearance, was large,
roomy, and was furnished with every consideration
for wealth and tasteful refinement. It was a two-story
and basement brick building, the parlors of which
were elevated several feet above the ground, and
entrance was obtained by ascending a flight of steps
in the center of the edifice. This lady was a widow,
her husband having died some years before, and
being possessed of considerable means, and mingling
with the highest circles of Washington society, her
home was the resort of most of the prominent people
of the city.

The instructions of the Secretary of War were,
that a strict watch should be kept upon this house,
and that every person entering or leaving the same
should come under the close surveillance of my men,
who should endeavor to ascertain who they were, and
if they attempted in any manner to communicate with
any suspicious persons. I was to report to him daily,
and to continue my espionage until I received definite

and official orders for its discontinuance. My further instructions were, that in case any of the visitors of Mrs. Greenhow should attempt to pass the lines of our troops, they should be arrested at once, and a rigorous search of their persons instituted, in order that nothing should be allowed to pass through without a thorough examination by the Secretary of War or Mr. Scott.

After the departure of the Secretary I took with me two of my men, and proceeded to the vicinity of the residence of Mrs. Greenhow.   I was then quite a stranger in Washington, and localities were not as familiar to me as they afterward became, and I therefore preferred to reconnoiter by daylight, to depending upon a survey after nightfall.

The entire day had been dark, gloomy and threatening ; clouds had been gathering in the heavens, and everything indicated the imminence of a severe storm. As I left my headquarters, a slight shower of rain was falling, which I knew was but the precursor of a storm more violent.   On arriving at the designated locality I found everything to be as they had already been described to me.   The inside shutters to the windows were closed, and no sign was apparent that the house was occupied, and after carefully noting the situation and the exposed condition of the premises, I left the two men within a convenient distance of the place, and returned for the additional aid which I thought might be needed.   Selecting three of my most discreet men, I again repaired to the scene of operations. We had not proceeded far, when the storm burst upon us in all its fury. The wind blew strong and chill, and the rain fell in deluging torrents. Umbrellas were a useless commodity, and, unprotected, we were compelled to breast the elements, which now were warring with terrible violence.

Arriving at Mrs. Greenhow's, under cover of the darkness I posted my men in such positions as I thought would be most advantageous for our purpose, and then calling in the two whom I had left there during the afternoon, I approached to within a short distance of the house. The darkness and storm, while decidedly uncomfortable, were of some benefit to us, as but few people were abroad, and these paid no attention to passing events, seeming to be only too anxious to reach their destination and to escape the pitiless rain.

The blinds at the windows were still closed, but a light was observed in two rooms upon the parlor floor, and I knew that the house was occupied. Of course I could see nothing within, as my view was entirely obstructed by the closed blinds, and, at length, becoming impatient at this unprofitable and unsatisfactory waiting, I determined to obtain a glimpse, at least, of the interior, and to ascertain, if possible, some knowledge of its occupants.

The parlor windows, through which the lights were gleaming, were too high from the ground to permit me to see within, and summoning the two men whc were awaiting instructions I made use of their strong, broad shoulders in a manner quite novel to me, and quite ludicrous, no doubt, to a passer-by who did not understand the situation.

Ranging the two men side by side under the broad windows in front of the house, I removed my boots and was soon standing upon their shoulders and elevated sufficiently high to enable me to accomplish the object I had in view. I was now on a level with the windows, and noiselessly raising the sash and turning the slats of the blinds I obtained a full view of the interior of the room. The furniture was rich and luxurious, valuable pictures hung upon the walls, and several pieces of statuary and various articles of artistic ornamentation were arranged about the apartment, but to my disapointment, it was unoccupied.

I was about to give expression to my chagrin at this discovery, when a warning "Sh!" from one of my sturdy supporters induced me to be silent. Some one was approaching the house, and hastily clambering down from my perch, we hid ourselves under the stoop which led up to the front door. Scarcely had we ensconced ourselves in this convenient shelter when we heard the footsteps of the newcomer, and to our satisfaction, he stopped in front of the house, and ascending the steps rang the bell and in a short time was admitted.

By this time we were drenched to the skin—the rain had fallen in copious showers and during all the time we had been exposed to its dampening influences —but paying but little heed to this, we again took our position in front of the window, and I was soon remounted upon the shoulders of my operatives, prepared to take notes of what transpired.

As the visitor entered the parlor and seated himself-awaiting the appearance of the lady of the house, I immediately recognized him as an officer of the regular army, whom I had met that day for the first time. He was a Captain of infantry and was in command of one of the stations of the Provost-Marshal, and not desiring to divulge the real name of the gentleman, who has since died, I will call him Captain Ellison.

He was a tall, handsome man of a commanding figure and about forty years of age. He had removed his cloak, and as he sat there in his blue uniform, and in the full glare of the gaslight, he looked a vertible ideal soldier. As I watched him closely, however, I noticed that there was a troubled, restless look upon his face; he appeared ill at ease and shifted nervously upon his chair, as though impatient for the entrance of his hostess. In a few moments Mrs. Greenhow entered and cordially greeted her visitor, who acknowledged her salutations with a courtly bow, while his face lighted up with pleasure as he gazed upon her.

17

Just at this moment I again received a warning from my supporters, and hastily jumping to the ground, we hid ourselves until the pedestrians had passed out of sight and hearing. When I resumed my station the Captain and Mrs. Greenhow were seated at a table in the rear part of the room, and their conversation was carried on in such low tones that, in consequence of the storm that was still raging, I could not catch but fragmentary sentences. At last, however, accustoming myself to the noise, I heard enough to convince me that this trusted officer was then and there engaged in betraying his country, and furnishing to his treasonably-inclined companion such information regarding the disposition of our troops as he possessed.

Presently, he took from an inner pocket of his coat a map which, as he held it up before the light, I imagined that I could identify as a plan of the fortifications in and around Washington, and which also designated a contemplated plan of attack.

My blood boiled with indignation as I witnessed this scene, and I longed to rush into the room and strangle the miscreant where he sat, but I dared not utter a word, and was compelled to stand by, with the rain pouring down upon me, and silently witness this traitorous proceeding.

After watching their movements for some time, during which they would frequently refer to the map before them, as though pointing out particular points

or positions, I was again compelled to hide myself
under the shelter of the convenient stoop, and when
I resumed my position the room was empty. The
delectable couple had disappeared. I waited impatiently for more than an hour, taking occasional
glimpses into the room and watching for their re-ap-
pearance. At the end of that time they re-entered
the parlor arm in arm, and again took their seats.

Again came the warning voice, and again I hastily
descended, and as the retreating figures disappeared
in the distance, I could hear the front door open and
the step of the traitor Captain above me.

With a whispered good-night, and something that
sounded very much like a kiss, he descended the
steps, and then, without paying any attention to the
fact that I was without shoes, I started in pursuit of
him, and through the blinding mist and pelting storms
kept him in view as he rapidly walked away. It was
then about half-past twelve o'clock, and the storm
evinced no sign of a discontinuance,

I was not sufficiently acquainted with the city at
that time to tell in what direction he was going, but
I determined to ascertain his destination before I left
him. I was compelled to keep pretty close to him,
owing to the darkness of the night, and several times
I was afraid that he would hear the footsteps of the
man who accompanied me—mine I was confident
would not be detected as, in my drenched stockings,
I crept along as steathily as a cat. Twice, I imagined

that he turned around as though suspecting he was followed, but as he did not stop I reassured myself and plodded on. I could not, however, disabuse my mind of the fear that I had been seen, I could not relax my vigilance, and I resolved to take my chances of discovery. I knew who my man was, at all events, and now I must ascertain where he was going.

As we reached the corner of Pennsylvania avenue and Fifteenth street I imagined that I saw a revolver glistening in his hand, but it was too dark for me to determine that fact with any degree of certainty. At this point he passed a guard on duty, and quickly passed into a building immediately in advance of me.

This movement was so unexpected, that I had no time to turn back, and I was so close to him that it would have been very unwise to have done so, but I was more surprised when, as I reached the building into which the Captain had disappeared, I was suddenly confronted by four armed soldiers, who rushed suddenly out upon me, with fixed bayonets pointed at my breast.

"Halt, or I fire!" called out the officer of the guard.

Realizing that an attempt at resistance or escape would be both foolish and useless, I attempted to make an explanation. All to no purpose, however. I informed them that I had been out late and had lost my way, but they refused to listen, and ordered my com-

"Halt, or I fire!"

panion and myself to march at once into the guard-house. I endeavored to make the best of my misfortune, and entering the building we seated ourselves and awaited developments.

After waiting for about half an hour, I was informed that my presence was required by the Captain; and the guard conducted me up-stairs to his room. As I entered, I found myself face to face with Captain Ellison, who was pacing excitedly up and down the floor ; stopping immediately in front of me, he glared fiercely at me for some minutes without uttering a word.

I was a sorry figure to look at, and as I surveyed my weather-soaked and mud-stained garments, and my bare feet, I could scarcely repress a laugh, although I was deeply angered at the sudden and unexpected turn affairs had taken.

"What is your name ?" imperatively inquired the Captain, after he had fully recovered himself, and had taken his seat at a table which stood in the room.

" E. J. Allen," I replied.

" What is your business ?"

" I have nothing further to say," I coolly replied, "and I decline to answer any further questions."

" Ah !" said the Captain, " so you are not going to speak. Very well, sir, we will see what time will bring forth."

He endeavored to impress me with his importance and played restlessly with the handles of two revolvers that lay before him on the table, but I saw too plainly through his bravado, and I knew that the scoundrel was really alarmed.

Finding that he could not compel me to answer his questions, he turned to the sergeant and ordered :

" Take this man to the guard-house, but allow no one whatever to converse with him; we will attend further to his case in the morning."

I made a profound bow to the discomfited officer as I departed, to which he replied with an oath, and then I was conducted down-stairs and placed among the other prisoners.

I found myself in a mixed and incongruous assembly indeed. Most of my fellow-prisoners were stupidly drunk, and lay about the floor like logs ; others were laughing and singing, while some were indulging in wild threats against the men who arrested them. Here I found my companion, who, representing himself as a Southern man had already become acquainted with two secessionists, who were laughing and talking about what they would have to tell when they obtained their release. He soon ingratiated himself with these men, and before daylight had obtained from them a revelation of certain matters that subsequently proved of great value to us in our operations.

As for myself, my feelings can better be imagined than described. Inwardly chafing against the unfortunate and disagreeable position in which I found myself, I was deeply concerned regarding the situation of affairs at the residence of Mrs. Greenhow. I had given no definite orders to my men, and they would be doubtful as to what course to pursue until they heard from me, and here was I a prisoner in the hands of the man against whom I had grave charges to prefer, and whom I had detected in treasonable correspondence. Added to this, my wet garments and the cold atmosphere of the room in which I was confined, affected me with a degree of chilliness that was distressing in the utmost. I shook like an aspen, and my teeth for a time chattered like castanets. It may be imagined that the hilarity of my fellow-prisoners had but little charm for me, until at length one of the guards very kindly brought me a blanket and an overcoat, which I wrapped about me, and soon began to feel more comfortable.

Despite the aggravating circumstances under which I suffered, I could not refrain from smiling at the ridiculous appearance I must have presented as I stood before the irate Captain who had caused my arrest. My hat was battered down over my face, and my clothing was spattered with mud from head to foot, and were dripping with water as I stood there. One might more readily imagine that I had been fished out of the Potomac than that I was the chief of the secret service of the government, in the performance of duty.

By the Captain's orders I was prevented from conversing with my fellow-prisoners, so I turned my attention to the guard. My chief desire was to apprise Mr. Scott of my captivity, as early as possible, in order that my release could be effected without unnecessary delay, and I therefore applied myself to the entertainment of my jailer.

The soldier who had charge of me I soon found to be a jolly, kind-hearted fellow, and I amused him immensely by relating some ridiculous anecdotes which I had heard, and before the time came for him to be relieved I had entirely won his favor.

Seizing a favorable opportunity I asked him if he would deliver a note for me after his time for standing guard had expired, at the same time offering to repay him for his trouble. To this he readily assented, and by the dim light afforded us I managed to scribble a few hasty lines to the Assistant Secretary of War, informing him of my imprisonment, and requesting him to order my release as soon as possible, and in a manner which would not excite the suspicion of Captain Ellison.

At about six o'clock the guards were changed, and my messenger departed upon his mission. He was fortunate enough to find the servants of Mr. Scott astir, and informing them that his message was of extreme public importance, he had it delivered to the Secretary in his chamber at once. At seven o'clock the guard returned, and coming to the door, he conversed a few minutes with the soldier who had succeeded him, when I called out :

"How is the weather outside ?"

"All right, sir !" replied the man, with a sly wink, and then I knew that my note had been safely delivered, and my liberation simply a question of time.

At about half-past eight o'clock the sergeant of the guard came to the door with a paper in his hand, and called out :

"E. J. Allen and William Ascot !"

Ascot was the name of my operative who had been arrested with me, and with whom I had not exchanged a word since I had been imprisoned. We responded to our names, and following the sergeant, were again taken to the room occupied by Captain Ellison.

"The Secretary of War has been informed of your arrest, and you will be conducted to him at once, and then we shall see whether you will remain silent any longer."

The manner of the Captain was imperious and commanding, and I laughed to myself as I thought of the possible result of our interview with the Secretary. The Captain led the way, and in the company of four soldiers, we left the place, arriving in a few minutes at the residence of Mr. Scott. He was awaiting our arrival, and as we entered the room he ordered the guard to release me, and directed me to accompany him to his room. I followed him immediately, and as the door closed behind us, he burst into a hearty laugh at my uncouth and unkempt appearance. I was a sorry spectacle indeed, and as I surveyed myself in the mirror, I joined in his merriment, for a more realistic picture of a " drowned rat" I never beheld.

I at once detailed what had transpired on the preceding night, and as I related the interview which I had witnessed between Captain Ellison and Mrs. Greenhow, his brow became clouded, and starting to his feet, he paced the room rapidly and excitedly.

" Mrs. Greenhow must be attended to. She is becoming a dangerous character. You will therefore maintain your watch upon her, and should she be detected in attempting to convey any information outside of the lines, she must be arrested at once. And now we will attend to Captain Ellison."

Tapping a bell which stood upon his table, he ordered :

" Request Captain Ellison to come here."

As the Captain made his appearance, he seemed to be very ill at ease, and gazed searchingly at Mr. Scott and myself, as though he suspected something was wrong.

" Captain," said Mr. Scott, addressing him, "will you give me the particulars of the arrest of this man ?" pointing to me.

The Captain answered that he had gone to visit some friends, who resided in the outskirts of the city, in the evening, and on returning at a late hour, he had noticed that he was being followed, and supposing me to be a foot-pad or a burglar, had ordered my arrest.

"Did you see any one last evening who is inimical to the cause of the government?"

The Captain became flushed and nervous under this direct question. He darted a quick glance at me, and after hesitating for some moments he answered in a faltering voice:

"No, sir; I have seen no person of that character."

"Are you quite sure of that?" sternly inquired Mr. Scott.

"I am, sir."

"In that case, Captain, you will please consider yourself under arrest, and you will at once surrender your sword to Captain Mehaffy."

The Captain was completely unmanned as these words fell from the lips of the Secretary, and sinking into a chair, he buried his face in his hands, seemingly overcome by his emotions.

But little remains to be told. Captain Ellison was arrested, and a search among his effects discovered sufficient evidence to prove that he was engaged in furnishing information to the enemy, and he was confined for more than a year in Fort McHenry. He was finally released, but broken in spirit and in health, and fully realizing the disgrace he had brought upon himself, he died shortly afterward.

After leaving the residence of Mr. Scott, I took a carriage and went directly to my headquarters, and dispatched new men to relieve those who had been on duty all night, and who had been so anxious for my safety that they had sent several times to make inquiries, and who were unable to account for my absence. They had, I was rejoiced to learn, taken care to recover my shoes, which I was afraid would be found by some one connected with the house, and thus lead to the suspicion that the premises were the object of espionage.

We continued our watching of the premises, and during its continuance a number of prominent gentlemen were received by the fascinating widow, and among the number were several earnest and sincere Senators and Representatives, whose loyalty was above question, and who were, perhaps, in entire ignorance of the lady's true character.

Almost every evening one particular individual was observed to call at the house, and his visits invariably were of long duration. He was therefore made the object of especial attention by me, and in a short time I succeeded in learning his true character, and the nature of the business which he followed. Ostensibly an attorney, I ascertained that he was undoubtedly engaged in the vocation of a Southern spy, and that he had a number of men and women under him by whom the information was forwarded to the rebel authorities. This gentleman, therefore, found himself, in a very few days, a prisoner of war.

About eight days after this, orders were given for the arrest of Mrs. Greenhow herself. She was confined in her own house, and all her papers were seized and handed over to the custody of the Department of War. The intention of the government was to treat her as humanely and considerately as possible, but disdaining all offers of kindness or courtesy, the lady was discovered on several occasions attempting to send messages to her rebel friends, and finally her removal to the Old Capitol prison was ordered, and she was conveyed there, where she was imprisoned for several months. After this she was conveyed across the lines, and reached in safety the rebel capital, where she was greeted by the more congenial spirits of rebeldom.

Mrs. Greenhow afterwards went to Europe, in some trustworthy capacity for the Confederacy, and while there was noted for her bitter animosity to the Union, and her vituperation of Northern men and measures, but retribution may be said to have followed her, and some time subsequent to this, having returned again to the South, she made her way to Charleston, S. C., from thence she took passage upon a blockade-runner, upon some secret mission for the Confederacy. Her person was loaded down with gold, which was packed in a belt close to her body. After passing

Fort Sumter, a severe storm arose, and the little vessel began to pitch and roll in the angry waters, which swept in huge waves over her deck. Mrs. Greenhow was, I was since informed, washed overboard, and the weight upon her person carried her down and she was lost. No trace of her was ever afterwards discovered.

A FEMALE SPY.

CHAPTER XVII.

Timothy Webster in Baltimore.—An Encounter with a Fire-eater.—Webster Defends Himself.—Treason Rampant in the Monumental City.

THE city of Baltimore at this time was also under military rule. It was garrisoned by United States troops, commanded successively by Butler, Banks and Dix, for the purpose of enforcing respect and obedience to the laws, and of presenting any violations of order within its limits, by the malignant and traitorous element of the people. Marshal Kane, the Chief of Police, as well as the active members of the police commissioners, were arrested and held in custody at Fort McHenry, because of the alleged encouragement and protection which were given to those unlawful combinations of men who were secretly aiding in numerous ways the people at war with the government. General Banks appointed a Provost-Marshal for the proper execution of the laws, in conjunction with the subordinate officers of the police department. This condition of things was of course a direct result of the great riot of the 19th of April, and the intention was to curb those mutinous spirits, whose passions otherwise would have led them into committing all sorts of crimes and outrages against the government. Notwithstanding these measures, however, the disturbing element was not by any means passive and inert, although appearances may have warranted such a conclusion. Secret bands of conspirators were still in existence, and were working assiduously for the advancement of the Southern cause.

By direction of General McClellan, I sent several of my best operatives to Baltimore, chief among whom was Timothy Webster, with whom the others were to co-operate whenever their assistance were required by him. The principal object in this was to enable Webster to associate with the secessionists of that city, and by becoming familiar and popular with them, to pave his way for an early trip into the rebel lines.

During his residence in Baltimore he was directed to represent himself as a gentleman of means and leisure, and to enable him the better to carry out this idea, I provided him with a span of fine horses and a carriage, for his own pleasure. He made his home at Miller's Hotel, lived in good style, and in his own irresistible way he set about establishing himself in the good graces of a large number of people, of that class whose confidence it was desirable to obtain. This task was made comparatively easy by the fact that he already had numerous acquaintances in the city, who introduced him about with great enthusiasm, representing him to be—as they really believed he was—a gentleman whose whole heart and soul was in the cause of the South. Thus, by easy stages, he soon reached the distinction of being the center and principal figure of an admiring crowd. Before a week had elapsed he had become a quietly-recognized leader in the clique with which he associated, and soon regarded as a man of superior judgment and power in all matters relating to political and state affairs.

During fair weather he would frequently drive out with one or more of his friends, and his handsome equipage became well known on the streets, and at the race-course. He was introduced into the houses of many warm sympathizers with the South, and by his agreeable and fascinating manners he became a favorite with the female members of the family. Through all, he was apparently an earnest and consistent advocate of Southern rights, never overdoing the matter by any exhibition of strained excitement or loud avowals, but always conversing on the subject with an air of calm conviction, using the strongest arguments he could invent in support of his pretended views. In compliance with the request of many of his Southern friends, he and John Scully, another of my operatives, went to a photograph gallery one day and had their pictures taken, holding a large Confederate flag between them, while Webster wore the rebel hat which the doughty Dr. Burton had presented to him in Memphis.

During all this time Webster was gathering information from every quarter concerning the secret plots and movements of the disloyal citizens, and promptly conveying it to me, and for this purpose he made frequent trips to Washington for verbal instructions, and to report in person the success of his operations. Sometimes he would be accompanied by one or more of his intimate associates, and these occasions were not without profit, for when thus accompanied, although necessarily prevented from reaching my office, he was enabled to increase his acquaintance with the traitorous element of Washington, and finally was enabled to unmask several guilty ones whose loyalty had never been impeached or suspected.

Once, on returning to Baltimore, after a longer absence than usual, his friends greeted him warmly.

" By Jove, Webster, we had begun to think you were in trouble," one of them exclaimed.

" No danger of that," was the laughing response. " I have no intention of being trapped before I fulfill my mission. I have some valuable work to do for the Southern Confederacy before the Yankees can get the upper hand of me."

They were in a saloon—a favorite rendezvous of these men—and Webster was in the midst of his crowd. He was telling them about some imaginary "points" which he had picked up in Washington, and assuring them he would in some manner transmit the information he had received to the rebel commanders before he was a week older. While thus entertaining his hearers, his attention was attracted by a man who entered the saloon with a swaggering gait, his hands in his pockets, and his hat tipped over one side of his head. He knew this man as a ruffian and bully of the worst stripe, Bill Zigler, and one of the ringleaders of the mob that had attacked the Union troops on the 19th of April; consequently, he entertained a wholesome contempt for the fellow, and avoided him as much as possible.

He was much surprised when the new-comer stopped in the middle of the room, and exclaimed, gruffly :

"Hello, Webster! You're *here*, are you? By G—d, I've been looking for you!"

Webster turned toward him a look of surprised inquiry.

"Did you speak to me, sir ?" he asked, quietly.

"Yes, I spoke to you, sir!" mimicked Bill Zigler, in a bullying voice. "I say I've been lookin' for you, and when I've spoke my piece I reckon this town will be too hot to hold you many hours longer."

"I don't understand you," protested Webster.

"Ha! ha! ha!" laughed the ruffian, a glitter of triumph and hatred in his eyes. "You've been playin' it fine on the boys here for the last three weeks, but d—n you, I'll spoil your little game!"

"What do you mean?" demanded Webster, his anger beginning to rise. "You speak in riddles."

"I'll tell you what I mean!" blustered the bully. "Gentlemen," turning toward the crowd, and pointing his finger toward the detective; "that man is leagued with the Yankees, and comes among you as a spy."

There was a general start of astonishment, and Webster himself was dumfounded.

"Oh, nonsense, Zigler," spoke up one of the men, after a death-like silence of several moments. "You must be drunk to make such an assertion as that. There is not a better Southern man in Baltimore than Mr. Webster."

"I am as sober as the soberest man here," declared Zigler; "and I reckon I know what I am talking about. I saw that fellow in Washington yesterday."

"I can well believe that you saw me in Washington yesterday," said Webster, quietly, "for I certainly was there. I have just been telling these gentlemen what I saw and heard while there."

"Maybe you have, but I'll bet ten dollars you didn't tell 'em that you had a conversation with the *chief of the detective force* while you were there!"

Webster, it must be admitted, was wholly unprepared for this, but he realized in an instant that the bully's insinuation must be denied and overcome. With an assumption of uncontrollable rage he cried out "You are a liar and a scoundrel!"

"The man reeled half way across the room, and fell prostrate between two tables."

P. 277

"I am, eh?" hissed Zigler through his clenched teeth, and before any one could make a movement to restrain him he sprang furiously toward Webster.

Quick as was this movement, however, Webster was prepared for him. Like a flash of lightning his fist flew straight out from the shoulder, striking the ruffian between the eyes, with a force that would have felled an ox. The man reeled half-way across the room, and fell prostrate between two tables.

With a roar like that of a baffled beast, Zigler gathered himself up and rushed at Webster, flourishing above his head a murderous-looking knife. But, as if by magic, a revolver appeared in the detective's hand, the muzzle of which covered his adversary's heart.

"Stop!" cried Webster, in a tone of stern command. "Hold your distance, you miserable cur, or your blood will be upon your own head!"

Zigler involuntarily recoiled. The frowning muzzle of the pistol, the unmistakable meaning of those words, and the deadly purpose expressed in the cold, calm face before him, were too much even for his boasted bravery. He turned pale and drew back, muttering and growling.

"Coward!" exclaimed Webster, "if I served you right I would shoot you down like a dog; and I am afraid I can't resist the temptation to do so anyway, if you don't immediately leave the room. Go! and

in future be careful who you accuse of being in league
with the accursed Yankees."

By this time a number of the other men had recovered from their astonishment, and they immediately joined their threats to those of Webster, commanding Zigler to leave the saloon at once, if he
desired to "save his bacon."

Zigler did not dare to disobey. Sullenly putting
up his knife, and muttering curses on the whole
crowd, he slunk out, stopping at the door long
enough to glance back at Webster, with the exclamation :

"I'll fix you yet, d—n you !"

When he was gone, Webster said :

" I cannot conceive what that fellow has against
me, that he should try to defame my character by such
an accusation."

Several of the men broke into a derisive laugh.

" I'd as soon suspect Jeff Davis of being a Yankee
spy," said one, with a boisterous guffaw.

"Lord, Webster," spoke up another, "you needn't
calculate that anything that fellow can say is going to
injure you with the people here."

" I reckon Zigler is mad because you won't
clique in with him and his gang," said a third.   " Nobody takes any stock in him.   It would have been
considered a good riddance if your pistol had gone off
while it covered his heart.   Bah ! he isn't worth a
thought. Come, boys, let's licker."

And the affair ended in a witty cross-fire of jokes, frequent explosions of hearty laughter, and numerous bumpers of sparkling wine.

So far from proving disastrous to Webster or his mission, this little episode with Bill Zigler rather elevated him in the estimation of his companions. The neat knock-down with which he had met the bully's unprovoked assault; his air of virtuous indignation in resenting the imputation of disloyalty to the South, and the manner in which he had defeated and put to flight a man who was much feared among his fellows, only won for him new laurels, and caused him to be regarded as brave as he was loyal. His intimate acquaintances reposed such firm faith in him, that not one of them entertained for a moment the thought that there might possibly be a grain of justice in Zigler's accusation.

One morning, not long after this little episode, Webster left his hotel to walk down town, when he noticed that there was some unusual excitement on the streets. On every corner on Baltimore street, from the Exchange office, large numbers of men were standing in groups, evidently absorbed in some particular topic of conversation.

While wondering what all this meant, the detective was accosted by a man named Sam Sloan, one of the most faithful of his adherents.

"Webster, I was just going up to see you. Have you heard the news?"

"I have heard nothing, Sam," was the reply. "Is there a new sensation this morning?"

"Another of Lincoln's outrages," said Sloan, with an indignant oath. "Major Brown, Ross Winans, and several others were arrested last night, and taken to Fort McHenry."

"What for?"

"For no other purpose, I suppose, than to break up the election, which is to take place next month."

"But how can that interfere with the election?"

"By making us all afraid to go to the polls, or speak our minds."

The two walked down the street together, and dropped into a drug store, which was known as one of the resorts of the unterrified. There they found a number of men conversing somewhat excitedly. The proprietor, a Mr. Rogers, turned toward the new-comers and said:

"Good morning, Mr. Webster; we were just talking over last night's proceedings."

"It beats anything I ever heard of," said Webster, warmly. "But what can we do?"

"Nothing just now," returned Rogers; "but I think there will soon be a time when we will have a chance to do something. In the meantime, gentlemen, we must make up our minds to say nothing. We have all been too free with our tongues. Hereafter, we must keep mum, or we will all get into Fort McHenry."

"'We must just lay low, and wait till Jeff crosses the Potomac," said one of the loungers.

"If we only had arms," said Webster, musingly.

"Arms!" echoed Rogers; "why, sir, we have from five to six thousand stand of arms right here in Baltimore."

"That may be true," said Webster, "but nobody seems to know where they are."

"I am satisfied they will turn up at the right time," said Rogers. "Marshal Kane, before he was arrested, put them in the hands of men who will take good care of them until they are wanted."

"And let us hope they will be wanted inside of two weeks," put in Sloan. "We can afford to be quiet now, boys, but when the Southern army comes this way, we'll rise ten thousand strong, and help take Washington."

The opinion seemed to have fixed itself in the minds of nearly all the Southern sympathizers in the city, that in a very brief space of time, three or four weeks at the utmost limit, Baltimore would be occupied by rebel soldiers, and Jeff Davis would be there in person.

"One thing is certain," said Webster, firmly. "If this thing goes on much longer, there will be a general uprising one of these days, and the streets of Baltimore will run with blood a thousand times worse than they did on the 19th of April."

"You are right, there," said Rogers; "but for

heaven's sake don't let any one outside of your circle hear you use that expression, or you will be the next one in limbo."

"If they want me, now is their time," replied the detective, with a smile, "for I have made up my mind to undertake a journey down into southern Maryland and Virginia, at an early day."

"The devil you have! You will find that a difficult and dangerous undertaking."

"Nevertheless, I shall attempt it. I find that if I can make the trip successfully I may be of service to some of our people here, by carrying letters and messages to their friends and relatives, with whom they are unable to communicate in any other way."

Webster made this intention known to all of his associates, and gave them to understand that he desired to sell his horses and carriage before leaving. The sale was accomplished in a manner that seemed legitimate enough to all, though it was a mere pretense. One of my operatives, whom I sent to Baltimore for that purpose, made a sham purchase of the team and turned it over to me in Washington.

CHAPTER XVIII.

*Webster Makes a Journey to the South.—A Secret Organiza-
tion.—The "Knights of Liberty."—Webster Becomes a
Member.—A Sudden Intrusion of the Military.—The
Conspiracy Broken Up.*

IN accordance with my instructions, Webster commenced his tour through southern Maryland,
on Thursday, September 26th. He was accompanied
by John Scully, who had been assisting him in his
Baltimore operations, and they followed a line of
travel which I laid out for them. Taking passage on
the steamboat "Mary Washington," they baffled the
officers who stopped them by showing a pass issued
by the Provost-Marshal of Baltimore, and were soon
steaming down the Chesapeake toward Fair Haven,
which was their pretended destination. Arriving at
that point they went ashore, and proceeded to the
village of Friendship. From there they worked their
way south-west to Prince Frederick, then across the
Big Patuxent to Bendict, from which place they proceeded to Charlotte Hall, and thence on foot to Leon-
ardtown, a distance of twenty miles. At the last-
named place they found Wm. H. Scott, another of

my operatives, awaiting them, and were accompanied by him during the remainder of the journey.

A number of messages, written and verbal, which had been intrusted to Webster by his Baltimore associates, were delivered at various points on the route, thus enabling them to form the acquaintance of certain secessionists who were men of prominence and influence in their respective neighborhoods, and who in turn provided them with letters of introduction to others of like ilk further on.   Through this medium they secured attention and hospitality wherever they stopped, and had the advantage of valuable advice and assistance in the matter of pursuing their journey safely.

They represented themselves to be rebel sympathizers on their way to the Potomac, for the purpose of finding a safe place where goods could be shipped across the river into Virginia.   They were frequently cautioned to be very careful, as there were Union soldiers stationed all along the river, and people whose hearts were with the South were not permitted to express their sentiments with impunity. They penetrated as far as a point called Allen's Fresh, and deciding that they had gained all the information that could be picked up in that part of the country, they returned to Washington and reported to me.

When Webster re-appeared on the streets of Baltimore, after completing this trip, he was more than ever lionized by his numerous friends who were in the secret of his Southern journey, and its supposed object. By endangering his life in the Southern cause, as it was believed he had done, he had made himself a hero in the eyes of the traitors who were attached to him.

"Are you still keeping mum?" he asked, as he stood in the center of a group at Dickinson's billiard hall, adjoining the Exchange.

"Those who have any regard for their personal safety are doing so," replied Rogers; "and I think the majority of the boys have learned that lesson. Baltimore is comparatively quiet now. Only one man has been arrested since you left, and we have hopes that he will be released?"

"Who is he?"

"A man from Washington. He was fool enough to think he could talk as he pleased in Baltimore."

"By the way," remarked some one present, "Webster must join our——"

"Sh," cautioned Dave Dickinson, the proprietor of the billiard room. "Have you no more sense than to reveal yourself *here?* Remember that your lips are sealed by an oath on that subject."

There was a moment's silence; Webster looked from one to another, and noticed that an air of mystery had settled upon every countenance present.

"What's this?" he demanded with a laugh. "Is it a conspiracy to betray me into the hands of the enemy?"

" Not exactly," replied Dickinson, whose laugh was echoed by the crowd. " Sloan, you will give Mr. Webster his cue when a favorable opportunity occurs. We want him with us, by all means."

Webster's curiosity was satisfied an hour later, when he and Sam Sloan walked toward Miller's Hotel together.

" The fact is," said Sam, in a guarded tone, "since you went away we've formed a secret organization."

" A secret organization?"

"Yes; and we have held several meetings."

" Is it a success?"

" A perfect success.   Some of the best in town are among our members.   We may be forced to keep silent, but, by Heaven! they can't compel us to remain idle.   We are well organized, and we mean undying opposition to a tyrannical government.   I tell you, Webster, *we will not down!*"

" Never!" responded Webster, copying the boastful tone and bearing of his companion.   " It does not lie in the power of these white-livered Yankees to make slaves of Southern men!   I should like to become a member of your society, Sloan."

" They all want you," said Sloan, eagerly.   " They passed a resolution to that effect at the last meeting. They want the benefit of your counsel and influence."

" What is your society called ?"

" The Knights of Liberty."

" When will your next meeting be held ?"

" To-night."

" So soon ?"

" And you are expected to attend. Have you any objections ?"

" None whatever. But how will I get there ?"

" I am delegated to be your escort," replied Sloan.

" What is your hour of meeting?"

" Twelve o'clock."

" Ah, a midnight affair. All right, Sam ; you'll find me waiting for you at the hotel."

Here they separated. Webster realized that quite an important period in his Baltimore experience was opening up before him, and that all his detective skill would probably be called into play to foil a band of conspirators. How to thwart the schemes of these Knights of Liberty, whose purpose, as he understood, was to assist in the overthrow of the Government of the United States, was now the question to be solved.

He did not, however, attempt to form any plans at this time, but waited for such developments as he had no doubt would be made that night. He resolved to learn the nature of the plots that were in existence, before he commenced counterplotting.

Promptly at eleven o'clock Sam Sloan put in an appearance at the hotel, and he and Webster proceeded toward the place of meeting. The night was dark and stormy, just the right sort of night, Webster thought, for the concocting of hellish plots and the performance of evil deeds.

> "That night, a chiel might understand,
>   The Deil had business on his hand."

The stars were hidden from view by masses of flying clouds; the wind whistled shrilly through the trees and spires; while the deep, threatening murmurs of distant thunder were accompanied by fitful flashes of lightning, which illumined the scene with a weird, quivering light. Few shops were open in the localities through which they passed. Occasionally a light was seen struggling through the screened window of a saloon, and the sound of midnight orgies within indicated that business had not been suspended there; but elsewhere all was dark and still.

Sloan led the way to a remote quarter of the city, and into a street which bore a particularly bad reputation. Here he stopped, and said :

"I must blindfold you, Webster, before proceeding further. This is a rule of the order which cannot, under any circumstances, be departed from."

Webster submitted quietly, while a thick bandage was placed over his eyes and securely fastened. Then Sloan took him by the arm and led him forward.

Blindfolded as he was, he knew that they turned suddenly into an alleyway, and he also knew when they passed through a gate, which Sloan closed behind them. He rightly conjectured that they were now in a sort of paved court, in the rear of a building.

"Come this way and make no noise," whispered Sloan.

The next moment the latter knocked on a door with a low, peculiar rap, that was like a signal. Immediately a guarded voice on the inside was heard:

"Are you white?"

"Down with the blacks!" responded Sloan.

Nothing more was said. A chain clanked inside, a bolt shot back, and the door creaked on its hinges as it swung open.

Webster was led through, and he and his conductor began to ascend a flight of stairs, so thickly carpeted that they emitted no sound from the footsteps upon them.

At the head of the stairs they were again accosted:

"Halt! Who comes there?"

"Long live Jeff Davis," muttered Sloan.

Passing on through another door, they found themselves in a small, square apartment, although, so far as Webster was concerned, there was no ocular proof of this. There seemed to be several persons here, and a voice, that was evidently meant to be tragical and impressive, demanded:

19

"Whom have we here?"

"Most Noble Chief," said Sloan, humbly, "I have a friend in charge, who wishes to become a worthy member of this league."

"His name?"

"Timothy Webster."

"Have the objects of the league been fully explained to him?"

"They have."

The gruff-voiced speaker then said:

"Mr. Webster, is it your desire to become a member of this knightly band?"

"It is," responded the detective, firmly.

There was a sound as of a number of swords leaping from their scabbards, and the clank and ring of the steel as the blades seemed to meet above his head. Then the Grand Chief continued:

"You will now kneel upon one knee, and place your right hand upon your heart, while I administer to you the binding obligation of our brotherhood."

Webster did as he was directed, and in this attitude repeated the following oath, as it was dictated to him:

"I, Timothy Webster, citizen of Baltimore, having been informed of the objects of this association, and being in full accord with the cause which it seeks to advance, do solemnly declare and affirm, upon my sacred honor, that I will keep forever secret all that I may see or hear, in consequence of being a member of this league; that I will implicitly obey all orders, and faithfully discharge all duties assigned to me, no matter of what nature or character they may be; and that life or death will be held subordinate to the success and advancement of the cause of the Confederacy and the defeat of the bloody tyrants who are striving to rule by oppression and terrorism. Should I fail in the proper performance of any task imposed upon me, or should I prove unfaithful to the obligations I have here assumed, may I suffer the severest penalty for treason and cowardice, as well as the odium and contempt of my brother knights."

The swords clanked again as they were returned to their scabbards, and the new-made member, having taken the oath, was commanded to rise. He did so in silence, and the bandage was removed from his eyes.

At first the light of the room almost blinded him, but his eyes soon became accustomed to the change, and he looked about him with some curiosity. He found that he was in the presence of seven stalwart men, besides Sloan, all of whom wore swords at their sides, dark cloaks drooping from their shoulders, and black masks upon their faces. The masks, however, were now removed, and Webster discovered, to his relief, that they were all familiar to him.

"Mr. Webster," said the Chief, dropping his tragic tone of voice, " without further ceremony, I pronounce you a Knight of Liberty. I greet you heart-

ily;" and then, extending his hand — "Come with
me."

As they emerged into the main council-chamber,
Webster quietly examined his surroundings. It was
a spacious apartment, very plain in its appointments,
with a low ceiling and bare walls, and furnished with
chairs arranged in rows around the room. At the
head of the hall was a low platform on which were
tables and chairs. Behind these, on the wall, were
suspended two Confederate flags, artistically draped,
above which were the initials "K. of L." Some forty
men were already assembled, and others were quietly
dropping in at intervals. Webster noticed that all
these men were from the better class of citizen secessionists, and that the low, rowdy element was not represented. They were mostly men who had not thus
far been suspected of disloyalty to the Union cause.

The Grand Chief and other officers now took
their positions on the platform, and Webster was
assigned to a seat where he could observe all that was
said or done.

Presently a clock in the room struck twelve. Instantly all the doors opening into the chamber were
securely locked, and the secret conclave was in session. The Grand Chief rose and opened the meeting in regular form; and again, after the secretary
had read the journal, made an address of some length.
At the conclusion of his remarks, some one arose and
said :

"Most Worthy Chief, I believe we can now claim Mr. Webster as a member of this body. I understand that he has just returned from an interesting and somewhat dangerous mission, and I now move that he be invited to address this meeting relative to his experiences during the journey he has just completed."

Webster, taken by surprise, undertook to combat the proposition, but the motion was unanimously concurred in, and no excuses were accepted. He therefore yielded good-naturedly, and mounting the platform, he proceeded to relate some of the particulars of his trip to the Potomac. He made the recital as entertaining and agreeable as possible, and although his statements did not always possess the merit of being strictly true, they were such as could not fail to meet the approval of his hearers, and were therefore received with great favor. Concluding with a well-timed panegyric on the "faithful" of Baltimore, he resumed his seat amid the congratulations of his many admiring friends.

After this, the regular business of the meeting was taken up, in which Webster took no other part than that of a close listener and observer. Motions were made, resolutions were adopted, and various duties assigned to volunteer committees. The proceedings grew more and more interesting to the detective as they progressed, and it was not long before he began to feel considerable surprise, if not alarm, at the unexpected revelations which were made. It became evident to him that these conspirators had by some means succeeded in placing themselves in direct communication with the Confederate leaders, and that a gigantic plot was now in preparation to make a united and irresistible movement against Washington. Nearly ten thousand Baltimoreans, it was alleged, were prepared to rise in arms at a moment's notice, and join the rebel army, whenever such a movement might seem feasible. It appeared, also, that the Baltimoreans were not alone in this plot against the government, but that branches of their organization existed in a number of the outlying towns, and that the secessionists of the entire State were working harmoniously together for the accomplishment of one great purpose. There was no lack of arms, for these had already been secured, but their place of concealment was known only to a few and they were not to be brought to light until they should be needed.

The main portion of the plot seemed to be well matured, and was most perfect in its details. The arrival of the rebel army in Maryland was expected in a very short time, as they had the promises of the Southern commanders themselves that they would soon cross the Potomac. Their coming was to be the signal for a simultaneous uprising of all the secessionists in the Western and Southern portions of the State, who were to unite in a movement that could scarcely fail to carry everything before it. There were also deep-laid schemes by which the Federals were to be kept in ignorance of the real designs of the Confederates, until too late to avert the blow.

The extent of the conspiracy rather startled Webster, although some of the projects sounded rather visionary, and he made up his mind to consult with me at once. Accordingly, the very next day, he proceeded to Washington, and was closeted with me for several hours. As soon as he had explained the situation, I devised a plan of procedure, and gave him full instructions as to the manner in which he should proceed. The great object, of course, was to break up the organization, and defeat the conspiracy in a manner that would not compromise Webster ; but it was not deemed prudent to go about this with any inordinate haste.

I advised Webster to continue attending the meetings, in the character of an active conspirator ; to learn all he could, and report to me as often as possible. In the meantime, I would send him two other operatives, and he was to secure their admission into the secret society, as members thereof. In a week or two the final act in the little drama would be introduced by first making a confidant of Mr. McPhail, the deputy Provost-Marshal of Baltimore, and then confronting the conspirators with a company of armed soldiers.

Webster returned to Baltimore with a clear understanding of the course he was to pursue, and he followed that course with the untiring zeal with which he performed every duty assigned to him. He attended the midnight meetings regularly, and gained much information concerning the plans and movements of the Southern commanders, which proved of incalculable value to the government. The two operatives soon contrived to join the society, not through Webster's recommendation, as that was to be avoided, if possible, but by making the acquaintances of men whom he pointed out to them, and representing themselves as secessionists who were capable of keeping their own counsel.

This done, the rest was comparatively easy. By the rules of the society, no one could enter the secret chamber of the conspirators without passing two guards, and giving sundry pass-words. These guards were appointed by the Chief from those who volunteered for the positions. At stated periods, new pass-words were arranged, by which every man was required to answer the questions of the guards, and any one who failed to commit these to memory sufficiently to satisfy these sentinels that he was a member of the society, found himself barred out of the meeting.

Our plan worked to perfection. There came a night when my two operatives were on duty, as guards, they having volunteered their services at the last preceding meeting. This was the night set apart for the surprise. It had been announced that Webster would speak that night, and it had been arranged with the guards, that a certain part in his speech should be taken as the signal for the grand finale that had been decided upon.

The hour of midnight approached. The old building in which the secret conclaves were held was shrouded in silence and darkness. At intervals one or more dark figures might have been seen to enter the covered archway leading thereto, and pass through the gate into the narrow court. Then, one at a time, they approached a certain door, and after a signal rap, and a low, muttered conversation with the guards, they passed in and ascended the dimly-lighted stairs. Another brief dialogue with the inside guard, and they entered the council-chamber, where they dropped their mysterious manner, and were ready to answer to their names at the calling of the roll.

The clock struck twelve. The sound rang through the apartment in solemn, measured tones, and as the twelfth stroke was still vibrating in the air, all the doors, even those communicating with the ante-rooms, were promptly locked, no one being admitted after that hour.

The meeting was opened after the regular form, and the business disposed of without interruption. When the time which was set apart for addresses arrived, Webster was called upon for his speech. He ascended the platform with a serious expression on his face, and after thanking his fellow-knights for the honor conferred upon him, he launched forth into a stirring address, the treasonable nature of which was calculated to fire the Southern blood of his hearers, and to add much to his own popularity. As the speaker appeared to warm up with his subject he lifted his voice and exclaimed:

"The dissolution of the Union is one of the inevitable necessities of Lincoln's election, and it will be our mission to strike directly at the heart of the abolition party, and bury its foul carcass beneath the smoking ruins of Washington city!"

This was the signal. The words had no sooner passed the lips of the speaker, than a startling noise, like that of a battering-ram being applied to one of the ante-room doors, cut short the speech, and caused every man present to spring to his feet in astonishment and alarm. Bang! bang! bang! sounded the heavy blows. The door burst open with a crash, and a stream of blue-coated soldiers, all fully armed, came pouring into the council-chamber, and quickly deployed around three sides of the room, effectually cutting off the retreat of the inmates before they could make a movement.

The sudden and unexpected appearance of these intruders had a paralyzing effect upon the conspirators. Had so many ghosts confronted them they could not have been more surprised. Horrified consternation was depicted on every blanched face;

"The door burst open and a stream of blue coated soldiers came pouring in."

startled eyes looked wildly around for some avenue of escape, and exclamations of terror or baffled rage broke from many white lips. Some of the most desperate seemed for a moment to entertain thoughts of breaking through the line of soldiers and reaching the door, but no such mad attempt was made. McPhail stepped forward with a revolver in each hand, and in a low, thrilling voice, said :

"Gentlemen, you are our prisoners. I advise you to give in gracefully. We are too many for you."

His advice did not go unheeded. They surrendered as gracefully as possible under the circumstances, and resigned themselves to the custody of their armed foes. The chamber in which they had maliciously plotted the overthrow of the government became the scene of their own downfall, and it was with dejected countenances that they submitted to the inevitable, and permitted themselves to be marched in a body before the Provost-Marshal. It was not observed, however, until they were being removed, that Timothy Webster had somehow contrived to make good his escape.

The leading spirits of this conspiracy—those who did the actual plotting, and who were known to be the arch traitors and prime movers in the secret enterprise—were taken to Fort McHenry. The rest, after taking the oath of allegiance, were released.

My two operatives disappeared from Baltimore immediately after this occurrence, as well they might, for of course the suspicion of the defeated conspirators fastened upon them at once. As they did not show themselves in that city again, however, they never were made the victims of the terrible vengeance which some of their late associates swore to bring down upon their luckless heads at the first opportunity. As for Webster, instead of being suspected of any complicity in the betrayal, he was congratulated upon his fortunate and remarkable escape from the fate which befell his unfortunate brother knights.

With the defeat of the " Knights of Liberty " in Baltimore, ended the existence of the branch lodges all over the State. The organization, which had so carefully planned the destruction of the Union at a single blow, was completely broken up. The conspirators, taking warning by the fate of their leaders, became mute and inactive, and although skilled detectives were sent to all outlying towns, no new signs of an uprising were discovered.

CHAPTER XIX.

Suspicions in Washington.—" Uncle Gallus."—Property Searched.—A Rebel Family sent South.—Webster starts for Richmond.

ASIDE from the operations of Timothy Webster and his assistants in Baltimore, there was work enough to do in Washington to keep myself and all the members of my large force constantly employed. Innumerable persons, suspected of treasonable designs, were closely shadowed; whole families became objects of distrust, and fell under the watchful eye of my department ; while the ungracious task of searching the homes of people who stood upon the highest round of the social ladder became of frequent occurrence.

Among the latter class were the wife and family of ex-Governor Morton, of Florida, who at this time were sojourning in Washington. Mrs. Morton was known to be in sympathy with the South, and the unceasing vigilance of my men soon developed the fact that she was in secret communication with certain off.cials of the rebel government, to whom she was giving information concerning affairs at the North. She was a lady of eminent respectability and refinement, and much esteemed by all who knew her, but this did not render it less advisable, under the circumstances, to have all her movements watched, and her house constantly shadowed by detectives. Her pleasant residence at No. 288 "I" street, was therefore placed under strict surveillance, and its inmates followed whenever they went out for a walk or drive, while all visitors at the house were invariably shadowed when they went away.

There was an old negro servant, known as Uncle Gallus, who went to and from the house oftener than any one else, on errands for the family. Finally one of my operatives drew the old fellow into conversation, and found him so cheerful and communicative, and so firm in his loyalty to the Northern cause, that when the fact was reported to me, I concluded to talk with Uncle Gallus myself. Accordingly, I gave orders to have him brought to my office, if it could be done without opposition on his part. The friendship I bore for the colored race, and my long experience as an underground railroad conductor, had given me such an insight into the character of the negro, that I believed I could gain his confidence and good-will if I should meet him.

Uncle Gallus came to my office quite willingly. He was a powerfully-built darky, though evidently well advanced in years, as attested by the bleached appearance of his wool and eye-brows. His skin was as black and shone as bright as polished ebony, and it took but little provocation to set him on a broad grin, which displayed two unbroken rows of glistening ivory.

This interesting specimen appeared before me one afternoon, when Timothy Webster was with me in my office. We had just finished a discussion concerning some delicate point in Webster's Baltimore operations, and had lapsed into a desultory conversation. My sable visitor stood bowing and scraping, and turning his hat round and round in his hands, till I bid him be seated.

"Your name is Gallus?" I said.

"Yes, sah," he replied, his mouth stretched from ear to ear. "Folks done got so dey call me *uncle* Gallus nowadays."

"You have been a slave all your life, I understand?"

"Yes, massa, eber sence I war knee-high to a hopper-grass. I'se done a mighty sight o' wu'k, too, 'kase I wus allus as big an stout as a sixty-dollah bull, an' I could stan' mo' hard-fisted labor dan any o' de udder niggahs on de plantation. But sence I been wid Massa Morton I ain't had nuffin' to do skursely, an' it seems as ef I'se gwine to git pow'ful lazy fur de want o' wu'k. H'yah! H'yah!"

"What is your native State, Uncle Gallus?"

"Ole Virginny, sah."

He held his head a little higher, and sat a trifle more erect as he said this, showing that inordinate pride in his State which I had so often noticed in other Virginia slaves, as well as in Virginia masters.

I asked him if the Mortons had offered him his freedom since the breaking out of the war. He shook his head and gravely replied :

" Dey hain't been nuffin' said to dis pusson on dat 'ar subjick, but I knows dey'd gimme my freedom in less'n twenty-fo' hours ef I done ax 'em fur it."

" Then you don't want to be free ?"

" Oh, yes, I does, massa ; yes, I does, fur sho'. But Massa Linkum an' de Yankee boys am gwine ter fetch dat aroun' all right by'm-bye. Bress your soul an' body, I can't b'ar fur to run away from missus an' ole massa, 'kase dey's been so good an' kyind to me ; an' I'se done tuk an oath dat I won't leave 'em till dey gimme leaf. When missus goes back down Souf I'se gwine ter go wid her, ef she don't tole me to stay heah. It won't be long, nohow, 'kase de time am soon comin' when de darkies will all be free."

" Your mistress intends to return to the South, then ?"

" Yes, sah ; we'll soon be off now, ef de good Lo'd will let us. Massa, he's in Richmond, an' he hab done sent fur de family."

" Is Mrs. Morton in communication with her husband ?"

" Spec' she is, sah. She writes letters, an' *gits* letters. She has ter be sorter keerful like, for dese 'yah Yankees is got eyes like a cat, an' kin see fru a stun wall in de dark."

" Do you know whether your mistress writes to any one besides her husband ?"

Uncle Gallus leaned back in his chair, and looked at me somewhat suspiciously, the whites of his eyes shining like polished china.

"'Deed, sah, I doesn't know whedder she dusdo, or whedder she doant," he said, hesitatingly. " Please, massa, doant ax dis chile any mo' questions. My missus is de bes' woman in de wu'ld, and nebber didn't do nuffin' wrong in all her bawn days. Ole Gallus wouldn't say nuffin' to bring trubble on her for fifteen cents," he added, earnestly.

I quieted the fears of the faithful old man by assuring him that I meant no harm to his mistress, and that I had no doubt she was the good lady he represented her to be. Satisfied with the result of my investigations, I permitted Uncle Gallus to depart, first charging him, however, to say nothing to any one concerning my interview with him. He promised secrecy, and bowed himself out with all his teeth visible, saying, as he went :

" Fo' de Lawd, gemmen, I'se hopin an' prayin' de No'thun folks will be de top dog in dis wrastle, an' ef eber dis niggah hes a chance to gib yu'uns a helpin' han', yu' kin bet a hoss agin' a coon-skin he'll do it ; but I hope an' trus' my missus not be boddered."

20

Nevertheless, I had learned enough to bring me to the decision, that Mrs. Morton's house must be searched, and under orders of the Secretary of War, I sent three of my men to No. 288 "I" street, to perform this unpleasant task. The operatives chosen to make the search were W. H. Scott, John Scully, and Pryce Lewis. Mrs. Morton received them very civilly, and told them they were at liberty to make a thorough search of the premises, which they immediately proceeded to do. They had instructions to read all letters that were found, but to keep only those that were of a treasonable nature, and in no case to destroy any property or leave anything in a disordered condition. These instructions were obeyed to the letter. Boxes that were packed ready for shipment were all carefully repacked and closed after they had been examined by my men, and when the operatives departed, they left no traces of their search behind them. Their polite and considerate conduct won for them the good will, not only of Mrs. Morton herself, but also of her daughter and two sons, who expressed themselves as being agreeably surprised, for they had been informed that the men from the Provost-Marshal's office were a set of ruffians, who did not scruple to break up boxes, and litter the house with their contents, and that their conduct towards ladies was insulting in the extreme. They even went so far as to assure the operatives, that if any of them should ever be taken prisoner and brought to Richmond, they would do all in their power to secure kind treatment for them.

Among the letters that were found, two of them were from ex-Governor Morton, to his son and daughter, requesting them to come to him at Richmond ; but nothing of a criminating character was discovered, and the family were not subjected to further annoyance.

Some two weeks afterwards, when John Scully boarded a train for Baltimore, whither I had sent him with a message to Webster, he chanced to meet Mrs. Morton and family in the car which he entered. They were departing from Washington, having been required to leave the North, by the authorities, who furnished them a safe passport to Richmond, and they were accompanied by the faithful Uncle Gallus. They recognized Scully, and greeted him with cordial courtesy, the eldest son rising in his seat to shake hands with him. They told him that on arriving at Baltimore, they were to take a flag-of-truce boat to Fortress Monroe, from which point they would continue their journey to Richmond. Scully as a matter of policy, gave them distinctly to understand that he had quitted the government service and was returning to his home in the North.

This little experience with the Morton family was trifling enough in itself, and was only one of many similar episodes with which I and my force were connected during those troublous times ; but I have been thus particular in detailing it because it has an important bearing upon other events which afterwards occurred.

It was about a month after the incident above mentioned, that Timothy Webster completed his preparations for making his first trip into Virginia and through the rebel lines. A large number of Baltimoreans had intrusted him with letters to their friends and relatives in the South, and he had assured them that their messages would be delivered safely and answers brought back in due time.

He left Baltimore on the 14th of October, and proceeded southward along the "Eastern Shore" of Virginia, seeking a convenient place to cross over to the mainland or "Western Shore." He arrived at Eastville, the county seat of Northampton county, on Tuesday, October 22d, where he found that he could effect a crossing with the assistance of a man named Marshall, who made a business of smuggling passengers and mails through the lines. He was compelled, however, to remain at Eastville several days, waiting for Marshall and his boat to come over from the other side, his trips being delayed on account of the bright moonlight nights, as the boatman did not dare to run the gantlet of the Federal guns, unless covered by darkness.

Some two or three months before, this man, Marshall, had owned a sloop, which he had used successfully in running the Federal blockade. One night he was caught in a calm near the western shore, and was run-down by a gunboat. His sloop was captured, and he narrowly escaped capture by deserting his vessel and reaching the shore in a smaller boat. Since that time Marshall had been pursuing his vocation with a sort of canoe, or " dugout," thirty-one feet in length and five feet in width, carrying three sails—main, fore and jib. His route was from Gloucester Point, York river, to Eastville, and his business was to transfer from one side of the bay to the other the Confederate mail and passengers, and sometimes a small cargo of merchandise. Marshall being an expert pilot and a thorough seaman, was frequently employed by the masters of sloops and schooners to pilot them past certain points, they giving him the privilege of putting his passengers and mail-bags aboard the vessel without charge. It was his invariable custom to place a stone or other heavy substance in his mail-bag before starting, for the purpose of sinking it in case of being pressed by the gunboats.

It was on a dark evening that Webster left Cherrystone Lighthouse in Marshall's canoe, to make the voyage across the Chesapeake. There were thirteen passengers, all told. Eight of these were Marylanders, mostly from Baltimore, every one of whom announced his intention of enlisting in the Confederate army or navy upon his arrival at Richmond.

On starting, Marshall rowed off a short distance from the light-house, and rested on his oars for some time, taking observations to ascertain if the bay was clear of hostile craft. The night was scarcely dark enough for safety ; the clouds were thin and scattered, and the stars were peeping through the dark, ragged curtain overhead. The wind was blowing strongly from the east, and the water was exceedingly rough.

Resolving, however, to make the effort, Marshall hoisted his sails, and as they rapidly filled, the little vessel sprung forward like a thing of life. It fairly skimmed over the waves, its sharp prow cutting the water and dashing up clouds of spray that caused the men to turn up their coat-collars and pull their hats down closer upon their heads. All conversation was forbidden, lest their voices should betray them to the enemy. With sealed lips and motionless forms, they might have been so many dark phantoms speeding before the wind on some supernatural mission.

Webster, by his own wish, had been put upon the look-out by the captain of the boat, and he keenly watched for signs of danger. When they had traveled nearly half the distance across the bay, he spied a point of light to leeward, and at once called Marshall's attention to it.

"It is a gunboat with a light on her bows," said the latter. "Let her come. She can't catch us, for with our present headway we are not to be overhauled by any boat on this water."

The canoe was headed due west for about fourteen miles, then south-west by west for ten or twelve miles, then due west again to Gloucester Point. The entire run was made in three and a half hours, the sailing distance being about thirty miles.

On nearing Gloucester Point, they were hailed by a sentinel, with the usual challenge :

" Who comes there ?"

The blockade-runner sent back the answer :

" Marshall—mail boat !"

" Stand, Marshall, and give the countersign !"

" No countersign," was the reply.

The sentinel then called out :

" Sergeant of the Guard, Post No. 1 !"

And another voice, further away, cried :

" Who's there ?"

" Marshall, with mail boat and passengers."

" Sentinel, let them pass."

A few minutes later the passengers disembarked, and found themselves in a rebel camp.

Webster, with others, went to Marshall's shanty— a rude, wooden structure, which that worthy had built on the Point for the accommodation of his passengers—and there the remainder of the night was spent in the refreshing companionship of Morpheus.

On the following morning Webster was up and astir at an early hour. He ascertained that the encampment at Gloucester Point consisted of two regiments of infantry, two companies of cavalry, and one field battery of six guns, all under the command of Col. Charles H. Crump. The entrenchments comprised an area of about fifteen acres, and the main breastwork on the beach consisted of a heavy earth-bank, walled on the inside with split pine logs set up on end. About the center of this breastwork was a sixty-four-pound gun, mounted on a high carriage, which traversed in a circle commanding a sweep of the whole land side of the entrenchments, where there was a clean field of about seven hundred acres bounded by timber on the north and York river on the south.

General Magruder had command of this division of the army, including the forces at Gloucester Point, Yorktown and all the peninsula bounded by the James and York rivers, extending down to Fortress Monroe. The division embraced thirty-three regiments of infantry and cavalry.

Webster called at Colonel Crump's headquarters and obtained from that officer a pass to Richmond, not only for himself, but for several others who had crossed the bay with him. At about the hour of noon on Saturday, the 26th, the party were ferried across the river to Yorktown, in a small boat. The landing at Yorktown was in front of a hill which rose with a gentle slope some twenty-five feet above the beach, on the top of which, in front of the town, was an earth-work mounting six or eight guns.

From this point the party proceeded in a south-westerly direction, across the peninsula, to Grove Wharf, on James river. The distance was about ten miles, and was accomplished without difficulty or delay. On their arrival at Grove Wharf, however, they were disappointed to learn that no boat was to leave there for Richmond until the following Monday. There was no help for it, and with a rueful attempt at resignation, they took quarters at a neighboring farm-house, where they waited and rested.

CHAPTER XX.

The Spy at Richmond.—Earthworks Around the Rebel Capital.—An Unexpected Meeting.—Pistols for Two.—A Reconciliation.—Safe Return to Washington.

ON Monday morning Webster left Grove Wharf, on the regular steam packet, for Richmond, where he arrived on the evening of the same day. Here he separated from his companions and made his way alone to the Spotswood Hotel, where he registered, and proceeded to make himself at home. He was now in the rebel capital, surrounded on all sides by the enemies of his country, with no friends to whom he could apply in case of danger, and burdened with a mission, upon the successful performance of which his life depended. It was a mission, too, requiring such delicate and skillful labor, that a man less iron-nerved would have trembled at the very contemplation of it ; but Webster, whose courage and self-command never deserted him in the most trying moments of his life, coolly reviewed the situation and laid his plans in a systematic manner for future operations.

The next day, he busied himself about the city, delivering his letters, forming acquaintances, and paving the way for an interview with the Secretary of War, his object being to obtain from that high official, if possible, a pass to Manassas and Winchester. He was informed by General Jones, Post-Adjutant to General Winder, the Provost-Marshal at Richmond, and commander of the forces there, that no interview could be obtained with the Secretary of War, except upon business especially connected with the military department, as they were daily expecting an attack from the Federal Army of the Potomac, and the Secretary was wholly engaged with officers of the army.

Among the acquaintances which Webster formed, was a young man by the name of William Campbell, originally a Baltimorean, to whom he brought a letter of introduction from the father of the young man. Campbell treated my operative with the utmost friendliness and courtesy, and invited him to a drive during the afternoon. The invitation was accepted, and as the weather was all that could be desired, they enjoyed a very pleasant afternoon. They visited the environs for the purpose of viewing the defenses, and Webster noted the fact that there were seventeen very superior earth-work batteries around the town, forming a rude semicircle with either end resting on the James river. The entrenchments around each of these batteries were from twelve to fourteen feet wide at the top, and about ten feet deep. Some of the batteries were designed for six guns and some for sixteen.   They were nearly all completed at this time, and the work upon them had been done exclusively by negro slaves.   In most cases they were mounted with their full complement of guns, varying in caliber, from thirty-two to sixty-four pounds. The land around Richmond consists of hills and valleys, and the batteries were planted on the most elevated and commanding points.   The heaviest of these commanded the turnpikes and railroads which formed the approaches from Manassas and Fredericksburg.

After visiting the batteries, Webster went with Campbell to the ordnance department, where he was introduced to several persons who had charge of the ordnance stores, and from whom he elicited much valuable information.   Among other things, he was informed by the Colonel in charge, that the "Bermuda," an English vessel which had recently run the blockade, had brought over for the Confederate government twelve thousand Enfield rifles, a large supply of cavalry swords and a number of rifled cannon; and that, upon trial, the rifled cannon were found to be more accurate than any of their brass pieces.

On the following day Webster concluded to make another inspection of the earth-works around the city. He went alone and on foot this time, as he desired to make some notes and calculations, which he was unable to do in the presence of others without running an unnecessary risk.   It was a fine, brisk morning, the air was slightly tinged with the coolness of approaching winter, and the spy occupied the entire forenoon in strolling leisurely from point to point, apparently with the single object of idling away a few leisure hours. Now he passed some men engaged in planting a cannon on one of the redoubts, and again he saw a group of slaves busily at work with pickaxes and shovels, but no one seemed to pay any attention to him.

About noon he came upon a scene, which, though characteristic of the time and place, was rather a novel sight to a Northern man, and he stopped to view it with considerable interest. In a sunny spot near the river bank about a dozen negro laborers were gathered, their surroundings showing that they had just left off work for the enjoyment of their allotted hour of rest, at noon. Having finished their mid-day repast, they were now filling their time by indulging in a species of amusement peculiar to their race. On a pine log sat a jolly-looking old negro, whose hair was white as snow and whose face was black as ebony, grinning, and rolling his head from side to side, while he patted "Juba" with great energy and skill, on his knees, chest and head. The other darkies were dancing to the "music," and apparently enjoying the sport to an unlimited degree.

The detective was amused at the spectacle, but this feeling gave way to one of surprise and curiosity, as he looked more intently at the white-haired old

man who was acting as *musician.* There was some·
thing strikingly familiar in those black, smiling features.
Surely this was not the first time he had seen that
face, or witnessed that tremendous grin. Where had
he met this darky before ?

Suddenly his recollection was quickened. The
person in question was none other than Uncle Gallus,
the servant of ex-Governor Morton, whom he had
seen in my office at Washington, on the day that I
had questioned him about his mistress. This fact
was clear enough to Webster, but somewhat surprising, withal. He remembered that Uncle Gallus had,
on that occasion, represented the Mortons as very
indulgent slave-owners, who never permitted him to
perform any hard labor; yet here he was, in the role
of a common workman, employed upon the fortifications around Richmond.

Whatever had caused this change, however, it did
not appear to weigh heavily upon the old darky, for at
this moment he was in the very ecstasy of delight, as he
patted inspiration into the nimble feet of his companions. The other darkies danced until their faces
shone with perspiration, and the manner in which
their loose-jointed limbs swung and wriggled, suggested the idea that those members were hung on
pivots. They leaped and vaulted, and flung their
heels in the airs, as if they were so many jumping-
jacks and Uncle Gallus was pulling the string.

The latter hummed snatches of plantation melodies

as he warmed up to his work, and finally he sung a series of characteristic verses, of which the following are a sample :

" Did you ebber see a woodchuck lookin' at a coon-fight ?
  Linkum am a-comin' by'm-bye ;
Did you ebber see a niggah gal dancin' in de moonlight?
  Glory, glory, glory hallelujerum !

" Possum up a gum-stump, chawin' slippery-ellum,
  Linkum am a-comin' by'm-bye ;
Nigga's in de market an' massa tryin' to sell 'em—
  Glory, glory, glory hallelujerum !

"Secesh in Richmon'—de Yankee boys has treed 'em—
  Linkum am a-comin' by'm-bye ;
All de little pickaninnies gwine to git dar freedom—
  Glory, glory, glory hallelujerum !"

Suddenly the merriment of the blacks was interrupted in a most unexpected manner.

Some tall bushes that covered the top of a slight elevation near by were suddenly parted, and a man, wearing the uniform of a Lieutenant in the Confederate army, leaped down among the astonished revelers. In a towering rage, he turned upon Uncle Gallus and shouted:

"Shut your head, you d——d old villain, or I'll fill your black hide with lead !" and he flourished a cocked revolver in the face of the terrified negro.

" Afo' God, Massa, we didn't mean no harm, we's jes passin' away de time," said Uncle Gallus, in a frightened voice.

"Well, then," said the officer, with an oath, " be a little more careful in the future about the kind of songs you sing, or I'll have every d——d one of you bucked and gagged, and whipped within an inch of your lives."

Replacing his weapon, and turning on his heel, he was striding angrily away when he came face to face with Webster.

The recognition was mutual and instantaneous between the two men. As quick as a flash Webster had his revolver cocked and pointed at the head of the blustering Confederate.

" Bill Zigler, what are you doing here? You move at your peril."

" I'd kill you, curse you, but you've got the drop on me now, as you had once before. But my time will come, you d——d Yankee spy!"

" Look here, Bill !" said Webster, anxious, if possible, to disarm at once and forever the suspicions of his enemy, "what is the use of our being continually at daggers' points? You were foolish enough to insult me in Baltimore by impeaching my loyalty to the South, and I resented it, as any man would. If you repeat the vile slander, I'll do the same thing. If, however, you have anything personal against me, and must fight, I'll put up my weapon and meet you hand to hand."

Zigler looked at the speaker a moment, and then advancing and extending his hand, said :

"Webster, put up your pistol; I guess I've made a d——d fool of myself. I did think you were a spy, but I knock under ; I don't want to be an enemy to such a friend to the cause as I now believe you to be."

Lowering his revolver, Webster good-naturedly received the friendly overtures of his former foe.

"I thought you would come to your senses at last ; but when did you come down here ?"

"Oh, I've been here several weeks. I enlisted in Baltimore and came down as a lieutenant, "answered Zigler. "But where are you from ?" he continued, "and what is the news from the Monumental City ?"

"I am just from that city," replied Webster, "and have brought a number of letters for parties here and at Manassas. I expect to go to the Junction to-morrow, if I succeed in getting a pass."

"Who do you want to see there ?"

"Well, I want to see John Bowen," replied Webster, naming a particular friend of Zigler's, whom he knew was at Manassas. "I understand he is down with typhoid fever, and will no doubt be glad to hear from home."

This straightforward story completely disarmed the suspicions of the bully as to Webster's true character, and finding that he had time to spare he invited the scout to his quarters.

Thus the quarrel was settled between these two

men, and the superior tact and coolness of Webster had succeeded in making a friend of a man who might have seriously interfered with his operations, and probably have jeopardized his life.

As they were leaving the place, Webster cast a look at the group of negroes, whose mirth had been so suddenly interrupted, and he noticed that they were regarding the Lieutenant with looks of sullen anger. He was, however, considerably relieved to find that Uncle Gallus had not recognized him, and that as far as the aged negro was concerned, he had nothing to fear. He accompanied Zigler to his quarters, where they chatted pleasantly for an hour, after which Webster returned to his hotel, a much wiser man than when he first started out upon his walk.

As he sauntered quietly back to the city, he felt quite elated at the success of his management of Zigler, whom he had made a fast friend. After supper, in company with Mr. Campbell, he strolled about the city for a short time, when his companion excused himself, and Webster pursued his way alone. He was walking along Utah street, apparently deeply absorbed in his own meditations, when he heard a voice behind him.

" Hole on dar, Massa !"

Turning around, he was surprised to see Uncle Gallus, approaching him as rapidly as his stiffened limbs would permit.

"Well, uncle," said Webster, as the old man caught up to him—"did you speak to me?"

"You'se de man dat I 'dressed, sah—done you know me?" said the old fellow, peering anxiously in the face of the detective.

"No, I don't remember you," said Webster, determined to ascertain whether the old darky did know him; "where have you ever seen me?"

"In Washington, sah," replied Uncle Gallus; "don' you remember you saw me at Majah Allen's, when I was dah libin wid Missus Morton?"

Webster looked at the negro a moment, and then, feeling assured of the friendliness of his interlocutor, he said:

"Your face does seem familiar to me; what is your name?"

"Dey calls me Uncle Gallus, sah," answered the old fellow.

"Oh, yes," said Webster, "now I remember you."

"Golly, massa," grinned Uncle Gallus, "wen I seed you gib it to Bill Zigler dis mo'nin', I dun knowed you right away, but I wouldn't say nuffin' for de world, fo' I knowed you was a pullin' de wool ober his eyes."

Knowing full well that he had nothing to fear from Uncle Gallus, he talked with him good-naturedly on various topics, and in the course of the conversation he learned that he was no longer with Mrs.

Morton, having been disposed of by her, some time before, and that he was now being used by the Confederate government to work upon the fortifications. Not deeming it advisable to remain long in conversation with the old darky on the streets, he told him that he would see him in a day or two, and placing a coin in the old man's hand, he bade him good-night.

The next morning Mr. Campbell and Webster visited General Jones, and obtained the sought-for passes to Manassas, for which place he left early in the forenoon. On his arrival there, he learned that John Bowen, for whom he had a letter, had been taken to Richmond, but having several other messages to deliver to parties of prominence there, he busied himself during the day in forming acquaintances, and in acquiring knowledge. From Manassas he went to Centreville, where he remained a few days, and from thence to Warrington, and finally back again to Richmond, where he delivered his remaining letters. Here he formed the acquaintance of a man by the name of Price, who was engaged in running the blockade, and who was making arrangements to return to Baltimore, to purchase a fresh supply of goods. Together they went to the office of the Provost-Marshal, where they obtained the necessary passes to insure their safe journey through the rebel lines.

Leaving Richmond, they went to Fredericksburg, where he stayed long enough to visit all the places of

interest around that city, and in company with Mr.
Price they went on to Brooks Station, the head-quarters of General Holmes, with whom Price was intimately acquainted. After remaining several days, he
left his companion, making his way to Yorktown and
Gloucester Point, and from thence to Washington,
where he reported to me.

This first visit of Timothy Webster to Richmond
was highly successful. Not only had he made many
friends in that city, who would be of service to him
on subsequent trips, but the information he derived
was exceedingly valuable. He was able to report
very correctly the number and strength of the fortifications around the rebel capital, to estimate the number of troops and their sources of supplies, and also
the forts between that city and Manassas Junction.
His notes of the topography of the country were of
the greatest value, and he received the warmest
thanks of the commanding general, for what he had
thus far been able to accomplish.

CHAPTER XXI.

*Again in Baltimore.—A Warning.—The Spy is Arrested,
and Escapes.*

AFTER the return of Timothy Webster from
Richmond and Manassas, I deemed it best
that he should again visit Baltimore and mingle
once more with his rebel friends in that city. Since
the summary collapse of the Knights of Liberty the
majority of them had been remarkably quiet, and no
indications were apparent that they contemplated
any further proceedings of a treasonable nature. It
will be remembered that on the night that the secret
meeting was disturbed, Webster managed in some
unaccountable manner to escape, and that he had disappeared almost immediately afterwards. As no suspicion existed as yet of his having been concerned in
the affair, and as his prolonged absence might give
rise to doubts of his loyalty, I concluded that it was
best for him to again show himself among his old
associates, and account for his escape in a manner
that would appear truthful and straightforward.

He accordingly took the train, and after arriving
in Baltimore, he went directly to Miller's Hotel.
Here he found several of his friends, and their greet-

ings were most cordial and hearty. In a few moments others of the party had been notified, and came thronging in to welcome him and to congratulate him upon his escape and present safety. Eager inquiries were made as to the manner in which he had so successfully eluded the soldiers, and how he had spent the time since the occurrence of that event. In reply Webster gave a satisfactory and highly interesting account of his movements, all of which was heartily enjoyed by his listening friends. Gratified beyond expression at the pleasant condition of affairs, he became quite jolly, and the balance of the evening was spent in convivial and social enjoyment.

On the following morning he started out in search of his old friend Sam Sloan, for whom he had a letter from his brother, who was in the rebel army, and stationed at Centreville. Having also a number of letters for other Baltimoreans, he desired to secure Sloan's services in their proper and safe delivery.

Sam looked in astonishment as Webster blandly approached him, and after an effusive greeting he remarked earnestly :

"Webster, you'll have to be mighty careful now, or you will be arrested yet. We are watched night and day—the least suspicious move we make is reported at once—and if repeated, the first thing the offender knows he finds himself in the guard-house."

"Well," replied Webster, laughingly, "I'll have to take my chances with the rest of you."

"I know your grit, Webster," said Sloan, "but by all means be careful. I was arrested myself since you went away."

"The deuce you were!" ejaculated Webster. "How did that occur?"

"Well, I went over to Washington to transact a little business, and while there I met some of the boys, and we had a little 'time.' I don't know what I did, but when I started to come home, the Provost-Marshal arrested me, and I had to take the oath of allegiance before I could get away."

"You don't tell me that you took the oath, Sam?"

"Yes, I did," laughed Sam. "I would take twenty oaths before I would be locked up;" and then he added : "I tell you, we are all spotted here in this city, and who is doing it we can't find out."

"What makes you think that?" inquired Webster, doubtfully.

"Many things. Why, only the other day I was taken before Lieutenant Watts, who has charge of the station-house, and the questions he put to me about the gang, convinced me that he knew a great deal more than was good for us."

"Did he ask anything about me?" queried Webster.

"No," replied Sam, "and if he had I wouldn't have told him anything, you may be sure."

"I can readily believe that," said the detective,

"but if it is so dangerous here, how am I going to deliver these letters?"

"I can help you there," said Sloan, after a moment's consideration; "John Earl, Richardson and I will see that they are delivered, and that will keep you from incurring suspicion."

"That will do," said Webster, "and you can tell the people you see to write their answers at once, and inclose them in two envelopes, one directed to their friend, and the other to John Hart, at Miller's Hotel."

"I understand; but who is this John Hart you mention—can we trust him?"

"I think so," replied the detective, laughing heartily; "his other name is Timothy Webster."

"By Jove, Webster, you're a good one; I begin to think myself that there isn't so much danger of your getting caught after all."

This being satisfactorily arranged, the two men started in search of John Earl and Richardson, who both agreed to assist in the delivery of the letters which Webster had brought with him from the South. They all went to the room occupied by the detective at the hotel, and after a friendly drink, the letters were properly assorted, and each man was given his particular portion. They were instructed to request answers from those only in whose friendship they could implicitly rely, and to take in person any that were prepared at the time.

In the afternoon, Webster called on Mr. Camp

bell, the father of the young man who had accompanied him on his trip from Richmond to Manassas
Junction. The old gentleman was rejoiced to hear
from his son, and after a few minutes' conversation
Webster discovered that he was quite as bitter a
secessionist as any one he had met, although he was
quite aged and not very active. He informed the
detective that he had once made a very handsome
horse-bit for General McClellan, and that he was now
making one for General Johnston, which he would like
Webster to take with him when he next went to
Richmond, and deliver it to the General in person.

"Have everything ready," said the detective, "and
I will see that it reaches its destination in safety."

Returning to the hotel, he went in to supper, and
after a hearty repast seated himself in the reading-
room to await the return of his mail-carriers. While
carelessly glancing over the columns of a daily paper,
he was approached by a gentleman, who stepped in
front of him, exclaiming heartily: "Why, Mr. Webster, how do you do? I am glad to see you; when
did you get back to Baltimore?"

Looking up hastily from his paper, Webster
recognized the speaker as Mr. Price, the blockade
runner whom he had met in Richmond, and with
whom he had traveled some distance through the
rebel country.

Their greeting was most cordial, and the return of
John Earl and Sam Sloan found the two men engaged

in animated conversation. From Price, Webster learned that a large amount of goods had been purchased by several wealthy gentlemen of Baltimore, who had adopted a very novel manner of transporting them into rebeldom, without danger from Federal pickets or gunboats. Their plan was to ship the goods upon a vessel bound for Europe and ostensibly the goods were intended for the same destination. In addition to this a small boat was purchased, which was to be taken in tow by the steamer. By an arrangement with the captain the vessel was to stand in as close as possible to the mouth of York river, when the small boat was to be brought alongside, then the goods were to be transferred to it, and the owners were to pull up the river to Yorktown, effect a safe landing, and the rest would be an easy task.

Webster complimented his companion on the shrewdness displayed in this suggestion, and that evening he wrote to me, conveying full particulars of the proposed blockade-running.

It is needless to say that this little plan, shrewd as it was, failed of execution. Men were at once placed upon the track of these merchants, and a more surprised coterie never existed than were these gentlemen, when their goods, carefully labeled for a foreign port, were seized by the government, and their conveyance to the South effectually stopped. An examination of the goods fully confirmed the correctness of Webster's information, and this venture, at least, was a losing speculation to those who had engaged in it.

After Mr. Price had taken his departure, John Earl called Webster aside, and informed him that a gentleman desired to send a draft for a large amount of money to Richmond, and that he had insisted on placing it in the hands of John Hart himself.

" Do you know this man, and that he is all right ?" asked Webster.

" No," replied Earl, " I know nothing about him except that he is vouched for by three parties who are true, and they say he is all right."

" I don't like this idea," said Webster, doubtfully ; " I guess you had better tell this man that you will deliver it safely for him, and then you can hand it to me."

" I did suggest that, but he said his orders were to intrust it to no one but John Hart himself."

After considering for some time, Webster finally concluded to see the individual in person. He was satisfied that no harm could come to him if the man was a Federal detective, as, by application to the authorities or to me he could readily extricate himself from any difficulty, and if he was a rebel, he would incur no risk whatever.

" Very well," he said, after he had fully deliberated the question, "you can bring him to my room and then we will see what is to be done. Meanwhile I will take a short walk and smoke a cigar."

On his return he found John Earl awaiting him.

"The gentleman is up-stairs in my room," said Earl; "will you go up now and see him?"

Webster signified his willingness, and the two men ascended the stairs. As they entered the room the stranger arose to greet them, and Webster scrutinized him carefully. The result of his scrutiny was decidedly unsatisfactory. The new-comer was a tall, well-formed man, of about forty years of age. His hair was dark, and he wore long side-whiskers of the same color. In appearance he was what would be ordinarily considered a handsome man, but there was a look of quiet curiosity about the eyes, and a peculiar curl about the mouth, which struck Webster very unpleasantly, and caused him to instinctively regret having accorded him the interview which he desired.

"Mr. Hart," said the stranger, pleasantly, after they had been formally introduced to each other, "I have a letter here, inclosing a draft, which I am desirous of having safely delivered to my sister-in-law in Richmond. You will find the address upon the envelope inside. Can you attend to this?"

"I guess so," replied Webster. "I can try, at all events."

Webster could not overcome a feeling of unrest and suspicion, as he conversed with the man, and he felt considerably relieved when, after expressing his thanks, he took his departure.

The next morning Webster was astir early, and after partaking of a hearty breakfast, he thought he would pay another visit to Mr. Bowen. Leaving the hotel, he walked rapidly down the street in the direction of the old man's residence. He had not proceeded far when, on turning around, he noticed that his friend of the night before was walking upon the opposite side of the street, and but a short distance behind him. Finding that he was observed, the man crossed the street, and after bidding Webster a very cordial good-morning, said :

"Mr. Hart, as we are walking in the same direction, if you have no objection, we will walk together."

Webster assented, and for a short distance they journeyed along, indulging in a very constrained conversation. Webster felt assured that the man had been following him, and that his apparent friendliness was assumed. Desiring to rid himself of his unwelcome and uncomfortable companion, he was upon the point of expressing himself very forcibly, when he was startled by the stranger grasping him firmly by the arm, and ejaculating :

"John Hart, you are my prisoner!"

Had a thunderbolt fallen at his feet he could not have been more surprised, but recovering himself quickly, he wrenched himself from the grasp of the man.

"What do you mean, sir?" he asked.

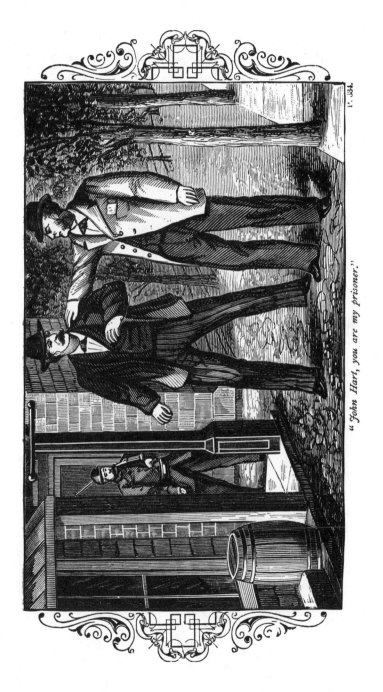

"John Hart, you are my prisoner."

" Just what I have said," replied the other, coolly ; "there is no occasion for any controversy upon the question, and as you are directly in front of the station-house, resistance would be worse than useless."

The cool manner in which these words were spoken exasperated Webster beyond control, but he saw that there were two soldiers standing guard in the doorway, and he realized at once that any attempt at escape would be foolhardy in the extreme. He therefore submitted quietly, and suffered himself to be led into the building, where an officer was seated at a table, examining the reports of the previous day.

The recognition between the Lieutenant and Webster's captor appeared to be mutual, and, indeed, the presence of my operative did not seem to be an unlooked-for event.

" Lieutenant, this is Mr. Hart," said the stranger.

" All right," replied that officer, " we will take good care of him."

After a short consultation, held in a tone too low for Webster to hear, the stranger took his leave, and the officer turned to the detective :

"Come with me, sir ; your case will be attended to in the course of the·day."

" Lieutenant, I would like to speak to you a moment, now that we are alone," said Webster, desirous of ending the matter, and of enabling the Lieutenant to ascertain his true character.

"I have no time to talk with rebels," said the officer, shortly, and then calling to the turnkey, he direected him to place Webster in a cell.

Deeply resenting the treatment of the officer, but feeling that opposition would only aggravate his annoyance, Webster followed the man, internally vowing vengeance against the fellow who had instigated his arrest. He was anxious to express himself forcibly to the officer in charge, but he considered that he would probably do the same thing under the same circumstances. The Lieutenant believed him to be a rebel, and as such his treatment was harsh and impolite, and after debating the matter in his mind he came to the conclusion that he was not much to blame after all. He was desirous, however, of communicating with some one who could intercede for him, and by that means secure his release, and he resolved to make friends with his jailer as the best possible way of obtaining what he wanted.

Shortly after he had been incarcerated, he heard the voices of Sam Sloan and John Earl, who had been informed of his arrest and had come to see him. Their request was denied, however, and they expressed themselves in very loud tones against the injustice they were compelled to submit to. All to no avail, however, and they reluctantly took their leave. The turnkey coming along the corridor at this time, Webster called to him, and requested his attention for a few moments. The man was about

sixty years of age, and had a very benignant countenance, which Webster argued was a good omen for
the work of propitiation which he had in hand.

"Will you tell the Lieutenant that I would like
to speak with him," asked Webster.

"It's no use," said the old man, with a shake of
the head; "the Lieutenant says he won't have anything to say to you, until your case is reported to
headquarters this evening."

"Well, then," smiled Webster, "I suppose I will
have to wait his pleasure; but can't a fellow get a little whisky and cigar? I'll make it worth your while
if you can help me in that particular."

The old man laughed, and said he would see what
could be done, as Webster slipped a bill into his
hand. He disappeared, and after about a half hour,
he returned and slipped a small bundle through the
grated door, admonishing Webster to be careful
about exposing himself to the other prisoners within
view.

"All right," said Webster, "you keep the change,
old man, for your trouble."

In the afternoon another officer, accompanied by
four men, came to his cell, and requested his appearance at the office. Here he was carefully searched, and
upon his person were found some letters addressed to
himself; a pass from Col. Cramp, and about seventy
dollars in money. They were about to take these
from him, when Webster inquired:

22

"Who was the man who arrested me this morning?"

"His name is McPhail, and he belongs to the secret service," was the reply.

At the mention of the name, Webster started in surprise. He had heard of him as connected with my force, and knew that everything would soon be all right.

"Well," said Webster, "will you be kind enough to send for Mr. McPhail, and ask him to telegraph to Major Allen, and inquire if Tim is all right?"

"What Major Allen is that?" asked the officer.

"Of the secret service," replied Webster. "McPhail will know all about him; and you will learn that I am no rebel, in a very short time."

"We will do what you request," said the officer, "and if you are all right, we will be glad to find it out."

Thanking the officer for his kindness, Webster was conducted back to his cell to await developments.

About ten o'clock that night, the officer again made his appearance.

"John Hart, come here."

Webster presented himself before the iron grating of his cell.

"Is your name John Hart?"

"No, sir, my name is Timothy Webster."

"Well, my orders are for a man named Hart, who is to be taken to Fort McHenry."

P. 389.

"Webster leaped from the wagon while it was in motion."

Something in the tone of the man's voice, and in the twinkle of his eye, told Webster that everything was understood, so he answered at once:

"Very well, I am the man!"

"Come with me, then."

They conducted him to the street, where he saw a covered wagon in waiting. They all got in and then in a loud voice the officer gave the order:

"Drive direct to Fort McHenry pier!"

After they had started, the officer explained to Webster that it had been arranged, in order to prevent suspicion, that he should be allowed to jump from the wagon as it was driven along, and after a pretended pursuit, he would make his escape to his rebel friends with whom he should remain quietly for a few days, and then return to Washington and report to me.

These directions he implicitly followed; and seizing a favorable opportunity, he leaped from the wagon and rapidly made his way in the direction of the city. Going directly to Sam Sloan's, he knocked loudly at the door. After a few minutes a window was raised and a voice inquired angrily:

"Who are you, and what do you want?"

"It is I—Webster—Sam, come down and open the door."

The window was shut, with an oath of joyful surprise, and in a twinkling, the door was opened, and

Sloan pulled Webster into the room, closing and locking the door behind him.

"Great G—d, Webster, how did you manage to get away from the Yanks?"

"Let me get warm, and I'll tell you," replied Webster, with a laugh.

"Come up stairs," said Sloan heartily, "and we'll have something to drink."

After refreshing themselves, Webster related the manner of his escape, carefully concealing the action of the officer, and the fact that he had been peaceably permitted to leave the vehicle—and when he had concluded, Sloan's admiration was unbounded. Promising to secrete him until he could safely get away, they all went to bed, and slept soundly.

Early the next morning Sloan left the house, and after an absence of an hour or two returned, bringing with him several of Webster's trusty friends, among whom was John Earl, who was decidedly crestfallen at the thought of having been instrumental in leading Webster into such danger by introducing the strange man to him, without learning more about his character for loyalty to the cause. They were all overjoyed at his escape, and spent the afternoon in a jollification over his safe return. The newspapers contained full particulars of the affair, and when they were brought before him Webster could not restrain his laughter at their contents, as he read:

"ESCAPE OF A STATE PRISONER.*

" It was rumored yesterday that the man Webster, who was arrested, stopping at the hotel of Messrs. McGee, upon the charge of being concerned in the regular transportation of letters between Baltimore and the seceded States, had succeeded in making his escape. It is learned upon the best authority that during a late hour of the night he was removed from the western police station and placed in a carriage under the charge of a special detective officer. The wagon was driven towards Fort McHenry, he having been previously ordered to that post, but while the vehicle was in motion, and when within a short distance of their destination, he gave a sudden bound from his seat, and before the officer could seize him, he was beyond his grasp. It is not known which direction he took, but he will scarcely be able to escape from the city. He is a citizen of Kentucky, but left there in the early part of April, and since that time has been residing in Baltimore."

In another paper he read :

†" We have learned from an entirely reliable source that Mr. Webster was arrested in endeavoring to procure replies to a number of letters which he had delivered from Marylanders now residing in Virginia to friends at home. A fact which, in view of the hazards of such an attempt, should content the unfortunate exiles from Maryland with the gratification of communication with their friends there and without

---

* The above is from the *Baltimore American* of November 22, 1861.
† The above is taken from the *Gazette* of November 22, 1861.

the reciprocal joy of hearing from the latter in return. We have reason to believe that Webster is beyond the reach of the Yankees."

Remaining with his friends until after midnight on the second day, he made his way to the train, and at 4.30 in the morning started for Washington, where he arrived about seven o'clock, and reported at my headquarters.

It may seem strange that Webster was arrested by one of my men, and that my intervention was necessary to effect his release, but a few words will serve as an explanation. McPhail, the operative who had caused Webster's arrest, had never seen that gentleman, and was entirely ignorant of his true character. Under such circumstances he very naturally was led to suspect him as a rebel spy, and to lay the trap for his capture. The delicate and important duties which had been assigned to Webster were such, that I deemed it advisable to inform but very few of my men of his immediate connection with me, hence the arrest, as far as McPhail was concerned, was a *bona fide* revelation of what he believed to be a dangerous crime. As it was, the arrest did no harm, but rather enabled Webster to cement more closely the bonds of friendship which existed between himself and those with whom he had previously associated.

CHAPTER XXII.

ON the first day of November, 1861, General McClellan was made the Commander-in-Chief of all the armies of the United States. Immediately on assuming this important position, the General turned his attention to the entire field of operations, regarding the Army of the Potomac as a branch, though the most important one, of the armies under his command.

Reliable information regarding the location and strength of the enemy was the most desirable thing to be obtained at present, and although Webster had been performing giant labor in this direction, his operations comprised but a minor portion of the work that devolved upon me. Numerous men of various callings and abilities were traveling through the South, gathering items of news wherever possible, and reporting the same as accurately and as rapidly as they were enabled to do so. So numerous were the methods which I employed in promoting the successful operations of the secret service, that it is possible within the limits of the present volume to enumerate but very few of the many events which occurred. Among the many men thus employed, was a negro by the name of John Scobell, and the manner in which his duties were performed, was always a source of satisfaction to me and apparently of gratification to himself. From the commencement of the war, I had found the negroes of invaluable assistance, and I never hesitated to employ them when, after investigation, I found them to be intelligent and trustworthy.

As I have previously stated, all refugees, deserters and contrabands coming through our lines were turned over to me for a thorough examination and for such future disposition as I should recommend. John Scobell came to me in this manner. One morning I was seated in my quarters, preparing for the business of the day, when the officer of the guard announced the appearance of a number of contrabands. Ordering them to be brought in, the pumping process was commenced, and before noon many stray pieces of information had been gathered, which, by accumulation of evidence, were highly valuable. Among the number I had especially noticed the young man who had given his name as John Scobell. He had a manly and intelligent bearing, and his straightforward answers to the many questions propounded to him, at once impressed me very favorably.

He informed me that he had formerly been a slave in the State of Mississippi, but had journeyed to Virginia with his master, whose name he bore. His master was a Scotchman, and but a few weeks before had given him and his wife their freedom. The young woman had obtained employment in Richmond, while he had made his way to the Union lines, where, encountering the Federal pickets, he had been brought to headquarters, and thence to me. He gave an intelligent account of his travels through the country, and appeared to be well informed as to the localities through which he passed, and of the roads and streams round about.

I immediately decided to attach him to my head-quarters, with the view of eventually using him in the capacity of a scout, should he prove equal to the task. For two weeks I employed him in various capacities of minor importance, but those in which secrecy and loyalty were essential qualifications, and his perform-ance of these duties was all that could be desired. At the end of that time I resolved to send him into the South, and test his ability for active duty. Calling him into my quarters, I gave him the necessary directions, and dispatched him, in company with Timothy Webster, on a trip to Virginia. Their line of travel was laid out through Centreville, Manassas, Dumfries, and the Upper and Lower Accoquan.

John Scobell I found was a remarkably gifted man for one of his race He could read and write, and was as full of music as the feathered songsters that warbled in the tropical groves of his own sunny home. In addition to what seemed an almost inexhaustible stock of negro plantation melodies he had also a charming variety of Scotch ballads, which he sang with a voice of remarkable power and sweetness. During the evenings his singing was the chief feature of the impromptu entertainments that were resorted to in order to while away the tedious hours before retiring, and he soon became a universal favorite. Possessing the talents which he did, I felt sure, that he had only to assume the character of the light-hearted, happy darky and no one would suspect the cool-headed, vigilant detective, in the rollicking negro whose only aim in life appeared to be to get enough to eat, and a comfortable place to toast his shins.

It was arranged that the two men should travel together until they arrived at Leonardstown, when they were to separate, Webster proceeding on to Richmond by way of Fredericksburg, while Scobell was to make his way to the rebel camp at Dumfries, and then up as far as Centreville.

Proceeding by stage to Leonardstown they parted company, each one depending upon his own exertions to get across the river. Although they had traveled in the same coach, they paid no attention to each other, nor gave any indication of a previous acquaintance. At Leonardstown Webster went to a hotel, kept by a Mr. Miller, who was a bitter secessionist.

and had known my operative for some time. His greeting was cordial, and his enthusiasm over his escape from the officers at Baltimore, an account of which he had read in the paper, was quite overpowering.

While they were conversing together a tall, dark-whiskered man came into the room, and after a quick, nervous glance at Webster, requested to see the land lord in another room. As they departed, Webster bestowed a searching look upon the new-comer and was at once impressed with the familiarity of his features. He recollected that while he was coming down on the stage, this man came riding rapidly behind them, seated in a buggy and driven by a young negro. They made several ineffectual attempts to pass the stage, and finally succeeded in doing so, and disappearing from view. Webster had forgotten all about him, until his sudden appearance at the hotel and his suspicious actions attracted his attention. After the lapse of a few minutes the two men again entered, and the stranger immediately took his departure.

Filled with curiosity as to the identity of the man, Webster carelessly observed to the landlord :

" That fellow seemed a little nervous, doesn't he ?"

"Yes," replied the landlord, "and he has cause to be ; he is a deserter from the Yanks."

" Was he an officer ?"

" He says he was a surgeon, and had served in the regular army on the Pacific coast for a number of years. His family are Southerners, and he says he concluded to throw up his commission and join our side."

" Which way is he going?"

"He wants to get to Richmond as soon as he can. He will be back shortly and I'll introduce you to him ; perhaps you can give him a helping hand."

" I'll do what I can," replied Webster, with a mental reservation. "What is his name?"

"He gave me his name as Doctor Gurley: he brought a letter from a friend of mine in Washington, and I believe he is carrying some messages to Mr. Benjamin, the Secretary of War, which he is very anxious to deliver as early as possible."

"Well, we may be fellow-travelers if he turns up in time to go over with me," said Webster, who was already attempting to devise some plan for intercepting the delivery of the dispatches which the titled deserter was carrying.

"I have made all arrangements," replied the landlord, "and will send you both down to-morrow in time to get the boat."

" All right," said Webster ; "and now, as I have a little time before dinner, I will take a short walk to give me an appetite."

Webster was intent upon finding John Scobell, if possible. He had formed a plan for getting possession of the dispatches, and he required the services of his colored companion in order to perfect it.

Keeping a sharp look-out about him, he strode on in the direction of the negro quarters, where he felt reasonably sure of meeting with the man he was in search of. As chance would have it, when within a short distance of the locality, he saw, to his intense delight, Scobell approaching him from the opposite direction. In a few words, he developed his plan to the intelligent darky, and from the broad grin which overspread his countenance, it was evident that he not only fully understood, but highly relished, the propositions that had been made. It was arranged, that Scobell should be in the neighborhood of the hotel during the afternoon, and that Webster should endeavor to point out to him the deserting surgeon, after which Scobell was to perform the duty which Webster had delegated to him.

That afternoon, the Doctor, who was stopping with some friends, a short distance out of town, made his appearance at the hotel, and Mr. Miller, having first assured him of my operative's loyalty, introduced the two men to each other. By reason of Webster's familiarity with the country, and his evident and hearty desire to serve his new-found friend, he soon won the kindly regards of the Doctor, who prolonged his visit until nearly dark. At length, promising to meet Webster on the morrow, and with a parting beverage, the Doctor started to go. Webster accompanied him to the door, and with apparent good-feeling, bade him good-evening. As Webster re-entered the hotel, he noticed with satisfaction that Scobell was on hand, and had posted himself in a secluded position, where, unobserved himself, he could watch the hotel, and notice what transpired.

"There is going to be a shower, and the Doctor will have to walk fast to escape it," said Webster, as he entered the bar-room.

He had been engaged in friendly conversation with Mr. Miller for about an hour, when they heard the hurried stamping of feet outside ; in a few moments, the door was thrown suddenly open, and the deserting Doctor stood before them. The appearance of the Doctor was most rueful. He was without his hat ; his clothing was disarranged, and torn and soiled ; his face was of a death-like paleness, while his lips trembled as if with fear.

Webster and the landlord sprang to their feet, and rushed toward the man, who was very near falling from exhaustion.

"What has happened !" inquired Webster, in a tone of solicitude.

"I've been attacked and robbed !" ejaculated the Doctor, weakly.

The landlord poured out a glass of spirits, which he gave to the demoralized Doctor, and after swallowing it, he seemed to regain his strength. After he had been sufficiently restored, he related his story. After leaving the hotel, he had started to walk toward the house where he was stopping. It becoming quite cloudy, and fearing a storm, he had hastened his pace in order to avoid the rain. Suddenly, as he was passing through a small patch of woods, he was stealthily approached from behind, by some one, who struck him a fearful blow on the back of the head. He was completely stunned and fell to the ground. When he recovered consciousness, he found that he had been thoroughly searched, and that his dispatches to the Secretary of War had been taken. Nothing else about his person was disturbed, and the attack had evidently been made by somebody who was aware of the fact that he had them in his possession. The Doctor's anxiety about his loss was pitiable in the extreme, but Webster could scarcely repress a smile of satisfaction, at the success which Scobell had achieved in capturing the precious documents.

"Never mind," said Webster, soothingly. "The loss of the papers won't amount to much ; when we arrive in Richmond you can communicate verbally the nature of the papers you have lost."

"That's the devil of it," blurted out the Doctor. "I don't know their contents ; they were intrusted to me by men who are working in the interest of the South, and as they were sealed, I have no more idea than you have what they contained."

This piece of information was an additional source of satisfaction to Webster, who had thus effectually prevented their transmission to the Rebel government. He sympathized with the Doctor, however, most sincerely, and although that individual was decidedly crestfallen at the turn of affairs, under Webster's ministrations he recovered some of his spirits, and finding that he was not seriously injured, he again started for his lodgings. He took the precaution, this time, to carry his revolver in his hand, and to keep a sharp look-out as he journeyed along.

Miller, the landlord, was somewhat alarmed at this adventure, but Webster endeavored to reassure him as best he could. He suggested that the attack was probably made by some one who was in the interest of the South, but who was fearful that, as the Doctor had deserted from the Northern army, he might not be as true to the good cause as he should be. However this may be, Miller's fears soon disappeared, and by nine o'clock he had recovered his usual good-humor, and set about making his arrangements for the morrow. Feeling anxious to learn from Scobell, Webster lighted a cigar and strolled out into the street. He walked slowly along, and after he had gone some distance from the hotel he turned around, and saw following him, at some distance behind, a figure which he instantly recognized as Scobell's. He therefore went on until he came to the outskirts of the town, and then awaited the arrival of his companion.

Scobell came up with a broad grin on his countenance, and extending his hand, said :

"Here dey is, Mister Webster. Dey is all right,

an' I reckon de Doctor don't know what hurt him by dis time."

Webster took the packet from the outstretched hand of the black man, and complimented him warmly upon his success. Scobell seemed quite elated over his exploit, and it was with some difficulty that Webster could restrain him from breaking out into loud laughter.

Scobell informed Webster that he had already made arrangements for forwarding the documents to me, provided they met with the approval of the scout. He suggested that they be intrusted to an intelligent and loyal colored man, who was to start for Washington on the following morning, and whose honor and truthfulness could be implicitly relied upon.

"I should like to see this man first," said Webster, when Scobell had concluded.

"Werry well; cum along of me," answered Scobell. "I'll show you sumfin you neber seed afore, I reckon.

"Go ahead, then," directed the scout.

Proceeding together a short distance, when the b'ack stopped before a dilapidated building that had evidently not been used for some time. It was a low, two-story structure, the windows of which were boarded up, and no sign of life was visible from without.

"Come this way," said Scobell, in a low voice,

23

taking Webster by the hand and through a low door, on which he rapped three times.

Webster had scarcely time to give vent to his astonishment by a low whistle, when the door was noiselessly opened. They entered without challenge and found themselves in utter darkness, while Webster could hear the bolts and bars being replaced upon the door. Listening intently, he thought he could hear voices overhead, and a noise as of the shuffling of feet. Presently he heard a shrill whistle from his conductor, which was replied to from above with the query:

" Who comes ?"

" Friends of Uncle Abe !" was the reply.

" What do you desire ?"

" Light and Liberty !" came the response.

Immediately a trap-door overhead was opened, revealing a dimly-lighted room, and a rope-ladder was let down before them.

" Mister Webster, you go up first," said Scobell, " and I will follow you."

Webster took hold of the ropes and, ascending easily, found himself in a dimly lighted room and surrounded by a body of negroes, numbering about forty. Some of them were young men who had barely attained their majority, while others were middle-aged, with a goodly number whose heads were as white as snow. The room in which they were assembled was quite large and entirely destitute of furniture. An upturned barrel, with an American flag draped over it, served as the desk of the President, and his seat was made of a box, which had once been used in packing merchandise for shipment.

It was not long before Webster realized that he was in a lodge of "the Loyal League," composed almost exclusively of colored men, and whose branches extended over the entire South. The trap-door being closed behind them, Webster was introduced to the assembly by John Scobell, who had already identified himself with the institution. His welcome was most cordial and hearty. Shortly after they had become quiet, the President, a tall, well-formed negro, about thirty-five years of age, took his position, and in a deep, full voice, addressed the meeting. He detailed the operations of the various lodges which he had visited, and gave an encouraging account of the good work that was being done by the colored men throughout the country. He was listened to intently, and when he had finished he was greeted with numerous remarks of approval and indorsement.

Scobell had meanwhile disclosed the nature and objects of the "Loyal League." Although as yet prevented from taking up arms in defense of their rights, these colored men had banded themselves together to further the cause of freedom, to succor the escaping slave, and to furnish information to loyal commanders of the movements of the rebels, as far as they could be ascertained.

The President of the League, Scobell said, was about undertaking a trip to Washington, and he was the person who had been selected to carry the packet to me. Webster conversed with him for some time after he had spoken, and finding him reliable and willing to undertake the task about to be imposed upon him, he signified his willingness to trust him with the delivery of the dispatches. Writing a hasty description of the manner in which they had been obtained, he safely sewed the package and his letter in the lining of the messenger's coat, and fully instructed him as to how the papers should be delivered.

Webster was called upon before the meeting adjourned, and he replied in a few words of encouragement and compliment, which elicited the most sincere tokens of appreciation from his sable auditors.

After thanking the colored men for their kindness to him, Webster and Scobell descended from the improvised lodge-room, and Webster made his way back to the hotel, feeling quite relieved as to the safety of the dispatches, and fully confident that they would reach their destination in safety. He shortly afterwards retired to rest, fully satisfied with the day's work, and slept soundly until morning.

The trusty messenger arrived in Washington in due time, and I received from his hands the papers intrusted to him. They were of a highly important nature, and conveyed information to the rebel authorities which would have been very dangerous had they reached their legitimate destination. As it was, through Webster's sagacity, Scobell's physical power, and the exertions of the President of the "Loyal League," the traitor surgeon was prevented from assisting the cause of treason and rebellion, and as a bearer of dispatches, his first venture was far from being successful.

A HOT CHASE.

CHAPTER XXIII.

A Negro Spy.—Passage on a Steam Packet.—Lyrical Melodies.—Scobell Deserts the Ship.—His Tramps Through Rebeldom.

THE next afternoon, Webster and Doctor Gurley started for their point of debarkation. The medical deserter was exceedingly downcast about the loss of valuable papers, although he had entirely recovered from the physical effects of his attack. He indulged in curses, loud and deep, upon the perpetrator of the theft, and speculated with grave seriousness as to the effect of their loss. Webster, who felt that he could be liberal in dealing out his sympathy, was profuse in his expressions of regret and condolence, though I am afraid, that an observer who was acquainted with the facts of the case, would have detected a sly twinkle of merriment in his eyes, that belied his words. They were driven to a farmhouse, situated on a little creek that ran in from the bay, where they were met by a man named James Gough, to whom Webster had a letter of introduction from Mr. Miller at the hotel. After reading the letter, Mr. Gough invited the travelers to enter, and informed them that the boat would attempt to cross the bay that night, if the weather would permit. After partaking of a bountiful supper, the party repaired to the landing, and although there were indications of a storm, the captain, who was in waiting, determined to make an effort to get across. A large amount of merchandise had already been placed on board, and soon after the arrival of Webster and the Doctor, who were to be the only passengers, they put off. Their trip was made in safety, and by midnight they reached the Virginia side. Here they went to the house of a Mr. Woodward, who was a partner with Mr. Gough, in shipping goods into the rebel country, and who took charge of the cargo that came over with our travelers in the boat.

Remaining at the house of Mr. Woodward during the night, on the following morning they went to Tappahannock, where they boarded a packet for Fredericksburg. Here they met a Colonel Prickett, who was an old acquaintance of Doctor Gurley, and from the general conversation that ensued, Webster obtained material information of the location of the rebel forces. That evening they proceeded to Richmond, and Webster, parting with his traveling companion, set about delivering some letters which he had brought with him. Finding that several of his friends, from whom he had hoped to receive information, were absent from the city, and that it would be impossible to do much good service, he resolved to return to Washington. He went to the office of the

Secretary of War, and, obtaining a pass to Norfolk, he returned by that route, taking notes by the wayside, and arrived in Washington in due time.

John Scobell remained in Leonardstown a few days after Webster's departure, mingling with the colored people of that locality, and posting himself upon several points that would be of benefit to him further on. The desire for freedom, and the expectation that the result of the war would determine that question, had now become universal among the colored men of the South. Although as yet debarred from taking up arms in defense of their rights, their efforts in behalf of the Northern troops were freely given when opportunity offered, and consequently, Scobell made hosts of friends among the black-skinned people, who advised him cheerfully and were profuse in their offers of assistance.

During the time that he remained in Leonardstown Scobell made his home with an old negro who was an active member of the League, and who had conceived a wonderful friendship for my bright and intelligent colored operative. Uncle Turner, as he was called, was a genuine Virginia darky, who, having been reared as a house servant, had been enabled to acquire more than the average amount of intelligence, and obtaining his freedom, had settled himself in Leonardstown, where he obtained a livelihood by performing a variety of duties for the people in the town. Here, with his aged wife, a fat, good-natured negress, he lived in comparative comfort, and a more thorough abolitionist never existed than was Uncle Turner.

Through this old negro, Scobell had made arrangements with a young colored man to set him across the river in a skiff, and after spending the day among his new-found friends, and amply provided with a substantial lunch from Aunt Judy, Scobell made his way to the river bank, where he found his man waiting for him, carefully concealed among some bushes that grew along the shore.

After remunerating the boatman, and bidding him a hearty farewell, Scobell started up the river. His first plan was to walk as far as Dumfries, and from that point commence his operations among the rebel camps, but after reflection, he concluded to make his way to the Rappahannock, and endeavor to work his way on one of the river boats as far as Fredericksburg, which would save him a walk of some fifty miles and materially expedite his journey. He accordingly set out for the river and, walking briskly, he found himself about noon at Leestown, a small landing-place on the Rappahannock. Feeling somewhat fatigued by his long tramp, he remained over night, and early on the following morning repaired to the wharf, where he was in hopes of finding a boat on which he could secure his passage. He had not long to wait, for shortly after his arrival the packet boat "Virginia" steamed up to the landing, and soon the men were engaged in putting on board a quantity of miscellaneous freight, that was destined for Fredericksburg. Finding that there was plenty of work to do, Scobell stepped quickly on board and seeking the captain politely asked permission to work his passage. The Captain, who was a kind and genial man at heart, although he carefully veiled these characteristics under a rough exterior, and a bluff and impetuous demeanor, listened to the request, and being in want of some extra help, turned to Scobell and said :

"You black rascal, what do you want at Fredericksburg? Come now, no lies, or I'll throw you into the river !"

" I done tell no lies, Massa Cap'n," replied Scobell, with a broad grin overspreading his face, "but I've bin back in de kentry to see some ob my folks dar, and I dun got no money fur ter git back."

"So you want me to take you to Fredericksburg, do you ?" ejaculated the Captain, good-naturedly. "Well, go below and tell the cook to put you to work !"

Scobell was about to express his thanks, when the Captain blurted out :

"Clear out, d—n you ! I've no time for talk now."

Scobell hurried below, and seeking out the cook was soon busily engaged at work ; before he had been very long employed he made a friend of his sable instructor, and was as merry as a cricket. The run to Fredericksburg was about twelve hours, but ow-

ing to shoal water they were obliged to stop at
Coulter's Wharf to wait for the rising of the tide. In
the evening the negro hands gathered on the deck
around the smoke-stack, and with the stars twinkling
overhead, they made the shores ring with their mirth-
ful melodies. Among the party was an old negro,
who had spent almost his entire life upon the river,
and who was an excellent performer on the banjo,
and he accompanied the singers with his instrument.
" Nelly Gray," " Bob Ridley," " Way down upon de
Swanee River," and a host of the most popular songs
of the day were rendered in a style that elicited the
heartiest applause from the delighted passengers.
The climax of enjoyment was reached, however,
when my Scobell, in his splendid baritone, and accompanied by the old negro and his banjo, sang that
sweet old Scottish ballad :

> " Maxwelton's braes are bonny,
> Where early fa's the dew."

The applause which greeted him upon its conclusion was most hearty and enthusiastic, and when he
gave them

> " A man's a man for a' that,"

the passengers crowded around him and began to
ply him with eager questions as to his knowledge of
the music of the beloved bard of Scotia. The idea of
a darky singing Scotch ballads, and with such true

emotional pathos and sweetness, was such a novelty to them that all were anxious to learn where he had heard them. Scobell briefly and modestly informed them that he had been raised by a gentleman who was a native of Scotland, who was himself a good singer, and that his master had taught him the music he loved so well. The Captain, who was also a Scotchman, and who had listened to the melodies with the tears trickling over his rubicund nose, now stepped forward and said heartily :

" Look here, young fellow, I need an extra man on this boat, and I'll give you forty dollars a month to work for me. The work is light—now what do you say ?"

Here was a dilemma entirely unexpected. Scobell had not only sung himself into the good graces of the passengers, but of the rough old Captain also. It was plain that this offer came from the very heart of the old salt, who was as deeply touched by the melodies as was any one else, and he wanted to secure Scobell's services as much for the songs he could sing as for the work he could do.

Scobell bowed his thanks to the Captain, and said :

" I'm werry much obliged to yer Cap'n ; I'se bin lookin' fur a job ebber since I left ole Mississippi, an' I'll do my best to please you, sure."

" All right,' replied the Captain. " It's time to turn in now, so go below and tell the mate to take your time ; your pay will commence from to-day."

"*The work isn't hard. Now, what do you say.*"

P. 354.

All hands went below, where Scobell duly reported to the mate, a bunk was assigned to him and he was made one of the crew of the steam-packet "Virginia." This was a rather different turn of affairs than he had expected, but he had done the best he could under the circumstances, and regretting that he was compelled to deceive the honest old Captain, he turned in for the night and slept soundly.

When he awoke the next morning, the boat was in motion, and he knew that he was on his way to Fredericksburg. How to get away was the next question to be decided, but he resolved to await the operation of events and adopt any chance that afforded for getting away. In due time the boat landed at her destination and soon all was bustle and confusion in discharging the freight. Scobell assisted manfully in landing the cargo, and earned the encomiums of the Captain for his diligent labor. Learning that the boat would not start on her return trip until the next morning, he requested permission to go on shore until they were prepared to start. This was readily granted by the unsuspecting and really good-natured Captain, who also gave him a small sum of money to defray his expenses, and cautioned him to report on time or the boat would start without him. Scobell promised to be punctual, and then took his leave.

It is not necessary to state that the "Virginia" on her down trip went without the ballad-singing negro, for by the time she was ready to put off, he was on his way to Dumfries and the Accoquan.

Carefully noting everything that came in his way he traveled through Dumfries, Accoquan, Manassas and Centreville, and after spending nearly ten days in these localities he finally made his way to Leesburg, and thence down the Potomac to Washington. His experiences on this trip were quite numerous and varied, and only a lack of space prevents their narration. Sometimes, as a vender of delicacies through the camps, a laborer on the earthworks at Manassas, or a cook at Centreville, he made his way uninterruptedly until he obtained the desired information and successfully accomplished the object of his mission.

His return to Washington was accomplished in safety and his full and concise report fully justified me in the selection I had made of a good, reliable and intelligent operative.

CHAPTER XXIV.

A Perilous Ride.—A Suspicious Peddler.—Uncle Gallus Again.—Scobell Investigating.—Doubts and Suspicions.

IT was on a beautiful morning in the early part of the month of April, 1862, when a lady, mounted upon a handsome and spirited black horse, and accompanied by a young and intelligent-looking negro, also excellently mounted, rode out of the city of Richmond, apparently for the purpose of enjoying a morning ride. Provided with the necessary passports, they experienced no difficulty in passing the guards, and after a short ride found themselves in the open country beyond the city.

The lady was young, handsome and apparently about twenty-five years of age. Her complexion was fresh and rosy as the morning, her hair fell in flowing tresses of gold, while her eyes, which were of a clear and deep blue, were quick and searching in their glances. She appeared careless and entirely at ease, but a close observer would have noticed a compression of the small lips, and a fixedness in the sparkling eyes that told of a purpose to be accomplished, and that her present journey was not wholly one of pleasure.

After leaving the city the colored attendant spurred to her side, and then, putting spurs to their horses, they broke into a swift canter. Their road lay along the river bank, which here led in a southeasterly direction. Turning to the negro at her side, the lady remarked:

"Now, John, we have a ride of ten miles before us, and we must be at Glendale as early as possible."

"All right, missus," rejoined her sable companion, "dese hosses will take us through in good shape, I know."

They followed the course of the stream, whose waters glistened in the rays of the morning's sun like polished silver. On either side the road was fringed with a growth of cottonwood trees, that cast a grateful shade along their path, while the cool breezes of the rippling river rendered their ride a most delightful one indeed. But as they sped along the most casual observer would have noticed from the expression of their faces that their ride was being undertaken for other purposes than pleasure.

The riders pressed on, scarcely slackening their speed until in the near distance could be seen the tall spire of the single church in the pleasant little village of Glendale. They now drew rein and brought their smoking steeds to a slow walk, and riding leisurely onward, they stopped before a neat little inn located on the outskirts of the town.

An old, white-headed negro took their horses and

led them away, while the landlady, a neat and tidy-looking matron, wearing widow's weeds, met the lady at the door, and cordially welcomed her into the house.

"Here, Jennie," she called to her daughter, a trim little girl of twelve years, "show this lady to her room."

Following the little girl, the lady was conducted into a cool and pleasant little parlor, with windows opening upon the garden, and through which came the fragrant breath of roses in full bloom.

Scobell accompanied the old man with the horses into the stable-yard, where he assisted in caring for the heated animals.

"I dun spose you's on de way to Yu'ktown?" queried the old darky, who was rubbing vigorously away upon the limbs of the glossy black horse. After waiting a short time, and hearing no response, he added:

"What'd you say? dis yer hoss is fidgettin' aroun' so I didn't har you."

"I didn't say anything," responded his companion good-naturedly, but in a tone that plainly indicated his intention not to submit himself to the pumping process at the hands of his garrulous friend.

"I tought you hearn what I dun axed you," replied the old man, a little taken aback by the cool demeanor of his new acquaintance.

Scobell, however, industriously worked away at his own horse and said nothing.

24

' Well," said the old darky after another pause, and apparently communing with himself—"it am a fac' dat now an den you meets people dat ain't got de cibbleness to answer a question—nor de grit to tell a feller 'tain't nun o' his business ; but dey jes let on like dey didn't har wat you sed—wen all de time dey kin har jes as well as I kin."

Still there was no satisfactory response, and at last the old man blurted out again :

" Now I dun spec' it am nun ob Uncle Gallus's bizness were dese folks am a goin', but Jemima ! I didn't tink it any harm to ax. Folks dat knows Uncle Gallus aint afeared tu tell him nuffin, coz dey knows he dun got a mitey close head when it am needcessary."

The old man was none other than the veritable old Uncle Gallus, whose experience in the South seemed to be very different from the easy life he had led as the house servant of Mrs. Morton. How he came into this position I am unable to say, but here he was, and the same smile of good-nature irradiated his face, as when his way of life was pleasant, and his duties lighter. Perhaps, it would be as well to state here, that the two persons already mentioned were Mrs. Carrie Lawton, a female operative on my force, and John Scobell, who has figured before in these pages. These two persons had been for a time employed in Richmond, and were now endeavoring to effect their journey North.

After finishing the last remark, Uncle Gallus straightened himself up and stood erect, with the air of a man who had been unjustly injured, and who was disposed to vindicate himself now and there.

" I tell you, uncle," finally replied Scobell, "there are times when one must be careful what you say, and who you say it to."

" Dat am a fac' !" ejaculated the old man.

" Now, if I knowed you was all right," Scobell continued, " I might talk, but 'tain't smart to tell your business to strangers."

" Dat am a fac', young man," observed Uncle Gallus, shaking his head with a knowing look ; " but den I spose you's a friend to Uncle Abe, ain't you now ?" he queried.

"And if I am," said Scobell, "what do you want ?"

" Light and Liberty," replied the old man impressively, "and fo' de L'ud I b'lieve de day am nigh when it am a comin'."

At these words, Scobell stepped forward and said in a low voice :

"Do you belong to the League ?"

" I does," answered Uncle Gallus ; " I dun jined it in dis berry place."

" How often do you meet ?" inquired Scobell.

"We meets ebery two weeks, down at Uncle Dicky Bassett's—he libs on de bluff ob de ribber 'bout a mile furder down de road to'rds Wilson's Landin'."

"How far is it to Wilson's landing?" asked Scobell, who, finding that Uncle Gallus was a member of the League, was now no longer loth to talk with him.

"A little grain de rise ob twenty mile," replied the old man.

"About sundown, then," said Scobell, "these horses must be saddled and ready for the missus and me, for we must be at the landing before midnight."

"All right," rejoined Uncle Gallus, "dey'll be ready when yu want 'em."

"See heah now, is yure name John?" suddenly asked the old man, as if an idea had just occurred to him.

"Yes, that's what they call me."

"An' you cum frum Richmun' dis mo'nin?"

Scobell nodded.

"An' dat young leddy am gwine to meet some-body, mebbe her husband, at de landin'?"

"Yes," said Scobell; "but how do you know these things? Has anybody been here to see you?"

"Yah! Yah!" chuckled the old man. "I dun tole you dat folks as knowed Uncle Gallus dun often come ter see him. I dun knowed you all de time, when you fust come—in fac', I was 'spectin' you and de missus all de mawnin'."

"Was the landlady looking for us too?" inquired Scobell.

"She knowed you was a comin'," replied Uncle Gallus; "dah was a gem'man heah las' night, as talked about you to her, an' lef' a note fur de lady."

"Is the landlady all right?" asked Scobell.

"True to de core," affirmed Uncle Gallus emphatically; "more'n one poor feller as 'scaped from Richmun' hes foun' a good bed an' supper at de 'Glen House.'"

"Well," said my operative, "you can finish your work here; I have an errand or two for the missus, and I must go and attend to them before dinner."

So saying, he started for the house, leaving Uncle Gallus to water and feed the horses, which had now sufficiently cooled, and were enjoying their needed rest.

Scobell's errand was simply to take a stroll about the village in order to ascertain whether there was any indication of their having been followed by anyone from Richmond. He strolled about the village, noting carefully every one whom he met, and, feeling comparatively secure, started to return to the hotel.

Turning the corner of a street he came suddenly face to face with a peddler, who addressed him in a rich Irish brogue and inquired the way to the tavern. Scobell gave him the required information and stood watching the fellow as he ambled off in the direction indicated. There was something in the appearance of this man that attracted the attention and excited the suspicions of my observant operative. He resolved to keep an eye upon his movements and endeavor to discover, if possible, whether the man was a genuine peddler, or a spy, who had adopted that disguise to conceal his true character.

In the few words that passed between them Scobell had noticed that while the man's hair was a fiery red his eyebrows and lashes appeared of a dark brown color, and his face was altogether of too florid a hue to be natural. These observations were sufficient to put Scobell upon the alert at once, and convinced him that the man was not what he appeared to be.

Following slowly he watched him until he reached the hotel and entered the bar-room, where, laying aside his pack, he ordered his dinner. Scobell entered the room immediately behind him, and passing through it, he made his way to the kitchen, where the landlady was superintending the preparations for a most savory dinner. Calling her aside, he informed her of the peddler's arrival and of his suspicions regarding him, cautioning her to convey the news to his missus before they met at the table.

In a few minutes dinner was announced, and the boarders, to the number of fifteen, including Mrs. Lawton and the peddler, with the landlady at the head, gathered around the long table in the low, old-fashioned dining-room. The lively clatter of the knives and forks soon attested the vigor with which they attacked the viands set before them. The peddler ate his meal in silence, undisturbed by the general conversation going on around him, and Mrs. Lawton noticed that he was keenly watching her whenever an opportunity occurred to do so, as he thought, unobserved. She, however, affected entire unconsciousness of the scrutiny she was subjected to, and kept up an animated conversation with the landlady upon various trivial topics until the meal was finished.

Scobell, who temporarily acted as an attendant at the table, lost no opportunity to carefully watch the movements of the peddler, and his searching glances, directed towards Mrs. Lawton, fully convinced him that his previous suspicions were well founded.

Mrs. Lawton returned to her room, not a little disturbed at the peddler's strange behavior, and having no doubt that the stranger was a spy, she determined to discover if she was the object of his visit, or whether his appearance bore any relation to her presence at the hotel. She accordingly sent for Scobell, and together they decided that he should carefully watch the movements of the peddler, and if nothing of a suspicious nature transpired, they would renew their journey after nightfall.

Scobell immediately left the room, and as he entered the bar-room he noticed that the peddler was settling his score, preparatory to taking his departure. He remarked to the landlady, with the same rich brogue which Scobell had observed, that business was dull, and that he would have to walk to Richmond.

"All right, my fine fellow," muttered my operative, "we'll see whether you are going to Richmond or not."

The peddler lighted a short-stemmed clay pipe, and swinging his pack over his shoulder, set off at a rapid pace on the road to Richmond.

Scobell hastened to the stable and, procuring a pole and line that he had observed there in the morning, started off in the direction which the peddler had taken, but taking a shorter cut to the river, which would enable him to reach the road about a mile below the village and in advance of the peddler. Sauntering along until he had gained the shelter of a belt of timber to his left, he then increased his pace until he was almost abreast of the peddler, though entirely concealed from view. He was now satisfied that with a little effort he could keep his man in sight, and he concluded not to pass him, as he had at first intended, but to follow him until he saw him on his way to the rebel capital.

When they were about three miles from the village, the peddler suddenly left the road and turned into the woods, leading directly to the banks of the river, which at this point were remarkably high and steep. This movement was entirely unexpected by my operative, and his only recourse was to drop hastily behind a tree to prevent being seen. He was not discovered, however, although the peddler, after entering the timber, gazed carefully around him, as if to see whether he was being followed. Apparently satisfied with his survey he resumed his walk, in happy ignorance of the fact that a pair of gleaming eyes were not far distant, noting his every movement.

Waiting until he had gone a sufficient distance to render it safe, Scobell rose slowly from the ground and stealthily followed his footsteps until the peddler paused at the edge of the bluff, which ran down into the river. Here he tightened the strap of his pack, and after another hasty glance behind him, he began the descent of the bluff, with the aid of the stout stick which he carried with him. The bank was almost perpendicular, and was covered with a heavy undergrowth of young timber and brush, which made the journey rather a hazardous undertaking.

" Wonder if he's going to swim to Richmond with that pack on his shoulders," said Scobell to himself, as he wonderingly watched these strange movements of the peddler.

Fully determined to see the end of this mysterious maneuver, but recognizing the necessity of exercising the utmost caution in his advance, Scobell slowly and noiselessly made his way to the spot where the peddler had vanished as completely from his view as if he had sunk into the bowels of the earth.

Advancing to within a few feet of the edge of the bluff, he threw himself upon his hands and knees, and drew himself forward until he could overlook the steep descent. He could see nothing of the peddler, however, for the dense growth of bushes completely obstructed his view, but he could readily discern the marks of footprints in the soft soil, which had been made by him in his descent to the bottom.

Here was a dilemma. He had lost his man, and he dared not follow directly after him, as the peddler might be lying in ambush, and an encounter might be fatal. After a few moments' consideration, he concluded to walk along the bluff a short distance and endeavor to find another path by which he might descend, and thus avoid the peddler, if he was waiting to surprise him. About a hundred yards further on he came upon a well-beaten path, and here he began his descent. Everything was as quiet as the grave around him, and he reached the base of the cliff in safety, but without seeing anything of the man he was after. Passing up along the lane by the river a short distance, he discovered a narrow path leading in the direction which the peddler had taken, and showing the mark of recent footprints. Passing cautiously along this path a short distance, he saw that the high bluffs were gradually giving to more level banks, and that a little further on the stream made a sharp detour to the right, and swept out into the open and level country.

In the bend of the river, and on the same side, he noticed a small cabin, half hidden by a clump of trees. Surmising that the peddler had entered this cabin, he resolved to hide himself and watch for a few minutes, hoping that the man would soon make his appearance. He had scarcely taken a position where he could unobservedly note all that was going on, when a man, whom he at once recognized as the peddler, made his appearance at the door, and stood anxiously gazing around, as though expecting some one. He still maintained his disguise, and appeared to be alone. Returning into the cabin, and after a few minutes, to the surprise of Scobell, another individual made his appearance. This new-comer, while about the same size as the peddler, was a very different-looking person indeed, for instead of the red hair and florid complexion, he noticed that this man had a closely-cropped head of black hair, while his complexion was dark and swarthy.

"So there's a pair of you!" thought Scobell.

The fellow, after apparently satisfying himself that the coast was clear, proceeded to a small stable that stood in the rear of the cabin, and almost on the edge of the river bank. Scobell thought he heard the faint whinny of a horse, and shortly afterwards the man, mounted on a dark iron-gray horse, appeared, and made his way over the hill and out into the direction of the river road.

It instantly flashed across Scobell's mind that this

man was no other than his peddler, and without hesitation he approached the cabin and knocked loudly at the door. There was no response, and after a moment's hesitation he lifted the latch and entered. As he had conjectured, the cabin was empty.

" GOOD-MORNING."

CHAPTER XXV.

The Journey Resumed.—A Midnight Pursuit.—A Brave Woman.—A Deadly Encounter.—Scobell Defends Himself.—Death of a Rebel Spy.

WHILE these events were occurring, General McClellan was advancing up the Peninsula towards Richmond. Yorktown had surrendered, the battle of Williamsburg had been fought, and the army was advancing to the Chickahominy.

Mrs. Lawton and John Scobell had been for some weeks in Richmond, during which time they had obtained much important information, Mrs. Lawton taking the role of a Southern lady from Corinth, Mississippi, and Scobell acting as her servant. Having determined to leave Richmond, they were on their way to join the Union forces, which, under General McClellan, had their headquarters on the Chickahominy at a point about ten miles from Wilson's Landing. Here, according to previous arrangement, they were to meet Mr. Lawton, who was also one of my operatives, and from that point were to proceed to the Union camp.

The landlady of the Glen House was a stanch friend to the Federals, and had on more than one occasion rendered valuable service to my operatives,

especially to Hugh Lawton. It was therefore at
his suggestion that his wife and Scobell adopted the
plan they did to leave Richmond and to reach our
lines. As Uncle Gallus had stated, a man had stopped at the tavern the night before and had informed
Mrs. Braxton, the landlady, that these parties would
take that route from Richmond—and had left a note
to be delivered to Mrs. Lawton, which contained instructions of her future line of travel.

The trip from Glendale was one attended with
great risk, as the country, on that side of the river,
was filled with the scouts of both armies, and if captured by the rebel scouts or pickets, the chances were
that detection would be followed by serious consequences. Among my female operatives, however,
none were clearer-headed or more resolute than Mrs.
Lawton, who prior to this time had been a most efficient worker and had been remarkably successful on
her trips into the lines of the enemy. In each case
she had escaped with rare good fortune.

When Scobell entered the structure which the
stranger had left, he found that it comprised but a
single room, and immediately proceeded to make a
thorough examination of its interior. A small fire-
place on one side, which showed no signs of having
been recently used, and a number of benches, were
scattered about, In the corner of the room he saw
the pack and several articles that had been worn by
the peddler, which left no further room for doubt in

his mind as to the character of the individual he had been watching for so long a time.

He accordingly set out for Glendale, where he arrived just as the sun was sinking behind the western horizon. He narrated the particulars of his chase to Mrs. Lawton, whow as convinced that the peddler was a rebel spy; but the question was—Was he upon their track? Did he suspect them? and if so, by what means had he discovered who they were and what their destination was?

Without attempting to settle these questions, however, they concluded to set out at once for the landing. The horses were brought to the door by Uncle Gallus, who was closely questioned as to whether a horseman answering the description given by Scobell had passed through the village that afternoon, did not remember having seen such a person. Believing that possibly the man might really have gone on to Richmond they concluded to start that night and hazard the consequences.

Both of them were well armed and were therefore fully prepared to defend themselves, unless attacked by numbers. They rode swiftly along at the free and sweeping gallop for which the southern saddle-horses are so famous, and feeling quite secure, they conversed pleasantly together on their way.

"I guess we will get through all right, notwithstanding our fears to the contrary," said Mrs. Lawton.

"I dunno about that," replied Scobell; "we're not through with our journey yet, and there's plenty of time for trouble yet. Perhaps we had better walk the horses a spell."

"That is a good suggestion," assented Mrs. Lawton, "we will walk them a mile or two, and then we will be enabled to go the faster."

"I tell you, missus," said Scobell, "I wish we was at the landin'; somehow I feel that there is yet danger ahead."

"What makes you think so?" inquired Mrs. Lawton.

"Well, I am afraid that confounded peddler will turn up before we get through."

"Why, I can manage him myself," laughed Mrs. Lawton, "and if that is all you fear, we are perfectly safe."

"Now you're pokin fun at me, missus; but you'll find that I can fight if I get the chance, and I was thinking more of you than of myself."

"Well, there's an old saying, John, don't cross a bridge until you reach it; so we won't borrow trouble until it comes."

Their journey now lay through a richly cultivated district; on either side were fine farms, whose growing crops had not yet been touched by the ravages of war, and the country, under the soft light of the moon presented a scene of rare beauty. Away to the left ran the river, now bathed in a flood of silvery light, which, emerging from a belt of woods, pursued its winding way until again lost to view in the woods that were sharply outlined at a distance. To their right the country was broken and hilly, and the landscape presented a rugged and picturesque appearance in marked contrast to the evidences of cultivation upon the other side. The night was soft and balmy, and the silence was only broken by the sound of the horses' hoofs as they slowly trotted along. It seemed difficult to believe that war was abroad in the land, and that even now, while in the enjoyment of apparent safety, danger was lurking on every hand.

Their horses being now sufficiently rested, they again pressed forward at a rapid pace until they were about five miles from the landing which was their point of destination. There Mrs. Lawton's husband was to meet her and the balance of the journey, to the Union camp would be free from danger, as the Federal pickets were posted across the river.

They were now approaching a patch of timber, through which they would be compelled to pass, and an instinctive feeling of dread came over both of them as they drew near to it. The trees grew close together, shutting out the light of the moon, and rendering the road extremely dark and gloomy.

"Just the place for an ambuscade," said Mrs. Lawton shiveringly; "draw your pistols, John, and be ready in case of attack."

Scobell silently did as he was directed, and riding

25

close together, they entered the wood. The darkness was so great, that they could distinguish objects but a short distance ahead of them. They passed safely through the wood, however, and as they emerged from the darkness, they congratulated themselves upon their good fortune, and began to think that they were unduly alarming themselves.

Their comforting reflections were of short duration, however, for scarcely had they left the wood, than they perceived four horsemen approaching them at a swift gallop. What to do now was a question to be decided promptly. To turn and retreat would certainly insure their capture, as the woods were just behind, and they were afraid to travel through them on a run—so they resolved to bravely continue their way, and trust to chance for their safe deliverance, should the new-comers prove to be foes.

A few hurried words were exchanged between them, as they arranged that each should select a man and fire on the instant they were challenged, and then they were to dash ahead, hoping by this bold and unexpected move to disconcert their assailants by killing or disabling two of their number, and thus effect their escape.

As the advancing party came closer, they divided, two going on each side of the road, leaving a space between them for our travelers to pass through. They were now close enough for my operatives to discover that two of them wore the uniform of Confederate gray, with heavy sabres at their sides, while the others were apparently in citizens' clothes.

Scobell, who had been intently regarding them, now exclaimed :

"'Fore God, missus, that one on your side is the peddler !"

He had scarcely uttered these words, when one of the men called out :

" Halt, and throw up your hands !"

They were now nearly face to face with each other, and in a flash two sharp reports rang out on the still night air, and two of the men reeled and fell from their saddles.

" At 'em !" hissed Scobell, through his clenched teeth, as he plunged the spurs into his steed. The two animals sprang forward, like arrows from the string, and in a moment they had dashed past the others, who seemed dazed at the suddenness of their actions, and before they recovered themselves, my operatives were speeding like the wind some distance away.

" Lay low to your saddle !" cried Scobell to his companion, "and turn your horse as far to the side of the road as you can," at the same time turning his own animal close to the fence that ran along the roadside.

His directions were immediately followed by Mrs. Lawton, who retained a wonderful control over herself and the beast she rode.

It was evident that their enemies had not been expecting such a result to their demand, and they sat for a time like statues; then, as if suddenly recollecting themselves, they wheeled their horses, and, discharging their revolvers in rapid succession, started in swift pursuit.

"They'll never get us now," said Scobell, "unless their horses are made of better stuff than I think they are."

The race now became an exciting one; the pursuers having emptied their weapons, without doing any harm to the escaping pair, did not take time to reload, but urged their horses to their utmost speed. They soon discovered that their horses were no match for those of the fugitives, and their curses were loud enough to be heard by both Scobell and his companion, as in spite of all their efforts they found themselves unable to lessen the distance between them.

Scobell several times ventured a look over his shoulder, to note the progress of their pursuers, and on each occasion, finding them still lagging behind, he uttered some encouraging remark to Mrs. Lawton, who was straining every nerve in the attempt to escape.

While indulging in one of these hasty observations, and forgetting for a moment the management of his horse, the animal suddenly swerved from the road, as if frightened at some object in advance of

"With a scream of anguish, the one nearest to him threw up his hands and fell heavily to the ground." P. 389.

them, and, stumbling, fell heavily to the ground, throwing Scobell over his head and into the ditch.

Scrambling quickly to his feet, the negro shouted to his companion :

" Go ahead, don't mind me ; save yourself !"

He then turned his attention to his horse, which had now recovered his feet, and stood panting and trembling in every nerve both from fright and excessive exertion. Listening intently, he could hear the clatter of hoofs of the horse rode by Mrs. Lawton, in the distance, while coming closer every instant was the noise of the approaching horsemen. They had discovered his misfortune, and were now shouting and yelling with triumph at the possibility of capturing at least one of the party. There was no time for mounting, even if his horse was unhurt, and Scobell determined to make a bold stand and sell his life dearly, while he would assuredly prevent the capture of Mrs. Lawton.

Leading his horse to the side of the road, he placed himself behind him, and resting his trusty weapon across the saddle, he awaited the coming of the approaching horsemen. He calmly waited until the two men were within a few yards of him, and then, taking as good aim as the light of the moon enabled him to do, he fired. The horseman nearest him uttered a scream of anguish, and, throwing up both hands, toppled from the saddle and fell upon the ground, while his frightened horse, with a snort of

terror, wheeled around and dashed off in the direction
from whence he had come.

The remaining man stopped his horse with a jerk
that drew him back upon his haunches, and then,
turning swiftly around, set off in the opposite
direction, while the bullets from Scobell's weapon
whistled in dangerously close proximity to his
ears.

Scobell, seeing that three of the pursuers were
either dead or badly wounded, proceeded to reload his weapon, and was preparing to remount his
horse and follow after Mrs. Lawton, when he heard
the tramp of horses' feet coming from the direction in
which she had gone.   From the noise they made, he
was convinced that the approaching party numbered
at least a score, and that they were riding at a
sweeping gallop.   A bend in the road, however, hid
them from his view, and he was unable to determine
whether they were friends or foes.   In an instant
later they swept into full sight, and, to his intense
relief, he discovered that they were Union cavalry-
men, and that Mrs. Lawton and her husband were at
their head.

" Hello, John !" exclaimed Lawton, as they came
up, " are you hurt ?"

" No," replied Scobell.

"What has become of your assailants ?"

" Two of them we left a mile or two back, one is
lying there in the road and the other, so far as I

know, is making tracks for Richmond," answered Scobell.

"You are a brave fellow, Scobell," said the Captain of the squad, coming forward. "You were lucky in escaping their bullets, and still more so that you didn't break your neck when your horse fell with you, at the speed you were going."

"He fell on his head, I reckon," ventured one of the soldiers, waggishly, "which accounts for his not being hurt."

"That's so," replied Scobell, in all serious-ness, "I landed right square on my head in that ditch."

A roar of laughter followed this remark, and Scobell added, good-naturedly:

"It might have killed one of you fellows, but it didn't even give me the headache. I am glad, though, it wasn't the missus' horse, or things might have turned out different."

The Captain now cut short the conversation by ordering four of the party to pursue the flying rebel, and, if possible, effect his capture, while the rest proceeded to hunt up those that had been injured. The man whom Scobell had shot last was soon found; he was dead, the ball having entered his skull. Riding back to the spot where the first encounter took place, they discovered the dead body of the peddler, or spy, who had met his doom from the bullet of Mrs. Lawton, while his companion, with a shattered arm, was sitting up, and nearly faint from loss of blood, and suffering intense pain.

Having captured two of the horses ridden by the party, and bandaging the shattered arm as well as they were able, the wounded man was placed on one of the animals and under an escort they were conveyed to the Union lines.

Two shallow graves were hastily dug, and in them were placed the bodies of the two dead men. The party sent after the escaped soldier soon returned, reporting that he had obtained too much the start of them to be overtaken, and they were compelled to give up the chase.

The entire party then returned to the Landing, and in the morning my operatives were put across the river, where they reported in due time at headquarters, where they detailed fully the information which they had gleaned in the rebel capital.

It was subsequently learned that the peddler was a rebel spy, and for some time past had been visiting the Union camps gathering information, which he had no doubt conveyed to the rebels. On his person were found papers which fully confirmed this, and that they failed to reach their destination on account of his death, was a fortunate occurrence for the Union cause.

How he had discovered the character of my operatives is a mystery yet unsolved, as his wounded companion, when examined the next day, stated that he had met him that night for the first time, and had at his request accompanied him in the trip which had ended so disastrously. He further stated that his party belonged to a band of independent scouts, which had but lately been attached to Lee's Army, and were assigned to Gen. Stuart's Cavalry. Mr. and Mrs. Lawton and Scobell soon afterwards returned to Washington, where they were allowed to rest themselves for a time before being again called upon.

A DEAD SHOT.

CHAPTER XXVI.

A Woman's Discoveries.—An Infernal Machine.—The Shipping in Danger.—Discovery and Destruction of the Submarine Battery.

THE destiny of nations, history tells us, sometimes turns upon the most trivial things. Rome was once saved by the gabbling of a flock of geese, whose cries awoke a sentinel sleeping at his post, just in time to give the alarm and enable the Roman soldiers to successfully repel the attack of an invading foe. A certain exiled and fugitive king took courage from watching a spider build its web, recovered his kingdom, and a crown that had been wrested from him by the misfortune of war. Darius, made King of Persia by the neighing of a horse— and in our own day historians agree, that had it not been for the opportune appearance of the "Monitor" when the rebel iron-clad "Merrimac" steamed out of Hampton Roads in March, 1862, the destruction of the Union might have been an accomplished fact. For had not that formidable battery met her match in the "Yankee cheese-box," as the "Monitor" was derisively called, she might have cleared the water of Union sloops of war, raised the blockade, opened

the way by river to Washington, shelled the national capital and turned the fortunes of war decidedly in favor of the South.

This battle was an important epoch in the history
of nations, and demonstrated to the world the formidable character of iron-clad war vessels, hitherto unknown; and placed the United States on record as
having produced the most invincible navy in the world.

In addition to the "Merrimac," the South, early in
1862, had devised a great many ingenious machines
in the shape of torpedoes and submarine batteries,
that were designed for the purpose of blowing up the
Union vessels that blockaded the Southern ports.

It was through the efforts of one of my operatives
that the existence of one of these submarine batteries
was discovered, and that, too, just in the nick of time
to save the Federal blockading fleet at the mouth of
the James River from probable destruction. It was in
the early part of November, 1861, that I dispatched
one of my lady operatives to Richmond and the
South, for the especial purpose of ascertaining as
much information as possible about these torpedoes
and infernal machines, which I had good reason to
believe were constructed at the rebel capital. The
Tredegar Iron Works, the largest factory of the kind
in the South, were located at this place, and since the
commencement of hostilities had been manufacturing
cannon and all kinds of shot and shell for the Confederacy.

The lady whom I selected for this task was Mrs.
E. H. Baker; she had been in my employ for years,
and at one time had resided in Richmond, although,
prior to the war, she had removed to the North, where
she had since dwelt.

This lady, fortunately enough, was well acquainted
with a Captain Atwater and his family, who resided
in Richmond, and after undertaking the mission, she
wrote to them from Chicago, apparently, stating that
notwithstanding the conflict between the two sections
of the country, she designed to pay a visit to them
and renew the acquaintance of years ago.

She accordingly started, and after a circuitous
journey, arrived in Richmond on the 24th day of the
month. The Captain and his family received her
most hospitably, and requested her to make her
home with them during her stay in that city.

Captain Atwater, although holding a commission
in the rebel army, was at heart a Union man, and
secretly rejoiced at the news of a Federal victory.
He soon expressed his views to my operative so
clearly and forcibly, that she believed, if he could do
so, without jeopardy, he would join the Union troops,
and fight for the cause that really had his heartiest
wishes for success.

While Mrs. Baker did not reveal to him her connection with the secret service of the United States,
she took no pains to conceal from him her real sentiments, and in their confidential conversations, was

quite free in expressing her desire for a speedy Union triumph. The Captain was firm in his belief that the South was wrong, and that the masses had been led into the war by designing and ambitious politicians, and that she must eventually fail. Moreover, he said, that, while born in a slaveholding State, he believed the institution to be wicked and cruel, and that the South should have given up her slaves rather than have gone out of the Union.

Loyal as he was, the Captain understood the Southern people thoroughly, and he felt sure that they would fight long and stubbornly, rather than yield to the blacks the boon of freedom. Many days thus passed in quiet enjoyment and in these stolen discussions upon the important topics of the day. Mrs. Baker found herself very comfortably situated beneath the Captain's hospitable roof, and nearly a week was passed in viewing Richmond and the strange sights it then afforded.

On every hand she saw preparations for war, and at every street she turned, she was confronted with armed soldiers, whose measured tread kept time to the music of fife and drum. In company with the Captain, she also visited the earthworks and fortifications around Richmond, and gained many valuable points of information in regard to their number and extent.

As yet, however, she had been unable to discover anything concerning the special object of her mission, and feeling the necessity of accomplishing something in that direction, she resolved to act. She had now established herself so firmly in the estimation of those with whom she associated, that she believed she could with safety turn her inquiries in the direction that would lead to the knowledge she desired to gain. Accordingly, one evening at the tea-table she remarked, incidentally, that she desired very much to visit the Tredegar Iron Works.

"Why, certainly," replied the Captain; "I will be most happy to go with you to-morrow."

"That will be delightful," said Mrs. Baker, enthusiastically.

"But stay a moment," said the Captain, musingly, "I am afraid I will not be able to go to-morrow, as I have to go down the river to witness a test of a submarine battery."

"Why couldn't I go, too?" demurely asked my operative. "I am sure I should enjoy it very much; that is, if there is no danger connected with it."

"Oh, there is no danger, whatever, and there will, doubtless, be a number of ladies present, and you can go if you wish to."

"I should most certainly wish to," laughingly answered Mrs. Baker.

"Very well," said the Captain; "if you and Mrs. Atwater will be ready by nine o'clock, we will have ample time to reach the place, which is some few miles below the city."

The ladies were both much pleased with this

arrangement, and expressed themselves in extravagant terms of thankfulness for a trip which, no doubt, would be exceedingly pleasant. The Captain then proceeded to explain to them the nature of the battery which was to be experimented with on the morrow. He explained the object to be obtained by this battery, which was to break up the blockading fleet at the mouth of the James River, and thus give the South an outlet to the sea.

The next day they started in a carriage for the scene of the exhibition, which was located about ten miles below the city. Arriving at the appointed spot, they found quite a large number of military men, many of them accompanied by ladies, assembled to witness the testing of the machine, from which so much was expected.

A large scow had been towed into the middle of the river, and the submarine vessel was to approach it and attach a magazine, containing nearly half a bushel of powder, to which was attached several deadly projectiles, and this was to be fired by a peculiarly constructed fuse, connected by a long wire coiled on board the submarine vessel.

At a given signal the boat was sunk into the river, about half a mile below the scow, and shortly afterwards it began to make its way under the water towards it. The only visible sign of its existence was a large float that rested on the surface of the water, and which was connected with the vessel below, designed to supply the men that operated it with air. This float was painted a dark green, to imitate the color of the water, and could only be noticed by the most careful observer. As my operative listened to a full explanation of the machine and its workings, she could scarcely control her emotions of fear for the safety of the Federal boats, in the event of its successful operation, and provided the government was not speedily warned of its existence.

It was learned that this vessel was but a small working model of a much larger one, that was now nearly completed, and would be finished in about two weeks, and would then be taken to the mouth of the James River, to operate on the war vessels guarding that port.

They had obtained an excellent position, where they had a full view of the river, and with the aid of a strong field-glass they could distinctly watch the large " float," which indicated the approach of the vessel.

" How do the men who operate the machine manage to attach the magazine to the vessel they design to destroy?" asked Mrs. Baker.

" Two or three men, who operate the boat," replied the Captain, " are provided with submarine diving armor, which enables them to work under the water and attach the magazine to the ship intended to be blown up. They then have only to quickly move away to a safe distance, fire their fuse, and the work is done."

The Captain also informed her, that the object was to break the blockade and allow the steamers "Patrick Henry" and "Thomas Jefferson" out to sea, these vessels being loaded with cotton and bound for England.

While they were talking, my operative was closely watching, by the aid of her glass, the movements of the boat, and she now noticed that having approached to within a few rods of the scow, it stopped, and the water "float" which indicated its position remained motionless. After remaining in this position for a few minutes, it slowly began to recede from the scow, in the direction from whence it came.

It moved steadily away some hundreds of yards, and Mrs. Baker was wondering at the seemingly long delay, when suddenly, and without any previous warning whatever, there was a terrific explosion, and the scow seemed lifted bodily out of the water and thrown high into the air. Her destruction was complete, and there was no longer any doubt that the submarine battery could be used with deadly and telling effect on the ships constituting the Federal blockading squadron.

Those who witnessed the experiment were, of course, much elated over the efficient work of destruction which had been accomplished, and even Captain Atwater, in his enthusiasm as a soldier, for-

26

got temporarily his real feelings, in his undisguised admiration of the ingenuity of the invention and the effectiveness of its operation.

Mrs. Baker, however, looked on with a heavy heart as she reflected upon the terrible consequences of the workings of this machine, and at once felt the urgent necessity of taking steps to inform me what she had witnessed. Unless something was done in this direction, she felt confident that the Federal ships would be destroyed, the blockade forever ended, and untold disaster would attend the Union cause.

After their return home that evening, she made copious notes of what she had learned and witnessed, which she safely secreted about her person. The next day, in company with the Captain, she visited the Tredegar Iron Works, and inspected the boat that was being built. It was truly a formidable-looking engine of destruction.

The next day, being Sunday, she remained at the residence of the Captain, and on Monday morning, having procured a pass, she bade farewell to her host and his amiable spouse, and left Richmond for Fredericksburg. From thence she made her way to Washington by the way of Leonardstown, and lost no time in reporting to me the success of her trip. She had made a hasty, though quite comprehensive, sketch of the vessel, which sketch is still in my possession, and which showed the position under the surface of the water, and explained its workings.

I immediately laid my information before General McClellan and the Secretary of the Navy, who at once transmitted the intelligence to the commanders of the squadron, instructing them to keep a sharp lookout for the "water-colored surface float," and to drag the water for the purpose of securing possession of the air tubes connecting the float with the vessel below.

Nothing was heard from this for about three weeks, but about that time I was informed that one of the vessels of the blockading fleet off the mouth of the James River had discovered the float, and putting out her drag-rope, had caught the air-tubes and thus effectually disabled the vessel from doing any harm, and no doubt drowning all who were on board of her.

This incident, and the peculiarity of the machine, was duly discussed in the newspapers at that time, who stated that "by a mere accident the Federal fleet off James River had been saved from destruction"—but I knew much better, and that the real credit of the discovery was due to a lady of my own force. The efficient manner in which this work was performed was of great service to the nation, and sustained the reputation of the Secret Service Department, as being an important adjunct in aiding the government in its efforts to suppress the rebellion.

CHAPTER XXVII.

*"Stuttering Dave."—His Tramp Through the Rebel Lines.
—An Ammunition Train.—"Dave's" Plan Succeeds in
its Destruction.—A Man Who Stuttered and "Had Fits."*

ONE morning, while the army was on the advance up the Peninsula, I was strolling about the camp, when I encountered a group of soldiers gathered around one of their number, who appeared to be entertaining them immensely with his droll anecdotes and dry witticisms. Approaching closer, I became one of the crowd that surrounded the narrator, and listened to an amusing incident admirably told, which had happened to him a day or two before while out with a scouting party.

He was a man about thirty years of age, of medium height, strongly and compactly built, and with a good, firm, intelligent face, over which he had the most perfect control. So perfect was his command over his facial expression that he could make his hearers roar with laughter, while he, to use a homely phrase, would "never crack a smile." I noticed on joining the little crowd that had gathered around him, that the fellow stuttered amazingly, which fact, together with his imperturbable gravity, seemed to be the secret of his always having a good audience about him to listen to his stories and to enjoy his droll humor. I was struck with the man's appearance at first sight and at once concluded that, unless I was much deceived in him, he was a man whom I could use to good advantage, and I determined to ascertain who he was and where he belonged.

Turning to a soldier at my side, I inquired the man's name. Looking at me as though surprised at my ignorance, he answered:

"Why, that's 'Stuttering Dave,' the drollest, smartest man in this regiment, and one of the best fellows you ever met."

"What regiment does he belong to?" I asked.

"To the Twenty-first New York," said the soldier, "but ever since I have known him, he has been with a scouting party. He used to live in Virginia before the war, and is well acquainted about here."

That day I called upon the Colonel of the regiment to which the man belonged, and informed him of my wishes, which, if agreeable to him, I would ask him to send "Stuttering Dave" to my quarters.

Shortly after sundown he came, and to my astonishment, I found that his stuttering propensity had entirely disappeared, and that he conversed with me with surprising ease and intelligence, and a quiet earnestness that betokened a solid and well-informed man. The fact was that stuttering with him was only a favorite amusement, and so naturally was it simulated, that no one would suspect he was sham‑ ming or that he was anything else but a confirmed stutterer of the most incorrigible type.   In the inter‑ view which followed he signified his willingness to enter the secret service, and a day or two later he was detailed to my force.   Here he served with such ability and credit that he was shortly discharged from his regiment altogether, and for the rest of the war was one of my most faithful and valued operatives.

A few days after this interview, David Graham, for that was his real name, otherwise known as " Stuttering Dave," set out under my instructions, on a trip within the rebel lines.   As he was about leav‑ ing my tent, he shook hands with me, and said in his dry manner :

" G-g-go-good-by, M-m-m-major, I'm g-g-g-oin to have s-s-some fun before I g-g-get home, if I d-d-don't I'm a g-g-goat, that's all."

Cautioning him against allowing his propensity for "fun" to get him into trouble, I accompanied him to the edge of the camp, and saw him set out in the direction of the Confederate forces.

Graham had adopted the disguise of a peddler of notions, and carried in his pack a goodly supply of but‑ tons, needles, thread, pins and such a trifling articles as he knew would be in great demand by the soldiers. Discarding his uniform, and dressed in a suit of but‑ ternut jean, with a broad-brimmed hat, a stout stick, and a pack across his shoulder, he appeared a verita‑

ble tramping peddler. No one, to have seen him, would have imagined that he was an emissary of the secret service, and they would little have suspected that the stuttering, harmless-looking fellow who was hawking his wares, knew aught about military affairs, or the plans and movements of an army.

It was in the fast deepening twilight of a beautiful evening, and but a few days after he had left the Union lines, that a party of rebel soldiers, weary and hungry with the toilsome march of the day, were resting around a camp-fire, engaged in the preparations of their evening meal.

While thus employed, they were approached by a strange-looking individual, who walked right into their midst, and without, ceremony, flung down his pack and seated himself among them.

"B-b-boys," said he, "I'm most d-d-darned hungry, w-w-w-what do you s-s-say to givin' me a b-b-b-bite to eat ; d-d-dang my buttons, I'm willin' to p-p-pay for it in t-t-trade or cash."

"How did you manage to get inside the camp ?" inquired one, who seemed to be the leader of the mess.

"F-f-f-followed my legs, and they b-b-b-brought me right in," replied Stuttering Dave, as he coolly produced a short-stemmed, dirty-looking pipe, which he deliberately filled, and then lighted with a coal from the glowing embers at his feet.

"What have you got to sell?" asked a soldier at his side.

"O, n-n-needles, p-p-pins, thread, b-b-buttons and n-n-notions."

"Did you come from the Yanks?" now asked the man who had first addressed him.

"D-d-d-am the Yanks!" ejaculated Dave, "I d-d-don't know anything about 'em. Ain't them your s-s-sentiments?" he added, nudging the fellow who sat nearest to him.

His companion evidently did not relish this sly poke, for he growled:

"I, for one, am gettin' most thunderin' tired of runnin' around the country, and nothin' would suit me better than for us to stop long enough to giv' 'em a good lickin'."

"You l-licked 'em like the d-d-devil at Williamsburgh, d-d-d-didn't you?" said Dave.

The fellow looked at him in surprise, but failed to detect any evidence of an intended sarcasm in the immovable gravity of his face, so mentally concluding that the peddler was a fool and one of nature's own at that, he dropped the conversation.

By this time the meal was ready, and Dave, being invited to join them, gladly assented, and fell to with an appetite that showed how thoroughly he enjoyed the repast. Supper over, the party spent the evening in chatting and telling yarns. The detective opened his pack, and displaying his goods, soon disposed of quite a large quantity, in return for which he demanded, and would take, nothing but silver or gold. When "taps" were called, he turned in with the party, and placing his pack under his head for a pillow, he soon slept soundly, until reveille in the early morning aroused him from his slumbers.

Having eaten his breakfast, he sauntered through the camp, taking keen notice of the number of troops, and finding out all he could concerning their intended plans and movements. During the day, he did a thriving business with his small stock of notions, and was everywhere followed by a crowd, who were attracted by his droll humor and witty sayings.

On one of these occasions, and while he was driving some lively bargains with the soldiers that were gathered around him, he was approached by an officer, who slapped him familiarly on the shoulder and exclaimed :

"Here, my good fellow, we can use men like you ; hadn't you better enlist with us ? You can do your country a great deal more good than you are doing, tramping around the country selling needles and pins."

The detective turned around, and seeing who it was addressing him, replied :

"C-Captain, I d-d-don't think you would want me ; I t-t-tried t-to enlist s-s-s-sometime ago, b-b-b-but the d-d-doctor said, m-my f-f-fits and stuttering b-b-being so b-b-bad, he c-c-couldn't p-p-pass me."

"Are you subject to fits ?" the officer now asked, as a sympathetic look came over his face.

"Had 'em ever s-s-since I was t-t-ten years old," replied Dave, "have 'em every f-f-full of the m-m-moon."

"Where do you live?" interrupted the officer.

"On t-t-the other s-s-side of the river," he answered.

"What is your name?"

"They c-c-call me St-st-stuttering Dave," replied the detective, with an idiotic grin.

The officer now turned and walked away, feeling no longer any interest in the fellow, except to pity his condition ; and thoroughly satisfied that there was no harm in him, and that he was utterly unfit for a soldier.

Well pleased to have shaken off the curious officer as easily as he had, Dave now turned again to the soldiers and resumed his occupation of dickering with the crowd about him ; having concluded his business here, he ambled off to another part of the grounds where a large quantity of ammunition was stored in the wagons.

Instantly, an idea occurred to him which he resolved to carry out if possible. It was to undertake the dangerous feat of firing the ammunition, and depriving his enemies of that much destructive material at all events. He lost all interest in disposing of his goods for a time, and proceeded to make a careful examination of the grounds about the wagons, and formed his plans for carrying out his project that very night.

He soon decided that by laying a train of powder from the wagons and running it to a safe distance, he could readily set fire to it, and make his escape in the confusion that would follow. At midnight, therefore, he stole around to the wagons and quietly commenced his work. He had taken the precaution that afternoon, to supply himself with a quantity of powder fuses, by rolling the powder up loosely in long strips of rags.

Placing these in position to connect with the ammunition in the wagons, and laying his train from one to another, the next thing was to lay a long train, that would enable him after firing it to get out of harm's way before the explosion occurred. Having completed his arrangements, he now took himself off, to wait until the whole camp should be quietly wrapped in slumber, before he started his "fireworks," as he called them.

About midnight, had the sentinel on guard at the wagons containing the ammunition been awake, and looking sharply about him, instead of dozing at his post, he might have observed a man stealthily steal up to the stores, and silently and quickly disappear into the woods beyond. Fortunately, however, for our friend, and the enterprise he had on hand, he only snored quietly and peacefully against a neighboring tree, little dreaming of the surprise that was in store for him.

A few minutes later, a long, quick flash of light

darted along the ground, which was immediately followed by a loud, stunning report, and the murky darkness was illumined with a brilliant, flaming light, and great volumes of smoke.

Instantly the entire camp was aroused, and the half-dressed and fully-frightened soldiers came rushing to the scene, which was now only a scattered pile of burning ruins. How it occurred, no one knew, or could tell aught about it, and wild conjectures were freely indulged in as to the probable cause of the disaster. In the meantime, the only man in the world who could tell anything about the affair, was traveling as fast as his legs could carry him in the direction of the Union camp.

In a few days he made his appearance at my headquarters, and related the success of his journey. I could not refrain from laughing heartily at his peculiar and independent system of warfare, but advised him to be more careful in the future as to how he tampered with the stores of the enemy.

I was not disappointed as to the ability of the man, however, and for months he served me faithfully and well, needing but little instruction, and always performing his work to the entire satisfaction of every one. He at times adopted various disguises, but generally depended upon his own natural shrewd-ness, and his natural adaptiveness for the role of an itinerant peddler to carry him through successfully.

He was always fortunate in his trips, and, so far

as I knew, his identity was never discovered, and in the peddler who stuttered and "sometimes had fits," the rebels never recognized an emissary of the Secret Service.

SHOT BY A CANNON-BALL.

CHAPTER XXVIII.

*Another Trip to Richmond.—A Rebel General Taken In.—
Curtis Makes Valuable Acquaintances.—"The Subterranean Headquarters."*

EARLY in 1862, it becoming necessary to obtain
more fully the plans and intentions of the
enemy, and their numbers around Richmond, I in
April of that year dispatched one of my keenest and
shrewdest operatives on this important mission.

The man selected for this delicate and dangerous
work was George Curtis, a young man about twenty-
five years of age, tall, well-formed, with dark complexion, clear gray eyes, and possessing handsome,
intelligent features. He was one of those men rarely
met, who was by nature a detective; cool-headed,
brave and determined, with ready wit and sagacious
mind, he was especially qualified for efficient work in
that important branch, the secret service.

He was a native of New York, and had at the
opening of the war enlisted in an infantry regiment
from that State.

Learning of his desire to enter the secret service,
I had procured his discharge from his regiment, and
he was detailed on my force, where he served until
the close of the war.

It was a beautiful April morning when, with his instructions carefully treasured in memory, for he dared take no written ones, he left my office on "I" street, in Washington, and set out on his perilous trip.

I had previously made arrangements that he should accompany General McClellan down the river on his boat, the "Commodore," and on which he had established his headquarters, to Fortress Monroe, and landing there, make his way to Richmond.

The morning of the first, he left Washington, and the next day he arrived at Old Point Comfort, and landed under the frowning walls of the old fort. He remained here until the morning of the second day after his arrival, where he was provided with a horse, and set across the river and proceeded on his way towards the rebel capital.

He had now a journey of near seventy miles before him, through a country filled with enemies to the cause he espoused, and from whom, should his true character and mission become known, he might expect anything but kind treatment at their hands. His object in crossing the James at this point was to place himself in less danger from suspicion as a spy, and to better enable him to learn the sentiment of the people, as well as to gain accurate knowledge of the condition of the country as to roads, bridges, streams, etc., all of which information is of essential importance for the General of an invading army to know.

He, therefore, on horseback, and apparently as a
man traveling for pleasure and recreation, proceeded
on his way up the valley of the river and towards the
objective point of his journey, the rebel capital.

Nothing worthy of note occurred during the day ;
he stopped at noon at a house by the wayside, and
obtained dinner for himself and horse.   In a conversation with his host, who was a well-to-do old farmer,
he apparently in a careless manner betrayed the fact
that he himself followed the same occupation, that he
lived on the river in the county of Norfolk, below,
and was on his way to visit among friends at Peters-
burgh.

It was towards evening that he neared the outskirts of the city, when he suddenly encountered the
rebel pickets, stationed outside the town, who halted
him and demanded to know his name and business.
" My name is Curtis," replied the operative, " and I
am from Norfolk ; my business I will state to your
commander when I am taken to him."

Without further ceremony he was turned over
to the officer of the guard, who sent him under escort
to General Hill, the general in command.

" Whom have you here ?" queried the General, as
in the company of his escort the detective was led
into his presence.

" A man who says he is from Norfolk," replied
the guard, " but who refuses to tell his business to
any one but yourself."

"You may retire," said the General, and the escort immediately left the room. "Now," he exclaimed, turning to Curtis, "What is your business? Please be as brief as possible, as I am very busy."

"Well, to come to the point at once," replied the detective; "in the first place, then, I spoke falsely to your pickets when I told them I was from Norfolk. My name is Curtis, and I am from Washington. As to my business, I deal in what the Yankees are pleased to term contraband goods; yet I don't see how gun-caps, ammunition of all kinds, and quinine should be considered contraband, for the simple reason that I, as a dealer, find a better market South than North for my goods. My desire," he continued, "is to get through to Richmond, where I hope to be able to effect contracts, with Secretary Benjamin, to furnish my goods to the Confederate government."

"How did you get through the Union lines?" asked the General, still, evidently, a little suspicious of the sincerity of the detective's story.

"I came down on the 'Commodore,' General McClellan's boat, three days ago," he answered, "was set across the river there, procured a horse from a friend, and here I am."

"Do you know anything of McClellan's plans for an advance?" asked the General.

"I can tell you nothing about them," answered Curtis, "as everything is kept secret from even his own staff, I am told."

27

The General mused, thoughtfully, a moment, and then said: "I will give you a pass to Richmond, and you can proceed on your way in the morning."

"Thank you, General," exclaimed the detective, "I assure you the cause shall suffer no loss by any efforts of mine. I shall, in all probability, return by this way, in a few weeks at farthest, when, if I can be of any service to you, you have only to command me."

"By the way," said the General, "I have some letters to parties in Richmond, which ought to go at once. If you will do me the favor to deliver them I shall be obliged to you."

"I shall be happy to serve you, General, and will take pleasure in seeing that your letters reach their destination all right."

"Very well, then; call at my quarters in the morning, before you start, and I will have them ready for you, and will give you also your pass to Richmond."

Curtis thanked him again, and, bidding him good-night, repaired to the hotel, and secured for himself and horse supper and lodging for the night.

After he had partaken of a hearty meal, and provided himself with an excellent cigar, he sauntered out on to the veranda of the hotel, and, taking a comfortable seat, prepared to enjoy his fragrant weed, and amuse himself with listening to the conversation of those around him.

He soon discovered that the war, and the prospects for a speedy victory for the South, were the subjects under discussion, and he listened with much interest to the ideas advanced, and the confidence that marked their assertions of the superiority of the Southern troops over the Northern mudsills, as they termed the Federalists.

"You may depend on it, that General Johnson will not permit the Yanks to approach any closer to Richmond than they now are, without contesting every inch of the ground as they advance," remarked one gentleman of the party near which he was sitting.

"No," emphatically rejoined another, "when they take Richmond, it will be when they have annihilated the Southern people, when not a thousand able-bodied men are left on Southern soil to rally to its defense."

"Well, I am satisfied," remarked another, "that right here is to be the contest, that is to decide this matter one way or the other."

"If the Yankees take Richmond, the South may as well surrender at once ; if however they fail, as they are extremely liable to do, *they*, on the other hand, may as well withdraw their forces and acknowledge our independence."

"If I am not greatly mistaken," now ventured my operative, "in the spirit of the Southern people, they will, to use a common phrase, 'fight to the bitter end.' And yet," he continued, "to the thoughtful observer, it is not pleasant to contemplate the spectacle of brother arrayed against brother, as they are in this war. I tell you, gentlemen," he added, "that while I am a Southern man, it grieves me to see our land so rent with strife and bloodshed and that the North has made it necessary for a resort to arms to settle a matter that should have been amicably adjusted."

At this juncture, the party was joined by a newcomer, who had evidently just left the supper-room, as he carried an unlighted cigar in one hand, while with the other he was picking his teeth, with the manner of a man who had just eaten a hearty meal and who had enjoyed it.

He was a man past the middle age, hair generously sprinkled with gray, and with a face, that while bronzed by exposure to the weather, was keenly intelligent, not unhandsome, and strongly expressive of force and decision of character. He seated himself and soon joined in the conversation, with that freedom and *nonchalance* that characterizes the experienced yet courteous traveler, who has seen the world and is familiar with its ways.

"We shall hear of some pretty hard fighting, shortly, I imagine," finally observed the stranger; "McClellan has arrived at Fortress Monroe, and will no doubt commence hostilities at once."

"And we shall also hear of his army getting badly whipped," put in one of the party.

"Well," rejoined the stranger, "that may be true; but, after all, the real contest will be before Richmond; the fighting that may occur now will only be the strategic moves preceding the final struggle. Lee and Johnson," he continued, "are not yet ready for McClellan to advance upon Richmond, and they will see to it that it is put in the best possible condition of defense before he succeeds in reaching it."

At this, my operative, who had taken little part in the conversation, except as an attentive listener, now arose and laughingly said : "Gentlemen, I guess we are all of one mind on this subject, let's adjourn down below and interview the bar-keeper; I don't profess to be a judge of military matters, but when it comes to a good article of whisky, I claim to be posted."

The party, numbering near a dozen gentlemen about him, good-humoredly took the interruption and laughingly followed the detective, who now led the way to the bar-room.

They filled glasses all around and Curtis proposed the rather ambiguous toast, "May the right prevail, and death and confusion, attend its enemies"—ambiguous in that it as much represented his real sentiments as it also met the approval of his secession friends.

After the party had drank, they separated, agreeing to meet later in the evening; Curtis was himself starting for a stroll about the town, when the stranger, who had last joined the party on the veranda approached him and said : " I have just drank the toast you proposed, and judging from it and your conversation up stairs, I take you to be, at least, a friend to the South, if indeed you are not a Southern man. I should like much to have your company for a short stroll about the city ; my name," he added, "is Leroy, and I hail from Baltimore."

" I shall be glad to accompany you, Mr. Leroy," said my operative, heartily : " I was just thinking of going for a walk alone, but I assure you I shall be only too glad to have a companion. And since you have so kindly told me your name, I may as well tell you, that mine is George Curtis, and I am from Washington. But before we start," he added, " let us have a fresh cigar."

He then ordered the cigars and they started for their walk.

They had not proceeded far, before his new companion revealed the fact, that he also was in the contraband trade, and singularly enough, was on his way to Richmond on precisely the same business my operative had represented himself as engaged. Of course, Curtis reciprocated the confidence of his new-found friend, and with such results, that he not only returned from his walk much better posted on how to get goods through to Richmond, but actually returned a partner in an enterprize to furnish their goods in large quantities to the Confederate government, provided they could succeed in making satisfactory arrangements with Mr. Benjamin, the Secretary of War. They returned to the hotel, where they had a long talk, completing their plans. It was arranged that my operative should leave his horse at Petersburg, and in the morning, they would proceed on their way to Richmond by rail.

On the following morning he arose early, and after breakfast, proceeded to call on General Hill at his quarters and obtained his pass, also the letters he was to carry for him to parties in Richmond. They then took a train for the rebel capital, and by noon found themselves in that city.

The day following his arrival, in company with Leroy, he called on Mr. Benjamin and succeeded in closing contracts to furnish large quantities of their goods to his government, and at prices that were highly satisfactory to Mr. Leroy, who jovially remarked, as they left the Secretary's presence, that if they only had good luck, their fortunes were made. Curtis, however, felt highly gratified over the result of the interview, more from the reflection of the aid it would give him in prosecuting the real object of his visit, than from any financial benefit he expected to derive from it. He had received a pass from the Secretary that would enable him to pass in and out of Richmond at his pleasure, a most important privilege, and one that really removed all practical hindrances, and left him free to more fully accomplish his work.

He had not been in the city a week before he discovered that through some source, the rebels had almost daily news from the front, concerning the movements and plans of the Union troops. This he now determined to ferret out, and the next day, he in a careless manner, inquired of his friend Leroy, how it was, they obtained news so promptly from the front.

"Why," replied his friend, laughingly, "haven't you heard of the subterranean headquarters?"

"I confess I have not," replied the detective.

"Then come along with me," said Leroy. "I ought to have told you about this before, as it is intimately connected with our business."

He then led the way to the very hotel at which they were stopping, and conducted Curtis to a large and elegantly furnished room on the third floor, and in which were seated a number of gentlemen—some reading, while others were engaged in writing at little tables that were ranged about the room.

"Here," said he, laughing, "are the subterranean headquarters, although they are above the top of the ground instead of beneath it. I need not tell you," he added, "that the name is given as much to mislead as for any other purpose."

They then took seats at one end of the room where they were alone, and he proceeded with his explanation:

"First," he said, "you must know that this is a bureau of intelligence, and is managed partly by the government and partly by wealthy merchants here and at Baltimore ; besides being used in getting information concerning the movements of the Federal troops, it is also used by the merchants in getting our goods through from Baltimore. We employ," he continued, " nearly fifty persons, some of whom are constantly in the field carrying dispatches, gaining and bringing in information from the Yankee lines. These persons are all under the control of a chief at their head, and are all known to that man yonder," pointing to a gentleman seated at a desk at the opposite end of the room.

"Strange as it may seem to you," he continued, " right here in this hotel, we have the most exclusive privacy. You noticed that man standing in the hall when we came in, the same one now sitting at the desk ?"

Curtis nodded, and he proceeded : " Well, he knew me, and consequently he knew you were all right. Had you come alone, that door would have been closed, and would not have opened, had you tried it. Now," he said, " I will call him here and introduce you."

Touching a small bell that stood on the table, the gentleman, to whom he had alluded, instantly answered its summons and crossed the room to where they were sitting.

" Mr. Wallace," said Leroy, " this is my friend and partner, Mr. Curtis." The two men bowed and shook hands, and Wallace seating himself proved to be a pleasant and well-informed gentleman.

In the course of the conversation, Leroy asked, " What is the latest news from the front, Mr. Wallace ?"

" We have nothing as yet to-day," he answered, " but yesterday it was reported that McClellan had laid siege to Yorktown ; the chances are, that we shall hear of a battle, in a few days at farthest." During the interview, Curtis learned also, that the persons operating for this bureau had confederates, both at Baltimore and at Washington ; these, he determined to discover, if possible, in addition to the information already gained.

To this end, he made himself very agreeable to Mr. Wallace, and in the course of the conversation, expressed his willingness to do what he could in aiding the force, and remarked that he should be passing back and forth, between Washington and Richmond, and could doubtless be of service.

Mr. Wallace thanked him heartily, and gave him a small plain badge of peculiar shape, that would at any time, if shown, admit him to the headquarters, and then taking him about the room, he introduced him to the gentlemen present, and after a short conversation with his new friends, he in company with Leroy took his departure, and together they went down to dinner.

That evening, as he was sitting in the bar-room

of the hotel, one of the men he had met up-stairs in the forenoon, came to him and told him that in a day or two, he was to start for Yorktown with important dispatches for General Magruder, but that owing, to sickness in his family, he did not want to leave home, unless it was impossible for him to get some one he could trust to undertake the task for him.

He then asked Curtis if he would object to making the trip for him. The detective thought a moment, and told him he would give him an answer in the morning. The two men then indulged in a friendly glass, after which they separated. The man had no sooner gone, than Curtis made up his mind to take the dispatches, not to General Magruder, but to me at Washington.

Accordingly, the next morning he informed his friend he would undertake the task for him, as he intended returning to Baltimore at any rate.

The next morning found him, with the dispatches carefully secreted about his person, at the depot, ready to take the first train for Petersburgh.

Here he arrived about noon, and proceeded to call on General Hill. After procuring his dinner at the hotel, he ordered his horse and started on his long ride for the Union camp, where he delivered his dispatches to Mr. Bangs, the superintendent of my headquarters in the field, and forwarded copies of the same to me at Washington, together with a full account of his trip and information he had gained;

not forgetting a full statement of his discovery of the " Subterranean Headquarters," and his enlistment as a member of its force of spies and agents, employed in transmitting intelligence of the movements and plans of the Union troops.

CHAPTER XXIX.

*A Virginia Home.—Unwelcome Visitors.—Mr. Harcourt
Arrested and Released.—Dan McCowan Makes Forcible
Love to Mary Harcourt.—The Girl in Peril.—A Timely
Rescue.—The Villain Punished.*

THE important information brought to my notice
by Operative Curtis, on his return from Richmond, concerning the character and working of the
"Subterranean Headquarters," at once determined
me on a plan of using the same body of men, or
rather the information they carried, for the benefit of
the Union forces, instead of allowing them to use it
in the interests of the Confederates. To accomplish
this, I detailed several members of my force, both at
Washington and Baltimore, to co-operate with Curtis,
whom I intended now should become an active agent
of the rebels in carrying dispatches to and from
Richmond. The plan was, in short, that all dispatches entrusted to him should be accurately copied,
the copies to be delivered to his confederates, and
the originals forwarded to their destination.

In war, as in game of chess, if you know the
moves of your adversary in advance, it is then an
easy matter to shape your own plans, and make your
moves accordingly, and, of course, always to your

own decided advantage. So in this case, I concluded that if the information intended for the rebels could first be had by us, after that, they were welcome to all the benefit they might derive from them.

In a few days, then, having completed my arrange-ments, Curtis started to Richmond, by the way of Wilson's Landing and Glendale, he having decided that, provided as he was with his pass from the Secretary, it would be perfectly safe, and at the same time a much shorter route than by the way of Peters-burgh.

Leaving him for the present, then, to make his way to Richmond as best he can, we will turn our attention to other persons and to other scenes. The interior of a comfortable farm-house, the place, and early evening the time.

The family are gathered around the tea-table, and are discussing earnestly the war, and the chances of the success of the Northern troops. The family con-sisted of five persons: the husband and wife, both traveling down the western slope of life, a young and beautiful daughter, apparently about twenty years of age, and two younger children, a boy and girl, aged, respectively, fourteen and twelve years.

These latter are listening attentively to the con-versation going on about them, and anon interjecting some childish observation, or asking some question commensurate with the quaint views and ideas of childish years.

"Well," finally observed the old gentleman, "it is hard that one dare not speak their own sentiments in a country like this ; my grandfather fought in the revolution, my father in the war of 1812, and I, myself, took a hand in the brush with Mexico ; but I never dreamed of seeing the day when a man dared not speak his honest convictions, for fear of having his roof burnt from over his head, and, worse than all, endanger even his own life, and those dearest to him."

"I have always told you, William," replied his good wife, "that the day would come when this fearful curse of slavery would have to be wiped out in blood, and you all know now that I prophesied truly. And," she added, "as for me, I have no fears for the result. *Our* only mistake has been in casting our lot and settling in the South, and in the very presence of an evil we could not avert."

"True, mother," rejoined her husband, "but you know I have ever been outspoken against slavery, and its attendant curses. I also flatter myself that I have had some influence in mitigating, at least, the condition of not a few of the black race. You remember Colonel Singleton liberated his slaves at the very outset of this war."

"And was compelled to flee to the North to save his own life," answered his wife ; "and had we been wise, we would have gone to a country more congenial to our views, and while we could have done so

with safety.   I am afraid," she continued, "if it becomes known that our son has joined the Union army,
serious trouble may befall us at the hands of men
who have long desired an excuse for arresting you
and confiscating your property ; if, indeed, they would
be content with sparing your life."

"If I were younger," said the old gentleman, "I
would defy them to do their worst; and, as it is,
my only fears are for my family, not for myself.
Still," he added, "my neighbors are all friendly,
and the majority of them, though thinking differently
from me on these questions, are under obligations to
me, so that I feel I have but little to fear at their
hands.   As to our boy, who has gone to fight for
the old flag, I am proud of him ; I fought for it, so
did my fathers before me, and I would disown the
child who would refuse, if necessary, to lay down his
life in its defense."

And here, fired with the sentiments he had just
uttered, he arose from the table in an agitated
manner and began to pace the floor.

"Ah," he continued, "I love that old flag, and
old as I am, would fight for it yet."

Going to a case that stood in a corner of the room,
he took from a shelf a beautiful silken banner, and
holding it aloft, he exclaimed, with great earnestness,
"There is the flag I fight under—the flag of the
Union and of the country our fathers fought to save."

"Father," exclaimed his eldest daughter, "you

forget yourself in your enthusiasm; even now some one may be outside listening; you forget that Dan McCowan and his desperate gang may be in the vicinity and give us a call at any moment."

Scarcely had the warning fell from her lips, when there came a loud knocking at the door, followed by a few vigorous and well-directed blows that threatened to take it from its hinges.

The whole family started up in alarm, and while one snatched the flag from the old gentleman and hastily deposited it in its hiding-place, another answered the summons from without.

The old man himself, while not frightened, was somewhat disconcerted by the noise, and remained standing in the center of the room, when the door was suddenly burst open, revealing a body of Confederate soldiers headed by a villainous-looking fellow, their leader, who now entered the room, and approaching him, said:

"Mr. Harcourt, I have orders to place you under arrest, so you will prepare to accompany us to Glendale at once!"

"What crime have I committed?" demanded the old man, now perfectly calm, "that you dare enter my house in this manner!"

"You will know that soon enough," replied the officer; "so hustle on your duds, as we must be going. Bill," he commanded, turning to a fellow near him, "you will search the house and take posses-

28

sion of anything contraband or treasonable that you can find."

This order was exactly what his followers wanted, as it meant really an order to plunder the house and appropriate to their own use whatever articles of value they found and that pleased them to take.

As none of the family had offered the slightest resistance, the unwelcome intruders had conducted themselves, so far, very orderly.   Mrs. Harcourt, a kind and matronly-looking woman, with a firmness and self-control, that under the circumstances was admirable, bustled about the room, getting together a small bundle of clothing for her husband to take with him on his enforced journey to Glendale; and anon, while doing this, spoke soothing words of comfort and encouragement to the younger children, who, white and speechless with terror, were crouching in the darkest corner of the room.

The eldest daughter, at a sign from her father, accompanied the two men detailed to search the premises, and proceeded with them from room to room, as they rummaged chests and drawers, appropriating various little articles to their own use, in spite of the indignant protest of the spirited girl at such barefaced robbery.

Finally, with much reluctance, she was compelled to admit them to her own room, and to witness their ruthless handling of the contents of a small trunk, in which were various little articles, trinkets and me-

mentoes, worthless to any one else, but, of course, priceless to her.

But what she most prized among them, and which caused her the most alarm should they be discovered, was a small packet of letters from her brother already mentioned as serving in the Union army, and a small locket containing his miniature. Judge of her dismay were one of the men picked up the letters, and with a laugh exclaimed : " These are from your feller, I suppose ;" and then, observing the locket, he opened it and with a leer on his face, said : " And this is his picture, I reckon, eh ?"

" Yes," said the girl eagerly uttering, or rather echoing, the falsehood. " Yes," she repeated, " please don't take them, as they are of no account to any one but myself."

" All right," said the fellow, good-naturedly, " I guess you can have them ;" as he handed them to her. She eagerly seized them, trembling at the narrow escape they had had from falling into the possession of those, who knowing their contents, would have given her poor old father much trouble indeed.

Having completed their search, and finding nothing that could be considered of a treasonable character, they returned to the room below, and reported to their Captain the result of their search. He then ordered his men to retire to the outside, where he followed them, and after consulting a short time, he returned to the house and brusquely informed Mr.

Harcourt that as he had found nothing to convict him of treason against the Confederate government, he might go this time, but to be d—d careful in the future, or he would get him yet. He then slammed the door behind him, rejoined his companions who mounted their horses and rode slowly away.

Satisfied that they had left, the family ventured to express their congratulations at the departure of their unwelcome visitors, and at once set to work re-arranging the disordered room. They, however, felt that this was only the commencement of their prose-cutions, and they well knew that another time, the chances were that they would not escape so easily; for should it become known that their son was in the Federal army, they could no longer hope to live in peace and safety. The men who had visited them on this occasion, were evidently strangers in the neighborhood, and were, no doubt, a scouting or for-aging party, who had stopped more from a want of having anything else to do, than from a desire to do them any injury. They, however, knew, that from those in their own vicinity, there was much more to be feared; and of one person in particular, they stood in especial dread. That person was Dan McCowan, the man whose name was mentioned by Mary Har-court, in her warning to her father, only a moment before the soldiers, had entered their dwelling. Dan McCowan was a man who for years had pur-sued the detestable calling of a negro-hunter.

He was about thirty-five years of age, tall, of an ungainly form, and slightly stoop-shouldered ; his hair and eyes were dark, and his complexion as swarthy as an Indian. His features, naturally coarse and repulsive, were rendered still more so, by being bronzed and hardened by long-continued exposure to the weather. His only associates and his most intimate friends appeared to be his blood-hounds, which he used in hunting and bringing back to their masters, the poor negroes who were seeking to escape from a life of continued toil and bondage. The following unique hand-bill, which he used to post up in various places over the country, will serve to show the nature of his business, and also the vast amount of intelligence necessary to carry it on.

NO TIS.

The undersind taiks this methed of makkin it none that he has got the best NIGGER HOUNDS in the state, and is always redy to ketch runaway niggers at the best rates.

My hounds is well trained, and I heve hed 15 yeres experience. My rates is 10 dollurs per hed if ketched in the beate where the master lives ; 15 dollurs in the coonty, and 50 dollurs out of the coonty.

DAN McCOWAN.

N. B.

Planters should taik panes to let me know, while the niggers tracks is fresh, if they want quick work and a good job.

It is scarcely necessary to say that his services were frequently employed to catch and bring back the poor runaways, and more than once had the Harcourt family been awakened in the night by his hounds, as they made the woods echo with their baying.   Often had they pictured to themselves the terror of the poor wretches, over whose trail, with unerring scent, swept the monsters, who would tear them limb from limb, and whose only choice was death at their hands or the old life of labor and the lash.

Mr. Harcourt was a strong anti-slavery man. Holding these views, he had ever spoken consistently against slavery.   He was also a man of deeds, as well as words, for many a poor fugitive had been assisted by him on his long and perilous journey northward in search of friends and the freedom he craved.

Owing to these proclivities, and to the fact that he had never taken pains to conceal his views, a mutual antipathy had long existed between Mr. Harcourt and Dan McCowan, the nigger-hunter.   While the latter had no direct proofs, yet he had long suspected Mr. Harcourt of being a friend to, and a sympathizer with the very runaways whom it was his business to catch and return to the bondage they were endeavoring to escape from.   Notwithstanding his dislike for the father, however, the fellow had conceived a violent attachment for Mary Harcourt, his daughter, and for a year past had greatly annoyed not only the poor girl herself, but the whole family, by his uncouth attentions.

Finally, Mr. Harcourt told him plainly that his attentions to his daughter were extremely distasteful to her, and added a polite, yet firm request, that he cease his troublesome visits.

Mary, who was a young lady of sweet and lovely disposition, possessing both intelligence and refinement, shrank from the fellow as she should from a viper in her path ; while his odious attempts to lavish his unsought affections upon her so disgusted and frightened her that she always avoided his presence.

Dan McCowan, however, was just the man, when thwarted in his plans, to at once take steps for revenge. For some time he had kept a close espionage of the house and the movements of its inmates. He had somehow obtained possession of the knowledge that young Harcourt was in the Union army, and he determined to use this in his well-laid plans to persecute the poor girl, who had been so unfortunate as to have been the object of his passion.

On the day following the incidents just related, Mary, who had been spending the afternoon with a neighbor's family, towards evening was returning to her home, when she was suddenly and most unexpectedly confronted by Dan McCowan. So startled was she by this unlooked-for meeting, that she involuntarily gave a slight scream, as she recognized who it was that stood before her.

"I see as how I have skeered you right smart now," said the fellow, grinning in her face with a wicked leer. "Your father told me as how he would be much obliged to me if I would stop my visits to his house, which, bein' a gentleman, I was bound to do, and as I had a little something to say to you, I thought this would be the time to say it."

The girl, who had now somewhat recovered her composure, yet fully realizing the character of the man with whom she had to deal, stood quietly looking him full in the face, and said, in a tone that betrayed her contempt, "I suppose I must listen to you, sir, but be brief, as it is getting late, and my folks will be uneasy at my long absence."

"Well, Miss Harcourt," he replied, "I will come to the point at once. You have a brother, who has been away from home fur some time. Do you know where he is?"

Mary was silent, and he muttered, half to himself, "I thought so; the whole family are traitors. No more than is to be expected from these d—d abolitionists. I can tell you where he is," he continued; "he is on the other side, and fighting against the South."

"And what if he is in the Federal army? He is fighting for the government you and yours are seeking to destroy," answered the spirited girl.

"It don't matter much to me which side he fights on; but suppose I tell it around, that he is fighting

"While she was struggling in his grasp, he was startled by a violent clutch upon his collar from behind." P. 441.

with the Yankees, do you think it would matter to you then ?"

"My brother is his own man," replied Mary, "and he alone is responsible for his acts ; surely they would not harm my father and us for that ; and surely you would not tell what you know, to injure us ?"

"That depends on you, Miss Mary," the fellow replied, now approaching closer, and attempting to take her hand.

"What do you mean, you scoundrel ?" demanded the girl, drawing back, while the fire flashed from her eyes. "Don't offer to touch me, Dan McCowan, or I'll——"

"What would you do, now ?" he exclaimed ; and, before she was aware of his intentions, he had sprang quickly forward, seized her about the waist, and placed one hand over her mouth, but not until she had given one long and piercing call for help.

The fellow's base designs were evident, and that he would have been successful there is no doubt ; but help, fortunately, was at hand. While he was yet struggling with the girl, he felt a violent clutch on his collar, from behind, and before he could see from whence it came he was thrown violently to the ground, and was writhing under the well-directed kicks, which were most lavishly bestowed upon him by the new comer, who was no less a personage than my operative George Curtis.

The girl had sank to the ground almost fainting

from fright, but so enraged was Curtis at the scene
he had witnessed, that he continued to shower his
kicks on the miserable wretch, who roared and begged
for mercy, until the girl interposed, and begged him,
for her sake, not to kill him, but to desist, and let
him go.

At this my operative ceased, more, however, from
mere lack of breath than from a feeling that the
fellow had been sufficiently punished, and allowed
him to regain his feet. "You contemptible, cowardly
brute," he exclaimed, as McCowan arose; "I have a
mind to finish you, while I have my hand in. Miss,"
he continued, turning to the girl, "I am happy to have
arrived in time to be of service to you. I do not know
anything about this difficulty, but from what I saw, I
concluded that I had not time to make any inquiries."

"I am very grateful to you, sir, for what you
have done in saving me from that villain. Look
out!" she exclaimed, "he has a pistol."

Curtis turned his head in time to see the fellow in
the act of drawing a revolver. Quicker than a flash,
his own weapon was in his hands, and covering the
man, he said, coolly:

"Drop your hands, you hell-hound, or I will blow
you to atoms in a second."

The fellow saw that he was foiled, and dropped
his hands at his sides.

Curtis advanced and disarmed him; then, stepping
back a pace, he said:

"Go now while I am in the humor to let you; another move like that, and I will shoot you as I would a dog."

McCowan reluctantly obeyed, and slunk away muttering threats of vengeance.

My operative, however, paid no attention to him now, but turned to the young lady who proceeded to relate the circumstance of her meeting with McCowan, from which his timely interference had saved her, and ended by a cordial invitation, blushingly given, that he would accompany her home, and spend the night under her father's roof. As he was anxious to find a lodging-place for the night, at any rate, the detective, gratefully accepted the invitation, feeling such an interest in this really beautiful girl that he could not resist the desire to cultivate further the acquaintance, so strangely begun. He hastily brought his horse from where he had left him by the roadside, and leading him by the bridle, walked by the side of his companion until they reached the house. As they strolled along, Mary frankly told him the secret of McCowan's attack, and proceeded to explain the man's character, and the detestable nature of the business in which he was engaged.

By this time, they had reached her father's house, where they were met at the gate by the old gentleman himself, who was alarmed and anxious at his daughter's absence so far beyond her usual time for return.

"Father," said the girl, "this is"—here she paused, visibly embarrassed, and gazed timidly into the face of the detective.

"Pardon me," said Curtis hastily, seeing the cause of her confusion; "my name is George Curtis; we have been so busy talking that I had not thought of names."

She then introduced them, and briefly related to her father the cause of her detention, and her adventure with McCowan, not forgetting to mention the part my operative had played in her timely rescue from the villain's hands.

The old man thanked him again and again, and so profusely, that Curtis begged that he would not mention it, as he had done nothing more than any gentleman, under the same circumstances, would have done, gone to the lady's rescue at her call for help.

His horse was ordered to be taken to the barn, and he himself was soon seated in the house, receiving the tearful thanks of good Mrs. Harcourt, and the object of the admiring gaze of Mary's younger brother and sister, who regarded him as a hero, and a person who had no small claim on their affection and esteem.

CHAPTER XXX.

Curtis Again on his Travels.—A Loving Episode.—Dan McCowan Again Turns Up.—The Capture of Curtis.— A Fight For Life, and Escape.—A Bit of Matrimony.

THE next day, my operative took his leave of the Harcourt family, and continued on his way to Richmond. He, however, gave them his promise, that he would visit them again before long, a promise he was in no wise loath to keep, as Mary had joined her request to that of her father, that he should not fail to give them a call, when he was in their vicinity.

The truth was my operative, who was a very excellent young man, and, notwithstanding his calling, susceptible to the charms of the fair sex, was not a little smitten by the fair Mary, whom he had met under circumstances that would have caused even a less romantic person than himself to have fallen in love with her at once.

On the other hand, the girl's feelings of gratitude and admiration for the young man, who had rescued her from McCowan's clutches, were those almost akin to love ; but with true maidenly modesty, she simply treated him with that delicate courtesy that, while it showed plainly her high regard for him, yet

it in no way overstepped the bounds of strict propriety. It was evident, however, that she regarded
him as one who certainly had strong claims upon her
friendship and esteem.

Bidding them good-bye, then, Curtis took leave of
the family, whom he had known but a single night,
yet who, in that brief space, had grown to be like old
acquaintances ; and his regret on leaving them, was
very much like that in parting from old and intimate
friends.

Taking the route by Glendale, he, towards evening, arrived at Richmond, without any event worthy
of notice, and put up at Miller's Hotel.

A few weeks later found him on his return to the
Army of the Potomac, and in his possession important dispatches that he had obtained in the rebel
capital. As he left Richmond, the news reached that
city of the evacuation of Yorktown by the rebels,
and their retreat up the peninsula towards Williamsburgh. The effect of these tidings was anything but
encouraging to those who had hoped that a final and
decisive battle would have been fought at Yorktown,
and the further advance of the Union troops effectually checked.

McClellan's vigorous preparations, however, for a
protracted siege, had decided the rebels that it
would be useless to risk a battle here, and they consequently determined to evacuate the place, which
they did on the fifth of May, and by noon of the

same day McClellan's army had broken camp and was in full pursuit. With such celerity did he make his movements, and so closely did he press the Confederates, that on the following day they were compelled to make a stand, and here was fought the battle of Williamsburgh, in which the rebels were defeated, and continued their retreat towards Richmond.

The army of the Potomac now continued its advance, with all the rapidity the terrible condition of the roads would permit, having for its base of supplies the York River, until two weeks later it rested between the Pamunkey and the Chickahominy. It was at this stage of affairs on the Peninsula, that Curtis was on his return trip from Richmond. With his passes in his pocket, his dispatches securely concealed about him, and his trusty horse as his only companion, he set out for his long ride to Wilson's Landing, and the headquarters of the Union army.

It was his purpose to stop by the way long enough to at least inquire after the health of the Harcourt family, and learn how they had fared during his absence. So, pushing rapidly ahead, towards the close of what had been a beautiful day in May, he, near nightfall, found himself at Farmer Harcourt's door, where he was most cordially welcomed.

His jaded horse was led to the barn to be watered and fed, while he was soon resting his tired limbs in an easy chair, while waiting a tempting supper that was almost ready for an appetite keenly whetted by his long and hard day's ride.

His object now, was to stop long enough to rest himself and horse, and then push on by night and endeavor to reach the Federal lines by daybreak. Mr. Harcourt informed him that they had not been molested by McCowan since his former visit, and that it was reported that he had formed a band of Guerrillas, and at their head was pillaging and robbing the people in an adjoining county.

"He is an unscrupulous villain," observed the old gentleman, "and I confess I stand in no little dread that he may pay us a visit at any time, in which case, if we escape with our lives, we may consider ourselves fortunate. I have," he added, "fully made up my mind to take my family, leave my home here, and, if possible, go North, where a man of my way of thinking can live in security and peace. If I were younger, I would enlist, myself, but my fighting days are past."

"I trust you may soon be able to get away from here," said Curtis; "and as the Union army is now advancing up the Peninsula, you can, I think, with little danger, make your way into its lines."

He then informed him of the evacuation of Yorktown, and of the retreat of the Confederates, and advised him to hasten his arrangements to go North, while this opportunity afforded him a way to do so with safety.

After the evening meal was over the family seated themselves on a pleasant little porch, that ran along one side of the old-fashioned house, facing the west, and in the deepening twilight they sat and talked over the trying times, and united in their wishes for a speedy termination of the fratricidal conflict.

Thus the evening passed until near ten o'clock, when my operative informed his friends that he must take his departure, as he was determined, if possible, to reach the Union lines by daybreak.

The whole family urged him to pass the night with them; but finding him bent on going, his horse was ordered to the door, and he prepared to take his leave.

He shook hands with the good farmer and his wife, and looked anxiously around for Mary; surely she would bid him good-bye before he went away, but she was nowhere to be seen. He even lingered a few moments, hoping she would return; she did not, however, put in an appearance; so, leaving his regards for her with her parents, he mounted his horse, and with a heavy heart rode along down the long, narrow lane that led from the house to the main road.

He could not understand why the girl should have absented herself just as he was taking his leave; could it be that he had in any way offended her, that she should avoid him on purpose? Revolving the matter in his mind, and feeling that hereafter he would take pains to avoid the Harcourt mansion, he

29

now approached the terminus of the lane, still buried
in thought, when his horse, becoming frightened, shied
slightly to one side ; hastily raising his eyes, he saw,
to his amazement, the object of his thoughts standing
by the roadside.

He checked his horse, and, in a tone that betrayed his astonishment, exclaimed, " You here, Miss
Mary !"

" Yes," she answered, evidently a little confused,
"I wanted to see you a little while alone. I trust you
will pardon me for adopting the means I have to
secure a short talk with you."

By this time Curtis had dismounted, and was
standing at her side.

" Well, what is it, Miss Harcourt ? I am happy
to be at your service in any way in my power."

" Thank you," she answered, hastily, "you have
placed me under obligations to you, but I venture to
night to ask one favor more."

" It is granted already," said Curtis.

Thanking him again, she proceeded : " You know
my brother is in the Union army, and I have not
heard from him for several weeks ; I wish you would
try to get this letter to him, and, if it is not asking
too much," she added, hesitatingly, "will you kindly
bring me his reply, or at least some word that I may
know he is safe and well ?"

Curtis took the letter from her hands, and, de-
positing it safely in an inside pocket of his coat, he

said · "I will do my best to deliver the letter, and, should I not return soon with an answer, you may know something unavoidable has detained me."

As he stood there, gazing earnestly into the sweet face of his fair companion, a sudden purpose to then and there declare his love for her came into his mind. With him, to resolve was to act; extending his hand, he took hers in a friendly clasp, and said: "Miss Harcourt, I am going to bid you good-bye, with the hope of seeing you again very soon; but I will not conceal from you the fact, that, in the fortunes of war, it is possible that we may never meet again. Under these circumstances, then, I make bold to tell you to-night something that, ordinarily, I would not mention until your longer acquaintance with me would make it appear more proper, at least so far as society rules are concerned.

"Miss Harcourt," he continued, still holding the hand that now lay passively in his, "in the short time I have known you I have learned to love you, and I am confident time only will strengthen that love. I do not ask your answer now; when we meet again, if we do, you can tell me my fate. If your answer then should be nay, I will try to bear it like a man, respecting you none the less even if I fail to win the love I would so highly prize. Good-bye, darling!" and lightly pressing her hand to his lips, he threw himself into his saddle, and giving his noble animal the rein, dashed away, leaving Miss Harcourt standing in a half-dazed manner, straining her eyes after his figure, that in the pale moonlight was rapidly disappearing from her view.

Curtis now set off for the headquarters of the Union army. Our friend pushed on, and shortly after midnight arrived at the Landing, and from here faced about to the east, and in the direction of Williamsburgh, where the Union army, victorious in the battle just fought, were encamped.

He now slackened his speed somewhat, to rest his jaded steed, and, dropping the reins, allowed him to take a moderate walk, while he himself fell into a deep reverie over the events of his trip.

On this occasion he had been very successful in his work in the rebel capital, and had, so far, effectually escaped any suspicion as a spy. Considering the watchful vigilance that at this time was maintained by the rebels, Curtis had indeed done well; and it was with feelings of thorough satisfaction that now, near the close of his arduous journey, and when he felt reasonably secure from being molested, that he relaxed somewhat his usual vigilance, and allowed himself and animal a much needed rest.

He was not, however, destined to get through so easily as he had anticipated. As he entered a small clump of timber, and while he was unsuspecting any danger at this nearness to the Union camp, two mounted men suddenly made their appearance from the side of the road, and from where they had been concealed in the bushes, and, holding their cocked weapons at his head, commanded him to halt.

At the same instant, men came pouring in from both sides of the woods, that here skirted his path, and almost before he could realize his situation, or who were his assailants, he was overpowered, taken from his horse, and securely bound.

He soon discovered his captors were a band of guerillas, who had been quartered in the grove, and he had by the merest chance stumbled right into their midst. While he was quickly debating in his mind his chances for escape, and his probable fate at their hands, he was led into the presence of the captain of the band, who, with a few of his followers, had evidently been sleeping about a camp-fire that had now burned low, leaving only a bed of glowing embers, that cast a faint light on the swarthy faces of the rough-looking men that now grouped yawningly about it awaiting his coming.

" Who have you here," asked the Captain, as the party escorting Curtis came up,

" Don't know, Capten," laconically answered one of the men ; " we jest now found him and handed him in here without askin' him enny questions ; but here he is, you can talk to him yourself."

Curtis was now unbound, and led forward, and stood facing the Captain. As their eyes met, the recognition was mutual and instantaneous ; in the man that stood before him, my operative recognized no less a personage than Dan McCowan, the man whom he had so unmercifully drubbed on a former occasion, which has already been described.

At the same moment, McCowan saw who it was that had so unexpectedly fallen into his hands, and with a wicked laugh and a horrible oath, he sprang forward, and clutching him by the throat, exclaimed :

" By G—d, I have been looking for you for some time ; it is my turn now."

It was evident that the fellow in his rage meant murder ; but Curtis, who was both brave and cool, besides being strong and active, wrenched loose from his grip, and springing hastily backward, he dealt him, with the rapidity of lightning, a powerful blow between the eyes, that felled him like an ox. Then, before the lookers-on could scarcely realize what had taken place, he leaped over the form of the prostrate man, and disappeared in the darkness of the wood.

The Captain by this time regained his feet, and showering curses upon his men for a pack of cowardly idiots, started off in pursuit, followed by a half a score of his fellows, who now, in order to conciliate their enraged leader, determined to retake the detective at all hazards.

Fortunately for Curtis, he had been allowed to retain his weapons, and being fleet of foot, he had but little to fear.

He soon succeeded in eluding his pursuers, and,

shortly after daylight, found his way into the Union camp.

He then reported to me with his dispatches from Richmond, and related his adventures here recorded.

I ought to state, however, that he did not, at that time, inform me of his proposal to Miss Harcourt; but after remaining with me until the close of the war, during which time he made many trips to and fro between Richmond and the headquarters of the Federal army, after the struggle was ended and we both had retired to the life of a citizen, he, as a salesman in a business house in Chicago, I to my business as a detective in the same city, then it was he related the story of his courtship, and the manner in which he wooed and won the woman who was then, and still is, his wife. As for the Harcourt family, they made their way to the North, by the aid of my operative and young Harcourt, and the courtship between Curtis and the daughter was kept up until the close of the war, when they were married.

I will also say, that they are still living happily together, surrounded by an interesting family of children, who with childlike eagerness clamber on their papa's knees to hear him tell them stories of the war, and his adventures before they were even born, a period that to them seems ages and ages ago.

Dan McCowan was killed in an attack that his party, led by him, made on a band of our scouts, shortly after the occurrence of the incidents described in this chapter.

I would fain have dwelt longer on the work of young Curtis, and noted more minutely the importance of his labors in the secret service, but a lack of space and time compel me here to drop him with the passing comment, that he was an excellent operative, and that he so faithfully and efficiently did his work, that the subterranean headquarters, with its corps of operatives, never did the Union cause any practical harm, but a great deal of good, in furnishing intelligence of the movements and intentions of the rebel forces.

NIGHT ON THE BATTLE-FIELD.

CHAPTER XXXI.

McClellan and his Enemies.—The Peninsula Campaign.—The Rebel Forces Before Richmond.—The Union Forces Outnumbered by the Enemy, and their Commander Hampered By Superiors.—An Honest Opinion.

I T is not my purpose to attempt to detail the various movements of the army, to describe the battles which were fought, or to chronicle the victories and defeats which were achieved and sustained by the brave soldiers who fought under the flag of the Union. That duty belongs to the historian ; mine simply to relate the experiences of my own men in the delicate, dangerous and laborious duties which devolved upon them. Far less is it my desire to enter into a discussion upon the various subjects that have, since that fratricidal conflict, engrossed the attention of the student of history.

I trust, however, that I may be pardoned, if, for a time, I depart from the main narrative and devote a brief space to the consideration of that much discussed subject, the campaign of the Peninsula. I make no pretension whatever to being a military scholar, nor in any sense a military man, but my connection with the government during the war, and participation in the movements of the Army of the Po-

tomac, together with my long and intimate acquaintance with its commander, General McClellan, may en-
title me to a brief expression of my own views of that
campaign. I may be pardoned, also, if I attempt to
ascribe to their proper source, some of the causes
which contributed largely to the disasters that attended it.

There can be no doubt of the fact, that the young
commander-in-chief was subjected to the persecu-
tions of the most malignant political intriguers, who
feared that his growing popularity would result in
political exaltation. Taking advantage of the fact,
therefore, that General McClellan was an avowed
Democrat, a scheming cabal was working to weaken
his influence with the people by vague insinuations
against his loyalty to the Union cause. To further
that end, his plans, so carefully and intelligently matured, for the speedy crushing of the rebellion, were
either totally disregarded by an unfriendly cabinet, or
were so frequently thwarted, that to successfully carry
them out was an utter impossibility.

As I have always been a faithful adherent of the
maxim, "speak the truth, though the heavens fall,"
and believing it to be a doctrine, that if practically
carried, will right all wrongs, uphold the innocent,
administer censure where deserved, and praise where
it is due, I have invariably attempted to form my
judgment of my fellow-men upon their own intrinsic
merits.

Whatever may have been his faults as a man, his mistakes as a General, he was throughout unflinchingly loyal to the cause of the North. With him it was but one sentiment, and one ambition—to whip the rebels into subjection—and manfully did he perform his duty toward the accomplishment of that object. Much of the censure which has been heaped upon him and his conduct as Commander of the Army of the Potomac, is due to a hasty and inconsiderate judgment of the man and his motives, or the result of direct prejudice and ill-will. In the eyes of his critics his great fault lay in what they considered his inexcusable delay in moving against the enemy in the Spring of 1862, after, as they supposed, he had ample time to prepare his army for the field.

From this point began the open and unfriendly criticisms which were designed to excite an impatient people, who did not, and could not, understand why active operations were not at once begun. This delay was adroitly used by scheming politicians to cast the shadow of disloyalty upon a man, who never for one moment entertained a disloyal thought, nor performed a single action which he did not believe would redound to the credit and honor of the Union troops, and of the Government which he served.

My acquaintance with General McClellan began before the war, and when he was the Vice-President of the Illinois Central Railroad. That corporation had, on frequent occasions, employed my services in various operations affecting their interests, and in this way I first met and became associated with the General. From this date began my warm regard for the man, which, during the many years that have passed, has known no diminution.

I knew the man so well, and my confidence in his integrity and patriotism was so thorough, that a doubt of his loyalty never entered my mind. Many of my old-line abolition friends went so far as to reproach me for my steadfast adherence to McClellan, and accused me of abandoning my principles. I, however, knew my own ground, and held it. I knew that the General was not an abolitionist, but that he was not a patriot I could not believe for a moment. I have always thought, and my opinion remains unchanged to this day, that had he been left free to carry out his plans in the Peninsula campaign, the Army of the Potomac would have escaped the disasters that befell it; Richmond would have been reduced, and occupied by the Federal troops; and victory instead of defeat would have crowned their heroic efforts from the river to the rebel seat of government.

" How do you account for General McClellan's 'masterly inactivity' during all these months that his army lay at Washington?" is asked. Ah, there is the mistake. It was anything but inactivity, and it is beginning to be pretty generally understood now what he was doing at that time.

More than one writer on the campaigns of the

Civil War, has taken occasion to say that the splendid achievements of the Army of the Potomac at subsequent periods, and under other commanders, were mainly due to the careful drilling and the rigid discipline inculcated under McClellan. At the time he was called to the command of the army it was nothing better than a band of disorganized men, who had not recovered from the defeat of Bull Run, and whatever efficiency it attained, was accomplished by the indefatigable efforts of General McClellan and the officers under his command.

The South, at the outbreak, was far better prepared for war than the North. For months preceding the election of Mr. Lincoln the people of the South were secretly preparing for a struggle. They had even then determined, if beaten by the ballot, to resort to the bayonet, and to decide upon the battle-field the questions which they failed to settle by fair discussion and honest leglslation in the National Congress. The people of the North, on the contrary, being so long accustomed to submit to the expressed will of the majority, apprehended no danger. While they were keenly alive to the important nature of the issues presented in the campaign, they did not dream that the new party, if successful, would have a gigantic civil war on its hands as the result of its triumph in a contest peaceably decided by the silent yet all-power· ful ballot. Resting in this fancied security from danger, the war was a surprise, for which they were but illy prepared.

I need not detail the situation of affairs when the news flashed over the wires that Fort Sumter was fired upon. Suffice it do say, that the South was up in arms, in full preparation almost, before the North could realize that war was at hand.

The first great battle of the war was fought, and the Union troops suffered a most humiliating defeat, falling back in disordered crowds upon Washington, and at this time General McClellan took command and brought order out of chaos.

The community did not seem to consider, or to understand, that it was necessary to spend so much time in drilling the troops and making elaborate preparations for the field. But the commanding officer was too good a general to imitate the impetuous actions of his predecessors, and to make an aggressive campaign with raw and undisciplined troops. It was in consequence of this, that months were spent in the patient and persistent task of properly organizing, drilling and equipping his men for the field, and in the spring of 1862, when the army did move, in the language of the General, it was one " from which much was to be expected."

Unfortunately, however, at the very outset, the General and the President had each matured a plan for the conduct of the war, and, in many respects, these where diametrically opposed to each other. At this point the question might be asked, whose plan should have been followed?

By the Constitution, the President is the Commander-in-Chief of all the armies and the navy of the United States, and is, of course, *ex-officio*, the highest military authority in the land. "But if a President disclaims all knowledge of military affairs," as President Lincoln did, "it then becomes a question how far he should defer the conduct of a war to his appointed Commander-in-Chief, who is supposed to be chosen on account of his skill and sagacity in military matters, and upon his presumed fitness for the position."

In President Lincoln's hesitation between the advice of his Generals in the field, and the views urged by his Cabinet lay the foundation of many of the blunders and mistakes of the war, the trouble being, as one writer affirms, that "instead of one mind, there were many minds influencing the management of military affairs." As the result of this there was a lack of concert and action between the two heads of the military department, and at the critical period of the campaign, McDowell's forces were held at Washington when McClellan expected him to re-enforce the army of the Potomac.

Notwithstanding all that has been said and written upon this subject, I have no hesitation in expressing the opinion, that had not the President and his advisors, stood in such ungrounded fear for the safety of Washington, and had not withheld McDowell's forces at a time when their absence was a most serious blow to the plans of General McClellan, the close of the year would have seen the Rebellion crushed, and the war ended.

At the commencement of the campaign I had an interview with General McClellan, and he expressed the utmost confidence in his ability, provided his plans were fully supported and carried out, to gain the objective point of the war, and to accomplish the reduction of the rebel capital. My force of operatives had been diligently at work in procuring what information that was possible of attainment, of the numbers of the enemy, and with such success that in March I was able to report the approximate strength of the rebel army at 115,500 men, apportioned about as follows:

At Manassas, Centerville and vicinity,	80,000
" Brooks' Station, Dumfries, &c., . .	18,000
" Leesburg, ...	4,500.
In the Shenandoah Valley, ...	13,000
Total, ...	115,500

In gaining this important information, Timothy Webster, Pryce Lewis, John Scobell and a host of other efficient members of my force, some of whom have already been mentioned in these pages, deserve especial credit for their sleepless energy in prosecuting the work that had been assigned to them.

On the 4th of April the forward movement was made, and the siege of Yorktown was begun. The result of this seige the student of history already knows, a simple detention of the Army of the Potomac, until the enemy could occupy and fortify Richmond. Here is where McClellan suffered from the detention of McDowell at Washington—he had prepared a plan with McDowell as one of its principal actors, and with that force withdrawn, the General's intentions were not only radically interfered with, but seriously deranged.

During this time the rebel army was being daily reinforced and strengthened, until, by June 26th, its numbers were swelled to nearly 200,000 effective men. McClellan, on the contrary, starting as he did, with a smaller army than he thought was necessary to cope with the enemy, found himself, when before their fortifications, after being deprived of McDowell's division, with an army of less than 90,000 effective troops.

Another element in this campaign must not be lost sight of. The Navy, whose co-operation and assistance had been promised and relied upon, was unable to aid him at all. Can it be wondered at, therefore, that his plans, however well laid, and whatever their merits, viewed from a military stand-point, or the stand-point of common sense, failed in their execution.

One writer, in speaking of the treatment of General McClellan, has well said : "A general of high spirit and sensitive soul might have found in the government's action the occasion for sending in his resignation ; but General McClellan continued in command, accepted the situation, and endeavored to make the best of it."

And still another has said, although inclined to be partial and unfair, in his account of the battles of Antietam and Fredericksburg :

"His capacity and energy as an organizer are universally recognized. He was an excellent strategist, and, in many respects, an excellent soldier. He did not use his own troops with sufficient promptness and vigor to achieve great and decisive results, but he was oftener successful than unsuccessful with them ; and he so conducted affairs that they never suffered heavily without inflicting heavy loss upon their adversaries. It may appear a strange statement to follow the other matter which this volume contains, but it is none the less true, that there are strong grounds for believing that he was the best commander the Army of the Potomac ever had." Concluding a comparison, that redounds much to the credit of General McClellan, both as a soldier and a patriot, the same writer says :

"A growing familiarity with his history as a soldier, increases the disposition to regard him with respect and gratitude, and to believe, while recognizing the limitations of his nature, that his failure to accomplish more was partly his misfortune, and not altogether his fault."

General McClellan knew much better than soem of his self-appointed critics the numbers and strength of the enemy. He knew from the reports 'of the secret service that the general estimate of the rebel army at, and around Richmond, was far below their real numbers.

My shrewd and daring operatives, men and women trained for the work, moved in and out among the Rebel troops at all times and places. From actual observation they gathered the location, character and strength of their fortifications, and from actual count the estimates were made of the numerical strength of the opposing army.

Suffice it to say, that I knew of my own knowledge, and General McClellan knew from the reports I laid before him, the fearful odds against which he had to contend in the bravely fought but disastrous campaign of the Peninsula.*

* See detailed statement in Appendix.

CHAPTER XXXII.

*Webster's Expedition.—His Gallantry.—A Stormy Passage.—
A Mysterious Package.—Treason Discovered and Punished.*

IT was Christmas morning, in Washington, and
the bells were ringing merrily throughout the
city. The sun was just peeping over the hills, and
lighting up the winter landscape with a beauty and
brilliancy that would defy the skill of an artist.
Washington was alive with soldiers. Throughout
the city the military was the predominating element,
and for miles around the country was dotted with the
white tents that marked the encampments of the
country's defenders. Thousands of muskets gleamed
in the morning light, as with the rattle of the drum
or the shrill blast of the bugle, the *reveille* awoke the
hills and valleys from the deathlike silence and slumber of the night.

The Union army was encamped around the
capital, and General McClellan was in command.
For months the process of drilling and disciplining
the volunteer troops had been going on under his
watchful eye and masterful hand, and the " Army of
the Potomac" was rapidly approaching a degree of

efficiency that was eminently calculated to make them formidable adversaries to their reckless and deter-mined enemies.

This morning, at my headquarters on I street, Timothy Webster was engaged in completing his arrangements for another extended journey into Rebeldom. By this time he had succeeded in thoroughly ingratiating himself into the favor of the rebel authorities, and at the War Department in Richmond he was regarded as a trusted emissary of the Confederate government.

Upon the trips which he had previously made he had carried numerous letters from Northern residents to their secessionist relatives in the South, and then, upon returning, he had delivered communications from Southern people to individuals north of the line. Of course these letters and communications, before being delivered to the parties to whom they were addressed, were first submitted to the inspection of trusted employees of my office, and anything which tended to convey information of the movements and intentions of the Southern leaders was carefully noted, and the Federal authorities duly notified. By this means a double purpose was served. Webster not only won the entire confidence of the Southern authorities, but he was very frequently the bearer of important dispatches, whose contents were often valuable to the Northern leaders.

After finishing his preparations, Webster came into my room, where Mr. Bangs and I were seated, and announcing his readiness to start, inquired if I had any further orders for him.

"I am ready now, Major," said he, cheerily, "have you any further commands?"

"No, Webster," said I, "I believe everything has been carefully arranged, and I have no commands to give except for you to take good care of yourself."

"I'll try to do that," he replied with a laugh, and then, tapping his breast lightly, where his letters were sewed into the lining of his waistcoat, "I will take care of my mail too."

With a warm clasp of the hand, and a hearty good-bye, Webster went out into the bright sunlight and frosty air of a winter's morning, and was soon lost to view.

Procuring a conveyance, Webster left Washington, passing the guards without difficulty, and made his way toward Leonardstown, in Maryland. This journey was accomplished without event or accident, and early on the following morning, he drove up before the hotel, and was warmly greeted by John Moore, the landlord of the hostelry at that place.

This Moore was a strong secessionist at heart, although openly professing to be a Union man, and regarding Webster as a Southern emissary his greeting was always cordial, and his hospitality unstinted. The air was cold and frosty, and riding all night in a stagecoach, which was far from being weather-proof,

Webster was chilled through when the stage stopped before the comfortable inn of John Moore. Very soon, however, a jug of steaming punch, and the genial warmth from a fire of crackling logs in the large open fire-place, were instrumental in loosening the stiffened joints of my tired operative, and contributing materially to his comfort.

"Well, John," said Webster at length, "what is the prospect for crossing the river to-night?"

"We can't cross here at all any more, Webster," replied Moore, with an oath; "the damned Yankees are too sharp for us."

"Is there no way of getting over about here at all?" asked Webster, somewhat troubled at the unexpected information.

"There's a way for some people," replied Moore with a laugh, and a significant wink, "and I guess you are included in the number."

"All right," said Webster, immeasurably relieved, "but how do we manage it?"

"Well," replied Moore, "you will have to go up to Cob Neck, and then I will see that you are taken care of."

Cob Neck is a point of land extending out from the main shore, about fourteen miles distant from Leonardstown, and was very well adapted for the purpose in view. On each side of the point, or neck, there was a wide bay or inlet where a boat could put out, and the ground, which was soft and marshy, was completely covered with a growth of pine thickets and underbrush, which prevented the placing of vigilant pickets at this point. Being perfectly acquainted with the locality named, Webster had no fears of being able to get safely across the Potomac into Virginia, and then continuing his way to the rebel capital.

" By the way," said Moore, " I have a favor to ask of you, Webster."

" Well," replied Webster, " anything I can do will be cheerfully done for you, Moore."

" I know that, Webster," said Moore, heartily, " and there is no one in the world I would rather oblige than you. The fact is, I have got two ladies here, who are wives of army officers, now stationed in Richmond, they have been living North for some time, and are anxious to get to their husbands ; they have three children with them, and I want you to take charge of the party, and see them safely on their way."

" I'll do that with pleasure," replied Webster, " and I'll take good care of them, too."

That night, about nine o'clock, a close-covered carriage was driven away from the hotel, in the direction of Cob Neck. John Moore and Timothy Webster sat on the driver's seat, while within were the families of the rebel officers, who had been placed in my operative's charge. Reaching their destination in safety, the party alighted, and walking out to the end of the point, Moore uttered a shrill whistle, which was immediately answered in the same manner. Soon they heard the splashing of oars, and in a few minutes a boat was discernable through the darkness, and the voice of a man called out :

" Here I am, Cap'n ! on time, as ye see."

" All right, Tom," replied Moore, " I've got a party here that you must take good care of."

" Very well, Cap'n, I'll do the best I can, but I'm afraid the wind ain't right for landin' on t'other side."

" Well," said Moore, " you must do your best, and I guess you will get over all right."

The night was dark and cold, the wind was blowing sharp and chill, and heavy clouds were shifting overhead. The river was running swiftly, and was of that inky blackness that invariably presages a storm. The wind through the low pines was sighing like a human being in distress, and the ladies gazed fearfully and shudderingly at the dark waters and the frail craft which was to carry them to the opposite shore. Webster uttered words of courage and assurance to the shrinking ladies, and assisted in comfortably bestowing them in the boat, and then, with a parting salutation to John Moore, the boat pushed off from the shore.

After getting clear of the land they hoisted sail, and were soon flying rapidly over the water, before the driving wind. As the wind was against them, they were obliged to make short and frequent tacks, and thus their approach to the opposite shore was accomplished by slow and labored degrees. The ladies were huddled together in the stern, clasping their frightened children nervously in their arms, while Webster, active and alert, rendered such assistance in managing the boat as was in his power.

"The storm's coming!" shouted the boatman, after a long silence, "and the women had better cover up."

The storm came, sure enough. A blinding rain, icy cold, which beat pitilessly down upon the unprotected voyagers, while the little vessel rocked to and fro at the mercy of the dashing waves. The wind suddenly changed, the frail yacht gave a sudden lurch, and in a twinkling the keel of the boat was heard scraping upon the bottom of the river, and they were aground. They had been blown out of their course, and had drifted into the shallow water, a mile below their landing place, and within a hundred feet of the shore.

Without a moment's hesitation, Webster bade the boatman lower his sail, and then, jumping into the water, which was waist deep, and as cold as ice, he took two of the children in his strong arms, and carried them safely to the river-bank. Returning again, he assisted in carrying the ladies and the remaining child ashore, although he was so chilled that his lips were blue and his knees knocked together with the cold. The nearest place of shelter was a mile away,

"Webster took two of the children in his strong arms, and carried them safely to the bank."

but unmindful of the cold and the pelting storm, Webster cheered his companions by his hearty words, and bidding the boatman take care of one of the children, he picked up another, and the weary party set out to walk through the icy rain to the little hut, whose welcome light was gleaming in the distance.

Thanks to a flask of good brandy, which Webster fortunately had with him, the ladies were strengthened and sustained sufficiently to make the journey; and when they arrived at last at the comfortable cabin, their words of gratitude to Webster were heartily and unstintingly uttered.

After warming themselves before the fire, and drying their drenched and dripping garments as far as practicable, the ladies retired to another room, leaving Webster, who, overcome with fatigue, was obliged to sleep in his wet clothing in the room to which they were first admitted. Unmindful of himself, however, his only solicitude was for the ladies who had been placed in his charge, and after they had been comfortably disposed of, he prepared to take his own much-needed rest.

He spread a blanket before the roaring blaze, and was about to stretch his weary limbs upon it, when he noticed, lying upon the floor, a short distance from him, a small packet, wrapped in oiled-cloth, and tied with red tape. It had evidently been dropped by one of the ladies, and its loss had escaped her notice. Picking it up, he examined it carefully by the light of the fire, and to his surprise he found that it was directed to Mr. Benjamin, the Rebel Secretary of War. As "all things are fair in love and war," Timothy lost no time in secreting the precious document about his own person. He had no objection at all to assisting two ladies to reach their husbands, even if they were enemies; but he objected decidedly to lend his aid to the forwarding of dangerous information to those who were fighting against the cause he held so dear. His conscience, therefore, gave him but little uneasiness as he pocketed the mysterious little packet, and with the resolve to discover its contents on the morrow, he stretched himself before the burning logs, and was soon sound asleep.

The next morning, when he arose, his clothing was dry, but he experienced acute pains in his limbs, and a sense of weariness, that boded no good to his physical condition. Ignoring his own ailments, however, he busied himself in securing the comfort of his charges, and after a hearty breakfast, the party set out upon their trip to Richmond. They traveled for several miles in an ox-cart, and then by team, to a place called Hop Yard Wharf, on the Rappahannock River. Here the party embarked on a steamboat, and traveled as far as Fredericksburg, where Webster was obliged to remain for two days, owing to an acute attack of rheumatism, which was caused by his exposure in behalf of the ladies, whose safety he had undertaken to insure. At this time he received a

Webster discovers a mysterious package.

P. 475.

striking illustration of the gratitude which one earns by the performance of a kindly act of self-sacrifice. No sooner had the boat landed at Fredericksburg, than these ladies expressed their impatient desire to push on directly to the rebel capital. Notwithstanding Webster's precarious condition, the danger in leaving him alone, and the fact that his sufferings had been occasioned by his efforts in their behalf, these high-toned Southern dames, intent only upon their selfish pleasures, left him to his own resources, and without displaying the slightest interest in his welfare they went their way, and Webster, unable to move himself, was obliged to depend upon the services of absolute strangers, for that care and attention of which he stood in so much need.

It was while he was detained at Fredericksburg, that he seized the opportunity of examining the package, which had come into his possession in the little cabin at Monroe's Creek. Removing the enfolding wrappers, he discovered that the contents of the bundle were complete maps of the country surrounding Washington, with a correct statement of the number and location of the Federal troops. Several items of information were also conveyed, in regard to the probable intentions of the Union Commanders in the coming spring. From the nature of this information, it was evident that a trusted officer of the Federal government was unfaithful to his duty, and was assisting the enemies of the country Webster congratulated himself upon the lucky chance which had thrown this little packet in his way, and he resolved to forward the same to me at the first opportunity that occurred.

On the second day, though suffering severely, he was able to resume his journey, and taking the train at Fredericksburg he was soon approaching the City of Richmond. Immediately upon his arrival, he repaired to the office of the Secretary of War, and delivered the letters which he had brought with him from the North, and which were to be forwarded to their various addresses by the Confederate authorities. Mr. Benjamin warmly congratulated Webster upon his success in passing through the Union lines, and for the information which he brought. He furnished him with passports, which would enable him to journey unrestricted and unquestioned throughout the Southern dominions, and requested a further interview at a later day.

Leaving the War Department, he went to the Monumental Hotel, where he engaged a room for himself, and where he found Mrs. Lawton, who had remained in the city during his absence. Mrs. Lawton informed Webster that she had just received a visit from Mr. Stanton, another of my operatives, who had arrived in Richmond from Nashville, Tenn., and that he was going to attempt to leave for Washington that night.

This was a lucky chance, and Webster resolved

to see Stanton, and entrust to him the conveyance of the packet that had so fortunately come into his hands. Knowing the places at which he would be most apt to be found, he made a tour of the city, and was at length fortunate enough to discover the man he was in search of. Selecting a secluded place, Webster confided his package to Stanton, instructing him to deliver it to no one but myself under any circumstances, and then, feeling the need of rest, he went back to the hotel, and shortly afterward retired to bed. The next day he was unable to move. His sufferings were excruciating, and for weeks he was compelled to endure the agonies of an acute attack of inflammatory rheumatism, which confined him a prisoner to his bed.

Leaving Webster at the Monumental Hotel, we will return to the movements of my operative, who had been delegated to deliver the package which Webster had found. Mr. Stanton arrived safely in Washington, and after rendering a report of his own observations upon his journey from Nashville to Washington, he produced this packet of Webster's, a careful examination of its contents revealed to me the author of the treasonable communications.

His name was James Howard, a native of the South, and he was a clerk in the Provost-Marshal's office. I had frequently seen his handwriting, and knew it perfectly. There could be no possibility of mistake about this, and I lost no time in laying before the commanding officer, the proof of the suspected man's guilt. Howard was confronted with the evidence against him, and finding it impossible to deny the truth, he confessed his treason, and implicated several others in the conspiracy. Before the shades of night had fallen over the tented city, James Howard, and his treasonable confederates, were placed within the enfolding walls of the old capital prison, and behind iron bars were left to meditate upon the heavy price they had paid for an attempt to betray their country.

"HAIL COLUMBIA!"

CHAPTER XXXIII.

Activity in Washington.—Webster's Journey Through The South.—His Return to the Capital.

DURING the month of January, 1862, I was actively engaged in the city of Washington. With a part of my force, I was acting in conjunction with General Andrew Porter, the Provost-Marshal of the district, while the remaining portion was assisting General McClellan in obtaining reliable information about the topography of the Southern country, and of the number and disposition of the Southern troops.

Almost every day witnessed some incident of importance to the national cause, and my time was fully occupied with the numerous and responsible duties which necessarily devolved upon me. Mr. George H. Bangs, who is now the general superintendent of my agencies, was detailed to the headquarters of the army, while I remained in charge of my office on " I " street, although I was kept fully informed by daily reports of whatever transpired at both places. As may readily be imagined, my office was no sinecure. Many times I was obliged to deprive myself of needed rest and sleep, engaged in laborious duties from early morn far into the waking hours of the succeeding day, and for weeks scarcely obtaining a peaceful night's slumber. The capital was filled with suspicious personages, with Southern spies, and their Northern allies, and frequently officers of the government, holding elevated positions, would be discovered in secret, but active correspondence with the rebel authorities. Arrests were numerous, and the searching of suspected premises of almost daily occurrence, while the large number of men employed by me required constant and unceasing personal surveillance.

In the army it was astonishing what rapid progress had been made in drilling and disciplining the large, and, for the most part, untried force of soldiery. The commanding general was engaged in perfecting his plans for a campaign against Richmond, and in order to do this intelligently, much information was required of the condition of the country through which the army must pass, and of the number of the enemy he would be likely to encounter. The obstacles that must be overcome, the defenses which would impede his passage, and all the minutia of war-like particularities, were mainly left to be discovered by the men in the secret service department, of which I was the authorized leader, and responsible head. Engaged in these duties the month of January passed away. Numerous operatives had been dispatched into the hostile country before us, and had made their examinations, and returned, conveying to me and to the commanding general items of valuable information which could have been obtained in no other way.

We will now follow the movements of Timothy Webster, whom we left in Richmond struggling with his old and relentless enemy, the rheumatism.

After a painful confinement to his bed for nearly a week, he was at last able to move about once more, and in a few days thereafter was strong enough to uundertake a journey which he had been contemplating for some time.

In company with one of the largest contractors for the rebel government, he left Richmond for Nashville, Tennessee. Mr. Campbell, the contractor, was engaged in the purchaser of leather and desirous of purchasing directly from the tanner, instead of depending upon the dealers, who might not be able to supply him in such quantities as he required. Traveling with this gentleman, and armed as he was, with an all powerful passport from the Secretary of War, Webster would have every opportunity for making his observations without incurring the slightest suspicion. During this journey he traveled through Knoxville, Chattanooga and Nashville, in Tennessee, then to Bowling Green, in Kentucky, and then, on his return, he passed through Manassas and Centreville, carefully noting in his passage through the country the number and condition of the various troops, the number and extent of batteries and fortifications, and eliciting an amount of information that seemed wonderful for one man to accomplish. He made the acquaintance of commanding officers, and conversed unreservedly with them upon the various matters connected with their divisions, and their movements, present and perspective. He carefully examined the fortifications that had been erected, and the number of guns they contained. He talked with the private soldier and the civilian, and in fact, on his return to Richmond, was as well informed with regard to the military resources of the enemy as were the generals themselves. Rejoiced at his success, and carefully noting what he had witnessed, Webster prepared to return North.

Visiting the War Department and the office of the Provost-Marshal, he received from Mr. Benjamin and General Winder a large number of letters and several important commissions, which were to be delivered and attended to after he should arrive in Washington and Baltimore.

Leaving Richmond, he safely passed the pickets and outposts of both Federals and rebels, and reported to me. His trip had been a most important and successful one, and the information he brought was most invaluable. Webster seemed as well pleased at his success as were either General McClellan or myself, and after a short rest announced himself as quite prepared to make another journey to the South, whenever his services should be required.

CHAPTER XXXIV.

Webster's Last Mission.—Anxiety at his Long Absence.—No Tidings of the Faithful Scout.—Operatives Sent in Search of him.—Webster Ill in Richmond.

IN the latter part of January, 1862, another packet of rebel mail matter had accumulated, and the various articles, which Webster had agreed to purchase for the residents of Richmond and vicinity, were ready for delivery, and Webster prepared himself for another journey into the South. While in Washington he had not experienced any painful reminders of his old disease, and he was impatient to be actively employed once more.

Accordingly, everything was arranged for his trip, and early one bright winter's morning he came, as was his custom, to bid me farewell.

I often recall, and with an emotion that I cannot control, the appearance of Timothy Webster, as I saw him that day. Brave, strong and manly, he stood before me. The merry twinkle in his eyes seemed to belie the sternness of the set lips, which were even now curved with a smile of good humor. No trace of fear or hesitancy was apparent in his manner. He seemed to be animated solely by an earnest desire to serve his country to the best of his ability. He well knew, as did I, that his journey lay through a hostile country; that danger was lurking everywhere around him, and that if his true character was discov-ered, the consequences would, no doubt, prove fatal to him. Notwithstanding this, there was no quivering of the compact muscles, the hand that grasped mine was as firm as iron, and the brave heart that throbbed in his bosom was insensible alike to a thought of shrinking, or a desire to evade, the responsibility that devolved upon him.

After a few words of necessary caution and with good wishes for his welfare and safe return, Timothy Webster took his departure, and went his way. I did not know then that I had looked upon his face and manly form for the last time, and no hint or warning of his subsequent fate came to me as I sat watching his retreating figure. But to this day, I can picture him with sentiments of pride, in his valor and services, and regrets, deep and heartfelt, for the brave man who but a few months afterwards laid down his life for his country.

For some time previous to this journey of Web-ster's, Mrs. Lawton had been located at Leonards-town, where she had assiduously cultivated the ac-quaintance of the most important people in that local-ity, whose sympathies were with the Southern cause, and whose assistance to Webster and herself would be valuable in time of need.

Among this number was a man whose name was Washington Gough, a wealthy secessionist, who was one of the most active in his efforts to assist the Southern blockade-runners in crossing over into Virginia, and in eluding the watchfulness of the Federal pickets. Through her acquaintance with this man, Mrs. Lawton was enabled to acquire much valuable information from those who sought the aid of Mr. Gough in obtaining the facilities for reaching the rebel lines in safety.

With Gough, Webster was a prime favorite, and so thoroughly had my operative ingratiated himself into the favorable opinion of this rebel gentleman, that any service which would be required would be performed without question or delay. Mrs. Lawton was invited to make the house of Gough her home, while in Leonardstown, and by her charms of mnaner and conversation proved a powerful ally to Webster in the discovery of important secrets relating to the movements and intentions of the enemy.

Webster's footing with the rebel authorities was also firmly established, and every one of them with whom he came in contact yielded to the magic of his blandishments and was disposed to serve him whenever possible.

An event which happened about this time fully justified this assertion. It appeared that during Webster's absence from Leonardstown, a gentleman by the name of Camilear had crossed over the river, and although a noted secessionist in his own immediate vicinity, was not known to any one upon the other side of the water. He was accordingly arrested and placed in confinement. The appeals of his friends and relatives were unavailing in securing his release, and the captive chafed terribly under the burden of his captivity. At length, on Webster's appearance, the matter was presented to him, and he was entreated by Camilear's relatives to intercede in his behalf. He promised to do so, and indited a letter to the officer who had the prisoner in charge, requesting his release, and giving assurances of the man's fealty to the Confederate government. In a few days the prisoner was returned to his home, and was informed by the officer, that only the protestations made by Webster had been sufficient to accomplish his release. From the highest to the lowest, the confidence in Webster was universal.

On this last mentioned trip Webster decided to take Mrs. Lawton with him, and having obtained my sanction to his proposition, he journeyed to Leonardstown and communicated his wishes to the lady, who was nothing loath to accompany him. They accordingly made their preparations, and in the darkness of the night they made their way to the river-bank where an oyster boat was in waiting to cross the river. Mrs. Lawton wore an overcoat and felt hat belonging to Webster, and to a casual observer appeared very masculine in her habiliments. The river was entirely clear of vessels, and the journey was made in perfect safety. As they neared the opposite bank the moon shone out brightly, and revealed the "pungy" to the rebel pickets, who were known by Webster, and from whom he expected no interference or opposition.

The lights on shore revealed the stations of these pickets, and as they were expecting his return Webster called out loudly : "Pickets ! Pickets ! !"

There was no response to this call, and to his dismay the lights were suddenly extingiushed. The boatman was greatly frightened at this proceeding, and was in momentary dread of being fired upon ; but Webster reassured him, and continued his loud, but ineffectual calls for the guard.

Finding it impossible to attract the attention of those who should have been upon the lookout for him, Webster assisted the boatman in landing their trunks, after which the "pungy" was pushed off from the shore, and soon afterwards disappeared in the darkness.

Webster and his companion wandered about for more than an hour, and it was nearly midnight when they came to a farm house, where their approach was heralded by the loud barking of numerous dogs, who were aroused by the unwonted presence of human beings, and were diposed to resent their approach.

The noise of the dogs brought the farmer to his

door, who demanded, in no very gentle terms, to know who they were, and what had brought them there at that unseasonable hour. In a few words Webster explained the situation, and the genial farmer bade them welcome, and safely bestowed them for the night.

They had scarcely retired, when they were aroused by a loud knocking at the door, which was discovered to have been made by the pickets from the adjoining camp, who demanded to know who the new-comers were, and stated that they had been ordered to bring them immediately before an officer of the guard, two miles away.

"Why didn't you tell them that, when they called out to you before?" inquired the farmer, in a contemptuous tone.

"Well we did not know who they were," answered the leader of the party, "and we did not think it was safe."

"Oho! you were afraid of them, were you, and ran away?"

At this point, Webster, who had heard the conversation, made his appearance at the door, and demanded to know what was wanted.

The leader of the guard again explained his mission, and demanded that Webster should accompany him to the camp.

"Tell your commander that I will not stir from this house until morning. My name is Timothy

Webster. I am in the employ of the Confederacy, and if you had answered my call, there would have been no difficulty

Finding that Webster was determined, the men went away, and left the household to their repose. The next morning Webster reported at the camp, and requested to see Major Beale, the officer in command. He was informed, that this gentleman was stationed twenty miles away, and upon telegraphing to him, the answer was returned : " Let Webster go where he pleases."

The day was cold and stormy, and the roads were in a wretched condition, but notwithstanding this Webster pushed on to Fredericksburg, and after delivering some letters and merchandise which he had brought for residents there, he pushed on to Richmond.

Taking up their quarters at the hotel, they resolved to wait until the following day before commencing their operations. During the night, however, Webster's malady returned, and he suffered terribly from his old enemy, the rheumatism. In the morning he was helpless, and unable to move.

From this time, I heard nothing further from him directly, and for weeks was utterly ignorant of his movements or condition. I began to grow alarmed. Hitherto, his visits had not occupied more than three or four weeks, and he had always succeeded in escaping suspicion, and evading being detained by either force through which he would necessarily be obliged to pass. As the days and weeks passed, and brought no tidings from him, my apprehensions became so strong that I resolved to send one or two of my men to the rebel capital, in order to ascertain the cause of his unusual and long-continued absence.

My anxiety was equally shared by General McClellan, with whom Webster was a great favorite, and who placed the utmost reliance upon his reports. One evening, early in February, the General called upon me, and advised the sending of one messenger, or two, for the sole purpose of hunting up Webster, or discovering some trace of him. I informed him that I had already considered the necessity of some such action, and was upon the point of submitting the matter for his approval. Finding the General thus fully in accord with the proposition, I at once selected two of my men for this important mission. After mature consideration, I decided upon despatching Price Lewis and John Scully upon this delicate quest. My reasons for this selection, were that both Scully and Lewis had been connected with other operations in Baltimore, in company with Webster, and had thus been enabled to form the acquaintance of a great number of secessionists in that city, some of whom had gone South, while others, who remained at home, had influential friends in Richmond. During these operations, both Lewis and Scully had pretended the most earnest and sincere sympathy for the cause of the Confederacy, and were known as ardent secessionists. This, I concluded, would materially assist them after reaching Richmond, particularly if they should be fortunate enough to meet any of their old Baltimore associates. They had also been engaged upon various investigations through the Southern States, and especially in Western Virginia, where they had rendered good service in the early campaigns in that section of the country. I had, therefore, no doubt of their ability to perform the task assigned to them, and felt perfectly satisfied that they would perform their duties to the best of that ability.

Requesting their presence in my private office, I broached the matter to them, and submitted the question of their undertaking this task to their own election. Upon operations of this kind, where there was danger to be incurred, where a man literally took his life into his own hands, and where death might be the result of detection, I invariably placed the question upon its merits, before the person selected for the mission, and then allowed him to decide for himself, whether he would voluntarily undertake its accomplishment.

I did this for various reasons. In the first place, I felt very loath to peremptorily order a man upon an enterprize where there was every possibility of danger, for in the event of fatal result, I should be disposed to reproach myself for thus endangering the

lives of those under my command. It is true, that
under their terms of service, and by virtue of the
authority vested in me, I had the undoubted right to
issue such order; but I always preferred that my men
should voluntarily, and without urging, signify their
willingness to undertake hazardous missions. Again,
I have invariably found, that the ready and cheerful
officer performs the most acceptable service, and that
the absence of fear or hesitation are sure passports
to success; while on the other hand, should there be
timidity or unwillingness, or a disposition to avoid
danger, success is rarely, if ever, attained.

It is but just, however, to state that during my
entire connection with the secret service of the government, I never found any of my men disinclined to
undertake an operation that was delegated to them;
but on the contrary, I alwa s experienced the utmost
cheerfulness and ready support from those who so
valiantly served under my orders. Nor was I disappointed in the present instance. On presenting
the case, with all its attendant dangers, to Price
Lewis and John Scully, both of them signified, without the slightest hesitation, their voluntary desire to
go to Richmond, and to make the inquiries, which
were considered of so much importance by both
General McClelkan and myself.

But few instructions, and very little preparation,
were required for this journey, and in the afternoon
both men were prepared to start. I did not deem it ad-

visable to provide them with any goods, as was some-times the case, in order to furnish an excuse for their blockade-running experiences, for the reason that their journey would be much delayed, owing to the impassability of many of the roads. I did, however, cause a letter to be written, apparently by a rebel spy, then in Washington, and which was directed to Webster. This letter introduced the two men to Webster as friends of the South, and informed him that his old route back was no longer a safe one, owing to the presence of Federal troops in that locality, and advising him to select some other and less hazardous one on his return to Washington. I did this to guard against their being suspected and detained after reaching the rebel lines, as, upon presenting this, they would at once be known as Southern emissaries, and given safe conduct to the capital. Provided with this letter, and with full verbal instructions as to their manner of proceeding, they started from Washington late on the evening of the 14th of February. As an additional safeguard, I sent along with them an operative by the name of William H. Scott, who was well acquainted with the various Federal commanders, and who was to see them safely across the Potomac river.

The three men departed in good spirits, and, though fully conscious of the danger before them, thoroughly resolved to successfully accomplish what they had undertaken.

Prior to despatching these men, I had some misgivings that there might be still remaining in Richmond some of those families who, while residing in Washington, had been suspected of sympathizing with, or furthering the cause of the Confederacy, and whose papers had been seized, and themselves transported beyond the lines. Among the most noted of these were the families of Mrs. Phillips, of South Carolina, and of Mrs. Ex-Gov. Morton, of Florida, who had been residing in Richmond for a short time. To satisfy myself upon this point, I made extensive inquiries from deserters, refugees and contrabands, and learned, from a variety of sources, that Mrs. Phillips had gone to Charleston, and that Mrs. Morton and her family had departed for their home in Florida. Believing my information to be reliable, I felt reassured, and then the men were selected.

While these men were making their way to Richmond, Webster was suffering excruciating pain, confined to his bed, and unable to move. During all this time, he was carefully attended and nursed by my resident operative, Mrs. Hattie Lawton, and through the long, weary days and sleepless nights, no patient ever had more careful nursing, or more tender consideration than did Timothy Webster, from the brave true-hearted woman who had dedicated her life and her services to the cause of her country and its noble defenders.

This was the state of affairs on the last day of

January, and when the information which Webster had gained would have been of vast importance and benefit to the cause of the Union, but which, lying an agonized invalid in a Richmond hotel, he was unable to communicate to those who were anxiously awaiting his return. And now, leaving Webster at Richmond, and with Price Lewis and John Scully on their way to the rebel capital, we will return to Washington, and watch the events which were transpiring at the capital.

32

EXCHANGE OF PRISONERS.

CHAPTER XXXV.

McClellan and the Government.—Lewis and Scully Arrested as Spies.—An Attempted Escape.—Trial and Conviction. — Condemned to Die. — Before the Gallows their Mouths are Opened.

THE month of February added its slowly passing days to those that had preceded it, and as yet no tidings were received from Timothy Webster, or from those who had gone in search of him. W. H. Scott had returned, and reported that they had safely passed over the Potomac River, and landed upon rebel soil, but further than this, I had no information that tended to allay my anxieties, or to give assurance of their safety.

In the meantime, the troops around Washington had not been idle. Reconnoissances had been made from time to time, by the advance-guard of the army, and skirmishes with the enemy were of frequent oc·currence. These movements were of great importance, not so much from the actual results of victories attained, as for the education which it imparted to the troops, in accustoming them to the presence of their foes, and giving them confidence while under fire.

General McClellan had completed his plans for the investment of the rebel capital, and the public mind was in a state of feverish anxiety and expectation for the forward movement of the troops. The popular cry of " On to Richmond," was echoed from lip to lip throughout the entire country. Every one, except those who knew and realized the danger and difficulties to be encountered and overcome, were filled with an enthusiasm which only regarded results and never considered the cost of their accomplishment. Extravagant ideas of a struggle which should be "short, sharp and decisive," were the only ones entertained by the great army of " stay at homes," and the question of caution, foresight and sagacity was left to the consideration of those who must brave the dangers of the field, and face the deadly fire of their determined enemies.

Added to this a feeling of dissatisfaction began to display itself in high circles at Washington. The delay, which General McClellan wisely deemed necessary for the perfect equipment and education of his army, was being used as a pretext by those who envied the young commander, to detract from his reputation, and to impair the confidence which a united people had reposed in his loyalty and ability. The President was besieged by importunate cavillers the burden of whose refrain was the defamation ot the hero of West Virginia, and it is not surprising, however much to be regretted, that Mr. Lincoln gradually permitted their clamors to disturb him, and eventually partook of some of the distrust with which they endeavored to impress him. From a legitimate and wise desire to prevent an untimely divulgence of his plans, General McClellan had, up to this time, kept his ideas and opinions to himself and confined his military discussions to but a few of his immediate officers, and those whom he had known and trusted for years. This manner of proceeding was not to the taste of some of the leading men in high places at that time, who deemed themselves as competent to confer with and advise the commanding general, as those whom he had chosen. In order to soothe their wounded self-pride they had recourse to a species of revenge not admirable, to say the least. They plied the ears of the President with comments derogatory to McClellan, and with innumerable suggestions of pet schemes of their own conception, which would, in their opinion, undoubtedly end the war with surprising alacrity. The result of these onslaughts was, that McClellan was required by Mr. Lincoln to unfold his own carefully arranged plans to a council of generals, for their consideration and approval. To this "wicked and ignorant clamor" he was obliged to yield, and it is not to be wondered at, that his proposed movements were betrayed, and that not long afterwards he was subjected to the mortification of having his army divided into corps, against his wishes, and their commanders appointed without consulting him, and without his knowledge. Subsequently he was compelled to sub mit to having the conduct of the war in Virginia placed in charge of inexperienced, irresponsible and jealous-minded officers, whose antipathy to him was as well known as it was unceasing and violent.

Notwithstanding all this, the general pursued his way. His army was organized, his plans prepared. The defense of Washington was provided for, as he thought, in the most complete manner possible, and in command of a noble army, which had grown up under his immediate guidance and control, the brave commander started upon his campaign.

During the month of March, 1862, the forward movement was commenced. By divisions the army was transported from Alexandria to their point of destination upon the Peninsula, and on the first day of April, General McClellan embarked, with his head-quarters, on the steamer "Commodore," reaching Fort Monroe on the afternoon of the following day.

At this point we will leave the army, to follow the movements of my operatives, and detail their experiences in the rebel capital, although the facts were not reported to me until a long time after their actual occurrence.

Price Lewis and John Scully reached the city of Richmond without accident or delay, and at once established themselves in the Exchange Hotel, where they remained quietly for the night. The next morning they started out to search for Timothy Webster, and for the purpose of obtaining reliable information of him they went to the office of the *Richmond Enquirer*, for the proprietors of which Webster had frequently carried letters, and purchased goods while in the North. Here they were informed that Webster was confined to his bed at the Monumental Hotel. Repairing at once to the place where they were directed, they were shown to Webster's room, and here they found the brave fellow, lying a weak and helpless invalid, attended by Mrs, Lawton, whose attentions to him were unremitting. There was also in the room, a Mr. Pierce, a warm Southern friend, whose friendship for Webster was of long standing, and whose visits to the sick man were of daily occurrence.

The recognition between them was a most formal and undemonstrative one, and no one would have suspected that they were engaged in the same vocation, and acting under the same authority. During the short interview that ensued, Webster was fretful and ill at ease. Knowing the sentiments of the people as he did, and associated as intimately as he was with the most prominent of the Confederate authorities, he was fearful that the precipitate and unheralded appearance of his companions might lead to their being suspected, as well as to attaching suspicion to himself.

The few words of conversation, therefore, that

ensued, were marked by a constraint which was uncomfortable to all parties, and the visit was of short duration. When they called again upon Webster, they found with him a rebel officer from the Provost-Marshal's office, who was a friend of Webster, and who visited him frequently.

Webster introduced his two friends to Captain McCubbin, for that was the man's name, and after a few minutes, that officer inquired :

" Have you gentlemen reported at General Winder's office ?"

" No, sir," replied Lewis, "we did not think it was necessary, having fully reported to Major Beale, and received his permission to travel."

" It *is* necessary for you to report to the Provost-Marshal here, and I now give you *official* notice of the fact," said McCubbin, laughingly.

" Very well," returned Lewis, "we will do so as early as possible."

" Any time within a day or two will answer," said the officer.

Webster watched the rebel captain carefully while he was speaking, and he thought he detected beneath his careless, laughing demeanor, an element of suspicion, which he did not like, and more than ever he deplored the fact that my men had visited him so soon, or had appeared to be acquaintances of his. However, the mistake had been made, if mistake it was, and he resolved to give the matter as little concern as possible, trusting that his anxiety was ill-founded, and that all would be right in the end.

On the following morning my two operatives presented themselves at the office of the Provost-Marshal, and meeting Captain McCubbin there, they were soon introduced to General Winder, who occupied that position in the rebel capital. After they had been formally introduced to General Winder, that officer made very minute inquiries, as to the antecedents and the business of the two men before him, although no word was mentioned, that led either of them to believe that they were suspected of being other than they seemed. They informed the Marshal that they were natives of England and Ireland, that Scully had been in America nearly three years, while Lewis had arrived only eighteen months before; that one of them had been connected with a prominent dry-goods house in New York city, and the other represented a London publishing firm, whose office was located in the same city. They also stated that in Baltimore they had become acquainted with W. H. Scott, who had informed them of great opportunities for making money by smuggling goods into the Confederacy, and that this visit had been made to afford them the knowledge requisite to embarking in such an enterprize. They had agreed to deliver the letter, which Mr. Scott gave them, to Mr. Webster, which they had done, and further than this their intimacy with either gentlemen did not extend.

This interview was conducted in a very pleasant manner by General Winder, and after they had fully answered all the questions which had been propounded to them, they took their leave, being politely invited by the General to call upon him whenever convenient.

Congratulating themselves upon the fortunate outcome of a visit which they had looked forward to with more or less solicitude, they repaired to Webster's room to give him an account of what had transpired.

They had not been seated very long, when a detective from the Marshal's office made his appearance, and after apologizing for his visit, inquired from what parts of England and Ireland the two men had come; stating also, that General Winder desired the information.

After this man had left, Webster turned to his companions and in as firm a voice as he could command, said :

"Get away from Richmond immediately! There is danger brewing. You are certainly suspected, and it may go very hard with all of us, unless you leave the city at once!"

"Why do you think so?" inquired Scully, in a skeptical tone. "We certainly cannot be suspected, and I am confident that you are alarming yourself unnecessarily."

A spasm of pain prevented Webster from replying immediately; but when the agony had somewhat subsided, he answered:

" I tell you that man never would have come here with that question unless there was something wrong. You must, indeed, get away, or the consequences will be serious."

Scarcely had he uttered these words, when there came a sharp rap at the door, which, upon being opened, revealed the forms of two men, one of them being George Cluckner, a detective officer attached to the Provost-Marshal's office, and the other no less a personage than Chase Morton, a son of ex-Governor Morton, of Florida, whose house in Washington my operatives had at one time assisted in searching.

The consternation of Lewis and Scully may well be imagined, and the latter, without uttering a word, walked rapidly towards the open doorway and disappeared, leaving Lewis, filled with astonishment and apprehension, to pass the ordeal of an introduction. The salutations between them were, as may be conjectured, not of a very cordial character; and after the merest form of politeness, Lewis bade Webster good-evening, and left the room. At the top of the landing he found Scully awaiting him, and they were about to descend the stairs, felicitating themselves upon having escaped a threatened danger, when the door of Webster's room was opened, and the Confederate detective again stood before them.

"Are your names Lewis and Scully?" he inquired.

"Yes, sir," answered Lewis, promptly, resolved to put as bold a face upon the matter as possible.

"Then," said the officer, "I have orders to convey you to General Winder's office."

There was no help for it, and they signified their readiness to accompany him at once, intending to make an effort to escape when they reached the street. This hope, however, was dashed to the ground; for, as they descended the stairs, they found three other officers awaiting their appearance, who immediately took them in charge, and accompanied them to the Provost-Marshal's office.

Several times, during their journey, Lewis noticed, with increasing apprehension, that the gaze of young Chase Morton was riveted fixedly upon them, and he had no doubt whatever that they had been recognized, and would certainly be apprehended. This prospect was far from being a cheerful one; but they mustered up all their latent courage, and conversed good-humoredly with their escort, as they walked briskly along.

Arriving at the General's headquarters, they learned that that functionary was absent upon some urgent business, but would shortly return, and had left orders that they should await his appearance. Lewis and Scully were accordingly admitted to a private room, and requested to make themselves comfortable until General Winder should desire ther presence. The door closed upon the retreating forms of their escort, and left them in a most uncomfortable condition of mind indeed. There was now no doubt of the correctness of Webster's suspicions, and they bitterly regretted their haste in visiting him, and also not having taken his advice at once. However, this was no time for regrets, and they resolved to firmly adhere to their original statements, and await the disposition of their case by General Winder.

While they were conversing together, the door was opened, and young Morton entered the room, accompanied by an officer. Stepping directly up to Price Lewis, he addressed him :

" Don't you remember me ?"

" I do not," responded Lewis ; " I do not remember to have seen you at any time before to-day."

He looked unflinchingly into the eyes that met his, and the determined tones of his voice betrayed no trace of the emotions that were raging within his bosom.

" Don't you remember," continued young Morton, " coming to my mother's house, in Washington, as an agent of the secret service of the Federal government, and making a thorough search of our premises and its contents ?"

" You are mistaken, sir," replied Lewis, firmly " I know nothing of what you are alluding to."

"I am not mistaken," said the young Southerner, "and you are the man!"

"Perhaps this gentleman will say that he recollects me, next," said Scully, resolved to be as bold as possible, under the circumstances.

Chase Morton gazed at him a few moments and then answered, decidedly:

"Yes sir, I recollect you also; you were one of the men who assisted in searching my mother's residence."

Both men insisted strongly upon their ignorance of any such proceeding, and indignantly repudiated the charges that had been made against them.

At this juncture General Winder came in, and walking up to Lewis he greeted him cordially, warmly shaking him by the hand, saying:

"How do you do, Mr. Lewis, and how is Mr. Seward?"

"I do not know what you mean," replied Lewis.

"Perhaps not," said Winder, with a disagreeable smile, "but I am inclined to think that you know a great deal more than you are willing to admit."

"I do not understand you."

"Very well," said the Provost-Marshal, "you will understand me, and all in good time. Do you know gentlemen, I suspected you were all wrong from the start, and you were not keen enough to impose your story upon me? George," he added, turning to one of his men, "go to the hotel, and get the baggage belonging to these gentlemen. We will see if that will throw any further light upon their true character."

The officer departed, and during his absence, General Winder plied them with questions about their mission; their knowledge of Timothy Webster; their visit to Richmond, and in fact about everything imaginable, and all of them showing conclusively that he believed them to be spies, and unworthy of credence. Their satchels were finally brought in, and a rigid examination failed to discover anything to justify his suspicions, and Winder finally left the room, angrily ordering them to remain where they were, and directing his officers and Chase Morton to accompany him.

A few minutes elapsed after their departure, during which the loud voice of Winder could be heard, angrily declaiming against the two men; he then came back again, and addressing my operatives said:

"Gentlemen, your stories don't agree with what I know about you, and we will give you time to think the matter over;" then turning to his deputy he commanded, "Take them away!"

"Where to?" inquired the officer.

"To Henrico Jail," was Winder's response.

They were then conducted to the jail and placed in a room in which six others were confined, where the officers left them to their meditations, which, as may be imagined, were far from pleasant. Not knowing what might be in store for them, and fearing that their presence in Richmond might result in danger to Webster, they resolved to say nothing whatever, and to adhere strictly to the story originally told by them, and then to abide by the consequences, no matter how serious they might be.

During the afternoon of the following day, an officer accompanied by an elder son of Mr. Morton made their appearance at the jail, and he, too, identified the two men, as being concerned in searching his mother's residence in Washington, and endeavored to recall several incidents which had taken place on that occasion. To all of his statements, however, Price and Scully made emphatic denials, and vehemently asserted their entire ignorance of anything connected with the Mortons, or their relations to the Federal government.

Finding it impossible to obtain any admission from the two prisoners, they took their departure, and left the confined detectives to their own unpleasant reflections.

For three days they remained in their place of confinement, and during that time no word came from the Marshals office or from any one concerning their disposition or future movements. It seemed as though the authorities had been content with simply placing them in durance vile, and then had dismissed them from their minds. This was the most favorable view they were able to take of the case, and they were solacing themselves with the fallacious hope of having escaped a fate which they dreaded, and also with the belief that Webster, their friend and companion, would not be associated with their presence in Richmond, and that their discovery would not operate to his injury.

On the fourth day, however, an attaché of the Marshal's office came to the jail, and calling for John Scully informed him that his presence was required by General Winder. Scully prepared himself for the visit, and taking leave of his companion followed the officer. He did not return that night, and for days afterwards Lewis was in ignorance of what had become of him, or what fate he was to expect at the hands of these minions of disloyalty and secession.

Lewis, meanwhile, had become acquainted with his fellow prisoners, all of whom were in a state of anxiety as to what measure of punishment would be meted out to them, and all nearly crazed with the uncertainty of their impending fate. For days they had been concocting a plan of escape, and finding Lewis disposed to make an effort to be released from his confinement, they developed their plans to him, and requested his aid in the accomplishment of their purpose.

Lewis hailed with delight a proposition that promised to enable them to exchange the damp and noisome air of a prison for the free breath of nature, and the dark hours of captivity for the freedom and liberty he longed for, and he became an energetic and careful coadjutor of those who suffered with him the degrading position of being imprisoned by a government which they despised, and by which their lives were menaced.

The part of the jail in which they were confined was separated from the main building, and contained four cells, two upon the ground floor and two immediately above them. These cells were reached through a corridor from the yard outside, and secured by two doors; one a heavy iron one fastened on the inside, and the other a stout wooden barricade, the lock of which was placed on the outside of the building. It was the custom of the old man, who acted as the jailer, to allow the prisoners a half hour's walk in the yard during the early evening, and then, locking them up safely again, he would leave them alone in the building, while he went to his home, several blocks distant.

One of the men had managed to secrete a file about his person, and with this they succeeded in making a saw out of a knife. These were the only implements which they had to work with. Notwithstanding the meagerness of their implements, but a few days had elapsed before the bolts on every cell-door were sawed through so that they only required a few minutes' labor to detach them from their fastenings altogether.

It is impossible to detail the hours of feverish

33

anxiety, of tireless energy, and of momentary fear of detection, through which these men passed while engaged in their difficult and dangerous work—or to depict their joy, when at last their labor was completed, and they awaited the time of carrying their plans into execution.

The outside door was now the only barrier between them and their coveted freedom, and various plans were suggested to overcome this obstacle. At length one was decided upon which promised to secure the object of their desires. In one corner of the yard in which they took their daily exercise, there was a large pile of ashes and garbage, which had been accumulating for a long time. It was resolved that one of their number should be buried under this rubbish, while several of the other prisoners engaged the old jailer in animated conversation.

The man selected for this purpose was a good, brave fellow, who was formerly a sailor, and had lately been a member of an artillery company from New York. His name was Charles Stanton, and he had come into the South upon his own inclination, and for the Quixotic purpose of obtaining command of a gunboat of the Confederacy, and then attempting to run it through to the Union lines. He had, however, been suspected, and remanded to prison, where he had remained without a trial, and without hope of release, for several months.

The prisoners were all turned out for their usual

exercise in the yard, on the evening which had been agreed upon ; and in accordance with their arranged plan, several of the prisoners surrounded the old turnkey, and engaged him in an earnest discussion, while others set actively to work to dig the grave of Stanton in the ashes. In order that he might not be unbearably uncomfortable, his body only was covered with the contents of the ash-heap, while his head and shoulders were concealed from view by some straw, which one of the men brought from his cell for that purpose.

In the jail, at this time, there were a number of negroes, who had been captured while attempting to make their way to the North, and although these faithful blacks were aware of the attempted escape, and knew full well that they were not included in the movement, their efforts were none the less active in behalf of the white men who were struggling for liberty.

They had been informed of the attempted escape, from the first, and had kept the matter a profound secret, at the same time rendering such service as they were capable of to the whites.

Everything worked to their entire satisfaction. The turnkey was unsuspicious ; the grave was made without discovery, and Stanton was carefully concealed. In a few minutes afterwards the call for retiring was heard, and the men, with throbbing hearts, rushed in a mass toward the door of the corridor. This was done in order to escape the counting of their number, in case the old man should attempt to do so. They passed quickly into their cells, and were not required to be counted. Thus far, all had been done as successfully as could be hoped for, or expected ; no suspicions were excited, nor was their missing comrade called for. It had been the custom of the old man to make a tour of the cells after the prisoners had retired, to see if they were all there before he went away for the night. In order to overcome this possibility of detection, a figure had been made of straw, stuffed into the garments of the men, and laid upon the bed, in order to look as much like a human being as possible.

This precaution proved to be a good one, for just before the time of closing up the prison arrived, the glimmer of the old turnkey's lantern was seen in the corridor, and shortly after, his face appeared at the door, as he eagerly scanned the occupants of the various cells. Apparently satisfied with his scrutiny, the jailer went his way, the heavy outside doors were closed and locked, and the retreating footsteps of the old man could be distinctly heard.

The critical moment had at last arrived, and they awaited in breathless silence the appearence of Stanton. Fortune favored them in a peculiar manner this evening. As the old man was passing the pile of ashes under which Stanton was concealed, he noticed the unusual appearance of the straw.

Stopping for a moment, he drew a match from his pocket, lighted it, and then walked toward the heap as though with the intention of setting fire to it. The match fortunately was extinguished by a blast of wind, and after searching in his pocket for another match, but finding none, he slowly turned, and walked out of the gate, locking it securely behind him.

Stanton's feelings, under this ordeal, may be imagined. If the old man had succeeded in igniting the straw, under which he was concealed, detection would have followed instantly, and no doubt serious injury would have been inflicted upon the brave fellow, who had willingly suffered the discomforts of his unpleasant confinement for the purpose of assisting his comrades to escape.

No sooner had the gate closed upon the jailor, than he crawled nimbly out from his place of concealment, and hastily made his way to the door. He at once began his operations upon the lock. The appearance of Stanton at the door was the signal for the others, and in less than an hour the locks upon the cell doors had been removed. Stanton had wrested the lock from the outside door, and only the iron inside one was now to be overcome. This barrier resisted all their efforts, and it was at last decided that the lock must be removed by main force. This was a proceeding which necessitated a great deal of noise, and they were in an agony of apprehension lest their clamor should attract the attention of people passing on the outside, and thus lead to their detection. To prevent this, the colored men, without any solicitation or instruction, came to the rescue in a very important, though unexpected manner. They commenced to sing in concert, at the top of their voices, snatches of plantation and camp-meeting melodies, which effectually drowned the sound of their blows, and enabled them to work without fear of detection.

The lock at last yielded to their combined efforts, and the men issued silently forth into the darkness of the night, breathing once more the stimulating atmosphere of hope and promised liberty. Only the wall around the prison yard was now to be surmounted, and with the aid of some old planks that were lying around, they succeeded in reaching the top, after which they noiselessly dropped themselves to the ground. Although this wall was very high, they all reached *terra firma* in safety, and with one impulse breathed a prayer of thankfulness for the success which had thus far attended their efforts.

Silently, and walking in couples, at long distances apart, they started out to leave the city. The sky was clear, and the moon was shining brightly overhead. The stars were twinkling merrily, as though enjoying the success which had attended these brave, patient men, in their labor and toil of days and weeks.

This was on the eighteenth day of March, and

Martial law had been proclaimed some time previously. It was now nearly eight o'clock, and by the provisions of the law any one found upon the streets after nine o'clock, must be in possession of a pass, or be liable to arrest. Great haste was therefore necessary, in order to leave the city before that hour. With only the stars for their guide, they set out in a northerly direction. Not one of the men was acquainted with the country, and their journey was all the more perilous on that account.

By midnight they had reached the Chickahominy, having succeeded, by the greatest good fortune, in escaping any one who was disposed to make inquiries or to molest them in any manner whatever. Across this swamp their way led through quagmires and deep pools, and was dangerous in the extreme. Sometimes waist deep in the soft mud and water, and scrambling over slipping places which furnished insecure footholds, and threatened instant danger from falling back into the pools through which they had made their way. Their journey was full of hardship and suffering. The air was cold and frosty, and their wet garments clung to them like ice; their limbs trembled; their teeth chattered with the cold, and their condition was really a pitiable one indeed.

At length they reached the woods upon the opposite side. Here they were obliged to stop and rest, completely exhausted. Some of the hardier of the party removed their dripping garments, and attempted to wring the water from them; while others, unable to stand the chilling air any longer, built a fire, around which they gathered in the effort to warm their bodies and to dry their water-soaked clothing.

They rested for about two hours, and then pushed on again until daylight, when they sought the shelter of the woods and laid down, hoping to get some sleep after their laborious and fatiguing journey of the preceding night. Sleep, however, was impossible; their clothing was wet, and the air was cold. Their sufferings became intense, and at length, finding it impossible to endure the freezing atmosphere longer, they determined to build a fire, regardless of the consequences. Proceeding further into the wood, they gathered some boughs, and soon the cheerful blaze afforded them sufficient heat to dry their frozen clothing and to warm their benumbed and freezing bodies. Thus passed the day, and when darkness came on again they resumed their journey.

Already they began to experience the pangs of hunger. They had eaten nothing since the evening before, and had walked many weary miles. They were foot-sore and tired and hungry. They had provided themselves with the remnants of the corn cake which had been served for their supper on the previous evening, but these had become thoroughly soaked with water on their journey through the swamps, and had crumbled to pieces. Notwithstanding their pitiable condition, their strong wills and brave hearts sustained them, and they plodded on.

The night was intensely dark; the stars were obscured, and a pall of inky blackness hung over them, which rendered their journey exceedingly hazardous, as they could not see the way before them, and were unable to tell in which direction they were traveling.

They had not proceeded far when the storm broke, and a drenching torrent of rain descended. The wind whistled and howled through the trees, and for hours the tempest raged with relentless fury. Seeking the shelter of the woods again, they crouched close to the trunks of the trees, and vainly attempted to screen themselves from the deluge. It was of no avail, however; the leafless timber afforded them no protection, and during the continuance of the storm the poor, tired and almost exhausted fugitives were exposed to the pitiless blast.

Shivering with cold, their teeth chattering, their garments drenched through to their quivering skin, they knelt or crouched upon the ground, and when daylight dawned, and the storm at last cleared away, they were almost too weak to help themselves.

Price Lewis looked around him as the faint streaks of sunrise illumined the horizon, and to his dismay saw that nearly all of his late companions had disappeared, and that only three others beside himself remained.

With the greatest difficulty they succeeded in building a fire, and were just preparing to enjoy its comforting warmth, when they were alarmed by the sound of the hasty tramping of feet, and in a moment they were surrounded by a number of Confederate soldiers, who commanded them to surrender at once

This sudden and unexpected appearance was a crushing blow to their hopes. They submitted without a word ; and although bowed to the ground with disappointment, they experienced a sensation almost amounting to relief, at the prospect of receiving the care and attention which even enemies would give to those in such distress as were these poor fugitives.

Limping along, they were marched to an outbuilding, connected with a farm-house near by, when, to their surprise, they saw the remainder of their party, who had been captured by another band of soldiers, huddled together in one corner of the room.

The soldiers were touched with pity, as they beheld the forlorn condition of the men whom they had secured, and in a short time they had provided them with a repast, which the famished fugitives devoured with a rapidity which gave ample testimony of their long and painful abstinence.

After dispatching this meal they were conveyed directly back to Richmond, and returned to their old quarters in Henrico jail. On their arrival each man was placed in a separate cell, and doubly ironed, to prevent a repetition of their efforts to escape.

The prisoners re-captured.

P. 522.

While Price Lewis had been engaged in this unsuccessful attempt to gain his liberty, John Scully had been undergoing a far different experience. A court-martial had been hurriedly convened, where he was fully identified by every member of the Morton family as the man who had searched their premises in the city of Washington, and had, after a very summary trial, been convicted and remanded back to prison to await his sentence.

On the second day after the return of Price Lewis he was conducted before a court-martial, and in a remarkably short space of time was accorded a trial, if trial it could be called, and his conviction followed as quickly as did that of John Scully.

They had been charged with being alien enemies, and at one time acting in the service of the Federal government in Washington. In addition to this, they were charged with loitering around the fortifications at Richmond and taking plans of the same. Notwithstanding the fact that no witness could be procured who would swear to having seen them in such localities, or engaged in any such occupation, the members of the court-martial, with singular unanimity, found them guilty of the second charge, with as much haste, and as manifest an air of solemnity, as they did of the first.

The next day they were each informed of their sentence, which was that they should be hung by the neck, as spies, and that their execution should take place in one week from the day of the communica-tion of the information to them.

This sentence was a heavy blow to the two pris-oners; and from the character of the men by whom they were surrounded, thay felt that hope was use-less. The spirit of animosity manifested toward them by the court, the indecent haste with which their trial had been conducted, and the rapidity with which their sentence had followed their conviction, gave them no reasons for hoping for clemency, or that they would be able to escape the dreadful fate which now was impending over them.

The conduct of the various members of the Mor-ton family in betraying my operatives to the author-ities, and in appearing as accusing witnesses against them, in face of their promises, long ago made, to be-friend them if possible, was an act which did not re-flect very favorably upon their regard for truth, or their appreciation of delicate treatment when they themselves were suspected of treachery.

Lewis and Scully had never seen each other from the time when the latter was removed from the cell a few days after their first imprisonment, and each was unconscious of the other's fate or of the state of their feelings under the fatal sentence which hung over them both.

After their conviction they had both been sent to a prison called Castle Godwin, and had been placed in irons, and in separate cells. During the first two days that elapsed after their conviction, they were visited by Judge Crump, who conducted the trial, and by several members of General Winder's staff, all of whom endeavored to obtain some admissions from the two prisoners which would justify their action in condemning them to death. All with no avail, however; the two men stoutly insisted upon their original story, except so far as to admit that they had searched the premises of Mrs. Morton, but each man was firm in stating that he had become disgusted with the service, and had left it very soon after that act had been committed.

On the day after their sentence had been communicated to them, a letter was brought to Lewis, from the commandant of the post, stating that Scully was suffering with a serious illness, and having requested that Lewis be allowed to visit him, the privilege had been granted. On entering the cell where Scully was confined, Lewis found his fellow-prisoner in a very depressed condition of mind, although his physical infirmities had been assumed in order to secure an interview with his partner in misfortune.

After discussing their situation as philosophically as possible under the circumstances, seeking for some ray of hope and finding none, they were at last compelled to the belief that their doom was sealed, and that their only plan was to bear up manfully to the end.

Scully, who was a Roman Catholic, desired the services of a priestly comforter, to whom he could make such statements as would relieve his mind in the coming trial, and made known this wish to Lewis.

"You will not tell him what you know of Webster, and his connection with this matter, will you?" said Lewis, fearful that Webster might be betrayed.

"I don't know what I will tell him," answered Scully ; "I have not decided what to say, nor do I know what I will be commanded to relate."

"For God's sake, Scully, don't say anything about Webster ; we can meet our fate like men, but to mention his name now, would be wrong indeed."

"I tell you," said Scully, "I don't know what I am going to say. I don't want to do wrong, but I cannot tell what I may have to do yet."

Lewis argued with his companion long and earnestly upon this matter, and when at last the priest arrived, and Scully followed him to another cell, the warning admonitions of his fellow-prisoner were ringing in his ears.

What transpired during that secret meeting between the condemned spy and his father-confessor, Lewis did not know, but when he was conducted to his own cell, late that night, he saw a man and woman closely guarded, in the lower hall, and his heart grew heavy and cold as his imagination conjured up the direful fate which a confession from his imprisoned comrade would bring to the faithful patriot Webster, who lay suffering and anxious upon his bed of pain.

After a long and restless night, in which he tossed

uneasily upon his hard prison bed, vainly attempting to court the rest-giving slumber of which he stood so much in need, Lewis arose from his couch, feverish and unrefreshed, as the first faint rays of the morning sun penetrated his damp and dingy cell.

His mind was in a state of confusion, and his heart was filled with fear. What had been done he knew not, and yet those guarded figures of the night before were ever in his mind. Could it be that they were Webster and his faithful attendant Mrs. Lawton? He shrank involuntarily from this thought; and yet, strive as he would, it recurred to him, with increased force, and with more convincing power, after each attempt to drive it from him.

In a little while, the prison was astir. The guards were making their accustomed rounds, breakfast was served, and another day, with all its solemn activity, and its bustle so death-like and subdued, had begun.

Unable to partake of the scanty meal that was set before him, Lewis impatiently awaited the hour when he would be permitted to visit his fellow-prisoner whom he had left upon the eve of consulting with his spiritual adviser, and, if possible, learn the result of his interview with the priest.

About ten o'clock the turnkey appeared, and he was conducted to Scully's cell. As he entered the dimly-lighted room, he noticed that the face of the man whom he had left the night before, had undergone a wonderful change. His cheeks were sunken and pale ; his eyes had a strange, wild expression, and the shadows under the lids were dark and heavy. His hair was unkempt, and his lips trembled with the emotions which he was struggling to repress. Whatever events had transpired since he had seen him last, it was evident that their effect upon Scully had been terrible and agonizing. He had been unable to sleep, and the tortures of his mind had been almost unbearable. His greeting to Lewis showed a degree of restraint which had been unknown before, and for a moment he seemed unable to speak.

At length he grew calmer, and related to his friend the events of the preceding night, and the influences that had been brought to bear upon him. The promise of freedom ; his loving family at home ; the certainty of an ignoble death if he refused ; the degradation of the impending scaffold; and the promise that his admissions should result in injury to no one, all combined against his weak condition of both mind and body, and at last, yielding to the influences which he could not control, he had told his story, and had given a truthful account of all his movements.

Who can blame this man ? Who, that has stood before the frowning scaffold, and with a free world before him, can utter words of censure ? Only those who have suffered as he did, prostrated as he was, can know the terrible agony through which he passed ere the fatal words were forced from his trembling lips. For myself, I have no judgment to utter. Now, as when the news was first communicated to me, I cannot express an unjust sentence. John Scully and his companion were not heroic martyrs. What then? They were simply men who, after having performed many brave acts of loyalty and duty to their country, failed in a moment of grand and great self-sacrifice. I cannot apologize for them—I cannot judge them. Their trial was a severe one, and they were in sore distress. If they succumbed to a controlling emergency, it was because of a lack of the heroic elements of humanity; and who, in our day, can claim their possession in the very face of death and dishonor?

Let us hasten over these unpleasant and disastrous events. Finding that the worst had occurred, and that further concealment was of no avail, Lewis, too, opened his mouth. He was again visited by the rebel authorities, and at last he, too, added his voice to that of Scully, and made a revelation of his true character, and of the nature of his mission to Richmond. The next day they were respited. They had escaped an ignominious death, but, perhaps, in their lonely cells they suffered a death in life, beside which an actual demise might have seemed a blessing. Leaving them to their reflections, we turn again to Timothy Webster.

34

CHAPTER XXXVI.

*Webster Arrested as a Spy.—A Woman's Devotion and a
Patriot's Heroism.—Webster is Convicted.—The Execution.—A Martyr's Grave.*

AFTER the departure of Lewis and Scully from
Webster's room, where they were so closely
followed by the Confederate detective and Chase
Morton, my trusty operative heard nothing of them
for some time. Fearing to make inquiries concerning them, lest he should compromise them still
further, as well as bring himself under the suspicion
of the rebel authorities, he maintained a strict silence
with regard to the movements of his companions.
Several days of anxious suspense followed, which, to
one in Webster's critical condition, were fraught with
agonizing doubts and heartfelt fears for the ultimate
safety of himself and his friends. Resolving, however, to utter no word which would compromise
them, he bore the solicitude with unmurmuring
firmness. Only to the heroic woman, who so faithfully nursed him, did he unburden his mind of the
weight of care which oppressed him, and her words
of womanly friendship and encouragement were the

only influences which supported him through the trying ordeal.

One day, Mrs. Lawton came into his room—as was her custom—but this time there was a gravity about her manner, which, to Webster's quick perceptions, boded no good. Finding him receiving some friendly visitors, the lady withdrew, and repressing his impatience as well as he was able to do, Webster dispatched his friends as quickly as politeness, and a due consideration for their kindly regard, would permit. When they had disappeared, Mrs. Lawton again entered the room.

"You have news for me," said Webster, impatiently; "what is it?"

"Be calm, my dear friend," said the devoted little woman; "what I have to tell, calls for the utmost calmness."

"Tell me what it is," said Webster; "I will be as calm as you could wish, but do not, I pray you, keep me in suspense."

"Well," replied Mrs. Lawton, "I learned this morning that Lewis and Scully have been arrested and taken to Henrico Jail."

"When did this occur?" asked the invalid, a great weight pressing upon his heart.

"The very day they were here last," answered the woman.

'Then all is lost," exclaimed the sick man. "I feared as much; and now the time has come I will meet it manfully; however," he continued, "it will be only a short time before I will share the same fate."

"Why do you think so?" anxiously inquired Mrs. Lawton. "Surely they cannot connect you with these men."

"I do not know why I think so, but I am as confident that I will be brought into this matter as though the officers were already here to arrest me."

While he yet spoke, there came a knock at the chamber door, which, on being opened, revealed the form of Captain McCubbin.

As he entered the room he gazed furtively around, and his salutation to Webster was very different from the cordiality which had marked his previous visits.

"Good morning, Webster," said he, as he took the offered chair, and for the first time since they had known each other neglecting to shake the invalid by the hand. "This is bad news about Lewis and Scully, isn't it?"

"What is it?" inquired Webster, apparently receiving the information for the first time.

"They have been arrested as spies, are confined in prison, and General Winder wants that letter which they brought to you from the North."

There was something so cold and imperious in the officer's tones, which confirmed Webster's fears for his own safety; but without evincing the slightest alarm, he cheerfully made reply :

"I am sorry to hear this news, and trust that they

will be able to exonerate themselves from the charge. Anything, however, that General Winder wants from me will be cheerfully given. Mrs. Lawton, will you get the letter, and hand it to Captain McCubbin."

There was no tremor of the voice, and the watchful Confederate looked in vain for any evidence of fear in the face of the man, who, stricken by disease as he was, still showed the bravery of a lion, and gazed unflinchingly at him. Though the hand of fate was upon him, Webster never lost his heroic courage, and bore the scrutiny of the officer without the quiver of a muscle.

Captain McCubbin received the letter, and almost immediately withdrew. As he closed the door behind him, Webster turned to his faithful companion, and, in a low, solemn voice, said: "That letter has sealed my fate!"

From this point, Webster's physical condition seemed to improve, and although depressed with fears for the fate of his companions, he gradually became stronger, and was at length able to leave his bed and move about his room.

The visits of his numerous friends had now almost ceased. From General Winder's officers, with whom he had previously been so intimate, he heard nothing, nor did they make inquiries about his health, as had been their custom. Of the many friends in private life, who had surrounded him, only two remained. These were Mr. Pierce and Mr. Campbell, with whom Webster had traveled for some time, and his family. This dropping away of old friends, and the breaking up of old associations, was significant to Webster of impending danger. It must be that he, too, was suspected, and that the favor of the rebel authorities had been withdrawn.

Day by day, during his convalescence, did the brave little woman who had nursed him back to life, endeavor to encourage him to a hopeful view of his situation, and to impress him with her own sanguine trust for a favorable outcome from this present dilemma. Webster listened to the bright promises of his devoted companion, but he was too profoundly aware of the danger that threatened him to permit himself to hope that the result to him would be a beneficial one.

After he was able to leave his bed, he accepted the pressing invitation of Mr. Campbell, and was removed to the residence of that gentleman, where he would be more quiet, and where he could receive that care and attention which could not be afforded him in a hotel. The kindness of Mr. Campbell and his family was heartfelt and unceasing. They did everything in their power to make him comfortable, and their courtesy to Mrs. Lawton was as marked and genuine, as was their regard and care for Timothy Webster.

Webster had been domiciled at the house of Mr. Campbell but two days, when one of Winder's men came to know if Webster was sufficiently recovered to go out, as his presence was imperatively demanded at the court room, as a witness in the trial of John Scully. The officer further stated that the evidence of Webster had been solicited by Scully himself. Finding him unable still to leave the house, the officer stated that arrangements would be made by which his testimony could be taken in his room. On the second day after the appearance of the officer, the court-martial adjourned to Campbell's house, and Scully accompanied them. Seating themselves around the bedside of the invalid, the court was formally opened, and Webster was requested to state what he knew of the antecedents of the accused.

Though very weak, and speaking with considerable difficulty, Webster made his statement. He said that he had known John Scully from April, 1861, to the time of his arrest. That the prisoner was in Baltimore when he first met him, and was always in the company of known secessionists, and was considered by them to be a good friend to the South. So far as he had any knowledge of the accused he was what he assumed to be, and that his appearance in Richmond was a surprise to him. He was not known to be in the employ of the government, and Webster had never met him under any circumstances which would indicate that fact.

This was all that he could say, and although closely questioned by the president of the court, and the attorneys present, he insisted that his knowledge of John Scully was confined to what he had already stated. Finding it impossible to obtain any further information upon this subject from the sick man, the court, in a body, left the room, and departed from the house.

Mrs. Lawton, who had been compelled to retire on the entrance of the Confederate authorities, and who had been in a wild state of excitement and apprehension during their visit, instantly repaired to Webster's room. When she entered the chamber, she found that the brave man, after the exciting experiences through which he had been compelled to pass, had fainted. His strength of will, which had supported him through the investigation, had given way, and he lay, limp and inanimate, upon the bed.

Several days of anxiety and solicitude now passed. Unable to learn any tidings of his unfortunate comrades, Webster tortured himself with all manner of vague fears and doubts as to their probable fate, all of which had their effect in retarding his recovery, and keeping him confined to his room.

At last, after days of weary and anxious waiting, the newspapers were brought in one morning, and the information of the conviction of Lewis and Scully was duly chronicled. The same paper also announced the day upon which their death was so speedily to follow. This filled the cup of Webster's misery to overflowing, and, sinking upon a chair, he wept like a child. Refusing to be comforted, although Mrs. Lawton exerted herself to the utmost, Webster paced the room, half frantic with his grief, at the horrible fate which had overtaken his friends.

Slowly the day passed, and when the shadows of evening were falling Webster was at last induced to lie down, and attempt to snatch a few hours sleep. He was soon slumbering quietly, although ever and anon he would start nervously and utter an inarticulate moan, as though his mind was stil troubled with the sad events of the day. While he lay thus, attended by Mrs. Lawton, Mr. Campbell suddenly entered the room, with a look of fear upon his face, which filled Mrs. Lawton with alarm.

" What is the matter ?" she hurriedly ejaculated.

" One of Winder's men is below, and I fear his presence indicates misfortune for Webster," was the reply.

" Who is it ?"

" Cashmeyer," answered Mr. Campbell. " He inquired for Webster, and says he must see him at once."

Webster, disturbed by this conversation, was awake in an instant and inquired what was wanted.

"Cashmeyer has called, and wishes to see you," said Mr. Campbell.

" Let him come up at once," replied Webster, in the hope that he might bring some tidings of Lewis and Scully.

Mr. Campbell departed, and in a few moments returned with the Confederate officer. Cashmeyer's salutation was cold and formal, and without any preliminary he addressed Webster.

"I have a painful duty to perform, Mr. Webster. I am directed by General Winder to arrest you, and convey you at once to Castle Godwin."

As he spoke, two soldiers appeared at the doorway.

"You cannot wish to take him away in this condition, and at this hour of the night," said Mrs. Lawton. "Such an action would be his death, and would be the worst of inhumanity."

Webster stood silent and unmoved. He did not utter a word, but gazed fixedly at the officer, whose visits heretofore had been those of sympathy and condolence.

"I cannot help it," said Cashmeyer, "my orders are to take him dead, or alive, and those orders I must obey."

"Then," said Mrs. Lawton, "I will go too. He needs care and attention, without it he will die, and no one can nurse him so well as I."

Cashmeyer gazed at the brave little woman for a moment, and a shade of pity came over his face.

"I am sorry to inform you, that my orders are to arrest you also, and to search your trunks."

"This is infamous," exclaimed Webster; "what can Winder mean by arresting this woman, and what am I charged with that renders your orders necessary?"

"Webster," answered Cashmeyer, "as God is my witness, I do not know; I only know what my orders are, and that I must obey them."

Without further parley, Webster and Mrs. Lawton prepared to accompany their guards, and Cashmeyer, demanding their keys, commenced a search of their trunks, which resulted in his finding nothing that would criminate his prisoners.

A carriage was procured, and Webster was assisted into it, while Mrs. Lawton, under the escort of Cashmeyer was compelled to walk. It was quite late when they arrived at the prison, and as Price Lewis was ascending to his cell, Webster and his faithful female companion entered the gloomy portals of the jail.

General Winder was present when they arrived, and after a hurried examination Webster was remanded to a room, in which a number of Union prisoners were already confined, and the atmosphere of which was reeking with filth and disease.

As he entered the room, pale and emaciated, and scarcely able to walk, the prisoners gathered around, in silent pity for his forlorn condition.

"My God!" excaimed one of their number, "they will send the dead here next."

Mrs. Lawton was conducted before the General, but she stoutly declined to answer a single question that was propounded to her. This so enraged the valiant officer that he ordered her to be taken away at once. She was then conducted to a room in which another lady was confined, and left for the night.

As midnight tolled its solemn hour over the city, and the tramp of armed men resounded through the streets, the noises within the prison died away. An awful and impressive silence brooded over the place. The dim light in the corridor shone faintly upon four miserable human beings, who tossed restlessly upon sleepless couches through the long, weary watches of the night.

Who can tell the thoughts that thronged through their brains, as the slow moving hours advanced toward the dawn? The brave woman who had been cruelly deprived of her privilege to administer to the needs of her suffering friend. The heroic Webster, wasted by disease, weakened by his long and painful illness, but still brave and defiant. Price Lewis and John Scully, tortured with the thoughts of their impending fate, and harassed with reflections of a more agonizing nature, which we may not analyse.

The trial of Webster was ordered for an early day. With a haste that was inhuman, the Provost-Marshal made his preparations for the farce of an investigation. It seemed as though he was fearful that his victim would die, ere he could wreak his vengeance upon him. The court was convened, and,

owing to Webster's weakened condition, their ses-
sions were held in the jail. For three long, weary
weeks did the investigation drag its slow length
along, although it was apparent that those who tried
him had already decided upon his fate. Numerous
witnesses were examined, and testimony was admitted
which would have been excluded by any righteous
tribunal whose ideas of justice were not obscured by
an insane desire for revenge.

Price Lewis and John Scully were compelled to
give their evidence; and although they attempted to
do their utmost to lessen the effect of their testimony,
it bore heavily against the poor prisoner, who sat
pale and emaciated before them, and whose heart
never failed him through the long and tedious ordeal.
What Webster's feelings must have been during
this harrowing experience is unknown to any one.
What thoughts were rushing through his brain, as the
damaging statements fell from the lips of his late associates, were never revealed by him. No murmurs
escaped his lips, no words of censure or blame
against the men whose evidence cost him his life,
were ever uttered. A heroic calmness, born of the
very despair which oppressed him from the first, was
manifest throughout the long, weary investigation.
Indeed so manfully had he borne himself, so completely had he controlled his feelings, that his
physical health perceptibly improved, so much so
that the tribunal removed their sittings to the court-

house, and Webster was able to be in daily attendance.

Webster had secured able counsel for his defence, and they did all that was possible for man to do. Although they were rebels, their efforts in behalf of the accused spy were such, that if pleadings could have availed him aught, his fate would have been averted.

It was not to be, however ; the trial came to an end at last. A verdict of guilty followed quickly upon the heels of the partial and antagonistic charge of the judge, and Timothy Webster was convicted of being a spy in the employ of the Federal authorities.

Not even then did the brave spirit break down. Firm and heroic he received the fatal verdict, and the satisfaction of his enemies was robbed of its value by the unflinching deportment of their victim.

After the trial, he was remanded to a cell, and closely watched. But a little time elapsed, and then came the warrant for his execution. An officer appeared in the cell, the paper was produced, and the faithful, brave, true-hearted man was condemned to be hung on the twenty-ninth day of April, but ten days after the approval of his sentence.

*   *   *   *   *   *

The Union army was before Yorktown. McClellan had already sustained two serious disappointments, and both of them at the hands of the government at Washington. In the first place, on his

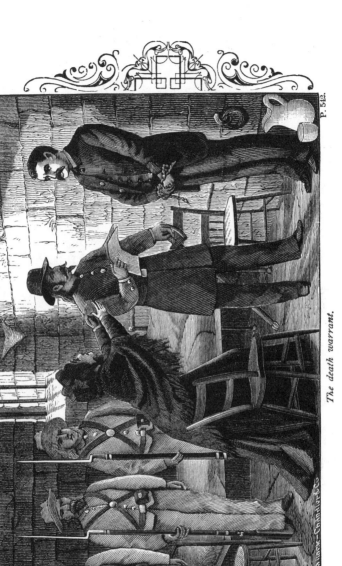

The death warrant.

arrival at Fort Monroe, he had ascertained that the promised assistance of the navy could not be relied upon in the least, and that their efficient co-operation with him would be an utter impossibility. This interference with his plans might have been overcome, although the loss of the naval support was a serious misfortune to him; but a more surprising and disheartening act of the authorities was yet in store for him. A few days later, he was thunderstruck at the unexpected information that General McDowell's entire corps, upon whose assistance he had confidently relied, was detached from his command, and had been ordered to remain in front of Washington, for the protection of the capital, which was erroneously believed to be in imminent danger of capture by the rebels. These events rendered a scientific siege of Yorktown a necessity; and while engaged in this laborious work, I was in constant consultation with the commanding General. Numerous scouts had been sent out through the rebel country, and the secret service department was taxed to its utmost. George H. Bangs was busily engaged in examining the rebel deserters and prisoners, Southern refugees and contrabands, who were either captured or came willingly into camp, and in preparing daily reports of our movements, which were required to be made to the General in command. I had accompanied McClellan upon this campaign, and gave my untiring personal supervision to the management of the large corps of men and women, white and black, then engaged in obtaining information.

During all this time, not a word had been received of my missing operatives. Tortured by the uncertainty of their fate, I passed many an anxious hour. At length all doubts were set at rest, and a dreadful certainty manifested itself to my mind. A newspaper, published in Richmond, was received by me, and in hastily perusing its contents, with a view of acquring such military information as it contained, my eye alighted upon a small paragraph, which filled me with dread and sorrow. This paragraph was the simple announcement that Price Lewis and John Scully had been arrested as spies in the rebel capital, and had been sentenced to be hung on the 6th day of April.

I cannot detail the effect which this announcement produced upon me. For a moment I sat almost stupefied, and unable to move. My blood seemed to freeze in my veins—my heart stood still—I was speechless. By degrees I was able to exercise a strong command over myself. I then sought my immediate associates, and communicated the fatal news to them. Their consternation and grief were equal to my own. Every man seemed to be impressed with the solemnity of the fate of their comrades. What was to be done? How to intercede in their behalf? I rushed to the tent of General McClellan, and relating the news to him, besought his aid in this direful extremity. His sympathy and sorrow were as acute as though the men had been joined to him by ties of blood. Anxiously we discussed the situation, in the vain attempt to seek some mode of obtaining their release, and all without definite or satisfactory conclusion.

All that night I paced the camp, unable to sleep —unable almost to think intelligently; and when morning dawned I was as far from devising any practical plan of relief as when I first received the information.

I telegraphed to Captain Milward, Harbor-Master at Fortress Monroe, and in charge of the flag-of-truce boat for exchanging prisoners, asking him to endeavor to ascertain from the Richmond papers, or from any other source, anything definite as to the fate of my unfortunate operatives.

Several messages were received from that officer, containing various statements of the case, and finally came the crushing intelligence that Lewis and Scully had been respited, after having given information which implicated Timothy Webster, whom the rebels now regarded as the chief spy of the three.

This was the crowning burden of all, and I was almost prostrated by the blow. Hurried consultations were held, every conceivable plan was suggested and discussed, which would avail in the slightest degree to avert so terrible a fate from the faithful patriot who now was in such deadly danger.

I suggested that General McClellan should send, by flag-of-truce boat, such a demand as would, if possible, save their lives; but to this the General demurred, fearing, and justly too, that such a course might be productive of more injury than good—that it would be a tacit acknowledgment of their real character as spies, and they would be hung without further delay.

It was at last decided that I should go to Washington, accompanied by Colonel Key, an eminent patriot, and an efficient member of General McClellan's staff. We were to confer with the President and the members of the Cabinet, lay the matter before them, and petition for the official interposition of the government in their behalf.

With Colonel Key, I started for Washington, about the middle of April. The interest of that officer was scarcely second to my own, and he was fully determined to exert every energy of his manly, sympathetic nature in the work of saving their lives, if possible.

The journey to Washington was quickly made. Mr. Lincoln was readily seen, and he, too, filled with sympathy for the unfortunate men, promised to call a special session of the Cabinet to consider the case, that evening.

In the meantime, Colonel Key and I occupied ourselves in visiting the various heads of the departments, in order to prepare them, before evening

arrived, for energetic and speedy action. We felt
that no time was to be lost; if, indeed, it was not
already too late to avert their dreadful doom.

Secretary Stanton, whom, among others, we saw,
expressed in strong terms his willingness to assist
Webster to the extent of the resources of the government, but he was but little disposed to assist the
others, who, he alleged, had "betrayed their companion to save their own lives."

In the evening the Cabinet was convened, and,
after a full discussion of the matter, it was decided
that the only thing that could be done, was to authorize the Secretary of War to communicate with the
rebel authorities upon the subject. He was directed
to authorize General Wool to send by flag-of-truce
boat, or by telegraph, a message to Jefferson Davis,
representing that the course pursued by the Federal
government toward rebel spies had heretofore been
lenient and forbearing; that in many cases such persons had been released after a short confinement, and
that in no instance had any one so charged been tried
for his life, or sentenced to death. The message concluded with the decided intimation that if the rebel
government proceeded to carry their sentence of
death into execution, the Federal government would
initiate a system of retaliation which would amply
revenge the death of the men now held.

Receiving a copy of these instructions, Colonel
Key and myself, feeling that we had exhausted the

power of the government in this matter, returned at once to Fortress Monroe. We arrived there on the 23d day of April. General Wool was immediately found, and without a moment's delay, he caused the required dispatches to be forwarded, by way of Norfolk, through General Huger, who was then in command of that place, with the urgent request that he would instantly transmit it by telegraph to the Richmond authorities.

This, I learned, was done as had been requested, and I learned further, that it reached the officers of the rebel government, and received their consideration in time to have been of avail, had there been one spark of manly sympathy animating the breasts of those who were the leaders of a vile conspiracy to destroy the noblest government under the blue canopy of heaven.

Feeling that all had now been done that was possible to save the lives of my men, and believing that the hate and malignity of the rebel officers would not carry them to such a murderous extent as this, I awaited the result of our mission with painful solicitude.

*　　　*　　　*　　　*　　　*　　　*

After the day of execution had been fixed, Mrs. Lawton was permitted to visit Webster in the room to which he had been assigned. During all the time that the trial had been in progress, they had never been allowed to communicate with each other, and the noble little woman had been compelled to suffer in silence, while Webster was undergoing the painful experiences of the investigation, which had resulted in his being condemned to be hung as a spy.

The meeting between Webster and Mrs. Lawton was a most affecting one. Tears filled the eyes of the faithful woman, as she gazed at the pale and emaciated form of the heroic patriot. Their hands were clasped in a warm pressure, and her words of heartfelt sympathy and grief were choked by the sobs which shook her frame. Even in the excess of his despair, Webster's fortitude never for a moment forsook him. He bore the burdens which had been imposed upon him with a courage and firmness that impressed all who witnessed it.

Under Mrs. Lawton's direction, the room in which he was confined was soon made cheerful and clean; with her own hands she prepared for him such delicacies as he needed most, and her words of comfort were of great effect in soothing his mind, and in preparing him for the dreadful fate which he was called upon to meet.

Nor did Mrs. Lawton stop here. She sought an interview with Jefferson Davis, but, finding him engaged with General Lee, she obtained the privilege of visiting the wife of the Confederate president. With Mrs. Davis she pleaded long and earnestly in behalf of the condemned man. Besought her by every holy tie of her own life to intercede for the pardon of the poor invalid, whose life hung by so slender a thread.

All in vain, however. While fully sympathizing with the fate of the unfortunate man, Mrs. Davis declined to interfere in matters of state, and Mrs. Lawton left the house utterly hopeless of being able to avert the dreadful fate which impended over Webster.

The hours flew swiftly by, and the day of execution drew near, and still a ray of hope glistened through the gloom which surrounded him. If McClellan only succeeded in capturing Richmond all would be well. But as the days passed, and this result seemed further from accomplishment than ever, even that flickering ember of hope died out, and he prepared to meet his fate like a man.

One thing, however, impressed the doomed man more than anything else—the thought of being hung. Any other mode of punishment would have been accepted with joy, but to be hanged like a murderer, was a disgrace which he could not bear to think about. On the day before his execution, he requested a visit from General Winder, and that officer, evidently expecting a revelation from the lips of his victim, soon made his appearance at the prison.

As he entered the cell where Webster was reclining upon his couch, he roughly accosted him:

"Webster you have sent for me; what is it that you desire?"

"General Winder," replied Webster, "I have

sent for you to make an appeal to your manhood;
my fate is sealed I know that too well—I am to die,
and I wish to die like a man. I know there is no
hope for mercy, but, sir, I beseech you to permit me
to be shot, not be hanged like a common felon,—
anything but that."

" I am afraid that cannot be done," said Winder,
coldly.

" It is not much to ask," pleaded Webster; " I am
to die, and am prepared, but, sir, for God's sake let
me not die like this; change but the manner of my
death, and no murmur shall escape my lips."

"I cannot alter the sentence that has been ordered."

Mrs. Lawton, who was present, and unable further to restrain herself, exclaimed :

" General, as a woman I appeal to you—you have
the power, and can exercise it. Do not, I pray you,
condemn this brave man to the odium of a felon's
death. Think of his family, and his suffering. Let
the manliness of your own heart plead for him.
It is not much that he asks. He does not sue for
pardon. He seeks not to escape your judgment,
harsh and cruel as it is. He only prays to be
allowed to die like a brave man in the service of his
country. You certainly can lose nothing by granting
this request, therefore, in the name of justice and
humanity, let him be shot instead of the dreadful
death you have ordained for him."

While she was speaking, the hard lines about the rebel's mouth grew still more harsh and rigid. He did not attempt to interrupt her, but when she had finished, he turned coolly upon his heel, and, as he reached the door he said :

"His request and yours must be denied. He hangs to-morrow."

"Then," ejaculated the undaunted woman, "he will die like a man, and his death will be upon your head, —a living curse until your own dark hour shall come !"

Without deigning to notice them further, he passed out of the cell, violently closing the door behind him.

The shadows of the night came down over the prison. The last night on earth to a brave man who had met death in a hundred forms ere this. How many times the gaunt, repulsive form of the fatal scaffold, appeared to the vision of the condemned man, as he sat firm and rigid in his dark cell, we may not know. How many times he lived over again the bright scenes of his past life ! The happy, careless days of childhood, when the fond eyes of a loving mother beamed upon him in his sportive gambols. His school days, the lessons conned by the evening lamp in the dear old home of long ago. The merry days of youth, which glided away amid scenes of mirth and jollity. The first dawnings of the passion of his life, when a soft hand nestled lovingly in his, and earnest eyes, full of love and trust, seemed to speak a world of affection. Then the stirring scenes of active life, he a man among men battling with the world, performing his daily duties, mingling honorably with his fellows, and upheld by a pride of honor and self-respect. His sacrifices for his country in the dark hour of her peril. The lonely marches, the weary burdens, the unflinching steadfastness of his fealty to his government The long nights of storm and danger, the varying episodes of pleasure and of pain, conflicts with enemies, and happy hours with friendly companions—all these thoughts came upon him with a distinctness which brought their actual presence near. Now he was listening to the sweet lullaby of his mother's voice, now he stood in the hall of the "Sons of Liberty," in the midst of affrighted conspirators and blue-coated soldiers—anon he strayed by a purling stream, with a loved one upon his arm—and again he breasted the dashing waters and the deluging storm on the bay, as he rescued the women and children from the stranded boat. So vivid were these pictures of his mind that he lived again a hundred scenes of his past life, partook of a hundred pleasures, shared in a hundred sorrows. Suddenly in the midst of some thrilling vision of by-gone days, the flickering of his lamp or the tread of the sentry outside would recall him from a delightful reverie to the dark and dreadful present. Then gloomy and despondent thoughts would come to him. He would picture minutely the scenes of the morrow, the rude platform, the dangling noose, the armed soldiers, the hideous black cap, the springing of the gallows trap.

Then, unable to bear the agony of his thoughts, he would start to his feet, press his hands to his ears, as if to drown the fearful sounds, and pace rapidly the narrow cell. Mrs. Lawton never left him; ever alert to his needs, ever ready with sustaining words, although her own brave, tender heart was breaking, she did her utmost to strengthen and sustain him. Gradually he became calmer. The slow moving hours passed on, and he resolutely performed the last duties that devolved upon him. Messages were confided to his unwavering nurse for the dear friends at home; expressions of love and regard for his kindred, and unswerving breathings of devotion to his country.

"Tell Major Allen that I met my fate like a man. Thank him for his many acts of kindness to me. I have done my duty, and I can meet death with a brave heart and a clear conscience."

The first faint streaks of the early dawn came in through the grated window; the sun was rising in the heavens, brightly and gloriously lighting up a day that should have been shrouded in gloom. Its beams illumined the little chamber, where Webster lay calm and wakeful, his hands clasped by the woman who had so nobly shared his captivity.

A silence had fallen upon them. Each was busy with thoughts which lips could not utter, and the deathlike stillness was undisturbed save by the tramp of the guards in the corridor.

Suddenly there came the sound of hurried footsteps. They paused before the door. The heavy bolts were shot back, and in the doorway stood Cap-Alexander, the officer in charge.

The little clock that ticked upon the wall noted a quarter past five o'clock.

" Come, Webster, it is time to go."

There was no sympathy in the rough voice which uttered these words.

" To go where ?" inquired Webster, starting up in surprise.

" To the fair grounds," was the laconic reply.

" Surely not at this hour," pleaded the condemned man ; " the earliest moment named in my death-warrant is six o'clock, and you certainly will not require me to go before that."

" It is the order of General Winder, and I must obey," answered Alexander. "You must prepare yourself at once."

Without another word Webster arose from his bed, and began his preparations. Not a tremor was apparent, and his hand was as steady and firm as iron. When he had fully arranged his toilet, he turned to Mrs. Lawton, and taking both her hands in his, he murmured :

" Good-bye, dear friend ; we shall never meet again on earth. God bless you, and your kindness to me.

I will be brave, and die like a man. Farewell, forever!" then turning to Captain Alexander, who stood unmoved near the door, he said :

" I am ready !"

As they went out through the door, a piercing shriek rent the air, and Mrs. Lawton fell prostrate to the floor.

Arriving at the entrance to the prison, they found a company of cavalry drawn up before them, and a carriage, procured by Mrs. Lawton, awaiting their appearance. Webster crossed the pavement with unfaltering step and entered the vehicle, the order to march was given, and the procession started for the scene of execution.

At Camp Lee, the scene was one of bustle and excitement. Soldiers were moving about in companies, and in small detachments. Eager spectators were there, curious to watch the proceedings, and the streets leading to the grounds were lined with people whose prevailing emotion seemed to be that of idle curiosity.

On arriving at the camp, Webster was conducted into a small room, on the ground floor of one of the buildings, and was left alone with the clergyman who had been requested to accompany him.

Thus he remained for several hours. At ten minutes past eleven, the carriage was drawn up before the door, and Webster appeared leaning upon the arm of the jailer, and attended by his spiritual adviser.

The doomed man wore a look of calm composure. His face was pale, and the feebleness of his condition was manifest in his tottering walk; but his eye was clear and steady and not a muscle of his face betrayed his emotion.

They reached the scaffold, which was erected on the north side of the parade ground. Slowly and painfully he ascended to the platform. Amid a breathless silence, he stood for a moment and gazed about him. The bright blue sky overhead, the muskets of the soldiers glistening in the rays of the sun, the white, eager faces which surrounded him. His last look on earth. Though much exhausted by his long illness, he stood alone and firmly whilst his arms were tied behind him and his feet were bound together.

The black cap was placed over his head, and then followed a moment of solemn stillness. The entire assembly seemingly ceased to breathe. The signal was given, the trap was sprung, and, with a dreadful, sickening thud, Webster fell from the gibbet to the ground beneath. The hang-man's knot had slipped, and the man, bound hand and foot, lay in a confused heap, limp and motionless, before the gathered throng. He was lifted up and carried to the scaffold.

"I suffer a double death," came from the lips of the dying man as he was again placed upon the readjusted trap. The rope was again placed around his neck, this time so tight as to be excruciatingly painful.

"You will choke me to death this time," came in gurgling tones from within the enveloping hood.

In a second the trap was again sprung, and the brave patriot was swinging in the air, between heaven and earth.

Rebel vengeance was at last satisfied, the appteite for human blood was sated.

Treason had done its worst, and the loyal spy was dead.

Early in the afternoon, Captain Alexander returned to the prison, and informed Mrs. Lawton that all was over. He found her deathly pale, but now firm, and giving no other outward sign of the agony of the past few hours.

"May I see him before he is taken away?" she asked.

"There is no objection to that."

Accompanying the officer, she went to the room in which the body lay, incased in a metallic coffin which Mrs. Lawton had procured. His face was not discolored in the least, and the features indicated the same Roman firmness which he exhibited when he left the prison. He died as he had lived—a brave man.

Several rebel officers stood around the coffin. Turning suddenly upon them, and facing Captain Alexander, Mrs. Lawton, in a burst of passion, exclaimed :

"Murderers! this is your work. If there is vengeance or retribution in this world, you will feel it before you die !"

As if stung to the quick by this accusation, Captain Alexander stepped up to the coffin, and laying his hand upon Webster's cold, white forehead, said :

"As sure as there is a God in Heaven, I am innocent of this deed. I did nothing to bring this about, and simply obeyed my orders in removing him from the prison to the place of execution."

Application was made to General Winder for the privilege of sending Webster's body to the North, where it might be buried by his friends ; but this the rebel officer peremptorily refused. A petition was then made that it be allowed to be placed in the vault in Richmond, with no better success. Not content with heaping ignominy upon him while living, the fiend was determined that even in death the patriot should be the subject of odium and contempt.

In the dead hour of the night, he ordered the remains to be carried away, and buried in an obscure corner of the pauper's burying-ground.

Farewell, brave spirit ! I knew thee well. Brave, tender and true; thou hast suffered in a glorious cause, and died a martyr's death. Thy memory will long be green in the hearts of thy friends. When treason is execrated, and rebellion is scorned and despised, the tears of weeping friends will bedew the sod which rests above the martyred spy of the Rebellion—Timothy Webster.

After the war was over, and peace once more reigned throughout the land, I procured his body, and it now lies in the soil of a loyal state—the shrine of the patriot—the resting-place of a hero.

But little more remains to be told. After weary months of captivity, Mrs. Lawton, Price Lewis and John Scully, were sent to the North, where their stories were told, and from whose lips I learned the particulars I have narrated.

CHAPTER XXXVII.

*The Defeat of General Pope at the second Battle of Manassas.
—McClellan Again Called to the Command.—The Battle
of Antietam.—A Union Victory.—A Few Thoughts about
the Union Commander.—McClellan's Removal from
Command and his Farewell Address.*

ON the second day of September, 1862, the
following order was issued:

> " War Department, Adj't-Gen.'s Office,
> " Washington, Sept. 2, 1862.
>
> " Major-General McClellan will have command of
the fortifications of Washington, and of all the troops
for the defense of the Capital.
> " By order of
> " Maj.-Gen. HALLECK.
>
> " E. D. TOWNSEND,
> Ass't. Adj't.-Gen."

At this time the Federal troops, under General
Pope, were retreating in great disorder from the disastrous defeat in the Virginia campaign, and the roads
leading to Washington were, for the second time during
the war, filled with stragglers from the ranks, making
their way to the capital. It will be remembered that
while McClellan and the main Eastern army were in
the Peninsula, the divisions of McDowell, Fremont

and Banks were, by orders of the government, held near Washington, for the protection of the national capital. On the 26th day of July, these forces were consolidated as the Army of Virginia, and placed under the command of General Pope. This army was guarding the line of the Rapidan.

Soon after the retreat of the Union army under General McClellan, the Confederates, in August, 1862, began to move towards Washington. Stonewall Jackson, leading the advance of the Southern army, attacked Banks' force at Cedar Mountain, on the 6th day of August. Banks, however, was able to hold Jackson in check for some time; but the main body of the rebels arriving, Banks was compelled to retreat. Lee now pressed heavily upon Pope, who retreated northward from every position then held by him.

When this movement became known to the authorities, General McClellan was ordered to hastily ship the Army of the Potomac back to Washington, and so persistent was General Halleck in his orders to that effect, that at the second battle of Manassas McClellan found himself completely stripped of his army—literally without a command—and compelled to submit to the mortification of listening to the roar of the battle from afar, and without being allowed to participate in its conflicts. Some idea of his feelings may be learned from a dispatch sent by him to General Halleck at this time:

" I cannot express to you the pain and mortification I have experienced to-day, in listening to the distant sound of the fighting of my men. As I can be of no further use here, I respectfully ask that if there is a probability of the conflict being renewed to-morrow, I may be permitted to go to the scene of battle with my staff, merely to be with my own men, if nothing more ; they will fight none the worse for my being with them. If it is not deemed best to intrust me with the command even of my own army, I simply ask to be permitted to share their fate upon the field of battle."

These appeals, however, were utterly disregarded. Gen. Pope was to command the army, and to do the fighting, and in the end the contemptuous superiors of the heroic commander suffered a crushing defeat in the bloodiest battle of this campaign. The second battle of Manassas was a most disastrous one, and on August 29–30 Pope's army was utterly defeated.

Lee was now pressing forward, flushed with victory, and threatening Washington. On the 1st of September the battle of Chantilly was fought, and in which those brave Generals, Kearney and Stevens, lost their lives.

Learning by bitter experience the culpable folly of ignoring the genius and bravery of Mc-Clellan, and with the rebel army besieging the capital, General Halleck, in the excess of fear, was forced to again call for the services of the gallant commander of the Army of the Potomac, and General

McClellan was once more placed in command of an army defeated and demoralized by the incompetency of its generals.

The broken army of Pope was now united with that of the Army of the Potomac, and the army of Virginia ceased to exist as a separate organization. With the intense enthusiasm of the soldiers for Mc-Clellan, he soon brought order out of chaos, and in an incredibly short space of time he faced them about, in orderly columns, and started to repel the invading army of Lee, who was now crossing the Potomac.

From reports made by my operatives at this time, it was ascertained that Lee had abandoned, if, indeed, he ever seriously entertained the idea of advancing directly upon the capital, and was now contemplating carrying the campaign into Maryland. Longstreet's division had left Richmond about the 5th day of August for Gordonsville, marching to Orange Court-house, he fell back to Gordonsville. Jackson fell back at the same time, and they both participated in the battle of Manassas, and in the fighting that followed. Jackson then crossed the river into Maryland, before Longstreet, who crossed a few days later, at or near Edwards' Ferry.

On the 4th day of September, my operatives, who were watching the movement of the rebel army, reported that Lee had his headquarters on the Aldie turnpike, near Dranesville ; while Jackson was near Fairfax Court-house. On the 9th, it was understood that the rebels had moved their entire army into Virginia, and it was presumed that his objective point was Baltimore.

General McClellan left Washington on the 7th day of September, and established his headquarters at Rockville, having first made all arrangements for the defense of Washington, and placing General Banks in command of the troops at that place. By this time it was known that the mass of the rebel army had passed up the south side of the Potomac river, in the direction of Leesburg, and that a part of the army had crossed the river into Maryland.

The uncertainty of Lee's intentions greatly distracted the authorities at Washington for the safety of that city, and they were fearful that he would make a feint towards Pennsylvania, and then suddenly seize the opportunity to attack the capital.

Some writers have animadverted freely upon the alleged " slowness " of McClellan's movements up the Potomac, and his " delay " in offering battle to Lee before the latter had time to unite his army and occupy the strong position he held at Antietam ; but they persistently ignore the fact that the dispatches from the commander-in-chief at Washington, to McClellan in the field, from the 7th to the 16th of September, were filled with cautions against a too hasty advance, and the consequent impropriety of exposing Washington to an attack. Indeed, it seems evident to me, when I regard the career of the Army of the Potomac, that had those in power in Washington been less concerned for their own safety, and trusted more to the skill and sagacity of the general in the field to direct its movements, the history of that army would have been widely different from what it is.   The campaign of the Peninsula terminated disastrously to the Union arms, and it was mainly due to this real or assumed fear of the authorities for the safety of Washington.

It is not presuming too much to say, that McClellan knew far better than those at Washington the movements and intentions of the enemy, and that he was apprised of them sooner ; but it is equally true that a certain element in the Cabinet was unfriendly to the secret service branch of the army, and, with characteristic stubbornness, placed but little reliance upon the information obtained from this source.

For instance, General Halleck was of the opinion, on the evening of the day before Antietam, that Lee's whole force had crossed the river, and so telegraphed McClellan, when the fact was that the rebel army was actually in our front, and ready for the battle that so speedily followed.

Still, the importance of moving with extreme caution was kept constantly in view, and the army was moved so that it extended from the railroad to the Potomac River, the extreme left flank resting on that stream.

On the twelfth of September, a portion of the

right wing of the army entered Frederick, Md., and on the following day the main body of the right and the center wings arrived, only to find that the enemy had marched out of the place two days before, taking the roads to Boonesboro' and Harper's Ferry.

Lee had left a force to dispute the possession of the passes, through which the roads across South Mountain ran, while he had dispatched Jackson to effect the capture of Harper's Ferry. In these plans he was partially frustrated, for, while Jackson succeeded in capturing Harper's Ferry, McClellan drove the rebel troops from the passes, after short but vigorous engagements at South Mountain, on September 14th, but failed in his efforts to relieve Harper's Ferry, and that place was surrendered on the following day.

Immediately following the actions at South Mountain, Lee, being closely pressed by McClellan, turned at bay in the beautiful valley of the Antietam. Here he resolved to endeavor to hold his position until he could concentrate his army. His forces at this time numbered about forty thousand men.

On the sixteenth, he was reinforced by Jackson's gallant corps, numbering about five thousand men, which, together with other reinforcements, received during the day, swelled his numbers to fifty thousand men, which, in the language of one of their own writers, constituted "the very flower of the Army of Northern Virginia."

Our own forces did not exceed eighty-five thousand men, and it is but correct to say that not seventy thousand were actually engaged on the day of the great battle. My own judgment is, that at no time during the fight was the Confederate army ever confronted by a force outnumbering their own.

Confederate writers have sought to make it appear that Lee, at Antietam, fought and practically defeated a force in excess of his own in the ratio of three to one. This assertion is proven to be a glaring error, for the facts are that the odds were less than three to two, even in point of actual numerical strength present, while, all things considered, these were reduced until the two armies faced each other on the morning of Antietam pretty evenly opposed, and with no decided advantage in favor of either contestant.

To explain : taking it for granted that McClellan had eighty-seven thousand men at roll-call on the morning of the seventeenth, it is now known that the battle was mainly fought by the First, Second, Ninth and Twelfth Corps, while the Fifth and Sixth Corps and the Cavalry Division were scarcely used at all. In addition to this, it should be remembered that ours was the attacking force; that the enemy occupied a chosen position, and therefore, in this view of the situation, the odds were by no means great in favor of the Federal troops.

On the morning of the sixteenth, being then at

"My horse was shot under me while crossing the stream."

headquarters, and desiring to learn from personal observation something of the position of the enemy, I accompanied a party of cavalry sent out to reconnoitre across the Antietam. Here it was discovered that the enemy had changed the position of some of their batteries, while their left and center were upon and in front of the Sharpsburg and Hagerstown turnpike, and their extreme left rested upon the wooded heights near the cross-roads to the north.

While returning from this reconnoitering expedition, fire was opened upon us from a masked battery upon the hill, and my horse, a beautiful sorrel, that had carried me for months, and to which I was much attached, was shot from under me while I was crossing the stream. Several of the men who accompanied me were seriously wounded, and I narrowly escaped with my life.

The next morning, at early dawn, the battle commenced, and raged with unabated fury until nightfall, when the rebels withdrew, and our soldiers slept that night upon a dearly won, yet decisively victorious field. McClellan determined not to renew the attack upon the following day, for which his critics have censured him severely; yet, I am satisfied, that not a few writers, who have fought, *on paper*, the battle of Antietam, just as it should have been fought in their own estimation, have not, in a single instance, given the subject more painful and anxious thought than did the General himself, during all that night, while his weary troops lay resting on their arms, on a field covered with their own and their enemy's dead.

No better reasons can be assigned, and, indeed, none better need be given for the course he pursued, than he, himself, has stated in his own report of that battle. He says: " I am aware of the fact, that, under ordinary circumstances, a General is expected to risk a battle if he has a reasonable prospect of success ; but at this critical juncture, I should have had a narrow view of the condition of the country, had I been willing to hazard another battle with less than an absolute assurance of success. At that moment, Virginia lost, Washington menaced, Maryland invaded, the National cause could afford no risks of defeat. One battle lost, and almost all would have been lost. Lee's army might then have marched as it pleased on Baltimore, Washington, Philadelphia or New York. It could have levied its supplies from a fertile and undevastated country, extorted tribute from wealthy and populous cities, and nowhere east of· the Alleghanies was there another organized force able to arrest its march."

The day after the battle, however, General McClellan gave orders for a renewal of the attack on the morning of the nineteenth ; but when morning dawned, it was discovered that the rebels had suddenly abandoned their position and retreated across the river, leaving nearly three thousand of their unburied dead on the late field of battle. Thirteen guns, thirty-nine colors, upwards of fifteen thousand stand of small arms, and more than six thousand prisoners, were taken in the battles of South Mountain, Crampton's Gap and Antietam, while not a single gun or color was lost by our troops in any of these encounters.

The Battle of Antietam, in its effects, was a brilliant and decisive victory for the Union arms, as it was a terrible blow to the South, who had expected much from Lee's sudden and daring invasion of a loyal state; and their losses, from the time they first invaded Maryland until the end of the Battle of Antietam, were in the neighborhood of thirty thousand men.

Whatever, therefore, has been said by unfriendly critics, concerning General McClellan's achievements, they must be regarded by the intelligent and fair-minded student of history, as far from being failures. Nor were they merely the achievements of an ordinary man. It is an easy, and no doubt a tempting task, nearly twenty years after a battle has occurred, and with the knowledge and materials now at hand, for writers to fight this battle over again, and point out alleged blunders here and there, and in their vivid, and not always truthful, imaginations conduct affairs as they should have been conducted.

It may be safely asserted, that no General in the history of the Nation was ever so shamefully treated by his government, as was General McClellan. With a brave and noble devotion, and with a self-sacrificing love for his country and her flag, he fearlessly offered his life and his services in sustaining the honor of the one, and the perpetuity of the other.

Reviewing his career from the date of his taking command of all the armies, down to the close of the battle of Antietam, he received the bitter opposition of the Cabinet, and the ill-concealed enmity of the politicians ; and scarcely had he been called to this important position, than his enemies began working to effect his downfall. With such persistence and success did they devote themselves to their task, that by the time he had his Army of the Potomac ready for the field, they had practically deposed him as the Commander-in-Chief.

His plans of the campaign were required to be submitted to a body of twelve of his subordinates for approval, and this ridiculous proceeding ended in their adoption by a vote of eight to four. The next day the enemy abandoned Manassas, a move which was the result of direct treason, or, at least, criminal indiscretion on the part of some member of that commission, either directly or indirectly. After his plans were adopted, and their execution commenced, he was hampered and distressed by orders from his superiors at Washington, conflicting with his own well formed ideas and deranging his carefully prepared plans in the field.

He, however, bore all these things patiently, and at all times faithfully endeavored to do the very best, under the adverse circumstances which surrounded him. He, however, at all times, had the courage to speak his convictions, knowing the purity of his own actions, notwithstanding the fact that he was frequently called upon to execute orders that his own better judgment convinced him were conceived in ignorance or malice, and which could but do harm to him and to the cause he loved.

On July 7, 1862, we find him writing to the President his views on the conduct of the war. He said :

" In carrying out any system of policy which you may form, you will require a Commander-in-Chief of the army, one who possesses your confidence, understands your views, and who is competent to execute your orders by directing the military forces of the nation to the accomplishment of the objects by you proposed. I do not ask that place for myself, I am willing to serve you in such position as you may assign me, and I will do so as faithfully as ever subordinate served superior. I may be on the brink of eternity, and as I hope for forgiveness from my Maker, I have written this letter from sincerity towards you, and from love for my country."

Through all his correspondence, while in the field, with his superiors, there breathed a spirit of earnest and sincere devotion to country ; and rarely was he tempted to utter words which proved how sorely he was tried and how much he resented the interference of incompetent authority. When pushed beyond all

control by the foolish, unfriendly and unjust course
of those at Washington, and when their interference
had caused the failure of his plans, he wrote to Secretary of War Stanton, "You have done your best
to sacrifice this army," and even then the words were
written more in a tone of regret than of anger.

Nearly a month later, when the order was issued
for the withdrawal of the Army of the Potomac before
Richmond, under the full force of his convictions, he
uttered a manly protest against such action. and entreated that the order might be rescinded. "All
points," said he, " of secondary importance elsewhere
should be abandoned, and every available man
brought here. A decided victory here and the
strength of the rebellion is crushed, it matters not
what partial reverses we may meet with elsewhere.
*Here is the true defense of Washington ; it is here, on
the banks of the James, that the fate of the Union
should be decided.* Clear in my convictions of right,
strong in the consciousness that I have ever been
and still am actuated by love of my country, ...
I do now, what I never did in my life before, I
entreat that this order may be rescinded."

How true these words were, and how prophetic
their scope, may be proven by the words of General
Sheridan several years later. When Grant was
compelled at last to adopt the very plans of Mc-
Clellan, thus giving as practical a vindication of that
general as could be desired, Sheridan sent a mes-

sage to Grant, but a little while before the surrender, urging him to come with all the force he could command in pursuit of Lee, saying, "*Here is the end of the rebellion.*" A fit corollary to McClellan's dispatch from James River to Halleck : "*Here, directly in front of this army, is the heart of the rebellion.*"

No general in this country, or in any other, was more universally beloved and admired by his troops, and no commander ever returned that affection with more warmth than did McClellan. Troops that under other commanders suffered defeat after defeat, until dismayed and discouraged they fled to Washington, followed by a pursuing and exultant enemy, were in a few days, by his magical influence over them, again transformed into brave and hopeful soldiers, ready to follow anywhere their trusted commander might lead.

It is a strange fact, but a fact, nevertheless, that the Army of the Potomac received all its good words, words of cheer and encouragement, from McClellan alone. Those in power at the capital were painfully blind to its sufferings on the toilsome march, or its deeds of valor on the bloody field. After the battle of Antietam, and after the Army of the Potomac had driven Lee from Maryland, General McClellan telegraphed his chief as follows : "I have the honor to report that Maryland is entirely freed from the presence of the enemy, who has been driven across the Potomac.   No fears need now be entertained for the safety of Pennsylvania ; I shall at once occupy Harper's Ferry."

Two days later, receiving no word of acknowledgement for his troops, whom he felt had earned them from the Commander-in-Chief, he, in a telegram of September 20th, said : " I regret that you have not yet found leisure to say one word in commendation of the recent achievements of this army or even to allude to them."

Before this, he had taken occasion to remind General Halleck of the fact that the army deserved some credit for its labors, and appreciated any acknowledgment of the same which the Commander-in-Chief might make.

On August 18th, 1862, and after the fighting before Richmond, he wrote to General Halleck as follows :

" Please say a kind word to my army, that I can repeat to them in general orders, in regard to their conduct at Yorktown, Williamsburg, West Point, Hanover Court-house, and on the Chickahominy, as well as in regard to the seven days, and the recent retreat. No one has ever said anything to cheer them but myself. Say nothing about me ; merely give my men and officers credit for what they have done. It will do you much good, and strengthen you much with them, if you issue a handsome order to them in regard to what they have accomplished. They deserve it."

Is it any wonder, then, that the army exhibited such splendid enthusiasm for their leader, when they, above all others, were fully acquainted with his character as a man and a general ?

Self was his last and least consideration. Always mindful of the comfort of his men, yet inculcating, by his splendid discipline, the essential requisites of the true soldier, he led his troops through the campaigns of the Peninsula and of Maryland, achieving a record that was a credit to him, his army, and the nation, and is an enduring monument to the faithful devotion and the gallant services of the Army of the Potomac. I cannot close this chapter in more fitting words than those used by General McClellan, in his brief and affectionate farewell to his officers and men, after the battle of Antietam, when, having won a victory at a critical period, he was, as a reward, relieved from his command.

" November 7th, 1862.

" Officers and soldiers of the Army of the Potomac :

" An order of the President devolves upon Major-General Burnside the command of this army. In parting from you I cannot express the love and gratitude I bear you. As an army, you have grown up under my care. In you I have never found doubt or coldness. The battles you have fought under my command will proudly live in our nation's history. The glory you have achieved, our mutual perils and fatigues, the graves of our comrades fallen in battle and by disease, the broken forms of those whom

37

wounds and sickness have disabled—the strongest associations which can exist among men—unite us still by an indissoluble tie. We shall ever be comrades in supporting the constitution of our country and the nationality of its people."

CHAPTER XXXVIII.

General Burnside in Command.—My Connection with the Secret Service Severed. — Reflections upon Important Events.—Conclusion.

ON the evening of the seventh of November, following the battle of Antietam, General McClellan was removed from the command of the Army of the Potomac. After having spent weeks in the laborious effort of reorganizing his forces, which had been severely shattered and weakened by the hard marching and the still harder fighting in the recent battles with Lee, the brave commander, upon the eve of an important forward movement was deprived of his noble army. General Burnside was named as his successor. Again had the political cabal at Washington succeeded in their opposition to the noble commander of the Army of the Potomac, and this time effectually.

McClellan's tardiness was the alleged cause of his removal. No one in authority seemed to consider for a moment the necessity, which was apparent to their immediate commander, of affording the Federal troops an opportunity to recuperate from their exhausted condition. The serious losses sustained at South Mountain, Crampton's Gap, and Antietam had left the army badly disorganized, and the privations and hardships to which they had been subjected, rendered a delay, for the purpose of allowing the worn and weary soldiers time to rest and recuperate, an absolute necessity. In the language of McClellan, "The Army had need of rest." After the terrible experiences of battles and marches, with scarcely an interval of repose, which they had gone through from the time of leaving the Peninsula; the return to Washington; the defeat in Virginia; the victory at South Mountain, and again at Antietam, it was not surprising that they were, in a large degree, destitute of the absolute necessities for effective duty. Shoes were worn out; blankets were lost; clothing was in rags; the army was unfit for duty, and time for rest and equipment was absolutely necessary.

McClellan at once notified the authorities of the condition of his troops, and made the necessary requisitions on the proper departments for the needed supplies. For some unaccountable reason—unaccountable to this day—the supplies ordered were so slow in reaching the men, that when, on the seventh of October, the command came for him to cross the river into Virginia, and give battle to the enemy, a compliance with the order was practically impossible.

Then, too, reenforcements were needed. In ordering the advance, the President, through the General-in-Chief, had submitted two plans, of which McClellan could take his choice. One was to advance up the valley of the Shenandoah with reenforcements of fifteen thousand troops, the other was to cross the river between the enemy and Washington, in which case he was be reenforced with thirty thousand men. McClellan's first inclination was to adopt the movement up the Shenandoah Valley, believing, that, if he crossed the river into Virginia, Lee would be enabled to promptly prevent success in that direction by at once throwing his army into Maryland. Owing, however, to the delay of the supplies in reaching the army, it was nearly the end of October before the troops were ready to move. About the twenty-sixth, the army commenced to cross at Harper's Ferry, and by the sixth of November the advance upon the enemy was begun. On the night of the seventh, therefore, when the order came relieving him from the command, McClellan's advance guard was actually engaged with the enemy.

I had already learned that Longstreet was immediately in our front, near Culpepper, while Jackson and Hill's forces were near Chester's and Thornton's Gap, west of the Blue Ridge. McClellan had formed the plan of attempting to divide the enemy, with the hope of forcing him to battle, when it was believed, an easy victory would be achieved.

At this junctnre, however, and when the army was in an exellent condition to fight a great battle, when officers and men were enthusiastic in their hopes of being able soon to strike an effective blow, McClellan was removed, and Stanton had, at last, accomplished his revenge, Not only this, but he had also secured the failure of, what was undoubtedly destined to be, a great and decisively victorious campaign.

McClellan's plan on discovering the position of the enemy's forces, was to strike in between Culpepper Court House and Little Washington, hoping by this means to separate the rebel army, or at least to force their retreat to Gordonsville, and then advance upon Richmond, either by way of Fredericksburg or the Peninsula.

Burnside, on assuming the command, submitted a plan of his own, which was to make a feint of doing, what McClellan really intended to do, before adopting the move upon Fredericksburg or the Peninsula, and then to advance from Fredericksburg.

This plan, however, did not meet the approval of General Halleck. That General had a long conference with Burnside, at Warrenton. Here their various plans were discussed, without either agreeing to the plan of the other, and the matter was finally referred to the President for his decision. After a further delay of several days, Mr. Lincoln adopted Burnside's plan, and the advance was ordered.

The success of this plan depended upon the immediate possession of Fredericksburg by the Federal army. The intelligent student knows full well that this was not even *attempted* until Lee had ample time to heavily re-enforce the rebel army already there. The subsequent results show Burnside's delay to have been fatal to his success.

There was a time when he could certainly have taken Fredericksburg, with but little loss ; but that time was passed when he permitted the enemy to fully garrison the place, and make ample provision for its defense with an army of nearly ninety thousand men.

At this time, however, my connection with the Army of the Potomac, and with the military concerns of the government, ceased. Upon the removal of General McClellan, I declined to act any further in the capacity in which I had previously served, although strongly urged to do so by both President Lincoln and the Secretary of War, Edwin M. Stanton.

From my earliest manhood, I had been an ardent and active abolitionist, and I have endeavored to demonstrate this fact throughout these pages. My deep admiration, therefore, for General McClellan, was the result of my knowledge, of my intimate acquaintance with him, and a consequent high regard, based upon his innate and intrinsic qualities, both as a man and a soldier, and not from any political affinity whatever.

Refusing longer to continue with the army under its new commander, I was afterwards employed by the government in the work of investigating the numerous claims that were presented against the United States. While acting in this capacity, I was instrumental in unearthing a vast number of fraudulent claims, and, in bringing to justice a large number of men who were engaged in the base attempt to swindle and defraud the nation in the dark hours of her need and peril.

In the Spring of 1864, I was transfered to the Department of the Mississippi, under General Canby, and my headquarters were located at New Orleans. Here I was engaged in looking after cotton claims, and the frauds which were sought to he perpetrated against the government in that region of the country.

In 1865, I severed my connection with the "Secret Service of the United States," and returned to Chicago, where I have since been engaged in the active prosecution of my profession as a detective.

Very often, as I sit in the twilight, my mind reverts back to those stirring scenes of by-gone days; to those years of war and its consequent hardships, and I recall with pleasure my own connection with the suppression of the rebellion. My subsequent life has been none the less happy because of my having assisted, as best as I could, in putting down that gigantic act of attempted disunion, and in upholding the flag of our fathers. More than all do I rejoice in the freedom it brought to nearly half a million of people, who, prior to that time, had been held in inhuman bondage,—striking the shackles from their bruised limbs, and placing them before the law free and independent.

My task is done. In a few brief pages I have attempted to depict the work of years. The war is over, the rebellion has been crushed, peace and plenty are everywhere apparent. The flag of the Union floats from every port in the United States, the slave is free, the South is recovering from the ravages of war, and the stories of those stirring times seem now like the legends of an olden time.

One more scene remains, and I will then draw the curtain.

It is a Sabbath morning, the air is fragrant with blossom and flower, the birds are carolling sweetly a requiem for the dead. Around us, sleeping the sleep that knows no waking, lie the forms of those whom we knew and loved. We are in the " city of the dead." The wind sighs through the waving branches of the trees, with a mournful melody, suggestive of the place. Near by is the bustling city, but here we are surrounded only by the mute, though eloquent testimonies of man's eternal rest. Here beneath a drooping willow let us pause awhile. Flowers are blooming over a mound of earth, saturating the atmosphere with a grateful aroma. Let us lean over while we read what is inscribed upon the marble tablet.

SACRED
TO THE MEMORY OF
TIMOTHY WEBSTER,
WHO
WAS EXECUTED AS A SPY,
BY THE
REBELS, IN RICHMOND, VA.,
APRIL 29, 1862,
AFTER GALLANT SERVICE IN THE WAR OF THE REBELLION.
HE SEALED HIS FIDELITY AND DEVOTION
TO HIS COUNTRY
WITH HIS BLOOD.

———

Alike to him are the heats of summer, or the snows of winter.
Peacefully and quietly he sleeps. The Spy of the Rebellion is at rest.

APPENDIX.

---◆---

THE HARDSHIPS AND PRIVATIONS
OF A DETECTIVE'S LIFE

EVERY person who may have survived the experience has undoubtedly a lively recollection of the wild groups of people which the building of the Union and Central Pacific Railroads brought together from all directions, and from all causes.

There were millions upon millions of dollars to be expended; and as the points of construction neared each other, and the twin bands of iron crept along the earth's surface like two huge serpents, spanning mighty rivers, penetrating vast mountains, and trailing through majestic forests, creeping slowly but surely towards each other, there was always the greatest dread at the most advanced points, which, like the heads of serpents, always contained danger and death; and the vast cities of a day that then sprang into existence, and melted away like school-children's snow-houses, were the points where such wild scenes were enacted as will probably never again occur in the history of railroad building.

Everything contributed to make these places typical of Babelic confusion, or Pandemoniac contention. Foreigners were told of the exhaustless work, and the exhaustless wealth, of this new country which was being so rapidly developed, and they came; men —brave men, too—who had been on the wrong side during the late irritation, and who had lost all, having staked all on the result of the war, saw a possible opportunity of retrieving their fortunes rapidly, and they came; the big-headed youth of the village whose smattering of books at the academy, or the seminary, had enlarged his brain and contracted his sense so that he was too good for the common duties and everyday drudgeries which, with patience, lead to success, learned of the glory and grandeur of that new land, and he came; the speculating shirk and the peculating clerk came; the almond-eyed sons of the Orient in herds—herds of quick-witted, patient, plodding beings who could be beaten, starved, even murdered—came; the forger, the bruiser, the counterfeiter, the gambler, the garroter, the prostitute, the robber, and the murderer, each and every, came; there was adventure for the adventurous, gold for the thief, waiting throats for the murderer; while the few respectable people quickly became discouraged, and fell into the general looseness of habits that the loose life engendered, and gradually grew reckless as the most reckless, or quickly acquiesced in the wild orgies or startling crimes which were of common occurrence. In fact, as in the human system, when any portion of it becomes diseased and all the poison in the blood flows to it, further corrupting and diseasing it until arrested by a gradual purification of the whole body, or by some severe treatment, so from every portion of the country flowed these streams of morally corrupt people, until nearly every town west of Missouri, or east of the mountains, along these lines, became a terror to honest people, and continued so until an irresistible conflict compelled a moral revulsion, sometimes so sweeping and violent as to cause an application of that unwritten, though often exceedingly just law, the execution of which leaves offenders dangling to limbs of trees, lamp-posts, and other convenient points of suspension.

As a rule, in these places, every man, whatever his business and condition, was thoroughly armed, the question of self-defense being a paramount one, from the fact that laws which governed older communities were completely a dead letter; and the law of might, in a few instances made somewhat respectable by a faint outline of ruffianly honor, alone prevailed, until advancing civilization and altered conditions brought about a better state of society; so that in these reckless crowds which pushed after the constantly changing termini of the approaching roads, any instrument of bloodshed was considered valuable, and stores where arms and ammunition could be secured did quite as large a trade as those devoted to any other branch of business; while so outrageous was the price extorted for these instruments of aggression or defense, that they have often been known to sell for their weight in gold; and just as, during the war, the army was followed by enterprising traders who turned many an honest penny trafficking at the heels of the weary soldiers, so the same class of people were not slow to take advantage of such opportunities for gigantic profits which, though often lessened by the many risks run in such trading, were still heavy enough to prove peculiarly attractive.

As a consequence, there were many firms engaged in this particular business, but probably the heaviest was that of Kuhn Brothers, who were reported to be worth upwards of one hundred thousand dollars, which had principally been made along the line of the road, and who, with headquarters at Cheyenne, had established various " stores " at different points as the Union Pacific was pushed on, always keeping the largest stock at the most advanced point, and withdrawing stocks from the paper cities which had been left behind, though only in those towns which had not been altogether destroyed by the periodical exodus occasioned by each change of terminus.

For this reason the firms were obliged to entrust

their business to the honesty of many different em-
ployés, who were subject to the vitiating influences
and temptations, which were unusual and severe under the circumstances already mentioned, while the
distances between the points, and the scarcity of
secure means of safely keeping the large sums of
money which would occasionally unavoidably accrue
at certain points, left Kuhn Brothers, in many instances, really dependent on those dependent on
them.

In this condition of affairs, and after a slight de-
falcation had occurred at one of their smaller stores
in the spring of 1867, the firm were seeking a man
whom they could place in actual charge of one or two
of their establishments at the larger towns, and give
a sort of general supervision over the others, when
the senior member of the firm, being in Laramie, casually met a young gentleman, who happened to be
able to do him so great a favor that the incident led
to a close friendship and ultimate business relations,
eventually resulting in this narrative of facts.

It was a pleasant May evening, and Mr. Kuhn
had decided to returned to Cheyenne in order to
secure a proper man for the superintendency nearer
home. He was to have left Laramie for the East at
a late hour of the evening and, being at a loss how
to pass the intervening time, strolled out from the
hotel with no particular destination in view and his
mind fully occupied with the cares of his business,

only occasionally noticing some peculiarity or strange sight more than usually striking among the thousands of weired things, to which his frontier business had compelled him to become accustomed, when suddenly he found himself in front of a mammoth dance-house, and, yielding to a momentary impulse of curiosity, turned into the place with the stream of gamblers, adventurers, greasers, and, in fact, everybody respectable or otherwise, who, so far from civilization, found such a place peculiarly attractive.

The dance-house was a sort of hell's bazaar, if the term may be allowed—and it is certainly the one most befitting it—and was really no "house" at all, being merely a very large board enclosure covered with a gigantic tent or series of tents, bedecked with flags and gaudy streamers. The entrance fee to this elegant place of amusement was one dollar, and you had only paid an initiatory fee when you had gained admission.

On either side as you entered were immense bars, built of the roughest of boards, where every kind of liquid poison was dispensed at the moderate sum of twenty-five cents a drink, five-cent cigars selling at the same price, and the united efforts of a half-dozen murderous looking bar-tenders at each side were required to assuage the thirst of the quite as murderous looking crowd that swayed back and forth within the space evedently prepared for that purpose.

Beyond this point, and to either side, as also

down the center for some distance, could be found almost every known game of chance, dealt, of course, "by the house," while surrounding the lay-outs were every description of men crazed with drink, flushed with success, or deathly pale from sudden ruin; while everywhere the revolver or the bowie intimated with what terrible swiftness and certainty any trifling dispute, rankling grudge, or violent insult would be settled, one way or the other, and to be marked by the mere pitching of an inanimate form into the street!

After these attractions came a stout partition which had evidently been found necessary, for beyond it there was the strikingly strange heaven of a mushroom city—a vast department where there were music and women; and it seemed that the "management" of this grand robbers' roost had shrewdly calculated on the fact that if a poor fool had not been swindled out of every dollar he might have had before he reached this point, those two elements, all powerful for good or evil the world over, would wring the last penny from him.

Here was another but a finer bar, where more time was taken to prepare a drink and drug a man with some show of artistic excellence, and where a half dollar was changed for a single measure of poison; women,—shrewd, devilish women who could shoot or cut, if occasion required, with the nicety and effect of a man,—"steering" every person giving token of having money in his possession to the more genteelly gotten up "lay-outs," and acting in the same capacity, only with far more successful results, as the ordinary "ropers-in" of any large city; a wild, discordant orchestra that would have been hooted out of the lowest of the "varieties" east of the Missouri; but in this place, and to these ears, so long unused to the music of the far-away homes beyond the Mississippi, producing the very perfection of enchanting harmonies; but above all, and the crowning attraction before which every other thing paled and dwindled to insignificance, a score of abandoned women, dancing and ogling with every manner of man, robbing them while embracing, cheering and drinking with them, and in every way bedeviling them; the whole forming a scene viler than imagination or the pen of man can conceive or picture; grouping of wild orgies and terrible debaucheries, such as would put Lucifer to a blush, and compel a revolution in the lowest depths of Hades.

Kuhn had strolled through the place, and now, out of compliment to general custom, purchased a cigar and was just turning to depart, when he suddenly found himself being hustled back and forth among several hard-looking fellows, who, evidently knowing his business, and surmising that he carried large sums of money upon his person, had determined to provoke him to resistance; when there would, according to the social codes then in existence at Laramie, have been a just cause for either robbing and beating him, or murdering him outright and robbing him afterwards ; when a tall, finely-formed man suddenly stepped into the crowd, and in a very decided tone of voice said :

"I say, gentlemen, that won't do. You must stand back !"

Then taking the terror-stricken ammunition dealer by the coat collar with his left hand, but keeping his right hand free for quick use and certain work, if necesssary, he trotted him through the now excited throng and out into the open air, hastily telling him to "cut for the hotel," which were quite unnecessary instructions, as he made for that point at as lively a gait as his rather dumpy legs could carry him.

The person who had thus prevented the merchant's being robbed, and had also possibly saved his life, was a tall, comely young man of about twenty-eight years of age, and with a complexion as fair as a woman's, pleasant, though determined, blue eyes, and a long, reddish, luxuriant beard, all of which, with a decidedly military cut to his gray, woollen garments, and long fair hair falling upon his shoulders—the whole crowned, or rather slouched over, by a white hat of extraordinary width of brim, gave him the appearance of an ex-Confederate officer, and right good fellow, as the term goes, perfectly capable of caring for himself wherever his fortune, or misfortune, might lead him · which proved the case as he turned and confronted the desperadoes, who had immediately followed him in a threatening manner, and whom he stood ready to receive with a navy revolver half as long as his arm, mysteriously whipped from some hiding-place, in each steady hand.

A critical examination of the man as he stood there, and a very casual survey of him, for that matter, would have instantly suggested the fact to an ordinary observer that a very cool man at the rear ends of two navy revolvers huge enough to have been mounted for light-artillery service, was something well calculated to check the mounting ambition on the part of most anybody to punish him for the character of the interference shown ; and the leader of the gang contented himself with remarking, " See here, Captain Harry, if it wasn't you, there'd be a reck'ning here ; lively, too, I'm tellin' ye !"

" Well, but it *is* me ; and so there won't be any reck'ning. Will there, now, eh ?"

The ruffians made no answer, but sullenly returned to the dance-house, when Captain Harry, as he had been called, rammed the two huge revolvers into his boot legs, which action displayed a smaller weapon of the same kind upon each hip ; after which he nodded a pleasant " good-night " to the bystanders, and walked away leisurely in the direction Mr. Kuhn had taken, pleasantly whistling " The Bonnie Blue Flag," or " The Star Spangled Banner," as best suited him.

The moment that Mr. Kuhn's protector appeared

at the hotel, the former gentleman expressed his live-
liest thanks for the opportune assistance he had been
rendered, and introduced himself to the Captain, who
already knew of him, and who in return gave his
name as " Harry G. Taylor, the man from some-
where," as he himself expressed it with a pleasant
laugh.

It was easy to be seen that there was a stroke of
business in Mr. Kuhn's eye, which his escape from
the dance-house had suggested, as he told Taylor
that he had intended to return to Cheyenne that
night ; but he further stated that as he had so unexpectedly been befriended, he should certainly be
obliged to remain another day in order to secure a
further acquaintance with the man to whem he already
owed so much.

Mr. Kuhn then produced some choice cigars, and
the gentlemen secured a retired place upon the hotel-
porch, at once entering into a general conversation,
which, from the merchant's evident unusual curiosity,
and Taylor's quite as evident good-humored, devil-
may-care disposition, caused it to drift into the Captain's account of himself.

He told Mr. Kuhn that his family resided at that
time in Philadelphia, where they had moved after his
father had failed in business at Raleigh, N. C., but
had taken so honorable a name with him to the
former city that he had been able to retrieve his fortunes to some extent. The Captain was born at

Raleigh, and had received his education in the South, and, being unable to share in his father's regard for the North, even as a portion of the country best adapted for doing business, sought out some of his old college friends in Louisville, Atlanta, and New Orleans, who had been able to secure him a fine business position at Atlanta, where by care and economy in 1860, though but a mere boy yet, he had accumulated property that would have satisfied many a man twenty years his senior.

Being impulsive, and a warm admirer of Southern institutions, he was one of the first men to join the Confederate army at Atlanta, and fought in a Georgia regiment under Johnson and Hood during the entire war, at Jonesville and Rough-and-Ready Station seeing the smoke ascend above the ruins of the once beautiful city, and realizing that the most of his earthly possessions had disappeared when the flames died away.

Having been promoted to a captaincy, he had fought as bravely as he could against the "blue-coats," like a man, acknowledging their bravery as well as that of his comrades; and at the close of the war, which of course terminated disadvantageously to his interests, he had sold his lots at Atlanta for whatever he could get for them, and with thousands of others in like circumstances, had come West and taken his chances at retrieving his fortunes.

This was told in a frank, straightforward way,

which seemed to completely captivate Mr. Kuhn, for he at once spoke to Taylor concerning his business in Laramie, and bluntly asked him, in the event of mutual and satisfactory references being exchanged, whether he would accept the engagement as superintendent of his business over that portion of the road, and take actual charge of the store in that place, and the one about to be established at Benton City.

The result of the evening's interview was the engagement of Taylor by the firm at a large salary ; his immediately taking supervision of the business without bonds or any security whatever ; and for a time his management and habits were so able and irreproachable that, with the gratitude for his protection of Mr. Kuhn at Lamarie still fresh and sincere, the firm felt that they had been most fortunate in their selection of an utter stranger, and were in every way gratified with the turn events had taken.

II.

DURING the early morning of a blustering December day of the same year, I was quite annoyed by the persistence of a gentleman to see me, on what he insisted, in the business office of my Chicago agency, on terming " important business."

It was not later than half-past eight o'clock; and, as I have made it a life-long practice to get at business at an early hour, get ahead of it, and keep ahead of it during the day, I was elbow-deep in the mass of letters, telegrams, and communications of a different nature, which, in my business, invariably accumulates during the night, and felt anxious to wade through it before taking up any other matter.

The gentleman, who gave the name of Kuhn, seemed very anxious to see me, however; and letting drop the statements that he greatly desired to take the morning train for Cheyenne, where he resided; might not be able to be in Chicago again for some time; felt very desirous of seeing me personally; and would require but a few moments to explain his business, which he agreed to make explicit; I concluded to drop everything else and see him.

On being ushered into my private apartments, he at once hastily gave me an outline of the facts related in the previous chapter, adding a new series of incidents which occasioned his visit, and to the effect that the firm had made the necessary arrangements for increasing their busines under their new superintendent, having added largely to their stock at Laramie, and placed about twenty thousand dollars' worth of goods at Benton City.

According to the agreement, he was required to forward money whenever the sales had reached a stated sum at each point, and was given authority to take charge of goods or moneys on hand at any of the less important stations, when convinced that things were being run loosely, or whenever it in any way appeared for the interests of the firm for him to do so.

It will be seen that under this arrangement, which was in every respect injudicious, no security having been given by Taylor, he immediately became possessed of great responsibility, as well as power; but appeared to appreciate the unusual confidence reposed in him, and conducted the business of Kuhn Brothers with unusual profit to them and credit to himself. Matters progressed in this way for some time, when suddenly, about the first of October, the firm at Cheyenne began to receive dispatches from different employees along the road, inquiring when Taylor was to return from Cheyenne, and intimating that business was greatly suffering from his absence. The members of the firm were astonished. They knew nothing of Taylor's being in Cheyenne. On the contrary, their last advices from him were to the effect that he should be at their city on the tenth of that month, with large collections; and the announcement was accompanied with glowing accounts of the prosperity of their business under his careful management.

After the startling intelligence of Taylor's unaccountable absence, a member of the firm immediately left for Laramie, Benton City, and other points, to ascertain the true condition of affairs, still unable to believe that the handsome, chivalrous captain had wronged them, and that everything would be found right upon examination of matters which was immediately and searchingly entered upon ; but the first glance at affairs showed conclusively that they had been swindled, and it was soon discovered that he had gathered together at the stores under his own charge, and at different points along the line, under various pretexts, fully fourteen thousand dollars, and had been given two weeks in which to escape.

Mr. Kuhn did not desire to give the case into my hands on that morning; but explained that he had returned from a fruitless trip to Philadelphia in search of his former superintendent, and had been advised by a telegram from his brothers to lay the case before me and request my advice about the matter ; at the same time securing information about the probable pecuniary outlay necessary for further prosecution of the search, and such other items of information as would enable him to counsel with the remainder of the firm concerning the case, and be able to give the case into my hands, should they decide to do so, without further delay.

This was given him ; and I, in turn, secured from Mr. Kuhn all the information possible concerning Taylor, which was scant indeed, as they had seen very little of him, could give but a very general description of the man, and here they had injudiciously given him over two months' start, during which time he might have safely got to the other side of the world.

Only one item of information had been developed by which a clue to his whereabouts could by any possibility be imagined. He had often spoken to Mr. Kuhn in the most glowing terms of life in both Texas and Mexico, as he had passed, so he had said, a portion of a year in that part of America, since the close of the war, and in connection with the subject, he had stated that he should have remained there had he been supplied with sufficient capital to have enabled him to begin business.

This was all ; and I dismissed the swindled merchant with little encouragement as to the result of a chase for a thief who had got so much the advantage , or, rather, intimated to him that though I had no doubts of being able to eventually catch him, it would be rather a poor investment for the firm to expend the amount of money which might be necessary to effect his capture, unless, in looking into the matter further, I should be able to see opportunities for securing much better knowledge as to his present whereabouts, or clues which could be made to lead to them.

With this not very cheering assurance, Mr. Kuhn returned to Cheyenne.

Not hearing from the firm for several days, I finally dismissed the matter entirely from mind ; but on arriving at the agency one morning, I received in-

40

structions from the Cheyenne firm to proceed in the matter, and with all expedition possible endeavor to cage the flown bird for them.

I at once detailed William A. Pinkerton, my eldest son, and at present assistant superintendent of my Chicago agency, to proceed to Cheyenne, and look over the ground thoroughly there, and also, if necessary, to proceed along the line of the Union Pacific, and, after ascertainig who were Taylor's friends and companions, work up a trail through them, which would eventually bring him down.

The latter course was not necessary to be followed, however, as on arriving at Cheyenne, with some little information gleaned from the firm, he was able to ascertain that a young lawyer there named La Grange, also orginally from the South, had been a quite intimate friend of Taylor's—so much so, in fact, that La Grange had for the last six months regularly corresponded with the Captain's sister, who had been described to him as not only an exceedingly beautiful woman, but as also a lady possessed of unusual accomplishments and amiability.

My son "cultivated" La Grange largely, but could secure but little information through him. He seemed to know nothing further concerning either Taylor or his family, save that he had incidentally met him along the line of the Union Pacific ; they had naturally taken a sort of liking to each other, and in that way became friends in much the same manner that most friendships were made in that country. He further recollected that he had always directed his letters to a certain post-office box, instead of to a street number; but seemed perfectly mystified concerning the action of the brother. He had just returned from a three months' absence in Kentucky, and it was the first intimation he had had of the Captain's crime. La Grange also said that as he had been very busy, he had not written to Miss Lizzie (evidently referring to the sister), nor had he received any communication from her during that time. He had had a photograph of Harry, taken in full-dress uniform while stationed at Atlanta, which had been copied in Philadelphia, but a thorough search among his papers failed to reveal it.

This was all that my son could secure, as La Grange, evidently suspecting that, in his surprise at Taylor's crime, he might say something to compromise himself and endanger Taylor or wound his beautiful sister, to whom he seemed greatly attached, positively refused to have anything further to say concerning the matter; and with what information he had, William returned to the hotel in a brown study, determined to take time to exhaust the material at Cheyenne before proceeding on the proposed trip along the Union Pacific.

After summing up and arranging the points he had got hold of, he telegraphed me fully, adding his own impression that Taylor was in Texas, but expressing a doubt as to whether he had better proceed along the Union Pacific for more information, or go on to Philadelphia at once, and in some way secure information of the family as to their son's whereabouts.

On the receipt of this telegram, which arrived in Chicago about noon, I at once resolved upon a little strategy, being myself satisfied that Taylor had proceeded, *via* St. Louis and New Orleans into either Texas or Mexico, and was then engaged under his own or an assumed name, in some business agreeable to his taste, as formerly explained to Mr. Kuhn, and immediately telegraphed to my son :

"Keep La Grange busied all day so he cannot write, or mail letters. Study La Grange's language and modes of expression. Get La Grange's and Taylor's handwriting, signatures, and Miss Taylor's address, and come next train."

Agreeable to these instructions, he secured several letters from Taylor to Kuhn Brothers, concerning business matters, with the last one, containing the announcement that he would be in Cheyenne on the tenth of October with collections ; and immediately sent by a messenger a courteous note to La Grange, desiring an outline of Taylor's life so far as he might feel justified in giving it, and requesting an answer, which was politely but firmly given in the negative over Adolph La Grange's own signature, which completed a portion of his work neatly.

The balance was more difficult. He ordered a

sleigh, and after settling his hotel bill, but reserving his room for the night, at once drove to La Grange's office, where he in person thanked him for his courteous letter, even if he did not feel justified in giving him the information desired. A little complimentary conversation ensued during which time my son's quick eyes noticed in the lawyer's waste-basket an envelope evidently discarded on account of its soiled appearance, addressed to " Miss Lizzie Taylor, Post-office Box ——, Philadelphia," which on the first opportunity he appropriated. The next move was to *prevent* La Grange's mailing any letter, as it was evident he had written several, including one to Taylor's sister, which were only waiting to be mailed.

Seeing that he had made a pleasant impression upon La Grange, who appreciated the courtesy of the call under the circumstances, and informing him that he had decided to make no further inquiries there, but was to proceed west on the following morning, he prevailed upon him to take a ride in his company about the city and its environs. In leaving his office, La Grange hesitated a moment as if deciding the propriety of taking the letters with him, or returning for them after the sleigh-ride; but evidently decided to do the latter, as he left them, much to my son's relief.

The drive was prolonged as much as possible, and the outlying forts visited, where, having letters of introduction from myself to several army-officers stationed there, both he and his companion were so hospitably treated that the afternoon slipped away quickly, and the two returned to town evidently in high spirits. La Grange felt compelled to reciprocate as far as in his power, and billiards, with frequent drinks for the lawyer and a liberal supply of water for the detective, were in order until within a half hour of the eastern bound train time, when La Grange succumbed to an accumulation of good-fellowship, and on his own suggestion, as he "wash rising y'n'g 'torny y'know !" accepted the hospitalities of my son's room, at the Rawlins House, where he left him sweetly sleeping at a rate which would prevent the mailing of the letters he had left locked in his office for at least two days to come ; as "rising young attorneys," as a rule, sober off in a carefully graduated diminishing scale of excesses of quite similar construction to the original.

On the arrival of my son in Chicago, I immediately caused to be written a letter addressed to Miss Lizzie Taylor, at her post-office box in Philadelphia, of which the following is a copy :

"SHERMAN HOUSE, CHICAGO, Jan. 1868.
" MISS TAYLOR,

"MY DEAR FRIEND :—You know of my intended absence from Cheyenne in the South. During that trip, I really never had the time when I could write you so fully as I desired, and even now I am only able to send you a few words. I am *en route* to Washington on business, and have now to ask you to send the street and number of your father's house, even if it is not a magnificent one, as you have told me, to my address, at the Girard House, in your city, on receipt of this, as I shall be in Washington but one day, and would wish to see both you and your people without delay. I not only greatly wish to see you for *selfish reasons*, which our long and pleasant correspondence will suggest to you as both reasonable and natural, but there are other good reasons, which you all will readily understand when I tell you that I met *him* accidentally just before my return to Cheyenne, and that I have a communication of a personal nature to deliver. While not upholding him in the step he has taken, I cannot forget that I am his friend, and he your brother.

"In great haste,

"Your true friend,

"ADOLPH LA G——.

"P. S.—I leave here for the East this morning. Please answer on immediate receipt.

A. L."

This was posted on the eastern-bound train not an hour after my son's arrival from the West; and another note was written upon the back of an envelope which had passed through the mail, and had got a very much used appearance, and ran thus :

"FATHER OF LIZZIE :

"Treat Adolph well, you can trust him. Give him one of the 'photos' taken at Atlanta in my full-dress uniform ; keep one other of the same for yourselves ; but destroy all the rest. Have been so hurried and worried that I don't remember whether I have said anything about photographs before. But this is a matter of *imperative necessity*. Adolph will explain how he met me. " Good-by,

"H. ———"

It was impossible to detect any difference between this handwriting and that of Captain Taylor's in his business correspondence to Kuhn Brothers ; and, armed with this document, with the assistance of the epistolary self-introduction which had preceded it, I directed my son to leave for Philadelphia that evening, secure admission to Taylor's residence and the family's confidence, agreeable to the appointment made by mail, and thus not only secure the man's photograph, but other information that would be definite.

On arrival at Philadelphia, he secured the services of an operative from my agency in that city, to follow any member of the Taylor family who might call for the letter, to their residence, in the event of an answer not being received at his hotel in due time from the one assumed to have been sent from the hotel in Chicago from La Grange, who found Taylor's home, an unpretentious house on Locust street, while my son remained at the hotel, fully expecting the coveted invitation to visit the Captain's beautiful sister, which arrived at his hotel only a half day after he did, and strongly urged him to call at his convenience.

He was satisfied from this that our theory regarding his being in Texas, or Mexico, was correct ; that the family had not the slightest suspicion of his identity, and that, wherever Captain Taylor might be, communication with his people had been very infrequent, and that, with what he would be able to invent after being received at Taylor's house, he could secure at least sufficient information to put him upon his son's trail. Not desiring to play upon their feelings and friendship as another person any longer than necessary, however, he sent word by a messenger, not daring to trust his own handwriting, that he would call that evening, though necessarily at a late hour ; and, accordingly, that evening, about nine o'clock, found him at the door of a pleasant Locust street cottage, ringing for admission.

A tall, handsome young woman greeted him at the door, and accordingly bade him enter, saying pleasantly, as she ushered him into the cozy little parlor, that she was Miss Lizzie Taylor, and presumed he was Mr. La Grange, with whom she had had so long and so pleasant a correspondence ; and of whom " poor Harry," as she said with a shade of sadness and tenderness in her voice, had so often written, before he had made his terrible mistake, and become a wanderer.

After hastily satisfying her that he was the genuine La Grange, and profusely apologizing for his not having written for so long a time previous to his arrival at Chicago, from Cheyenne, he took up the thread she had dropped, as quickly as possible, and said that he felt sure that Harry would retrieve himself soon, and return the money, as he had no bad habits, and everything would be all right again.

"But yet, Mr. La Grange," she continued, "it makes me shudder whenever I think of all my brothers being away off there on the Rio Grande, among those terrible people!"

"But, you must remember," he replied, encouragingly, "they are strong men, and can well defend themselves under any circumstances."

"Harry is strong and brave, I know," answered Miss Taylor, rather admiringly; "but brother Robert is not fit for such a life. Why, he is but a boy yet."

"Ah, a younger brother?" he thought, making a mental note of it, in order to assist in shaping his conversation after which he said aloud: "I almost forgot to give you this note;" and he took the piece of envelope out of his note-book, as if it had been sacredly guarded, and handed it to her.

Miss Taylor read the hastily written lines with evident emotion; and after studying a moment, as if endeavoring to reconcile matters, while her face was being searchingly read by an experienced detective, she rose, and, apologizing to him for the absence of her father, who was in New York, on business, and of her mother, who was confined to her apartment, a confirmed invalid, she asked to be excused so as to show the note to her mother.

The instant the door closed, my son had seized the album, which he had located during the preceding conversation ; and rapidly turned its leaves to assure himself that he was not treading on dangerous ground. He found a half-a-dozen different styles of pictures of the Captain, including three of the copies taken in Philadelphia of the original Atlanta picture, and felt reassured beyond measure at the lucky turn things had taken. He would have abstracted one of these, but it was impossible, and had barely time to return the album to the table, and himself to his seat, when he heard the woman's step along the hall, and in a moment more she entered the room.

III.

GIVING the door a little impulsive slam, as she closed it, Miss Taylor at once came to where my son was sitting upon the sofa, and seated herself beside him. She said that her mother was anxious beyond measure to learn how and where he had met Harry, how he was looking, and what he had said.

The imagination and resources of the able detective are fully equal to those of the most brilliant newspaper reporters, and a pleasant and plausible fiction was invented, how he (as La Grange, of course), having taken a run from Louisville down to New Orleans, by boat, was just landing at the levee, when he suddenly came across Harry, who had hastily told him all ; how great had been his transgression, how deeply he had regretted it ; but that now he was situated in his business matters so that, if let alone, he would be able to return to Kuhn Brothers every dollar which he had taken, and have a fine business left ; how it had been necessary for him to come to New Orleans on imperative business, and that he should not come east of the Mississippi again under any circumstances. He further said, that Harry seemed hopeful ; that he had stated that his younger brother Robert was well and enjoying the frontier life ; and that, further than that, he had no time or disposition to talk, as he was on the very eve of departure for Texas, only having time to write the little note concerning the photographs.

Miss Taylor excused herself for a moment to convey the truthful intelligence to her anxious mother ; and on her return suggested that they go through the album together at once, and attend to the photographs, an invitation which was accepted with unusual readiness.

Every gentleman who has had the experience, and there are few who have not, know that looking over an album with a beautiful woman who has some interest in her companion, is a wonderfully pleasant diversion. In this instance it was doubly pleasant, for it meant success to my son, whose zeal is as untiring as my own when once on the trail of a criminal.

"I wonder why," asked Miss Taylor, as if wondering as much about Mr. La Grange as about any other subject; "I wonder why Harry desires those photographs destroyed?"

He was turning the leaves for her and, as La Grange, of course, had a perfect right to take plenty of time to explain the matter soothingly and sympathetically.

"But do those horrid detectives track a man out and run him down, when, if he were let alone, he might recover from his misfortune, and right the wrong he has done?"

Mr. La Grange remarked that he had heard that some of them were very much lacking in sentiment and sensibility, and would go right forward through the very fire itself to trace the whereabouts of a criminal; and all those little things helped, he could assure her.

She began to see how it was, she said; but suddenly firing up, she shook her pretty fist at some imaginary person, exclaiming:

"Oh, I could kill the man who would thus dog my brother Harry." And then, after a little April shower of tears, quite like any other woman's way of showing how very desperate they can be under certain circumstances, began slowly taking the Captain's pictures from the album, commenting upon them, and then handing them to the bogus La Grange to burn, who would occasionally step to the fire-place for that purpose, where he would quickly substitute miscellaneous business cards, which answered the purpose excellently.

An hour or two was passed with Miss Taylor in conversation upon various topics which might lead the really estimable young lady to divulge all she knew about the Captain, or concerning his whereabouts and business, which was certainly not much.

It appeared that, immediately after the embezzlement, and while at St. Louis, Taylor had telegraphed to his brother Robert to meet him at New Orleans at a certain time, as he was going into business in that section, and should need his services, for which he would be able to pay him handsomely; the brothers had met there and had proceeded to some other point; the Captain claiming that it would be injudicious to make that fact known, as he had also sent a full and complete confession to his parents of his embezzlement from Kuhn Brothers, which he had directed them to burn, and which he finished by requesting his family not to write to either himself or his brother for some time to come; or at least until he should indicate to them that it would be safe to do so; and under no circumstances to give any person an iota of information concerning himself or his brother.

My son left Miss Taylor's hospitable home with a pang of regret for the deception which had seemed necessary in this case; for whatever may be the opinion of the public regarding the matter, a detective has often quite as large and compassionate a soul as men of other and apparently more high-toned professions.

So long as intelligent crime is the result of a high standard of mental culture and a low standard of moral conscience—conditions which now exist and have for some years existed—intelligent minds must be trained to battle criminals with their own weapons; and these two questions, of speedy detection of crime and swift punishment of criminals will be found quite as essential to a preservation of law and society as lofty arguments or high moral dissertations on the right or wrong of the expediencies necessary to bring wrong-doers to immediate and certain justice.

As soon as I had received a full telegraphic report of the success of the Philadelphia experiment, I directed him to proceed to Louisville, where he would be met by operative Keating, from Chicago, who would bring letters of introduction from myself to Colonel Wood, commanding the First Infantry at New Orleans; Captain White, chief of the detective force of that city; General Canby, commanding the

Department of Texas, at Austin; Col. Hunt, Chief
Quartermaster of the Department of Texas, and
other army officers, requesting them to render my
son and his assistant any aid in their power should
the necessity for such assistance arise; the requisition
from Governor Foulke, of Dakotah Territory, for
Henry G. Taylor, upon Governor Pease, of Texas,
and general instructions concerning his conduct of the
search for the handsome captain after he had got
beyond mail and telegraphic communication.

I was sending him into a country which was at
that time in many portions utterly unsafe for the
securing of a criminal should the pursuer's mission
become known, so as to allow the person desired time
to apprise his friends of his danger, or give him even
an opportunity to rally any number of acquaintances
for defense; for the reason that, as Texas had become
a sort of refuge for ruffians, they became clannish
through the general peril of being pursued each experienced; and would, as a rule, on the slightest provocation, assist in the rescue of any person under arrest, not knowing how soon it might be their turn to
cry for help; but I have invariably sent my sons into
danger with the same expectation that they would do
their duty regardless of consequences, as I have had
when sending other men's sons into danger. Happily
I have never mistaken their metal; and, in this instance, felt sure that I could rely upon him to exercise
both discretion and intrepidity in exigencies to which

his long experience and careful training have at all times made him equal.

The two detectives met in Louisville, and at once proceeded to New Orleans, where they arrived early in the morning of the 7th of January, 1868, and were driven to the St. Charles Hotel. No time was lost; and while my son presented his letters to different parties, and made cautious inquiries regarding the recent appearance in New Orleans of Taylor, Keating, in the character of a provincial merchant, investigated as far as possible the business houses dealing in stock, leather, or wool, as to whether any such person had made arrangement for consignments from the interior or seaport Texan cities. No trace of their man was found, however, until my son was able to get at the register of the St. Charles Hotel for the preceding three months, which was attended with some difficulty, on account of the crowded condition of things at that house; and any detective, or other expert, will understand how much time and patience are required to discover one signature from among ten thousand, when that one may be an assumed name, and perhaps five hundred of the ten thousand be so similar to the one sought, that a disinterested person could scarcely be convinced it was really not the person's handwriting desired; but after a good deal of trouble and searching, the names of " H. G. Taylor & clerk," were discovered on the last half line at the bottom of a page under date of November 30th, 1867, which,

41

by constant wear and thumbing in turning pages, had been nearly defaced, but which, in his handwriting, beyond a doubt told the story of their presence.

Further inquiry of the clerk on duty at that time, and with his memory refreshed by a glance at Taylor's photographs, developed the facts that he had certainly been at the St. Charles on the date shown by the register, and that he was accompanied by a young man about nineteen years of age, who was recognized as Taylor's clerk.

The peculiar register then kept at the St. Charles Hotel in New Orleans was also instrumental in assisting the detectives. It gave the guest's name, residence, hour of arrival, and hour of departure, with name of conveyance at arrival and departure, in the following manner :

H. G. Taylor and Clerk, | *Mobile,* | 12 *m.* | *Ped.* 2 *Dec.* | 7 *a. m.* | *'Bus.*

This told anybody curious about the matter that H. G. Taylor and clerk, assuming to reside in Mobile, arrived at the St. Charles Hotel, New Orleans, at noon on Saturday, the thirtirth day of November, 1867, either afoot or by some mode of conveyance unknown to the clerk of the house, and that they left the house in an omnibus at seven o'clock on the morning of the third day following.

Naturally the next inquiries were directed to ascertaining to what boat or railroad lines omnibuses could be ordered at that hour of the morning; if to different ones, then to discover who had driven the particular omnibus which conveyed Taylor and his brother from the hotel ; and then make an effort to learn to what point they had been conveyed. This, however, proved less difficult than had been feared ; for it was found that on the morning in question the omnibus had gone from the hotel to but one point, and that was to the ferry connecting with Berwick Bay route, by the New Orleans and Opelousas Railroad and the Gulf, to Galveston, although a large number of passengers had been booked, and it was impossible to ascertain whether Taylor and his brother had actually gone that route or not, though everything was in favor of that presumption.

The death of General Rosseau had caused quite a commotion in New Orleans, and it seemed a pretty hard matter to get anything further of a definite character in that place ; and I therefore instructed my son and detective Keating to proceed slowly to Galveston, stopping at Brashear City, where Taylor might have diverged,—supposing he had taken that route with the other passengers from New Orleans,— and to particularly search passenger lists aboard any lines of boats, and all hotel registers, before arriving at Galveston, so as to have the work done thoroughly nearest the base of operation ; as I knew that for any party to get on the wrong scent in that vast state, thinly settled as it was, with no means of quickly conveying needful intelligence, was to enter upon both a needless waste of money for my patrons, and an objectless and wearying struggle against insurmountable obstacles for my detectives, whom, whatever may be said to the contrary, I have never in a single instance needlessly or injudiciously exposed to privation or danger.

In Brashear conductors of trains were applied to; the hotel and omnibus men were questioned, the postmaster was appealed to, and even the passenger-lists of the boats which had been in port, and to which they were able to gain access for a period of three months, had been searched in vain. Every trace of the man seemed lost; and I was appealed to for a decision as to whether they should proceed to Galveston by boat, with the presumption that Taylor had taken passage under an assumed name, or take a few days' trip up along the line of the New Orleans and Opelousas Railroad and seek for information of their man at different points through Central Louisiana.

I decided on the former course, and they accordingly embarked from Brashear immediately after the receipt of my telegram of instructions, on the handsome steamer "Josephine," the only boat whose books they had had no opportunity of examining; and, having received my telegram but a few minutes before the steamer left, were obliged to do some lively running to reach it; for, in anticipation of a message from me

to take that route, my son had directed Keating to settle the hotel bill, and with both valises in hand wait at
a convenient corner, where, should William receive
a dispatch from me of the character expected, within
a certain time, they might yet make the boat.
Everything transpiring as my son had hoped, they
were just in time, after a lively run, to be hauled up
the gang-plank by two stalwart negroes, and were
soon steaming down the bay and thence out to sea.

IV.

As the two ascended to the cabin they were congratulated by the officers of the boat and many of the
passengers on their graceful and expeditious board-
ing of the steamer; and being something of objects
of interest on account of the little incident, they concluded not to lose the opportunity to blend the good
feeling evoked into a thoroughly pleasant impression,
and consequently took the shortest way to accomplish
that desired end by at once walking up to the bar
where the assembled gentlemen, to a man, apparently
in compliance to general custom, seemed to understand that they had been invited before a word had
been uttered by either of the detectives, so that when
my son asked, " Gentlemen, won't you join us ?" it

was an entirely superfluous request; for on either side, behind, and extending a solid phalanx beyond, the "gentlemen" had already joined and were describing the particular liquor that in their minds would do honor to the occasion in the most lively and familiar manner possible, and interspersing their demands upon the leisurely bar-keeper with such remarks as "Gen'lemen had narrow 'scape;" "Gen'lemen made a right smart run of it;" "Gen'lemen not down from Norlens (New Orleans), reckon come down Opelousas route," and other similar comments; but invariably prefacing each and every remark with the stereotyped word "Gen'lemen," which men were, without exception, assumed to be in that country at that time, at least in conversation; as any neglect to preface a remark with the word laid one liable to become immediately engaged in a discussion regarding the propriety of the use of the term, behind navy revolvers, rifles, double-barreled shot-guns, or any other available pointed or forcible means of argument.

After the thirst of the crowd, which upon a Gulf-coasting steamer is something terrible to contemplate, had been in a measure assuaged, my son excused himself, and with Keating repaired to the office, remarking to the clerk:

"I presume you would like to transact a little business with us now?"

"Any time to suit your convenience," returned the clerk, but getting at his books with an alacrity which showed that he would be a little more willing to attend to the matter of fares then than at any other time.

William handed him an amount of money large enough to pay for both the fares of himself and Keating from Brashear to Galveston ; and, while the clerk was making change, said, by way of getting into conversation with him, " I'm afraid we're on a fool's errand out here."

The clerk counted out the change, inked his pen to take the names, and then elevating his eyebrows, although not speaking a word, plainly asked, " Ah, how's that ?"

"Well, you see," replied the detective, " we're hunting a man that's had right good luck."

" He can't be in these parts," replied the clerk, with a slightly satirical smile. " Names ?" he then asked.

" James A. Hicks and Patrick Mallory."

" Where from ?"

" Pittsburg."

" Which is which ?" asked the clerk, in a business tone of voice.

" I am Hicks, and that pretty smart-looking Irishman by the baggage-room is Mallory," was the reply.

" Your age and weight ?" asked the clerk mechanically, at the same time looking at my son keenly, and getting the rest of his description at a glance.

These questions were properly answered, and as the clerk was noting them he asked, "Might I ask what was the gentleman's good luck?"

"Certainly; he has fallen heir to a coal mine in Pennsylvania, and we are endeavoring to hunt him up for the executors of the estate."

"Ah?" said the clerk, driving away with his pen; "will you be so good as to ask Mr. Mallory to step this way?"

My son stepped up to Keating and remarked aloud, "Mr. Mallory, Mr. Mallory, the clerk would like to see you;" and then as Keating stepped to his side, remarked as if for his better information, "He knows your name is Patrick Mallory and that we are from Pittsburg, hunting Taylor, so he can come home and enjoy the property the old man left him; but he wants your entire description."

"Quite so," said the quick-witted Irishman, dryly.

"You've got me, now," said Keating, winking familiarly at the clerk, "when we came over we went under; and so many of us was lost that those saved wasn't worth mendin' as to age, ye see; but concerning heft, why I'd not fear to say I'd turn an honest scale at a hundred an' sixty."

The clerk smiled, but concluded not to ask Mr. Mallory from Pittsburg any more questions.

As soon as he had made his notes, however, William told him that he had examined the lists of all other boats plying between Brashear and Galveston save those of the "Josephine," and requested him to look through them, concluding by describing Taylor, and stating that he might register either as H. G. Taylor and clerk, or under an assumed name, as he was somewhat erratic, and through family troubles, not necessary to explain, he had got into a habit of occasionally traveling *incognito.*

The clerk readily complied with his request, scanning the pages closely, and repeating the name musingly as if endeavoring to recall where he had heard it. By the time he had got on with the examination of a few pages, William had selected a photograph of Taylor, and on showing it to the clerk the latter seemed to have a certain recollection of having seen him, but a very uncertain recollection as to where, or under what circumstances. He went on repeating the name, however, turning back the pages with his right hand and tracing the names back and forth with the index finger of his left hand, occasionally looking at the photograph as if to assist in forcing a definite recollection, but without any result for so long a time that Messrs. Hill and Mallory of Pittsburg became satisfied that their last hope before arriving at Galveston was gone, when suddenly the clerk carelessly placed the picture beside a certain name and in a manner very similar to a dry-goods clerk on securing a successful "match," in two pieces of cloth, quietly remarked :

"Yes, can't be mistaken. There you are; I've got him."

"Then *we've* got him!" exclaimed my son, in the excess of his gratification, shaking the hand of Mr. Mallory, from Pittsburg.

"It's a joy," said the latter, beaming.

"Think of the immense property!" continued my son.

"And the surprise to his friends!" murmured Keating.

"The surprise to himself, I should say," interrupted the clerk.

"Quite so," said Mr. Keating.

It appeared that Taylor and his brother had missed one or two boats at Brashear from some cause, but had finally taken passage on the "Josephine," November 7th; and as the detectives had not been able to ascertain whether the "Josephine" had carried the fugitives or not, on account of her being belated by adverse weather, and was now returning to Galveston, after having had barely time to touch at Brashear, they had felt that perhaps they might be upon the wrong trail, which, with unknown adventures before them, had been peculiarly discouraging; so that now, when they ascertained that his apprehension was only a question of time and careful work, they could not repress their gratification.

Nothing further worthy of note transpired on the voyage from Brashear to Galveston, save that the trip was a pretty rough one, and they finally arrived in the latter city, hopeful and encouraged, notwithstanding the unusually dismal weather, which seemed to consist of one disconnected but never-ending storm, the " oldest inhabitants" of the place contending with great earnestness that "it 'peared like's they'd never had nothin' like it befoah !"

Arriving in Galveston early Sunday morning, they went to the Exchange Hotel, and after breakfast set about examining the hotel registers of the place, ascertaining that Taylor and brother had been in the city, stopped a day or two, and then, so far as could be learned, had gone on to Houston. They were satisfied he had made no special efforts to cover his tracks, although he had not made himself at all conspicuous, as the difficulty encountered in getting those who would be most likely to recollect him, to recollect him at all, clearly showed ; and it was quite evident that he had not anticipated pursuit, at least of any nature which he could not easily compromise, and intended going into some legitimate business under his own name, and with his brother's assistance.

Before he could be arrested in Texas, however, it would be necessary to secure Governor Pease's warrant, which obliged a long, tedious trip to Austin, the capital of the State ; nearly the whole distance having to be done by stage, which at that time seemed a forbidding piece of work, as it had rained every day of the year, so far; and it might be a question of helping the stage through rather than being helped through by it. Besides this, according to my son's reports, which gave a true description of things in Texas at that time, everything beyond Houston had to be paid for in gold, as sectional sentiment and counterfeiting had pronounced a ban upon greenbacks, and not only in gold, but at exorbitant prices; hotel rates being five dollars per day; single meals from one to two dollars; railroad fares eight cents per mile, and stage rates nearly double that amount; with no assurance that you would ever reach a destination you had paid to be conveyed to; all attended by various kinds of danger, among which was the pleasant reflection that you might be called upon at any time to contribute to the benefit of that noble relic of chivalry, the Ku Klux Klan, who at that day were particularly busy in Texas.

All of these pleasant considerations made the departure from Galveston for Austin, in a Pickwickian sense, unusually agreeable.

At Houston they discovered from different persons, including the postmaster, that Taylor had been there, but had made inquiries about points further up country; and the general impression was that he had gone on, though at Brenham, the terminus of the railroad, where they arrived Monday evening, they could find no trace of him.

The next morning, when my son arose and looked

on the vast sea of mud,—a filthy, black earth below ; a dirty, black sky above ; with nothing but driving rain and wintry gusts between ; while the lackadaisical Texans slouched about with their hands in their pockets, with only energy enough to procure tobacco or "licker ;" their sallow faces, down-at-the-heels, snuff-dipping wives desolately appearing at the doors and windows, only to retire again with a woe-begone expression of suspended animation in their leathery faces,—he fully realized the force of the remark attributed to General Sheridan, and more expressive than polite : "If I owned Texas and hell, I would live in hell and sell Texas !"

The stage was crowded, however, and the dreary conveyance splashed and crunched on until noon, when dinner was taken at Wilson's Ranche, a long, low, rambling, tumbledown structure, which, like its owner, who had at one time been a "General" of something, and now retained the thriving title out of compliment to his departed glory, had gone to a genteel decay with a lazy ease worthy of its master's copy. The dinner was one long to be remembered by the detectives, as it was their first genuine Texan dinner, and consisted merely of fat boiled pork, and hot bread of the consistence of putty cakes of the same dimensions, which, when broken open after a mighty effort, disclosed various articles of household furniture, such as clay pipes, old knife handles, and various other invoices, probably playfully dumped into the flour barrel by some one of the half-score of tow-headed, half-clad children, which the " General" and his buxom helpmeet had seen fit to provide for torturing another generation with rare Texan dinners at a dollar a plate.

It was an all-day's labor getting to La Grange, but thirty-five miles from Brenham, where they arrived at ten o'clock, tired and exhausted from the day's banging about in the stage and out of it, for they were obliged to walk many times in order to rest the jaded horses so that they could get through to La Grange at all; but before retiring made all the inquiries necessary to develop the fact that their man had not been at that point.

The next day, Wednesday, was rather more trying than the previous one. Two miles out of town the stage got "bogged," and the entire load of passengers were obliged to get out and walk through three miles of swamps, the stage finally sticking fast, necessitating prying it out with rails. After this Slough of Despond was passed, the Colorado river had to be forded three times, and then came a "dry run," which now, with every other ravine or depression, had became a "wet run," and was "a booming" as the drunken driver termed it between oaths. There was at least four feet of water in the dry run, and the horses balking, the buckskin argument was applied to them so forcibly that they gave a sudden start, and broke the pole off short, which further complicated matters. My son, being on the box, sprang to the assistance of the driver, and stepping down upon the stub of the pole, quickly unhitched the wheel horses, so that the stage could not be overturned, and then disengaged the head team, finally appropriating a heavy wheel horse, with which he rode back to Keating, who was perched upon a rear wheel to keep out of the water, which was rushing and seething below, sweeping through the bottom of the stage, and at every moment seeming to have lifted the vehicle preparatory to sweeping it away like feathers, and also holding on to the baggage, which he had got safely upon the roof of the stage; and, taking him aboard his improvised ferry, after securing the valises, rode to the muddy shore, forming with his companions about as fine a picture of despairing "carpet-baggers" as the South has ever on any occasion been able to produce. The bedraggled passengers ascertained that the next town, Webberville, was several miles distant, and that there was no house nearer, save on the other side of the rapidly rising stream; and as night had come on, the best thing that could be done was to penetrate the woods, build a rousing fire, and shiver and shiver through as long, wet and weary a night as was ever experienced.

There was never a more longed-for morning than the next one, and the moment that the sickly light came feebly through the mist and rain, and straggled into the dense cotton-wood trees, where the discouraged passengers had a sort of fervent out-doors prayer-meeting, they started forward for Webberville, hungry, drenched, and so benumbed as to be scarcely able to walk. It was five miles into town, but one mile of that distance stretched over a quagmire known and described in that section as "Hell's half-acre;" and the truthful inhabitants of Webberville related of this delectable ground that during the rainy season its powers of absorption were so great that it would even retain the gigantic Texan mosquito, should it happen to take a seat there.

This bog was impassable to the travelers, who finally bartered with the owner of a hog wagon to be carried over the marsh for a silver half dollar each. This was far better than remaining on the other side, and they finally trudged into the town more dead than alive.

Fortunately for the detectives, the brother of ex-Governor Lubbock, of Texas, was one of the party, and as they had all become so thoroughly acquainted, as common misery will quickly make travelers, he took my son and Keating to the residence of Colonel Banks, a merchant of Webberville, whose good wife never rested until she had provided the party with a splendid meal, something with which to wash it down, and beds which seemed to them all to have been composed of down.

After they had a good rest, the passengers for Austin were got together, and explained the situation